PREVENTING BULLYING

Through
Science, Policy,
and Practice

Committee on the Biological and Psychosocial Effects of
Peer Victimization: Lessons for Bullying Prevention

Frederick Rivara and Suzanne Le Menestrel, *Editors*

Board on Children, Youth, and Families
and
Committee on Law and Justice

Division of Behavioral and Social Sciences and Education

Health and Medicine Division

The National Academies of
SCIENCES · ENGINEERING · MEDICINE

THE NATIONAL ACADEMIES PRESS
Washington, DC
www.nap.edu

THE NATIONAL ACADEMIES PRESS   500 Fifth Street, NW   Washington, DC 20001

This study was supported by contracts between the National Academies of Sciences, Engineering, and Medicine and the Centers for Disease Control and Prevention (Contract 200-2011-38807, Task Order 26), the Eunice Kennedy Shriver National Institute of Child Health and Human Development (Contract HHSN263201200074I, Delivery Order HHSN26300072), the Health Resources and Services Administration of the U.S. Department of Health and Human Services (Contract HHSH250200976014I, Delivery Order HHSH25034018T), the Highmark Foundation (Grant 1026727), the National Institute of Justice of the U.S. Department of Justice (Grant 2014-MU-MU-0011), the Robert Wood Johnson Foundation (Grant 72186), the Semi J. and Ruth W. Begun Foundation, and the Substance Abuse and Mental Health Services Administration of the U.S. Department of Health and Human Services (Contract HHSP233201400020B, Delivery Order HHSP23337031). Any opinions, findings, conclusions, or recommendations expressed in this publication do not necessarily reflect the views of any organization or agency that provided support for the project.

International Standard Book Number-13:   978-0-309-44067-7
International Standard Book Number-10:   0-309-44067-X

Library of Congress Control Number: 2016948504
Digital Object Identifier: 10.17226/23482

Additional copies of this report are available for sale from the National Academies Press, 500 Fifth Street, NW, Keck 360, Washington, DC 20001; (800) 624-6242 or (202) 334-3313; http://www.nap.edu.

Printed in the United States of America

Suggested citation: National Academies of Sciences, Engineering, and Medicine. (2016). *Preventing Bullying Through Science, Policy, and Practice*. Washington, DC: The National Academies Press. doi: 10.17226/23482.

The National Academies of
SCIENCES · ENGINEERING · MEDICINE

The **National Academy of Sciences** was established in 1863 by an Act of Congress, signed by President Lincoln, as a private, nongovernmental institution to advise the nation on issues related to science and technology. Members are elected by their peers for outstanding contributions to research. Dr. Ralph J. Cicerone is president.

The **National Academy of Engineering** was established in 1964 under the charter of the National Academy of Sciences to bring the practices of engineering to advising the nation. Members are elected by their peers for extraordinary contributions to engineering. Dr. C. D. Mote, Jr., is president.

The **National Academy of Medicine** (formerly the Institute of Medicine) was established in 1970 under the charter of the National Academy of Sciences to advise the nation on medical and health issues. Members are elected by their peers for distinguished contributions to medicine and health. Dr. Victor J. Dzau is president.

The three Academies work together as the **National Academies of Sciences, Engineering, and Medicine** to provide independent, objective analysis and advice to the nation and conduct other activities to solve complex problems and inform public policy decisions. The Academies also encourage education and research, recognize outstanding contributions to knowledge, and increase public understanding in matters of science, engineering, and medicine.

Learn more about the National Academies of Sciences, Engineering, and Medicine at **www.national-academies.org**.

Acknowledgments

The committee thanks, first, the sponsors of this study for their guidance. Support for the committee's work was provided by the Centers for Disease Control and Prevention; the Eunice Kennedy Shriver National Institute of Child Health and Human Development; the Health Resources and Services Administration of the U.S. Department of Health and Human Services; the Highmark Foundation; the National Institute of Justice of the U.S. Department of Justice; the Robert Wood Johnson Foundation; the Semi J. and Ruth W. Begun Foundation; and the Substance Abuse and Mental Health Services Administration of the U.S. Department of Health and Human Services.

Many individuals volunteered significant time and effort to address and educate the committee during our public information-gathering meeting (see Appendix A for the names of the speakers) and our site visit. Their willingness to take the time to share their perspectives was essential to the committee's work. We also thank the many stakeholders who offered input and shared information and documentation with the committee over the course of the study. In addition, we appreciate the generous hospitality of the institution that hosted us and provided space to us on our site visit. In particular, we are immensely grateful for the planning assistance and logistical support for our site visit provided to us by Sharon Kramer.

The committee also expresses its deep appreciation for the opportunity to work with the dedicated members of the staff of the National Academies of Sciences, Engineering, and Medicine on this important project. We are thankful to the project staff: Suzanne Le Menestrel, Francis Amankwah, Kelsey Geiser, Annalee Gonzales, Cyan James, and Mariana Zindel. The committee is also grateful to Lisa Alston, Pamella Atayi, and Faye Hillman for their administrative and financial assistance on this project. The committee gratefully acknowledges Natacha Blain, Kimber Bogard, and Bridget Kelly of the Board on Children, Youth, and Families; Kathi Grasso and Malay Majmundar of the Committee on Law and Justice; Robert Hauser, executive director of the Division of Behavioral and Social Sciences and Education (DBASSE); Mary Ellen O'Connell, deputy executive director of DBASSE; Dr. Victor Dzau, president of the National Academy of Medicine; Clyde Behney, executive director of the Health and Medicine Division (HMD); and Chelsea Frakes, director of policy of HMD, for the guidance they provided throughout this important study. The committee would like to thank the Office of Reports and Communication staff of DBASSE: Eugenia Grohman, Viola Horek, Patricia L. Morison, Kirsten Sampson-Snyder, Douglas Sprunger, and Yvonne Wise. We also wish to thank Daniel Bearss and Rebecca Morgan for their tremendous research and fact-checking assistance.

We are grateful to Ann Moravick and Tamar Sekayan of Rx4good and Lauren Tobias of Maven Messaging & Communications for their thoughtful work as communications consultants for this study. We are also very appreciative of Sally Cohen's contributions of her expertise in public health and policy. We thank Chad Rose for his valuable commissioned work. We are appreciative of Robert Katt for the diligent and thorough editorial assistance he provided in preparing this report. We also thank Jay Christian for his skilled and creative design work.

This report has been reviewed in draft form by individuals chosen for their diverse perspectives and technical expertise, in accordance with procedures approved by the Academies. The purpose of this independent review is to provide candid and critical comments that will assist the institution in making its published report as sound as possible and to ensure that the report meets institutional standards for objectivity, evidence, and responsiveness to the study charge. The review comments and draft manuscript remain confidential to protect the integrity of the deliberative process.

We thank the following individuals for their careful, considerate, and thorough review of this report: Theodore J. Corbin, Department of Emergency Medicine, Health Management and Policy, and Healing Hurt People, Center for Nonviolence and Social Justice, Drexel University; Dewey Cornell, Curry School of Education, University of Virginia; Wendy Craig, Department of Psychology, Queen's University, Kingston, Ontario; Kenneth A. Dodge, Center for Child and Family Policy, Duke University; Elizabeth K. Englander, Massachusetts Aggression Reduction Center, and Department of Psychology, Bridgewater State University; Dorothy Espelage, Educational Psychology, University of Illinois, Champaign; Paula Goldberg, Director's Office, PACER Center, Inc., Bloomington, MN; Julie Hertzog,

National Bullying Prevention Center, PACER Center, Inc., Bloomington, MN; Bruce S. McEwen, Harold and Margaret Milliken Hatch Laboratory of Neuroendocrinology, The Rockefeller University; Stephen T. Russell, Department of Human Development and Family Sciences, University of Texas at Austin; Deborah Temkin, Education Research, Child Trends, Bethesda, MD; and Joseph L. Wright, Department of Pediatrics and Child Health, Howard University College of Medicine.

Although the reviewers listed above have provided many constructive comments and suggestions, they were not asked to endorse the conclusions or recommendations, nor did they see the final draft of the report before its release. The review of this report was overseen by Hugh H. Tilson, Gillings School of Global Public Health, University of North Carolina, and Alan F. Schatzberg, Department of Psychiatry and Behavioral Sciences, Stanford University School of Medicine. Appointed by the Academies, they were responsible for making certain that an independent examination of this report was carried out in accordance with institutional procedures and that all review comments were carefully considered. Responsibility for the final content of this report rests entirely with the authoring committee and the institution.

Contents

Boxes, Figures, and Tables

BOXES

FIGURES

TABLES

Summary

"I think in the early high school years I just tried to stay in the background, I was like 'Hopefully no one notices me.' And I would just walk through the halls like a ghost. And it seemed to work for a while but I mean with that you don't get the full benefits of a social experience."
—Young adult in a focus group discussing bullying

Bullying has long been tolerated by many as a rite of passage among children and adolescents. There is an implication that individuals who are bullied must have "asked for" this type of treatment, or deserved it. Sometimes, even the child who is bullied begins to internalize this idea. For many years, there has been a general acceptance when it comes to a child or adolescent with greater social capital or power pushing around a child perceived as subordinate—such that you can almost hear the justification: "kids will be kids." The schoolyard bully trope crosses race, gender, class, ethnicity, culture, and generations, appearing in popular media ranging from *Harry Potter* to *Glee*, and *Mean Girls* to Calvin and Hobbes cartoons. Its prevalence perpetuates its normalization. But bullying is not a normal part of childhood and is now appropriately considered to be a serious public health problem.

Although bullying behavior endures through generations, the milieu is changing. Historically, bullying has occurred at school—the physical setting in which most of childhood is centered and the primary source for peer group formation—or really anywhere that children played or congregated. In recent years, however, the physical setting is not the only place bullying is occurring. Technology allows for a new type of digital electronic aggression, cyberbullying, which takes place through chat rooms, instant messaging, social media, and other forms of digital electronic communication. Simultaneously, the demographics of cities and towns in the United States are in flux, with resulting major changes in the ethnic and racial composition of schools across the country. Numerical-minority ethnic groups appear to be at greater risk for being targets of bullying because they have fewer same-ethnicity peers to help ward off potential bullies. Ethnically diverse schools may reduce actual rates of bullying because the numerical balance of power is shared among many groups.

Composition of peer groups, shifting demographics, changing societal norms, and modern technology are contextual factors that must be considered to understand and effectively react to bullying in the United States. Youth are embedded in multiple contexts, and each of these contexts interacts with individual characteristics of youth in ways that either exacerbate or attenuate the association between these individual characteristics and being a target or perpetrator of bullying. Even the definition of bullying is being questioned, since cyberbullying is bullying but may not involve repetition—a key component in previous definitions of bullying—because a single perpetrating act on the Internet can be shared or viewed multiple times.

Although the public health community agrees that bullying is a problem, it has been difficult for researchers to determine the extent of bullying in the United States. However, the prevalence data that are available indicate that school-based bullying likely affects between 18 and 31 percent of children and youth, and the prevalence of cyber victimization ranges from 7 to 15 percent of youth. These estimates are even higher for some subgroups of youth who are particularly vulnerable to being bullied (e.g., youth who are lesbian, gay, bisexual, and transgender [LGBT]; youth with disabilities). Although these are ranges, they show bullying behavior is a real problem that affects a large number of youth.

STUDY CHARGE AND SCOPE

Recognizing that bullying behavior is a major public health problem that demands the concerted and coordinated time and attention of parents, educators and school administrators, health care providers, policy makers, families, and others concerned with the care of children, a group of federal agencies and private foundations asked the National Academies of Sciences, Engineering, and Medicine to undertake a study of what is known and what needs to be known to reduce bullying behavior and its consequences. The Committee on the Biological and Psychosocial Effects of Peer Victimization: Lessons for Bullying Prevention was created to carry out this task under the Academies' Board on Children, Youth, and Families and the Committee on

Law and Justice. The committee was charged with producing a comprehensive report on the state of the science on the biological and psychosocial consequences of peer victimization and the risk and protective factors that either increase or decrease peer victimization behavior and consequences (see Chapter 1 for the committee's detailed statement of task).

This report builds on a workshop held in April 2014 and summarized in a report from the Institute of Medicine and National Research Council, *Building Capacity to Reduce Bullying and Its Impact on Youth Across the Lifecourse*. The committee that authored the current report, several members of which participated in the initial workshop, began its work in October 2014. The committee members represent expertise in communication technology, criminology, developmental and clinical psychology, education, mental health, neurobiological development, pediatrics, public health, school administration, school district policy, and state law and policy.

The committee conducted an extensive review of the literature pertaining to peer victimization and bullying and, in some instances, drew upon the broader literature on aggression and violence. To supplement its review of the literature, the committee held two public information-gathering sessions and conducted a site visit to a northeastern city.[1]

Given the varied use of the terms "bullying" and "peer victimization" in both the research-based and practice-based literature, the committee chose to use a current definition for bullying developed by the Centers for Disease Control and Prevention (CDC):

> Bullying is any unwanted aggressive behavior(s) by another youth or group of youths who are not siblings or current dating partners that involves an observed or perceived power imbalance and is repeated multiple times or is highly likely to be repeated. Bullying may inflict harm or distress on the targeted youth including physical, psychological, social, or educational harm.

Not only does this definition provide detail on the common elements of bullying behavior but it also was developed with input from a panel of researchers and practitioners. The committee also followed the CDC in focusing primarily on individuals between the ages of 5 and 18. The committee recognizes that children's development occurs on a continuum, and so while it relied primarily on the CDC definition, its work and this report acknowledge the importance of addressing bullying in both early childhood and emerging adulthood. The committee followed the CDC in not including sibling violence, dating violence, and bullying of youth by adults, as those subjects were outside the scope of the committee's charge.

---

[1] The location of the city is not identified in order to protect the privacy of the focus group participants.

THE SCOPE AND IMPACT OF THE PROBLEM

While exact estimates of bullying and cyberbullying may be difficult to ascertain, how their prevalence is measured can be improved. The committee concluded that definitional and measurement inconsistencies lead to a variation in estimates of bullying prevalence, especially across disparate samples of youth. Although there is a variation in numbers, the national surveys show bullying behavior is a real problem that affects a large number of youth (Conclusion 2.1). Chapter 2 describes the definitional, measurement, and sampling issues that make it difficult to generate precise, consistent, and representative estimates of bullying and cyberbullying rates. Moreover, the national datasets on the prevalence of bullying focus predominantly on the children who are bullied. Considerably less is known about perpetrators, and nothing is known about bystanders in that national data (Conclusion 2.2). Further, there is currently a lack of nationally representative data for certain groups that are at risk for bullying, such as LGBT youth and youth with disabilities.

Although perceptions and interpretations of communications may be different in digital communities, the committee decided to address cyberbullying within a shared bullying framework rather than as a separate entity from traditional bullying because there are shared risk factors, shared negative consequences, and interventions that work on both cyberbullying and traditional bullying. However, there are differences between these behaviors that have been noted in previous research, such as different power differentials, different perceptions of communication, and differences in how to best approach the issue of repetition in an online context. These differences suggest that the CDC definition of traditional bullying may not apply in a blanket fashion to cyberbullying but that these entities are not separate species. The committee concludes cyberbullying should be considered within the context of bullying rather than as a separate entity. The Centers for Disease Control and Prevention definition should be evaluated for its application to cyberbullying. Although cyberbullying may already be included, it is not perceived that way by the public or by the youth population (Conclusion 2.3).

The committee also concludes that different types of bullying behaviors—physical, relational, cyber—may emerge or be more salient at different stages of the developmental life course (Conclusion 2.4). In addition, the committee concludes that the online context where cyberbullying takes place is nearly universally accessed by adolescents. Social media sites are used by the majority of teens and are an influential and immersive medium in which cyberbullying occurs (Conclusion 2.5).

As described in Chapter 3, research to date on bullying has been largely descriptive. These descriptive data have provided essential insights into a

SUMMARY 5

variety of important factors on the topic of bullying, including prevalence, individual and contextual correlates, and adverse consequences. At the same time, this descriptive approach has often produced inconsistencies due, in part, to a lack of attention to contextual factors that render individual characteristics, such as race/ethnicity, more or less likely to be related to bullying experiences. **Youth are embedded in multiple contexts, ranging from peer and family to school, community, and macrosystem. Each of these contexts can affect individual characteristics of youth (e.g., race/ethnicity, sexual orientation) in ways that either exacerbate or attenuate the association between these individual characteristics and perpetrating and/ or being the target of bullying behavior (Conclusion 3.1)**

The committee also concludes that **contextual factors operate differently across groups of youth, and therefore contexts that protect some youth against the negative effects of bullying are not generalizable to all youth. Consequently, research is needed to identify contextual factors that are protective for specific subgroups of youth that are most at risk of perpetrating or being targeted by bullying behavior (Conclusion 3.2).**

Finally, the committee notes that stigma[2] plays an important role in bullying. In particular, the role of stigma is evident not only in the groups of youth that are expressly targeted for bullying (e.g., LGBT youth, youth with disabilities, overweight/obese youth) but also in the specific types of bullying that some youth face (i.e., bias-based bullying). Despite this evidence, the role of stigma and its deleterious consequences is more often discussed in research on discrimination than on bullying. In the committee's view, **studying experiences of being bullied in particular vulnerable subgroups (e.g., those based on race/ethnicity or sexual orientation) cannot be completely disentangled from the study of discrimination or of unfair treatment based on a stigmatized identity. These are separate empirical literatures (school-based discrimination versus school-based bullying) although often they are studying the same phenomena. There should be much more cross-fertilization between the empirical literatures on school bullying and discrimination due to social stigma (Conclusion 3.5).**

Bullying is often viewed as just a normal part of growing up, but it has long-lasting consequences and cannot simply be ignored or discounted as not important. It has been shown to have long-term effects not only on the child who is bullied but also on the child who bullies and on bystanders. While there is limited information about the physical effects of bullying,

---

[2] As noted in a 2016 report *Ending Discrimination Against People with Mental and Substance Use Disorders: The Evidence for Stigma Change* from the National Academies of Sciences, Engineering, and Medicine, some stakeholder groups are targeting the word "stigma" itself and the Substance Abuse and Mental Health Services Administration is shifting away from the use of this term. The committee determined that the word stigma was currently widely accepted in the research community and uses this term in the report.

existing evidence suggests that children and youth who are bullied experience a range of somatic disturbances, including sleep disturbances, gastrointestinal concerns, and headaches. Emerging research suggests that bullying can result in biological changes. The committee concludes that **although the effects of being bullied on the brain are not yet fully understood, there are changes in the stress response systems and in the brain that are associated with increased risk for mental health problems, cognitive function, self-regulation, and other physical health problems (Conclusion 4.3).**

As described in Chapter 4, being bullied during childhood and adolescence has been linked to psychological effects, such as depression, anxiety, and alcohol and drug abuse into adulthood. The committee concludes that **bullying has significant short- and long-term internalizing and externalizing psychological consequences for the children who are involved in bullying behavior (Conclusion 4.4).** Studies suggest that individuals who bully and who are also bullied by others are especially at risk for suicidal behavior due to increased mental health problems. Individuals who are involved in bullying in any capacity (as perpetrators, targets, or both) are statistically significantly more likely to contemplate or attempt suicide, compared to children who are not involved in bullying. However, there is not enough evidence to date to conclude that bullying is a causal factor for youth suicides. Focusing solely on bullying as a causal factor would ignore the many other influences that contribute to youth suicides.

With regard to the linkages between bullying and school shootings, several characteristics of the research that has been conducted on school shootings bear mentioning. First, to date, research has not been able to establish a reliable profile or set of risk factors that predicts who will become a school shooter. Second, it is important to keep in mind that multiple-victim school shootings are low base rate events, and thus caution should be used in generalizing findings from these rare events to broad populations of students. There is also a lack of reliable evidence about school shootings that may have been successfully prevented or averted.

Given that school shootings are rare events, most of what is known about them comes from studies that aggregate events over many years. These studies mostly employ qualitative methods, including descriptive post-incident psychological autopsies of the shooters, analysis of media accounts, or in-depth interviews of a small subset of surviving shooters. Most investigations have concluded that bullying may play a role in many school shootings but not all. It is a factor, and perhaps an important one, but it does not appear to be the main influencing factor in a decision to carry out these violent acts. Further, there is not enough evidence to date (qualitative or quantitative) to conclude that bullying is a causal factor for multiple-homicide targeted school shootings nor is there clear evidence on how bullying or related mental health and behavior issues contribute to school shootings. The committee concludes that **the data are unclear on the role of bullying as one of or a precipitating cause of school shootings (Conclusion 4.5)**.

Although the research is limited, children and youth who do the bullying also are more likely to be depressed, engage in high-risk activities such as theft and vandalism, and have adverse outcomes later in life, compared to those who do not bully. However, whereas some individuals who bully others may in fact be maladjusted, others who are motivated by establishing their status within their peer group do not evidence negative outcomes. Thus, the research on outcomes for children who bully is mixed, with most research on the short- and long-term outcomes of bullying not taking into account the heterogeneity of children who bully. The committee concludes that **individuals who both bully others and are themselves bullied appear to be at greatest risk for poor psychosocial outcomes, compared to those who only bully or are only bullied and to those who are not bullied (Conclusion 4.6)**.

Existing evidence suggests that **both social-cognitive and emotion regulation processes may mediate the relation between being bullied and adverse mental health outcomes (Conclusion 4.8)**. Regardless of mechanism, being bullied seems to have an impact on mental health functioning during adulthood. Prior experiences, such as experiences with early abuse and trauma; a chronically activated stress system due to home, school, or neighborhood stress; the length of the bullying experience; and the child's social support system, all interact to contribute to the neurobehavioral outcome of bullying.

A PIVOTAL TIME FOR PREVENTION: NEXT STEPS

This is a pivotal time for bullying prevention. Reducing the prevalence of bullying and minimizing the harm it imparts on children can have a dramatic impact on children's well-being and development. Many programs and policies have been developed, but more needs to be known about what types of programs or investments will be most effective. The committee concludes that **the vast majority of research on bullying prevention programming has focused on universal school-based programs; however, the effects of those programs within the United States appear to be relatively modest. Multicomponent schoolwide programs appear to be most effective at reducing bullying and should be the types of programs implemented and disseminated in the United States (Conclusion 5.1)**.

Universal prevention programs are aimed at reducing risks and strengthening skills for all youth within a defined community or school setting. Through universal programs, all members of the target population are exposed to the intervention regardless of risk for bullying. Examples of universal preventive interventions include social–emotional lessons that are used in the classroom, behavioral expectations taught by teachers, counselors coming into the classroom to model strategies for responding to or reporting bullying, and holding classroom meetings among students and teachers to discuss emotionally relevant issues related to bullying or equity. They may also include guidelines for the use of digital media, such as youth's use of social network sites.

Selective preventive interventions are directed either to youth who are at risk for engaging in bullying or to youth at risk of being a target of bullying. Such programs may include more intensive social–emotional skills training, coping skills, or de-escalation approaches for youth who are involved in bullying. Indicated preventive interventions are typically tailored to meet youth's needs and are of greater intensity as compared to the universal or selective levels of intervention. Indicated interventions incorporate more intensive supports and activities for those who are already displaying bullying behavior or who have a history of being bullied and are showing early signs of behavioral, academic, or mental health consequences.

There is a growing emphasis on the use of *multi-tiered approaches,* which leverage universal, selective, and indicated prevention programs and activities. These combined programs often attempt to address at the universal level such factors as social skill development, social–emotional learning or self-regulation, which also tend to reduce the chances that youth would engage in bullying or reduce the risk of being bullied further. Multi-tiered approaches are vertical programs that increase in intensity, whereas multicomponent approaches could be lateral and include different elements, such as a classroom, parent, and individual components bundled together.

Research indicates that positive relationships with teachers, parents, and peers appear to be protective. The committee concludes that **most of the school, family, and community-based prevention programs tested using randomized controlled trial designs have focused on youth violence, delinquency, social–emotional development, and academic outcomes, with limited consideration of the impacts on bullying specifically. However, it is likely that these programs also produce effects on bullying, which have largely been unmeasured and therefore data on bullying outcomes should be routinely collected in future research (Conclusion 5.2).**

Families play a critical role in bullying prevention by providing emotional support to promote disclosure of bullying incidents and by fostering coping skills in their children. And some research points to an opportunity to better engage bystanders, who have the best opportunity to intervene and minimize the effects of bullying.

Chapter 5 offers a number of specific ways to improve the quality and efficacy of preventive interventions. As concluded by the committee, **there has been limited research on selective and indicated models for bullying intervention programming, either inside or outside of schools. More at-**

tention should be given to these interventions in future bullying research (Conclusion 5.3).

There remains a dearth of intervention research on programs related to cyberbullying and on programs targeted to vulnerable populations, such as LGBT youth, youth with chronic health problems such as obesity, or youth with developmental disabilities such as autism. Schools may consider implementing a multicomponent program that focuses on school climate, positive behavior support, social–emotional learning, or violence prevention more generally, rather than implementing a bullying-specific preventive intervention, as these more inclusive programs may reach a broader set of outcomes for students and the school environment.

Moreover, suspension and related exclusionary techniques are often the default response by school staff and administrators in bullying situations. However, these approaches do not appear to be effective and may actually result in increased academic and behavioral problems for youth. Caution is also warranted about the types of roles youth play in bullying prevention programs. The committee concludes that **the role of peers in bullying prevention as bystanders and as intervention program leaders needs further clarification and empirical investigation in order to determine the extent to which peer-led programs are effective and robust against potentially iatrogenic effects (Conclusion 5.5).**

As the consequences of bullying become clearer and more widely known, states are adopting new laws and schools are embracing new programs and policies to reduce the prevalence of bullying. As noted in Chapter 6, over the past 15 years all 50 states and the District of Columbia have adopted or revised laws to address bullying. Forty-nine states and the District of Columbia include electronic forms of bullying (cyberbullying) in their statutes. The committee concludes that **law and policy have the potential to strengthen state and local efforts to prevent, identify, and respond to bullying (Conclusion 6.1).** However, there are few studies that have examined the actual effect of existing laws and policies in reducing bullying. The committee concludes that **the development of model anti-bullying laws or policies should be evidence based. Additional research is needed to determine the specific components of an anti-bullying law that are most effective in reducing bullying, in order to guide legislators who may amend existing laws or create new ones (Conclusion 6.2).** Further, **evidence-based research on the consequences of bullying can help inform litigation efforts at several stages, including case discovery and planning, pleadings, and trial (Conclusion 6.6).**

Some policies and programs have been shown to be ineffective in preventing bullying. The committee concludes **there is emerging research that some widely used approaches such as zero tolerance policies are not effective at reducing bullying and thus should be discontinued, with the resources redirected to evidence-based policies and programs (Conclusion 6.7).**

In Chapter 7, the committee makes seven recommendations. The first three recommendations are directed to the cognizant federal agencies and their partners in state and local governments and the private sector, for improving surveillance and monitoring activities in ways that will address the gaps in what is known about the prevalence of bullying behavior, what is known about children and youth who are at increased risk for being bullied, and what is known about the effectiveness of existing policies and programs. Another four recommendations are either directed at fostering the development, implementation, and evaluation of evidence-based preventive intervention programs and training or directed to social media companies and federal partners to adopt, implement, and evaluate policies and programs for preventing, identifying, and responding to bullying on their platforms. The committee's recommendations are provided below:

Recommendation 7.1: The U.S Departments of Agriculture, Defense, Education, Health and Human Services, and Justice, and the Federal Trade Commission, which are engaged in the Federal Partners in Bullying Prevention interagency group, should foster use of a consistent definition of bullying.

Recommendation 7.2: The U.S. Departments of Education, Health and Human Services, and Justice, and other agencies engaged in the Federal Partners in Bullying Prevention interagency group should gather longitudinal surveillance data on the prevalence of all forms of bullying, including physical, verbal, relational, property, cyber-, and bias-based bullying, and the prevalence of individuals involved in bullying, including perpetrators, targets, and bystanders, in order to have more uniform and accurate prevalence estimates.

Recommendation 7.3: The U.S. Department of Education's Office of Civil Rights, the state attorneys general, and local education agencies together should (1) partner with researchers to collect data on an ongoing basis on the efficacy and implementation of anti-bullying laws and policies; (2) convene an annual meeting in which collaborations between social scientists, legislative members, and practitioners responsible for creating, implementing, enforcing, and evaluating anti-bullying laws and policies can be more effectively facilitated and in which research on anti-bullying laws and policies can be reviewed; and (3) report research findings on an annual basis to both Congress and the state legislatures so that anti-bullying laws and policies can be strengthened and informed by evidence-based research.

Recommendation 7.4: The U.S. Departments of Education, Health and

Human Services, and Justice, working with other relevant stakeholders, should sponsor the development, implementation, and evaluation of evidence-based programs to address bullying behavior.

Recommendation 7.5: The U.S. Departments of Education, Health and Human Services, and Justice, working with other relevant stakeholders, should promote the evaluation of the role of stigma and bias in bullying behavior and sponsor the development, implementation, and evaluation of evidence-based programs to address stigma- and bias-based bullying behavior, including the stereotypes and prejudice that may underlie such behavior.

Recommendation 7.6: The U.S. Departments of Education and Health and Human Services, working with other partners, should support the development, implementation, and evaluation of evidence-informed bullying prevention training for individuals, both professionals and volunteers, who work directly with children and adolescents on a regular basis.

Recommendation 7.7: Social media companies, in partnership with the Federal Partners for Bullying Prevention Steering Committee, should adopt, implement, and evaluate on an ongoing basis policies and programs for preventing, identifying, and responding to bullying on their platforms and should publish their anti-bullying policies on their Websites.

In addition, the committee identified a set of current research gaps and recognized the value of future research in addressing issues raised in the report and important for a more comprehensive understanding of bullying behavior, its consequences, and factors that can ameliorate the harmful effects of bullying and foster resilience. These research needs are listed in Table 7-1 and are connected to general topics addressed in the report such as "Law and Policy," "Prevalence of Bullying," and "Protective Factors and Contexts."

The study of bullying behavior is a relatively recent field, and it is in transition. Over the past few decades, research has significantly improved understanding of what bullying behavior is, how it can be measured, and the critical contextual factors that are involved. While there is not a quick fix or one-size-fits-all solution, the evidence clearly supports preventive and interventional policy and practice. Tackling this complex and serious public health problem will require a commitment to research, analysis, trial, and refinement, but doing so can make a tangible difference in the lives of many children.

1

Introduction

Bullying, long tolerated by many as a rite of passage into adulthood, is now recognized as a major and preventable public health problem, one that can have long-lasting consequences (McDougall and Vaillancourt, 2015; Wolke and Lereya, 2015). Those consequences—for those who are bullied, for the perpetrators of bullying, and for witnesses who are present during a bullying event—include poor school performance, anxiety, depression, and future delinquent and aggressive behavior. Federal, state, and local governments have responded by adopting laws and implementing programs to prevent bullying and deal with its consequences. However, many of these responses have been undertaken with little attention to what is known about bullying and its effects. Even the definition of bullying varies among both researchers and lawmakers, though it generally includes physical and verbal behavior, behavior leading to social isolation, and behavior that uses digital communications technology (cyberbullying). This report adopts the term "bullying behavior," which is frequently used in the research field, to cover all of these behaviors.

Bullying behavior is evident as early as preschool, although it peaks during the middle school years (Currie et al., 2012; Vaillancourt et al., 2010). It can occur in diverse social settings, including classrooms, school gyms and cafeterias, on school buses, and online. Bullying behavior affects not only the children and youth who are bullied, who bully, and who are both bullied and bully others but also bystanders to bullying incidents. Given the myriad situations in which bullying can occur and the many people who may be involved, identifying effective prevention programs and policies is challenging, and it is unlikely that any one approach will be appropriate in all situations. Commonly used bullying prevention approaches include policies regarding acceptable behavior in schools and behavioral interventions to promote positive cultural norms.

STUDY CHARGE

Recognizing that bullying behavior is a major public health problem that demands the concerted and coordinated time and attention of parents, educators and school administrators, health care providers, policy makers, families, and others concerned with the care of children, a group of federal agencies and private foundations asked the National Academies of Sciences, Engineering, and Medicine to undertake a study of what is known and what needs to be known to further the field of preventing bullying behavior. The Committee on the Biological and Psychosocial Effects of Peer Victimization:

BOX 1-1
Statement of Task

The Board on Children, Youth, and Families of the Institute of Medicine and the National Research Council (NRC), in conjunction with the NRC's Committee on Law and Justice will convene a committee of experts to conduct a consensus study that will produce a comprehensive report on the state of the science on: (1) the biological and psychosocial consequences of peer victimization and (2) the risk and protective factors that either increase or decrease peer victimization behavior and consequences. Given the limited research on bullying specifically and potential to learn from other areas of victimization, the study committee will review the relevant research and practice-based literatures on peer victimization, including physical, verbal, relational, and cyber, from early childhood through adolescence. The committee can also draw upon research in other areas of victimization to inform the core questions of this study. A particular focus on children who are most at risk of peer victimization—i.e., those with high risk factors in combination with few protective factors—such as children with disabilities, poly-victims,[1] LGBT youth, and children living in poverty will be included in the study. The work of the committee will build on the workshop, *Building Capacity to Reduce Bullying*, as appropriate. The following questions are of particular interest:

• What is known about the physiological and psychosocial consequences of peer victimization for both the perpetrator and target? Specifically, what is the state of research on the neurobiological and mental and behavioral health effects of peer victimization?

Lessons for Bullying Prevention was created to carry out this task under the Academies' Board on Children, Youth, and Families and the Committee on Law and Justice. The study received financial support from the Centers for Disease Control and Prevention (CDC), the Eunice Kennedy Shriver National Institute of Child Health and Human Development, the Health Resources and Services Administration, the Highmark Foundation, the National Institute of Justice, the Robert Wood Johnson Foundation, Semi J. and Ruth W. Begun Foundation, and the Substance Abuse and Mental Health Services Administration. The full statement of task for the committee is presented in Box 1-1.

Although the committee acknowledges the importance of this topic as it pertains to all children in the United States and in U.S. territories, this report focuses on the 50 states and the District of Columbia. Also, while the committee acknowledges that bullying behavior occurs in the school

- How are individual and other characteristics (e.g., cognitive and social skills and affective dispositions) related to the dynamic between perpetrator and target and the subsequent initial signs and long-term outcomes for both?
- What factors contribute to resilient outcomes of youth exposed to, and engaged in, peer victimization (e.g., safe and supportive school climate, relationships with adults and peers)?

Based on currently available evidence, the committee will address the questions above and provide findings, conclusions, and recommendations that can inform future policy (e.g., state legislatures, school districts), practice (e.g., school safety, disciplinary actions, health care provision, law enforcement), and future research on promising approaches to reduce peer victimization, particularly for vulnerable populations and those most at-risk of experiencing peer victimization. The committee will also identify 3-5 key research gaps, that if filled would significantly inform the knowledge base about how to reduce peer victimization.

[1]The terms "poly-victim" and "poly-victimization" have been coined to represent a subset of youth who experience multiple victimizations of different kinds, such as exposure to (1) violent and property crimes (e.g., assault, sexual assault, theft, burglary), (2) child welfare violations (child abuse, family abduction), (3) the violence of warfare and civil disturbances, and (4) bullying behavior, and who manifest high levels of traumatic symptomatology (Finkelhor et al., 2007). See Chapter 4 for more information about children who are poly-victims.

environment for youth in foster care, in juvenile justice facilities, and in other residential treatment facilities, this report does not address bullying behavior in those environments because it is beyond the study charge.

CONTEXT FOR THE STUDY

This section of the report highlights relevant work in the field and, later in the chapter under "The Committee's Approach," presents the conceptual framework and corresponding definitions of terms that the committee has adopted.

Historical Context

Bullying behavior was first characterized in the scientific literature as part of the childhood experience more than 100 years ago in "Teasing and Bullying," published in the *Pedagogical Seminary* (Burk, 1897). The author described bullying behavior, attempted to delineate causes and cures for the tormenting of others, and called for additional research (Koo, 2007). Nearly a century later, Dan Olweus, a Swedish research professor of psychology in Norway, conducted an intensive study on bullying (Olweus, 1978). The efforts of Olweus brought awareness to the issue and motivated other professionals to conduct their own research, thereby expanding and contributing to knowledge of bullying behavior. Since Olweus's early work, research on bullying has steadily increased (see Farrington and Ttofi, 2009; Hymel and Swearer, 2015).

Over the past few decades, venues where bullying behavior occurs have expanded with the advent of the Internet, chat rooms, instant messaging, social media, and other forms of digital electronic communication. These modes of communication have provided a new communal avenue for bullying. While the media reports linking bullying to suicide suggest a causal relationship, the available research suggests that there are often multiple factors that contribute to a youth's suicide-related ideology and behavior. Several studies, however, have demonstrated an association between bullying involvement and suicide-related ideology and behavior (see, e.g., Holt et al., 2015; Kim and Leventhal, 2008; Sourander, 2010; van Geel et al., 2014).

In 2013, the Health Resources and Services Administration of the U.S. Department of Health and Human Services requested that the Institute of Medicine[1] and the National Research Council convene an ad hoc planning committee to plan and conduct a 2-day public workshop to highlight relevant information and knowledge that could inform a multidisciplinary

---

[1] Prior to 2015, the National Academy of Medicine was known as the Institute of Medicine.

road map on next steps for the field of bullying prevention. Content areas that were explored during the April 2014 workshop included the identification of conceptual models and interventions that have proven effective in decreasing bullying and the antecedents to bullying while increasing protective factors that mitigate the negative health impact of bullying. The discussions highlighted the need for a better understanding of the effectiveness of program interventions in realistic settings; the importance of understanding what works for whom and under what circumstances, as well as the influence of different mediators (i.e., what accounts for associations between variables) and moderators (i.e., what affects the direction or strength of associations between variables) in bullying prevention efforts; and the need for coordination among agencies to prevent and respond to bullying. The workshop summary (Institute of Medicine and National Research Council, 2014c) informs this committee's work.

Federal Efforts to Address Bullying and Related Topics

Currently, there is no comprehensive federal statute that explicitly prohibits bullying among children and adolescents, including cyberbullying. However, in the wake of the growing concerns surrounding the implications of bullying, several federal initiatives do address bullying among children and adolescents, and although some of them do not primarily focus on bullying, they permit some funds to be used for bullying prevention purposes.

The earliest federal initiative was in 1999, when three agencies collaborated to establish the Safe Schools/Healthy Students initiative in response to a series of deadly school shootings in the late 1990s. The program is administered by the U.S. Departments of Education, Health and Human Services, and Justice to prevent youth violence and promote the healthy development of youth. It is jointly funded by the Department of Education and by the Department of Health and Human Services' Substance Abuse and Mental Health Services Administration. The program has provided grantees with both the opportunity to benefit from collaboration and the tools to sustain it through deliberate planning, more cost-effective service delivery, and a broader funding base (Substance Abuse and Mental Health Services Administration, 2015).

The next major effort was in 2010, when the Department of Education awarded $38.8 million in grants under the Safe and Supportive Schools (S3) Program to 11 states to support statewide measurement of conditions for learning and targeted programmatic interventions to improve conditions for learning, in order to help schools improve safety and reduce substance use. The S3 Program was administered by the Safe and Supportive Schools Group, which also administered the Safe and Drug-Free Schools and Communities Act State and Local Grants Program, authorized by the

1994 Elementary and Secondary Education Act.[2] It was one of several programs related to developing and maintaining safe, disciplined, and drug-free schools. In addition to the S3 grants program, the group administered a number of interagency agreements with a focus on (but not limited to) bullying, school recovery research, data collection, and drug and violence prevention activities (U.S. Department of Education, 2015).

A collaborative effort among the U.S. Departments of Agriculture, Defense, Education, Health and Human Services, Interior, and Justice; the Federal Trade Commission; and the White House Initiative on Asian Americans and Pacific Islanders created the Federal Partners in Bullying Prevention (FPBP) Steering Committee. Led by the U.S. Department of Education, the FPBP works to coordinate policy, research, and communications on bullying topics. The FPBP Website provides extensive resources on bullying behavior, including information on what bullying is, its risk factors, its warning signs, and its effects.[3] The FPBP Steering Committee also plans to provide details on how to get help for those who have been bullied. It also was involved in creating the "Be More than a Bystander" Public Service Announcement campaign with the Ad Council to engage students in bullying prevention. To improve school climate and reduce rates of bullying nationwide, FPBP has sponsored four bullying prevention summits attended by education practitioners, policy makers, researchers, and federal officials.

In 2014, the National Institute of Justice—the scientific research arm of the U.S. Department of Justice—launched the Comprehensive School Safety Initiative with a congressional appropriation of $75 million. The funds are to be used for rigorous research to produce practical knowledge that can improve the safety of schools and students, including bullying prevention. The initiative is carried out through partnerships among researchers, educators, and other stakeholders, including law enforcement, behavioral and mental health professionals, courts, and other justice system professionals (National Institute of Justice, 2015).

In 2015, the Every Student Succeeds Act was signed by President Obama, reauthorizing the 50-year-old Elementary and Secondary Education Act, which is committed to providing equal opportunities for all students. Although bullying is neither defined nor prohibited in this act, it is explicitly mentioned in regard to applicability of safe school funding, which it had not been in previous iterations of the Elementary and Secondary Education Act.

The above are examples of federal initiatives aimed at promoting the

---

[2]The Safe and Drug-Free Schools and Communities Act was included as Title IV, Part A, of the 1994 Elementary and Secondary Education Act. See http://www.ojjdp.gov/pubs/gun_violence/sect08-i.html [October 2015].

[3]For details, see http://www.stopbullying.gov/ [October 2015].

healthy development of youth, improving the safety of schools and students, and reducing rates of bullying behavior. There are several other federal initiatives that address student bullying directly or allow funds to be used for bullying prevention activities.

Definitional Context

The terms "bullying," "harassment," and "peer victimization" have been used in the scientific literature to refer to behavior that is aggressive, is carried out repeatedly and over time, and occurs in an interpersonal relationship where a power imbalance exists (Eisenberg and Aalsma, 2005). Although some of these terms have been used interchangeably in the literature, peer victimization is targeted aggressive behavior of one child against another that causes physical, emotional, social, or psychological harm. While conflict and bullying among siblings are important in their own right (Tanrikulu and Campbell, 2015), this area falls outside of the scope of the committee's charge. Sibling conflict and aggression falls under the broader concept of interpersonal aggression, which includes dating violence, sexual assault, and sibling violence, in addition to bullying as defined for this report. Olweus (1993) noted that bullying, unlike other forms of peer victimization where the children involved are equally matched, involves a power imbalance between the perpetrator and the target, where the target has difficulty defending him or herself and feels helpless against the aggressor. This power imbalance is typically considered a defining feature of bullying, which distinguishes this particular form of aggression from other forms, and is typically repeated in multiple bullying incidents involving the same individuals over time (Olweus, 1993).

Bullying and violence are subcategories of aggressive behavior that overlap (Olweus, 1996). There are situations in which violence is used in the context of bullying. However, not all forms of bullying (e.g., rumor spreading) involve violent behavior. The committee also acknowledges that perspective about intentions can matter and that in many situations, there may be at least two plausible perceptions involved in the bullying behavior.

A number of factors may influence one's perception of the term "bullying" (Smith and Monks, 2008). Children and adolescents' understanding of the term "bullying" may be subject to cultural interpretations or translations of the term (Hopkins et al., 2013). Studies have also shown that influences on children's understanding of bullying include the child's experiences as he or she matures and whether the child witnesses the bullying behavior of others (Hellström et al., 2015; Monks and Smith, 2006; Smith and Monks, 2008).

In 2010, the FPBP Steering Committee convened its first summit, which brought together more than 150 nonprofit and corporate leaders, researchers, practitioners, parents, and youths to identify challenges in bullying prevention. Discussions at the summit revealed inconsistencies in the definition of bullying behavior and the need to create a uniform definition of bullying. Subsequently, a review of the 2011 CDC publication of assessment tools used to measure bullying among youth (Hamburger et al., 2011) revealed inconsistent definitions of bullying and diverse measurement strategies. Those inconsistencies and diverse measurements make it difficult to compare the prevalence of bullying across studies (Vivolo et al., 2011) and complicate the task of distinguishing bullying from other types of aggression between youths. A uniform definition can support the consistent tracking of bullying behavior over time, facilitate the comparison of bullying prevalence rates and associated risk and protective factors across different data collection systems, and enable the collection of comparable information on the performance of bullying intervention and prevention programs across contexts (Gladden et al., 2014). The CDC and U.S. Department of Education collaborated on the creation of the following uniform definition of bullying (quoted in Gladden et al., 2014, p. 7):

> Bullying is any unwanted aggressive behavior(s) by another youth or group of youths who are not siblings or current dating partners that involves an observed or perceived power imbalance and is repeated multiple times or is highly likely to be repeated. Bullying may inflict harm or distress on the targeted youth including physical, psychological, social, or educational harm.

This report noted that the definition includes school-age individuals ages 5-18 and explicitly excludes sibling violence and violence that occurs in the context of a dating or intimate relationship (Gladden et al., 2014). This definition also highlighted that there are direct and indirect modes of bullying, as well as different types of bullying. Direct bullying involves "aggressive behavior(s) that occur in the presence of the targeted youth"; indirect bullying includes "aggressive behavior(s) that are not directly communicated to the targeted youth" (Gladden et al., 2014, p. 7). The direct forms of violence (e.g., sibling violence, teen dating violence, intimate partner violence) can include aggression that is physical, sexual, or psychological, but the context and uniquely dynamic nature of the relationship between the target and the perpetrator in which these acts occur is different from that of peer bullying. Examples of direct bullying include pushing, hitting, verbal taunting, or direct written communication. A common form of indirect bullying is spreading rumors. Four different types of bullying are commonly identified—physical, verbal, relational, and damage to property. Some observational studies have shown that the different forms of bullying that youths commonly experience may overlap (Bradshaw et al., 2015;

Godleski et al., 2015). The four types of bullying are defined as follows (Gladden et al., 2014):

- Physical bullying involves the use of physical force (e.g., shoving, hitting, spitting, pushing, and tripping).
- Verbal bullying involves oral or written communication that causes harm (e.g., taunting, name calling, offensive notes or hand gestures, verbal threats).
- Relational bullying is behavior "designed to harm the reputation and relationships of the targeted youth (e.g., social isolation, rumor spreading, posting derogatory comments or pictures online)."
- Damage to property is "theft, alteration, or damaging of the target youth's property by the perpetrator to cause harm."

In recent years, a new form of aggression or bullying has emerged, labeled "cyberbullying," in which the aggression occurs through modern technological devices, specifically mobile phones or the Internet (Slonje and Smith, 2008). Cyberbullying may take the form of mean or nasty messages or comments, rumor spreading through posts or creation of groups, and exclusion by groups of peers online.

While the CDC definition identifies bullying that occurs using technology as electronic bullying and views that as a context or location where bullying occurs, one of the major challenges in the field is how to conceptualize and define cyberbullying (Tokunaga, 2010). The extent to which the CDC definition can be applied to cyberbullying is unclear, particularly with respect to several key concepts within the CDC definition. First, whether determination of an interaction as "wanted" or "unwanted" or whether communication was intended to be harmful can be challenging to assess in the absence of important in-person socioemotional cues (e.g., vocal tone, facial expressions). Second, assessing "repetition" is challenging in that a single harmful act on the Internet has the potential to be shared or viewed multiple times (Sticca and Perren, 2013). Third, cyberbullying can involve a less powerful peer using technological tools to bully a peer who is perceived to have more power. In this manner, technology may provide the tools that create a power imbalance, in contrast to traditional bullying, which typically involves an existing power imbalance.

A study that used focus groups with college students to discuss whether the CDC definition applied to cyberbullying found that students were wary of applying the definition due to their perception that cyberbullying often involves less emphasis on aggression, intention, and repetition than other forms of bullying (Kota et al., 2014). Many researchers have responded to this lack of conceptual and definitional clarity by creating their own measures to assess cyberbullying. It is noteworthy that very few of these definitions and measures include the components of traditional bullying—i.e., repetition, power imbalance, and intent (Berne et al., 2013). A more recent study argues that the term "cyberbullying" should be reserved for incidents that involve key aspects of bullying such as repetition and differential power (Ybarra et al., 2014).

Although the formulation of a uniform definition of bullying appears to be a step in the right direction for the field of bullying prevention, there are some limitations of the CDC definition. For example, some researchers find the focus on school-age youth as well as the repeated nature of bullying to be rather limiting; similarly the exclusion of bullying in the context of sibling relationships or dating relationships may preclude full appreciation of the range of aggressive behaviors that may co-occur with or constitute bullying behavior. As noted above, other researchers have raised concerns about whether cyberbullying should be considered a particular form or mode under the broader heading of bullying as suggested in the CDC definition, or whether a separate defintion is needed. Furthermore, the measurement of bullying prevalence using such a definiton of bullying is rather complex and does not lend itself well to large-scale survey research. The CDC definition was intended to inform public health surveillance efforts, rather than to serve as a definition for policy. However, increased alignment between bullying definitions used by policy makers and researchers would greatly advance the field. Much of the extant research on bullying has not applied a consistent definition or one that aligns with the CDC definition. As a result of these and other challenges to the CDC definition, thus far there has been inconsistent adoption of this particular definition by researchers, practitioners, or policy makers; however, as the definition was created in 2014, less than 2 years is not a sufficient amount of time to assess whether it has been successfully adopted or will be in the future.

THE COMMITTEE'S APPROACH

This report builds on the April 2014 workshop, summarized in *Building Capacity to Reduce Bullying: Workshop Summary* (Institute of Medicine and National Research Council, 2014c). The committee's work was accomplished over an 18-month period that began in October 2014, after the workshop was held and the formal summary of it had been released. The study committee members represented expertise in communication technology, criminology, developmental and clinical psychology, education, mental health, neurobiological development, pediatrics, public health, school administration, school district policy, and state law and policy. (See Appendix E for biographical sketches of the committee members and staff.) The committee met three times in person and conducted other meetings by teleconferences and electronic communication.

Information Gathering

The committee conducted an extensive review of the literature pertaining to peer victimization and bullying. In some instances, the committee drew upon the broader literature on aggression and violence. The review began with an English-language literature search of online databases, including ERIC, Google Scholar, Lexis Law Reviews Database, Medline, PubMed, Scopus, PsycInfo, and Web of Science, and was expanded as literature and resources from other countries were identified by committee members and project staff as relevant. The committee drew upon the early childhood literature since there is substantial evidence indicating that bullying involvement happens as early as preschool (see Vlachou et al., 2011). The committee also drew on the literature on late adolescence and looked at related areas of research such as maltreatment for insights into this emerging field.

The committee used a variety of sources to supplement its review of the literature. The committee held two public information-gathering sessions, one with the study sponsors and the second with experts on the neurobiology of bullying; bullying as a group phenomenon and the role of bystanders; the role of media in bullying prevention; and the intersection of social science, the law, and bullying and peer victimization. See Appendix A for the agendas for these two sessions. To explore different facets of bullying and give perspectives from the field, a subgroup of the committee and study staff also conducted a site visit to a northeastern city, where they convened four stakeholder groups comprised, respectively, of local practitioners, school personnel, private foundation representatives, and young adults. The site visit provided the committee with an opportunity for place-based learning about bullying prevention programs and best practices. Each focus group was transcribed and summarized thematically in accordance with this report's chapter considerations. Themes related to the chapters are displayed throughout the report in boxes titled "Perspectives from the Field"; these boxes reflect responses synthesized from all four focus groups. See Appendix B for the site visit's agenda and for summaries of the focus groups.

The committee also benefited from earlier reports by the National Academies of Sciences, Engineering, and Medicine through its Division of Behavioral and Social Sciences and Education and the Institute of Medicine, most notably:

- *Reducing Risks for Mental Disorders: Frontiers for Preventive Intervention Research* (Institute of Medicine, 1994)
- *Community Programs to Promote Youth Development* (National Research Council and Institute of Medicine, 2002)

- *Deadly Lessons: Understanding Lethal School Violence* (National Research Council and Institute of Medicine, 2003)
- *Preventing Mental, Emotional, and Behavioral Disorders Among Young People: Progress and Possibilities* (National Research Council and Institute of Medicine, 2009)
- *The Science of Adolescent Risk-Taking: Workshop Report* (Institute of Medicine and National Research Council, 2011)
- *Communications and Technology for Violence Prevention: Workshop Summary* (Institute of Medicine and National Research Council, 2012)
- *Building Capacity to Reduce Bullying: Workshop Summary* (Institute of Medicine and National Research Council, 2014c)
- *The Evidence for Violence Prevention across the Lifespan and Around the World: Workshop Summary* (Institute of Medicine and National Research Council, 2014a)
- *Strategies for Scaling Effective Family-Focused Preventive Interventions to Promote Children's Cognitive, Affective, and Behavioral Health: Workshop Summary* (Institute of Medicine and National Research Council, 2014b)
- *Investing in the Health and Well-Being of Young Adults* (Institute of Medicine and National Research Council, 2015)

Although these past reports and workshop summaries address various forms of violence and victimization, this report is the first consensus study by the National Academies of Sciences, Engineering, and Medicine on the state of the science on the biological and psychosocial consequences of bullying and the risk and protective factors that either increase or decrease bullying behavior and its consequences.

Terminology

Given the variable use of the terms "bullying" and "peer victimization" in both the research-based and practice-based literature, the committee chose to use the current CDC definition quoted above (Gladden et al., 2014, p. 7). While the committee determined that this was the best definition to use, it acknowledges that this definition is not necessarily the most user-friendly definition for students and has the potential to cause problems for students reporting bullying. Not only does this definition provide detail on the common elements of bullying behavior but it also was developed with input from a panel of researchers and practitioners. The committee also followed the CDC in focusing primarily on individuals between the ages of 5 and 18. The committee recognizes that children's development occurs on a continuum, and so while it relied primarily on the CDC definition, its work and this report acknowledge the importance of addressing bullying in both early childhood and emerging adulthood. For purposes of this report, the committee used the terms "early childhood" to refer to ages 1-4, "middle childhood" for ages 5 to 10, "early adolescence" for ages 11-14, "middle adolescence" for ages 15-17, and "late adolescence" for ages 18-21. This terminology and the associated age ranges are consistent with the Bright Futures and American Academy of Pediatrics definition of the stages of development.[4]

A given instance of bullying behavior involves at least two unequal roles: one or more individuals who perpetrate the behavior (the perpetrator in this instance) and at least one individual who is bullied (the target in this instance). To avoid labeling and potentially further stigmatizing individuals with the terms "bully" and "victim," which are sometimes viewed as traits of persons rather than role descriptions in a particular instance of behavior, the committee decided to use "individual who is bullied" to refer to the target of a bullying instance or pattern and "individual who bullies" to refer to the perpetrator of a bullying instance or pattern. Thus, "individual who is bullied and bullies others" can refer to one who is either perpetrating a bullying behavior or a target of bullying behavior, depending on the incident. This terminology is consistent with the approach used by the FPBP (see above). Also, bullying is a dynamic social interaction (Espelage and Swearer, 2003) where individuals can play different roles in bullying interactions based on both individual and contextual factors.

The committee used "cyberbullying" to refer to bullying that takes place using technology or digital electronic means. "Digital electronic forms of contact" comprise a broad category that may include e-mail, blogs, social networking Websites, online games, chat rooms, forums, instant messaging, Skype, text messaging, and mobile phone pictures. The committee uses the term "traditional bullying" to refer to bullying behavior that is not cyberbullying (to aid in comparisons), recognizing that the term has been used at times in slightly different senses in the literature.

Where accurate reporting of study findings requires use of the above terms but with senses different from those specified here, the committee has noted the sense in which the source used the term. Similarly, accurate reporting has at times required use of terms such as "victimization" or "victim" that the committee has chosen to avoid in its own statements.

---

[4]For details on these stages of adolescence, see https://brightfutures.aap.org/Bright%20 Futures%20Documents/3-Promoting_Child_Development.pdf [October 2015].

ORGANIZATION OF THE REPORT

This report is organized into seven chapters. After this introductory chapter, Chapter 2 provides a broad overview of the scope of the problem. Chapter 3 focuses on the conceptual frameworks for the study and the developmental trajectory of the child who is bullied, the child who bullies, and the child who is bullied and also bullies. It explores processes that can explain heterogeneity in bullying outcomes by focusing on contextual processes that moderate the effect of individual characteristics on bullying behavior.

Chapter 4 discusses the cyclical nature of bullying and the consequences of bullying behavior. It summarizes what is known about the psychosocial, physical health, neurobiological, academic-performance, and population-level consequences of bullying.

Chapter 5 provides an overview of the landscape in bullying prevention programming. This chapter describes in detail the context for preventive interventions and the specific actions that various stakeholders can take to achieve a coordinated response to bullying behavior. The chapter uses the Institute of Medicine's multi-tiered framework (National Research Council and Institute of Medicine, 2009) to present the different levels of approaches to preventing bullying behavior.

Chapter 6 reviews what is known about federal, state, and local laws and policies and their impact on bullying.

After a critical review of the relevant research and practice-based literatures, Chapter 7 discusses the committee conclusions and recommendations and provides a path forward for bullying prevention.

The report includes a number of appendixes. Appendix A includes meeting agendas of the committee's public information-gathering meetings. Appendix B includes the agenda and summaries of the site visit. Appendix C includes summaries of bullying prevalence data from the national surveys discussed in Chapter 2. Appendix D provides a list of selected federal resources on bullying for parents and teachers. Appendix E provides biographical sketches of the committee members and project staff.

REFERENCES

Berne, S., Frisén, A., Schultze-Krumbholz, A., Scheithauer, H., Naruskov, K., Luik, P., Katzer, C., Erentaite, R., and Zukauskiene, R. (2013). Cyberbullying assessment instruments: A systematic review. *Aggression and Violent Behavior, 18*(2), 320-334.

Bradshaw, C.P., Waasdorp, T.E., and Johnson, S.L. (2015). Overlapping verbal, relational, physical, and electronic forms of bullying in adolescence: Influence of school context. *Journal of Clinical Child & Adolescent Psychology, 44*(3), 494-508.

Burk, F.L. (1897). Teasing and bullying. *The Pedagogical Seminary, 4*(3), 336-371.

Currie, C., Zanotti, C., Morgan, A., Currie, D., de Looze, M., Roberts, C., Samdal, O., Smith, O.R., and Barnekow, V. (2012). Social determinants of health and well-being among young people. Copenhagen, Denmark: World Health Organization Regional Office for Europe.

Eisenberg, M.E., and Aalsma, M.C. (2005). Bullying and peer victimization: Position paper of the Society for Adolescent Medicine. *Journal of Adolescent Health, 36*(1), 88-91.

Espelage, D.L., and Swearer, S.M. (2003). Research on school bullying and victimization: What have we learned and where do we go from here? *School Psychology Review, 32*(3), 365-383.

Farrington, D., and Ttofi, M. (2009). School-based programs to reduce bullying and victimization: A systematic review. *Campbell Systematic Reviews, 5*(6).

Finkelhor, D., Ormrod, R.K., and Turner, H.A. (2007). Poly-victimization: A neglected component in child victimization. *Child Abuse & Neglect, 31*(1), 7-26.

Gladden, R.M., Vivolo-Kantor, A.M., Hamburger, M.E., and Lumpkin, C.D. (2014). *Bullying Surveillance among Youths: Uniform Definitions for Public Health and Recommended Data Elements, Version 1.0.* Atlanta, GA: Centers for Disease Control and Prevention and U.S. Department of Education.

Godleski, S.A., Kamper, K.E., Ostrov, J.M., Hart, E.J., and Blakely-McClure, S.J. (2015). Peer victimization and peer rejection during early childhood. *Journal of Clinical Child & Adolescent Psychology, 44*(3), 380-392.

Hamburger, M.E., Basile, K.C., and Vivolo, A.M. (2011). *Measuring Bullying Victimization, Perpetration, and Bystander Experiences: A Compendium of Assessment Tools.* Atlanta, GA: Centers for Disease Control and Prevention, National Center for Injury Prevention and Control.

Hellström, L., Persson, L., and Hagquist, C. (2015). Understanding and defining bullying— Adolescents' own views. *Archives of Public Health, 73*(4), 1-9.

Holt, M.K., Vivolo-Kantor, A.M., Polanin, J.R., Holland, K.M., DeGue, S., Matjasko, J.L., Wolfe, M., and Reid, G. (2015). Bullying and suicidal ideation and behaviors: A meta-analysis. *Pediatrics, 135*(2), e496-e509.

Hopkins, L., Taylor, L., Bowen, E., and Wood, C. (2013). A qualitative study investigating adolescents' understanding of aggression, bullying and violence. *Children and Youth Services Review, 35*(4), 685-693.

Hymel, S., and Swearer, S.M. (2015). Four decades of research on school bullying: An introduction. *American Psychologist, 70*(4), 293.

Institute of Medicine. (1994). *Reducing Risks for Mental Disorders: Frontiers for Preventive Intervention Research.* Committee on Prevention of Mental Disorders. P.J. Mrazek and R.J. Haggerty, Editors. Division of Biobehavioral Sciences and Mental Disorders. Washington, DC: National Academy Press.

Institute of Medicine and National Research Council. (2011). *The Science of Adolescent Risk-taking: Workshop Report.* Committee on the Science of Adolescence.Washington, DC: The National Academies Press.

Institute of Medicine and National Research Council. (2012). *Communications and Technology for Violence Prevention: Workshop Summary.* Washington, DC: The National Academies Press.

Institute of Medicine and National Research Council. (2014a). *The Evidence for Violence Prevention across the Lifespan and around the World: Workshop Summary.* Washington, DC: The National Academies Press.

Institute of Medicine and National Research Council. (2014b). *Strategies for Scaling Effective Family-Focused Preventive Interventions to Promote Children's Cognitive, Affective, and Behavioral Health: Workshop Summary.* Washington, DC: The National Academies Press.

Institute of Medicine and National Research Council. (2014c). *Building Capacity to Reduce Bullying: Workshop Summary.* Washington, DC: The National Academies Press.

Institute of Medicine and National Research Council. (2015). *Investing in the Health and Well-Being of Young Adults.* Washington, DC: The National Academies Press.

Kim, Y.S., and Leventhal, B. (2008). Bullying and suicide. A review. *International Journal of Adolescent Medicine and Health, 20*(2), 133-154.

Koo, H. (2007). A time line of the evolution of school bullying in differing social contexts. *Asia Pacific Education Review, 8*(1), 107-116.

Kota, R., Schoohs, S., Benson, M., and Moreno, M.A. (2014). Characterizing cyberbullying among college students: Hacking, dirty laundry, and mocking. *Societies, 4*(4), 549-560.

McDougall, P., and Vaillancourt, T. (2015). Long-term adult outcomes of peer victimization in childhood and adolescence: Pathways to adjustment and maladjustment. *American Psychologist, 70*(4), 300.

Monks, C.P., and Smith, P.K. (2006). Definitions of bullying: Age differences in understanding of the term and the role of experience. *British Journal of Developmental Psychology, 24*(4), 801-821.

National Institute of Justice. (2015). *Comprehensive School Safety Initiative. 2015.* Available: http://nij.gov/topics/crime/school-crime/Pages/school-safety-initiative.aspx#about [October 2015].

National Research Council and Institute of Medicine. (2002). *Community Programs to Promote Youth Development.* Committee on Community-Level Programs for Youth. J. Eccles and J.A. Gootman, Editors. Board on Children, Youth, and Families, Division of Behavioral and Social Sciences and Education. Washington, DC: National Academy Press.

National Research Council and Institute of Medicine. (2003). *Deadly Lessons: Understanding Lethal School Violence.* Case Studies of School Violence Committee. M.H. Moore, C.V. Petrie, A.A. Barga, and B.L. McLaughlin, Editors. Division of Behavioral and Social Sciences and Education. Washington, DC: The National Academies Press.

National Research Council and Institute of Medicine. (2009). *Preventing Mental, Emotional, and Behavioral Disorders among Young People: Progress and Possibilities.* Committee on the Prevention of Mental Disorders and Substance Abuse Among Children, Youth, and Young Adults: Research Advances and Promising Interventions. M.E. O'Connell, T. Boat, and K.E. Warner, Editors. Board on Children, Youth, and Families, Division of Behavioral and Social Sciences and Education. Washington, DC: The National Academies Press.

Olweus, D. (1978). *Aggression in the Schools: Bullies and Whipping Boys.* Washington, DC: Hemisphere.

Olweus, D. (1993). *Bullying at School. What We Know and Whal We Can Do.* Oxford, UK: Blackwell.

Olweus, D. (1996). Bully/victim problems in school. *Prospects, 26*(2), 331-359.

Slonje, R., and Smith, P.K. (2008). Cyberbullying: Another main type of bullying? *Scandinavian Journal of Psychology, 49*(2), 147-154.

Smith, P. ., and Monks, C. . (2008). Concepts of bullying: Developmental and cultural aspects. *International Journal of Adolescent Medicine and Health, 20*(2), 101-112.

Sourander, A. (2010). The association of suicide and bullying in childhood to young adulthood: A review of cross-sectional and longitudinal research findings. *Canadian Journal of Psychiatry, 55*(5), 282.

Sticca, F., and Perren, S. (2013). Is cyberbullying worse than traditional bullying? Examining the differential roles of medium, publicity, and anonymity for the perceived severity of bullying. *Journal of Youth and Adolescence, 42*(5), 739-750.

Substance Abuse and Mental Health Services Administration. (2015). *Safe Schools/Healthy Students. 2015.* Available: http://www.samhsa.gov/safe-schools-healthy-students/about [November 2015].

Tanrikulu, I., and Campbell, M. (2015). Correlates of traditional bullying and cyberbullying perpetration among Australian students. *Children and Youth Services Review, 55,* 138-146.

Tokunaga, R.S. (2010). Following you home from school: A critical review and synthesis of research on cyberbullying victimization. *Computers in Human Behavior, 26*(3), 277-287.

U.S. Department of Education. (2015). *Safe and Supportive Schools.* Available: http://www.ed.gov/news/press-releases/us-department-education-awards-388-million-safe-and-supportive-school-grants [October 2015].

Vaillancourt, T., Trinh, V., McDougall, P., Duku, E., Cunningham, L., Cunningham, C., Hymel, S., and Short, K. (2010). Optimizing population screening of bullying in school-aged children. *Journal of School Violence, 9*(3), 233-250.

van Geel, M., Vedder, P., and Tanilon, J. (2014). Relationship between peer victimization, cyberbullying, and suicide in children and adolescents: A meta-analysis. *Journal of the American Medical Association. Pediatrics, 168*(5), 435-442.

Vivolo, A.M., Holt, M.K., and Massetti, G.M. (2011). Individual and contextual factors for bullying and peer victimization: Implications for prevention. *Journal of School Violence, 10*(2), 201-212.

Vlachou, M., Andreou, E., Botsoglou, K., and Didaskalou, E. (2011). Bully/victim problems among preschool children: A review of current research evidence. *Educational Psychology Review, 23*(3), 329-358.

Wolke, D., and Lereya, S.T. (2015). Long-term effects of bullying. *Archives of Disease in Childhood, 100*(9), 879-885.

Ybarra, M.L., Espelage, D.L., and Mitchell, K.J. (2014). Differentiating youth who are bullied from other victims of peer-aggression: The importance of differential power and repetition. *Journal of Adolescent Health, 55*(2), 293-300.

2

The Scope of the Problem

Although attention to bullying has increased markedly among researchers, policy makers, and the media since the late 1990s, bullying and cyberbullying research is underdeveloped and uneven. Despite a growing literature on bullying in the United States, a reliable estimate for the number of children who are bullied in the United States today still eludes the field (Kowalski et al., 2012; Olweus, 2013). Estimates of bullying prevalence vary greatly, and there is little consensus on the value and accuracy of existing estimates.

This chapter describes the current state of research focused on estimating rates of bullying and cyberbullying in the United States and based on the findings from four major, federally funded, nationally representative samples. The committee considers overall trends in these prevalence estimates, as well as areas of inconsistencies and potential reasons for these discrepancies across the particular studies. The committee also draws upon other large-scale studies to provide insight into various demographic factors—such as gender, age, and ethnicity—as potential risk or protective factors for youth involvement in bullying. Although perceptions and interpretations of communications may be different in digital communities, the committee decided to address cyberbullying within a shared bullying framework rather than treating cyberbullying and traditional bullying as separate entities because there are shared risk factors, shared negative consequences, and interventions that work on both cyberbullying and traditional bullying. However, there are differences between these behaviors that have been noted in previous research, such as different power differentials, different perceptions of communication, and questions of how best to approach the issue of repetition in an online context. These differences suggest that although the Centers for Disease Control and Prevention (CDC) definition, developed in the context of traditional bullying, may not apply in a blanket fashion to cyberbullying, these two forms are not separate species. This chapter offers insights into the complexities and limitations of current estimates and underscores the challenges faced by policy makers, practitioners, advocates, and researchers.[1] Although exact estimates are challenging to identify and require more comprehensive measurement of bullying that addresses the current prevalence research limitations, it is clear that a sizable portion of youth is exposed to bullying.

Perspectives from the Field

"[Bullying is] emotionally, or mentally, or physically putting down someone and it happens everywhere, it never stops."

—Young adult in a focus group discussing bullying
(See Appendix B for additional highlights from interviews.)

NATIONALLY REPRESENTATIVE STUDIES OF BULLYING IN THE UNITED STATES

Several national surveys provide insight into the prevalence of bullying and cyberbullying in the United States. In this section, the committee focuses specifically on the School Crime Supplement (SCS) of the National Crime Victimization Survey (NCVS), the National School-Based Youth Risk Behavior Survey (YRBS), the Health Behaviour in School-Aged Children (HBSC) survey, and the National Survey of Children's Exposure to Violence (NatSCEV) because their samples of youth are nationally representative and epidemiologically defined. The committee notes that there are a number of methodological differences in the samples and measurement across the four studies. The prevalence of bullying behavior at school ranged from 17.9 percent to 30.9 percent, whereas the prevalence of cyberbullying ranged from 6.9 percent to 14.8 percent of youth (Centers for Disease Control and Prevention, 2014b; Finkelhor et al., 2015; Iannotti, 2013; U.S. Department of Education, 2015; see Table 2-1 for a summary of these nationally representative surveys and Appendix C for detailed results from these surveys). The discussion below considers in greater detail the strengths

---

[1] Additional information about strategies for overcoming these limitations can be found in Chapter 7.

TABLE 2-1 Comparison of Current National Data Sources on Bullying for School-Aged Children and Adolescents

	NCVS	YRBS	HBSC	NatSCEV II
Year of most recent report release	2015 release (data 2012-2013 school year)	2013	2010 (data 2009-2010 school year)	2013
Funding organization	U.S. Department of Education	CDC and state and large urban school district school-based YRBSs conducted by state and local education health agencies	World Health Organization (WHO-Euro)	U.S. Department of Justice and CDC
Estimate of school bullying from most recent report	21.5%	19.6%	30.9%	17.9% (for assault by a non-sibling peer)
Estimate of electronic bullying from most recent report	06.9%	14.8%	14.8%	06.0% (for Internet / cell phone harassment)
Past years of survey that included bullying	2013, 2011, 2009, 2007, 2005, 2003, 2001, 1999	2015 will be released 6/2016 2013 2011 2009	2009-2010 2005-2006 2001-2002 1997-1998	2011 2008
Purpose of study	To show the relationship between bullying and cyber-bullying victimization and other crime-related variables.	To monitor priority health-risk behaviors that contribute to the leading causes of morbidity and mortality among youth and adults.	To increase understanding of health behavior, lifestyles, and their context in young people.	To support a more regular and systematic national assessment of children's exposure to violence, crime, and abuse.
Sample size	6,500 participants (for SCS - larger for NCVS)	13,583 participants	12,642 participants	4,503 participants
Age of participants	Age 12 - Age 18	Age 14 – Age 18	Age 10 –Age 16	1 month to Age 17 (parent report for children under 10 years old)
Geographic coverage	Nationally representative	Nationally representative	Nationally representative	Nationally representative

continued

Table 2-1, continued

Study method	NCVS	YRBS	HBSC	NatSCEV II
Study method	Randomly selected students are administered face-to-face or telephone interviews using computer-assisted personal interviewing.	Randomly selected students are administered a self-report questionnaire regarding health-risk behaviors plus obesity, overweight, and asthma.	Randomly selected students are administered a self-report questionnaire about nutrition, physical activity, violence, bullying, relationships, perceptions of school, and alcohol and drug use.	After a short interview is conducted with an adult caregiver for family demographic information, randomly selected students are administered a telephone questionnaire on sexual assault, child maltreatment, conventional crime, Internet victimization, peer and sibling victimization, and witnessing indirect victimization.

NOTES: NCVS = National Crime Victimization Survey; YRBS = National School-Based Youth Risk Behavior Survey; HBSC = Health Behaviour in School-Aged Children Survey; NatSCEV = National Survey of Children's Exposure to Violence.
SOURCES: Centers for Disease Control and Prevention (2010, 2012, 2014b), DeVoe et al. (2010, 2011), Finkelhor et al. (2012, 2015), Iannotti (2012, 2013), U.S. Department of Education (2013, 2015), U.S. Department of Health and Human Services (2008), World Health Organization (2003).

and weaknesses of the methods employed by each of these surveys, in an effort to elucidate factors that may contribute to the variation in reported prevalence rates.

School Crime Supplement of the National Crime Victimization Survey

The SCS is a national survey of 4,942 students ages 12 through 18 in U.S. public and private elementary, middle, and high schools as well as home-schooled youth (U.S. Department of Education, 2015). Created as a supplement to the NCVS and co-designed by the Department of Education, National Center for Education Statistics, and Bureau of Justice Statistics, the SCS survey collects information about victimization, crime, and safety at school (U.S. Department of Education, 2015). The survey was designed to assist policy makers as well as academic researchers and practitioners at the federal, state, and local levels so they can make informed decisions concerning crime in schools. NCVS crime data come from surveys administered by field representatives to a representative sample of households in the United States throughout the year in person and over the phone (U.S.

Department of Education, 2015).[2] In 2015, the SCS administration tested two different ways of asking about bullying to better align with the CDC definition of bullying.

The SCS asked students a number of key questions about their experiences with and perceptions of crime and violence that occurred inside their school, on school grounds, on a school bus, or on the way to or from school.[3] Additional questions not included in the NCVS were added to the SCS, such as students' self-reports of being bullied and perceived rejection at school. This survey's approach to bullying and cyberbullying is far more intensive than the other national surveys; however, it is limited by its focus exclusively on reports of being bullied (being a target of bullying behavior), with no information on perpetration. Additional information is also available regarding differences in rates of being bullied and cyberbullied by student characteristics such as gender, race and ethnicity, school and grade level, school enrollment, geographic region, eligibility for reduced-price lunch, household income, and student-teacher ratio. Other characteristics of the events assessed include whether or not an adult was notified of the bullying incident, injury, frequency of bullying, form of bullying, and location of the bullying (U.S. Department of Education, 2015). The SCS data showed that in 2013, 21.5 percent of students ages 12-18 were bullied on school property and 6.9 percent of students were cyberbullied anywhere (U.S. Department of Education, 2015; see Appendix C, Tables C-1 through C-3).[4]

Although the SCS provides the most recent and in-depth assessment of bullying and cyberbullying prevalence in the United States, it has several major limitations. The questions about being bullied or cyberbullied are only included in the SCS, a supplement to the NCVS; therefore, its sample size is only a fraction of that of the larger NCVS.[5] The SCS and NCVS data, similar to the other national datasets, are voluntary self-report surveys. These surveys focused on students ages 12-18 and on their experience be-

---

[2]Households are selected through a stratified, multistage, cluster sampling process. Households in the sample are designed to be representative of all households as well as noninstitutionalized individuals ages 12 or older.

[3]For the SCS, being "bullied" includes students being made fun of, called names, or insulted; being the subject of rumors; being threatened with harm; being pushed, shoved, tripped, or spit on; being pressured into doing things they did not want to do; being excluded from activities on purpose; and having property destroyed on purpose. "At school" includes the school building, school property, school bus, or going to and from school. Missing data are not shown for household income.

[4]In 1995 and 1999, "at school" was defined for respondents as in the school building, on the school grounds, or on a school bus. In 2001, the definition for "at school" was changed to mean in the school building, on school property, on a school bus, or going to and from school.

[5]The NCVS has a nationally representative sample of about 90,000 households comprising nearly 160,000 persons, whereas the sample size of the SCS is just 4,942 students.

ing bullied; data are not available from younger children and from children who have bullied others or children who have witnessed bullying instances. The survey also fails to address rates of bullying among various subpopulations of youth, such as groups differentiated by their sexual orientation or gender identity, by weight status, or by religious minorities.

School-Based Youth Risk Behavior Survey

The YRBS is one component of the Youth Risk Behavior Surveillance System (YRBSS), an epidemiological surveillance system developed by the CDC to monitor the prevalence of youth behaviors that most influence health (Centers for Disease Control and Prevention, 2014b). The YRBS is conducted biennially and focuses on priority health-risk behavior established during youth (grades 9-12) that result in the most significant mortality, morbidity, disability, and social problems during both youth and adulthood.[6] State and local education and health agencies are permitted to supplement the national survey to meet their individual needs.

National YRBS

Bullying and cyberbullying estimates include responses by student characteristics, such as gender, race and ethnicity, grade level, and urbanicity of the school.[7,8] The data showed that 19.6 percent of children ages 14-18 were bullied on school property and 14.8 percent of children ages 14-18 were electronically bullied (Centers for Disease Control and Prevention, 2014b; see Appendix C, Table C-4). The data captured by the national YRBS reflect self-report surveys from students enrolled in grades 9-12 at public or private schools. As with the other nationally representative samples, it does not identify many subpopulations that are at increased risk for bullying such as lesbian, gay, bisexual, and transgender (LGBT) youth and overweight children. The YRBS gathers information from adolescents approximately ages 14-17; but it offers no nationally representative information on younger children (Centers for Disease Control and Prevention, 2014b). The survey gathers information on Hispanic, black, and white students but does not identify other races and ethnicities.

---

[6]The YRBS uses a cluster sampling design to produce a nationally representative sample of the students in grades 9-12 of all public and private school students in the 50 states and the District of Columbia.

[7]The 2014 YRBS does not clarify whether this includes school events held off campus or the children's journey to and from school.

[8]Electronically bullied includes being bullied through e-mail, chat rooms, instant messaging, Websites, or texting.

State and Local YRBS

The YRBSS is the only surveillance system designed to monitor a wide range of priority health risk behavior among representative samples of high school students at the state and local levels as well as the national level (Centers for Disease Control and Prevention, 2014b).[9] There is a smaller sample of middle school youth that is included in various state YRBS results, but national-level estimates are not available. The 2014 CDC report includes state- and local-level surveys conducted by 42 states and 21 large urban school districts. Of the 42 states that conducted their own YRBS survey, 26 asked questions about bullying and cyberbullying.[10] The state-specific results for bullying prevalence ranged from a high of 26.3 percent in Montana to a low of 15.7 percent in Florida (Centers for Disease Control and Prevention, 2014b). Whereas this state-level high is relatively similar to the prevalence of 19.6 percent reported by the national YRBS, the state-level low is less than a third of the national prevalence. For cyberbullying, the state results ranged from a high of 20.6 percent in Maine to a low of 11.9 percent in Mississippi. The national YRBS cyberbullying prevalence of 14.8 percent is about in the middle of these extremes (Centers for Disease Control and Prevention, 2014b).

At this time, the available state and local data are highly variable due to major limitations caused by self-reports, variable definitions of bullying, and the limited age range of students, making it difficult to gauge differences in bullying prevalence among states and in comparison to national estimates.

The Health Behaviour in School-Aged Children Survey

The HBSC survey is an international study that generally addresses youth well-being, health behavior, and their social context (Iannotti, 2013). This research is conducted in collaboration with the World Health Organization Regional Office for Europe, and the survey is administered every 4 years in 43 countries and regions across Europe and North America. The HBSC survey collects data on a wide range of health behaviors, health indicators, and factors that may influence them. These factors are primarily characteristics of the children themselves, such as their psychological attributes and personal circumstances, and characteristics of their perceived social environment, including their family relationships, peer-group associations, school climate, and perceived socioeconomic status (Iannotti, 2013).

---

[9] Each state-based and local-school-based YRBS employs a two-stage, cluster sample design to produce representative samples of students in grades 9-12 in the survey's jurisdiction.

[10] States and cities could modify the national YRBS questionnaire for their own surveys to meet their needs.

The most recent survey focused solely on the United States was conducted in the 2009-2010 school year. The 2009-2010 HBSC survey included questions about nutrition; physical activity; violence; bullying; relationships with family and friends; perceptions of school as a supportive environment; and use of alcohol, tobacco, marijuana, and other drugs (Iannotti, 2013).[11,12] Regarding bullying and cyberbullying, the HBSC asked questions only about the frequency with which children were bullied in the "past couple of months," with follow-up questions about the frequency of a certain type of bullying a student experienced (called names or teased, left out of things, kicked or pushed, etc.). The survey found that 30.9 percent of children ages 10-16 were bullied at school and 14.8 percent of children ages 10-16 were bullied using a computer or e-mail (Iannotti, 2013; see Appendix C, Tables C-6 and C-7).[13] The survey is the only nationally representative survey that asked students how often they bullied another student and the type of bullying they carried out. It found that 31.8 percent of students bullied others and 14.0 percent of students cyberbullied other children (Iannotti, 2013). It is the only national survey that asked students to report on the reason they thought they were bullied (e.g., how often were you bullied for your race/color?; how often were you bullied for your religion?). (For additional detail, see Appendix C, Tables C-6 and C-7). Nevertheless, like the other surveys reviewed here, the HBSC survey is limited by the nature of self-reported and voluntary data from minors, as well as by its decision to limit questions only to frequency of incidents.

National Survey of Children's Exposure to Violence

The National Survey of Children's Exposure to Violence II (NatSCEV II) was designed to obtain up-to-date incidence and prevalence estimates for a wide range of childhood victimizations (Finkelhor et al., 2015). The first such assessment, the National Survey of Children's Exposure to Violence I (NatSCEV I), was conducted in 2008. This updated assessment, conducted in 2011, asked students to report on 54 forms of offenses against them. The offenses include sexual assault, child maltreatment, conventional crime, Internet victimization, peer and sibling victimization, witnessing victimiza-

---

[11]The student survey was administered in a regular classroom setting to participating students by a school representative (e.g., teacher, nurse, guidance counselor, etc.).

[12]Three versions of the self-report questionnaire were administered: one for fifth and sixth graders; one for students in seventh, eighth, and ninth grade; and one for students in tenth grade. The tenth grade questionnaire contained the complete set of questions asked.

[13]This is the highest prevalence rate for both bullying and cyberbullying reports among the four national surveys.

tion, and indirect victimization (Finkelhor et al., 2015).[14] While this survey asked questions regarding bullying-type incidents, many of the questions referred to the offenses as "assault" rather than bullying, which typically includes a wider scope of victimization. It addressed these offenses by age and gender of the child who was bullied. NatSCEV II found that 17.9 percent of children ages 1 month to age 17 had experienced an assault by a nonsibling peer, 1.8 percent of children had experienced a bias assault, and 6.0 percent experienced Internet/cell phone harassment (Finkelhor et al., 2015; see Appendix C, Table C-5). It is not clear whether Internet or cell phone harassment meets the CDC definition of bullying.

Trends over Time

Although attention to bullying and cyberbullying has increased, the extent to which rates of bullying have changed in recent years is unclear (Figures 2-1 and 2-2) (Kowalski et al., 2012; Limber, 2014). As illustrated in Figure 2-1, data from the SCS-NCVS indicate a sharp reduction in the percentage of 12-18 year olds who reported being bullied at school—from 27.8 percent to 21.5 percent in just 2 years (U.S. Department of Education, 2015).

While the YRBS and NatSCEV mirror this decline, neither found so large a change (Finkelhor et al., 2015; Centers for Disease Control and Prevention, 2014b; see Figure 2-1). Findings from the HBSC survey show an increase in bullying among 11-, 13-, and 15-year-old youth in the United States of about 1 percentage point between 2006 and 2010 (Iannotti, 2013). As illustrated in Figure 2-2, the trend in cyberbullying over time is even less clear. According to the SCS-NCVS data, the percentage of students ages 12-18 who were cyberbullied doubled between 2001 and 2007 but declined by 2 percentage points between 2011 and 2013 (U.S. Department of Education, 2015).[15] While the HBSC survey and the YRBS also showed a decline in the percentage of students who have been cyberbullied, the NatSCEV showed an increase in the percentage of students who experienced Internet and/or cell phone harassment (see Figure 2-2).

Because the available national trend data are limited in the range of years for which data are available and because findings vary somewhat

---

[14] For NatSCEV II, data were collected by telephone interview on 4,503 children and youth ages 1 month to 17 years. If the respondent was between the ages of 10-17, the main telephone interview was conducted with the child. If the respondent was younger than age 10, the interview was conducted with the child's primary caregiver.

[15] The statistical standard for referring to "trends" is at least three data points in the same direction. In the SCS, the decrease from 2011 to 2013 is one data point, and conclusions should not be drawn at this point in time.

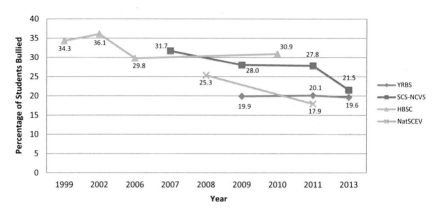

FIGURE 2-1 Trends in bullying over time as reported by national surveys.
NOTES: HBSC = Health Behaviour in School-Aged Children; NatSCEV = National Survey of Children's Exposure to Violence, NCVS = National Crime Victimization Survey; SCS = School Crime Supplement of the NCVS, YRBS = National School-Based Youth Risk Behavior Survey.
SOURCES: Centers for Disease Control and Prevention (2010, 2012, 2014b), DeVoe et al. (2010, 2011), Finkelhor et al. (2012, 2015), Iannotti (2012, 2013), U.S. Department of Education (2013, 2015), U.S. Department of Health and Human Services (2008), World Health Organization (2003).

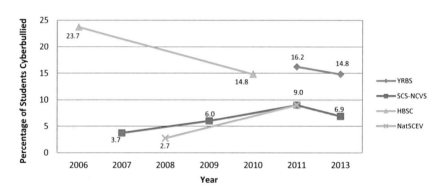

FIGURE 2-2 Trends in cyberbullying over time as reported by national surveys.
NOTES: HBSC = Health Behaviour in School-Aged Children; NatSCEV = National Survey of Children's Exposure to Violence, NCVS = National Crime Victimization Survey; SCS = School Crime Supplement of the NCVS, YRBS = National School-Based Youth Risk Behavior Survey.
SOURCES: Centers for Disease Control and Prevention (2010, 2012, 2014b), DeVoe et al. (2010, 2011), Finkelhor et al. (2012, 2015), Iannotti (2012, 2013), U.S. Department of Education (2013, 2015), U.S. Department of Health and Human Services (2008), World Health Organization (2003).

among the major national samples, it is difficult to gauge the extent to which bullying may have increased or decreased in recent years. Additional data points will be necessary to determine national trends in the prevalence rates for children and youth who are bullied.

EXISTING ESTIMATES OF BULLYING IN THE UNITED STATES BY SUBPOPULATION

In an effort to understand the nature and extent of bullying in the United States, some studies have examined specific subpopulations or subsets of children involved in bullying incidents. Because the major national surveys that include bullying do not uniformly or fully address the bullying experience of subpopulations of interest,[16] in this section the committee also draws upon findings from meta-analyses and independent large-scale research. Although these studies are limited by inconsistent definitions, survey data based on self-reports, differing age ranges, and a lack of questions seeking responses from children who have bullied or have witnessed bullying incidents, they do provide valuable insight into particular risk factors or protective factors for involvement in bullying, insights that are generally not available from the surveys of nationally representative samples. The committee expands on risk and protective factors in Chapter 3.

Prevalence of Bullying by Age

A majority of bullying research has shown that children's experiences with bullying vary significantly according to their age. Decreases with age in rates of being bullied were reported in the SCS.

As reported by Limber (2014), a meta-analysis by Cook and colleagues (2010) found that the likelihood of both being bullied and perpetrating bullying behavior peaked in the early adolescent years (ages 12-14) before decreasing slightly in later adolescence (Limber, 2014). Decreases with increasing grade level in rates of being bullied were also reported in the SCS-NCVS.

For example, whereas 27.8 percent of sixth graders reported being bullied at school in 2013, 23.0 percent of ninth graders and 14.1 percent of twelfth graders said they had been bullied (U.S. Department of Education, 2015; see Figure 2-3). Although these data suggest that the overall chances

---

[16] The committee's Statement of Task (See Box 1-1) requested "a particular focus on children who are most at risk of peer victimization—i.e., those with high-risk factors in combination with few protective factors . . ." At-risk subpopulations specifically named in the Statement of Task were "children with disabilities," poly-victims, LGBT youth, and children living in poverty . . ."

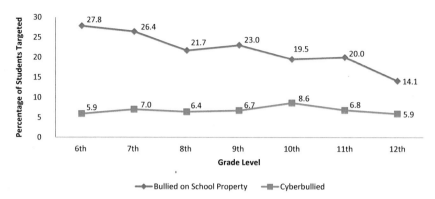

FIGURE 2-3 Prevalence of bullying and cyberbullying among students, ages 12-18, by grade level, as reported by the 2013 School Crime Supplement of the National Crime Victimization Survey.
SOURCE: Data from U.S. Department of Education (2015).

of being bullied are particularly likely in middle childhood, children are more or less likely to be involved in specific forms of bullying at different ages, depending on their verbal, cognitive, and social development (Limber, 2014).

Reports of being bullied through an electronic context appear to peak later than reports of being bullied by a more traditional context; the SCS, for example, reported a peak for cyberbullying in tenth grade (U.S. Department of Education, 2015). According to a 2015 overview of teen's social media and technology use, the Pew Research Center found that 68 percent of teens ages 13-14 had access to a smartphone and 84 percent had access to a desktop or laptop computer, whereas 76 percent of teens ages 15-17 had access to a smartphone and 90 percent had access to a desktop or laptop computer (Lenhart et al., 2015). Today's youth are often referred to as "digital natives" due to their upbringing immersed in technological tools including smartphones and social media, while adults are often referred to as "digital immigrants." This report found that approximately three-fourths of teens ages 13-17 reported access to a cell phone and 94 percent of teens reported going online daily, including 24 percent who said they go online "almost constantly" (Lenhart et al., 2015). Owning a mobile phone allows for ongoing access to the Internet, including social media and other communication tools that may foster opportunities for bullying. Approximately one-quarter of teens surveyed described themselves as "constantly connected" to the Internet (Lenhart et al., 2015). Among teens 13-17 years old, most reported using several forms of social media including Facebook,

Instagram, Snapchat, and Twitter (see Figure 2-4). A previous study found that older adolescents viewed Facebook as a powerful source of influence through four major processes: connection to others, comparison with peers, building an online identity, and an immersive multimedia experience (Moreno et al., 2013).

This increasing access to and use of technologies with age may help explain rising rates of cyberbullying as adolescents age. An older study of 10-17 year olds found an "online harassment" prevalence of approximately 9 percent (Wolak et al., 2007). However, a more recent study, which focused on middle school adolescents, found a lower prevalence of cyberbullying: 5 percent reported being a perpetrator of cyberbullying, and 6.6 percent reported being a target of cyberbullying (Rice et al., 2015).

Smith and colleagues (2008) found rates of cyberbullying to be lower than rates of traditional bullying, but appreciable, and reported higher cyberbullying prevalence outside of school than inside. It is possible that reported cyberbullying rates are lower than traditional bullying rates because

Percentage of all teens 13 to 17 who use ...

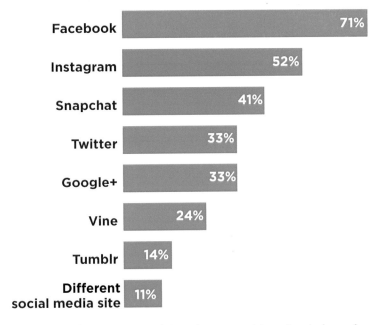

FIGURE 2-4 Facebook, Instagram, and Snapchat top social media platforms for teens (*n* = 1,060 teens ages, 13-17).
SOURCE: Adapted from Lenhart (2015, p. 2)

much of technology use occurs outside of school and current approaches to measuring bullying are designed mostly to assess rates of traditional bullying in school (Smith et al., 2008). Previous work has suggested that increased Internet use is associated with increased risk for cyberbullying (Juvonen and Gross, 2008).

Although research has suggested that the prevalence of bullying among older adolescents is lower than that of younger adolescents, researchers have proposed that cyberbullying among older students may represent a continuation of behaviors from previous grades but with a focus on technological tools for more subtle bullying techniques (Cowie et al., 2013).

Prevalence of Bullying by Gender

Research has confirmed that there are gender differences in the frequency with which children and youth are involved in bullying. A recent meta-analysis found that although boys and girls experienced relatively similar rates of being bullied, boys were more likely to bully others, or to bully others and be bullied, than girls were (Cook et al., 2010; Limber, 2014). Research has suggested that there are gender differences in the frequency with which children and youth are involved in bullying. The SCS, YRBS, and NatSCEV found that rates for self-reports of being bullied range from 19.5 to 22.8 percent for boys and from 12.8 to 23.7 percent for girls (Centers for Disease Control and Prevention, 2014b; Finkelhor et al., 2015; U.S. Department of Education, 2015). All three of these national surveys found that girls were more likely to report being bullied than were boys (see Figure 2-5 for SCS data).

Research has suggested similarities and differences, beyond just overall frequency, in how often boys and girls experience different forms of bullying (Felix and Green, 2010). As noted in Chapter 1, there are two modes of bullying (direct and indirect) as well as different types of bullying (physical, verbal, relational, and damage to property). As illustrated in Figure 2-6, being made fun of or called names and being the subject of rumors are the two most common forms of bullying experienced by children and youth, and both are much more frequently experienced than physical bullying (Iannotti, 2013; Limber, 2014; U.S. Department of Education, 2015). For example, the 2013 SCS found that 13.2 percent of youth ages 12-18 reported being the subject of rumors and 13.6 percent said they had been made fun of, called names, or insulted, compared with 6.0 percent who reported being pushed, shoved, tripped, or spit on (U.S. Department of Education, 2015; see Figure 2-6). Notions of gendered forms of bullying are common because physical aggression has been regularly associated with boys, whereas relational aggression has been considered to be the domain

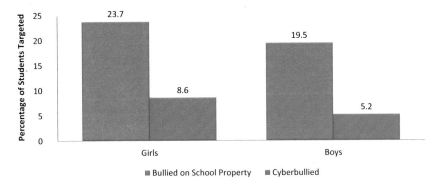

FIGURE 2-5 Prevalence of being bullied among 12-18 year olds by gender, as reported by the 2013 School Crime Supplement of the National Crime Victimization Survey.
SOURCE: Data from U.S. Department of Education (2015).

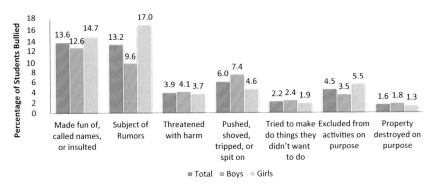

FIGURE 2-6 Prevalence of different types of bullying among students, ages 12-18, bullied in a school year, as reported by the 2013 School Crime Supplement of the National Crime Victimization Survey.
SOURCE: Data from U.S. Department of Education (2015).

of girls (Oppliger, 2013). For example, studies have shown that indirect aggression is normative for both genders, while boys are more strongly represented in physical and verbal aggression (see review by Card et. al., 2008). As for differences in different forms of cyberbullying, according to the 2013 SCS, girls experienced a higher prevalence of being bullied in nearly all types, except for receiving unwanted contact while playing online games and facing purposeful exclusion from an online community (Limber, 2014; U.S. Department of Education, 2015; see Figure 2-7). However, because there is not yet a common definition of cyberbullying, there is no agreement on what forms of online harassment fall under the umbrella term of "cyberbullying."

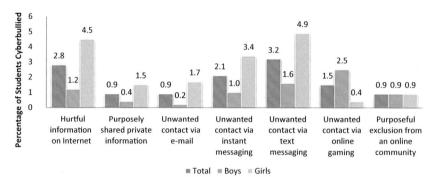

FIGURE 2-7 Prevalence of different types of cyberbullying among students, ages 12-18, bullied in a school year, as reported by the 2013 School Crime Supplement of the National Crime Victimization Survey.
SOURCE: Data from U.S. Department of Education (2015).

Limber and colleagues (2013) observed that age trends for self-reports of bullying others varied for boys and girls. Among boys, bullying others increased from grades 3 through 12, but among girls, rates of bullying others peaked in eighth grade (Limber et al., 2013). Among older adolescents and college students, cyberbullying may be more common than traditional bullying. Prevalence rates of cyberbullying among young adults and college students have been estimated to be around 10-15 percent (Kraft and Wang, 2010; Schenk and Fremouw, 2012; Wensley and Campbell, 2012).

Prevalence of Bullying by Race and Ethnicity

There has been only limited research on the roles that race and ethnicity may play in bullying (Larochette et al., 2010; Peskin et al., 2006; Spriggs et al., 2007).[17] Data from the SCS indicate that the percentage of students who reported being bullied at school in 2013 was highest for white students (23.7%) and lowest for Asian students (9.2%), with rates for black students (20.3%) and Hispanic students (19.2%) falling between (see Figure 2-8; data from U.S. Department of Education, 2015). Data from the national YRBS were highest for white students (21.8%), next highest for Hispanic students (17.8%), and lowest for black students (12.7%) (Centers for Disease Control and Prevention, 2014b). The YRBS data did not include any other ethnicities/races.

It is challenging to interpret the percentages of children and youth who are bullied across different racial and ethnic groups, due to the limited

---

[17]The committee expands on this topic in Chapter 3.

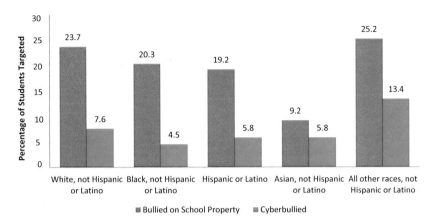

FIGURE 2-8 Prevalence of being bullied and cyberbullied among students, ages 12-18, by race/ethnicity, as reported by the 2013 School Crime Supplement of the National Crime Victimization Survey.
SOURCE: Data from U.S. Department of Education (2015).

information currently available on racial and ethnic differences in definitions of bullying and on whether and how bullying may vary according to the racial/ethnic diversity and density of schools and communities. See Chapter 3 for a discussion of contextual factors, including the school and community contexts, and their modulation of the relations between individual characteristics and prevalence of involvement in and consequences of bullying by race/ethnicity.

DISPARITIES IN BULLYING PREVALENCE IN THE UNITED STATES AMONG VULNERABLE GROUPS

In addition to exploring standard demographic differences in bullying (i.e., gender, age, race/ethnicity), researchers have identified specific populations that are at increased risk for being bullied. This section reviews the research on groups for which there is consistent epidemiologic evidence of disparities in being the target of bullying, including LGBT youth, overweight/obese youth, and youth with disabilities. The committee also identified groups for which the evidence of increased risk is not currently consistent and which therefore warrant greater research attention (U.S. Government Accountability Office, 2012). In this chapter, we report descriptive data on prevalence rates; see Chapter 3 for a discussion of factors that contribute to these disparities in rates of bullying (e.g., stigma) as well as research evidence on specific forms of bullying (e.g., bias-based bullying) that are more likely to occur among some of the groups covered in this section.

Differences in Bullying by Sexual Orientation and Gender Identity

LGBT youth, youth questioning their sexuality, and youth who do not conform to gender stereotypes frequently face bullying by their peers (Eisenberg and Aalsma, 2005; Espelage et al., 2008; Garofalo et al., 1998; Rivers, 2001; Russell et al., 2014). The prevalence of bullying of lesbian, gay, and bisexual (LGB) males and females ranges from 25.6 percent to 43.6 percent (Berlan et al., 2010).

Most research on bullying related to sexual orientation and gender identity comes from nonprobability samples. For example, the 2003 Massachusetts Youth Risk Behavior Survey found that 42.0 percent of sexual-minority youth reported being bullied in the 12 months prior to survey administration (Hanlon, 2004). Similarly, the cross-sectional analysis of the 2001 questionnaire from the Growing Up Today study, a national longitudinal study involving 7,559 youths (ages 14-22) who were children of nurses participating in the Nurses' Health study found that the prevalence of bullying victimization was lowest in heterosexual female respondents (15.9%) and highest in gay male respondents (43.6%) (Berlan et al., 2010). Girls identifying as "mostly heterosexual" and "mostly bisexual" were at increased risk for perpetrating bullying compared to heterosexual girls, while boys identifying as gay were less likely to perpetrate bullying than were heterosexual boys (Berlan et al., 2010).

A growing body of research has aimed to assess the experiences of transgender youth specifically. The existing quantitative research suggests that most transgender youth experience regular bullying and harassment at school (Grant et al., 2011; Kosciw et al., 2012; McGuire et al., 2010). For instance, in a sample of 5,542 adolescents sampled online, 82 percent of the transgender or gender nonconforming youth reported any bullying experience in the past 12 months, compared to 57 percent among cisgender boys and girls (Reisner et al., 2015).[18]

Measures of sexual orientation—including sexual attraction, sexual behavior, and sexual identity—have been recently incorporated into large surveillance systems, such as some state and local versions of the YRBSS, which have provided population-based estimates of bullying among LGB youth. Two of CDC's large surveillance systems—School Health Profiles and the School Health Policies and Practices studies—assess school health policies and practices relevant to LGB students including the prohibition of harassment and bullying (Centers for Disease Control and Prevention, 2014a). The results from these sources provide a means to assess sexual-orientation differences in bullying perpetration and victimization among

---

[18]Reisner and colleagues (2015, p. 1) define cisgender youth as youth "whose gender identity or expression matches one's sex assigned at birth."

youth by location within the United States (Centers for Disease Control and Prevention, 2014a).[19] Recent analyses by Olsen and colleagues (2014) were conducted by creating two datasets: one that combined 2009-2011 YRBS data from 10 states (Connecticut, Delaware, Hawaii, Illinois, Maine, Massachusetts, North Dakota, Rhode Island, Vermont, and Wisconsin) and the other that combined YRBS data from 10 school districts (Boston, Chicago, District of Columbia, Houston, Los Angeles, Milwaukee, New York City, San Diego, San Francisco, and Seattle). Adjusted prevalence rates for being bullied on school property were lowest for both heterosexual boys and girls (18.3% and 19.9%, respectively, based on the state dataset; 11.4% and 11.8%, respectively, based on the district dataset) and highest among gay boys (43.1% and 25.7%, respectively, based on the state and district datasets) and bisexual boys (35.2% and 33.2%, respectively, based on the state and district datasets) (Olsen et al., 2014). Rates of being bullied on school property were intermediate for the lesbian girls (29.5% in the state dataset, and 14.0% in the district dataset) and bisexual girls (35.3% in the state dataset, and 18.8% in the district dataset).

Given the absence of measures of gender identity disaggregated from sex in these large state and local datasets, population-based estimates of the prevalence of bullying among transgender youth are not currently available. However, recent research has conducted cognitive testing to determine the most reliable and valid way of assessing gender identity among both adults (GenIUSS Group, 2013) and youth (e.g., Conron et al., 2008). Further, population-based datasets have very recently begun to include measures of gender identity among youth (e.g., the 2013-2014 California Healthy Kids Survey), which will enable researchers to examine gender identity–related disparities in bullying using representative samples of youth.

Using data from the first wave (1994-1995 school year) of the National Longitudinal Study of Adolescent Health, which included 10,587 youth between 13 and 18, Russell and colleagues (2002) examined differences in experiencing, witnessing, and perpetrating violence, depending on the respondent's self-reported category of romantic attraction (same-sex, both-sex, or other-sex), a measure of sexual orientation. Youth who reported same-sex or both-sex attraction were more likely to experience and perpetrate the most dangerous forms of violence (e.g., pulling a gun or knife on someone, shooting or stabbing someone) and to witness violence (Russell et al., 2002). These findings were not disaggregated by sex or gender identity.

---

[19] The National YRBS data available at the time of publication did not include questions about sexual identity and sex of sexual contacts, but these topics are included in the YRBS report released in June 2016.

Differences in Bullying Among Youth with Disabilities

Much of the existing data suggests that students with disabilities are overrepresented within the bullying dynamic (McLaughlin et al., 2010; Rose, 2015; Rose et al., 2010), whether as children who have bullied (Rose et al., 2009), children who have been bullied (Blake et al., 2012; Son et al., 2012), or children who have both bullied and have been bullied (Farmer et al., 2012).[20] Specifically, national prevalence data suggest that students with disabilities, as a whole, are up to 1.5 times more likely to be bullied than youth without disabilities (Blake et al., 2012); this disproportionate bullying begins in preschool (Son et al., 2012) and continues through adolescence (Blake et al., 2012; Rose, 2015).

However, variability exists in reported prevalence rates of involvement for various subgroups of youth with disabilities. For example, Rose and colleagues (2015) conducted a prevalence study of a large sample of youth with and without disabilities in middle and high school (n = 14,508) and determined that 35.3 percent of students with emotional and behavioral disorders, 33.9 percent of students with autism spectrum disorders, 24.3 percent of students with intellectual disabilities, 20.8 percent of students with another health impairment, and 19.0 percent of students with specific learning disabilities experienced high levels of victimization. In addition, 15.3 percent of youth with emotional and behavioral disorders, 19.4 percent of youth with autism spectrum disorders, 24.1 percent of youth with intellectual disabilities, 16.9 percent of youth with other health impairment, and 14.4 percent of youth with specific learning disabilities perpetrated bullying behavior. These estimates are in contrast to 14.5 percent of youth without disabilities who experienced high rates of being bullied and 13.5 percent who engaged in high rates of perpetration. The authors of this study acknowledge that the study has a number of limitations—mainly self-report, cross-sectional data, and data that were examined at the group level.

This literature on bullying and disabilities has several inconsistencies, which stem from differences in three basic factors: (1) measurement and definition, (2) disability identification, and (3) comparative groups. For instance, separating subclasses of youth with specific typographies of learning disabilities proves difficult, resulting in the general assessment of a combined class of specific learning disabilities (Rose, 2015). This confounding factor leads to conflicting measures of bullying involvement, with some studies suggesting that rates of bullying perpetration are relatively comparable among youth with and without disabilities (Rose et al., 2015), while others found that students with specific learning disabilities were almost six

---

[20]This section is adapted from a study (Rose, 2015) commissioned by the committee for this report.

times more likely to engage in bully perpetration than their peers without disabilities (Twyman et al., 2010). These conflicting results suggest further assessment or disaggregation of subgroups of youth with specific learning disabilities may be necessary to better understand bullying involvement among this subpopulation of youth.

Differences in Bullying by Weight Status

Weight status, specifically being overweight or obese, can be a factor in bullying among children and youth (Puhl and Latner, 2007). The CDC defines childhood overweight as a body mass index (BMI) at or above the 85th percentile and below the 95th percentile of a CDC-defined reference population of the same age and sex. It defines childhood obesity as a BMI at or above the 95th percentile of this reference population for the same age and sex (Centers for Disease Control and Prevention, 2015b).

In 2012, 31.8 percent of U.S. children and youth 6 to 19 years of age were overweight or obese, using the CDC weight status categories. Eighteen percent of children 6 to 11 and 21 percent of youth 12 to 19 years of age were obese (Centers for Disease Control and Prevention, 2015a). Although the 2012 National Health and Nutrition Examination Survey (NHANES) data showed a decrease in obesity rates for children 2 to 5 years of age, the obesity rates for 2-19-year olds between 2003-2004 and 2011-2012 remained unchanged at 31.8 percent (Ogden et al., 2014). Thus, weight-based bullying can affect a substantial number of youth.

In 2007, Puhl and Latner reviewed the growing literature on social marginalization and stigmatization of obesity in children and adolescents, paying attention to the nature and extent of weight bias toward overweight youth and the primary sources of stigma in their lives, including peers.[21] The researchers found that existing studies on weight stigma suggest that experiences with various forms of bullying is a common experience for overweight and obese youth; however, determining specific prevalence rates of bias is difficult because various assessment methods are used across the literature (Puhl and Latner, 2007). For example, Neumark-Sztainer and colleagues (2002) examined the prevalence of weight-based teasing among middle and high school students (n = 4,746) and found that 63 percent of girls at or above the 95th percentile for BMI and 58 percent of boys at or above the 95th percentile for BMI experienced "weight-based teasing." However, in a recent longitudinal study of weight-based teasing (n = 8,210),

---

[21] In this review, weight stigma included "verbal teasing (e.g., name calling, derogatory remarks, being made fun of), physical bullying (e.g., hitting, kicking, pushing, shoving), and relational victimization (e.g., social exclusion, being ignored or avoided, the target of rumors")" (Puhl and Latner, 2007, p. 558).

Griffiths and colleagues (2006) found that 34 percent of girls at or above the 95th percentile for BMI and 36 percent of boys at or above the 95th percentile for BMI reported being victims of "weight-based teasing and various forms of bullying" (Griffiths et al., 2006). Griffiths and colleagues (2006) found that obese boys and girls were more likely to be victims of overt bullying one year later.

Janssen and colleagues (2004) found that among 5,749 children, ages 11-16, girls with a higher BMI were more likely to be targets of bullying behavior than their average-weight peers. They found that the likelihood of these girls being targeted in verbal, physical, and relational bullying incidents only increased as BMI rose. Among boys, however, the researchers found no significant associations between BMI and physical victimization. When they looked at the older portion of the sample, they found that among 15-16-year-old boys and girls, BMI was positively associated with being the perpetrator of bullying behavior compared with BMI among average-weight children (Puhl and Latner, 2007). In this sample of 15 and 16 year olds, girls still faced an increased likelihood of both being bullied and being a perpetrator of bullying (Puhl and Latner, 2007).

In their review of the literature on peer victimization and pediatric obesity, Gray and colleagues (2009) summarized evidence since 1960 on stigmatization, marginalization, and peer victimization of obese children. They concluded that obesity in children and youth places them at risk for harmful physical, emotional, and psychosocial effects of bullying and similar types of peer mistreatment. They also noted that "over time, a cyclical relationship may emerge between obese individuals and victimization such that children who are victimized are less likely to be active, which in turn leads to increased weight gain and a greater likelihood of experiencing weight-based victimization" (Gray et al., 2009, p. 722).

In summary, although numerous studies indicate that overweight and obese youth are at increased risk of being bullied, it can be difficult to attribute weight-based bullying to a single physical attribute, given that being overweight or obese often co-exists with other factors (see also the subsection below on "Youth with Intersectional Identities"). Additional research is needed to identify the relative importance of weight as a reason for being bullied or being a perpetrator of bullying among children and youth.

Other Disparity Groups Requiring More Research

Although most research on groups that are at disproportionate risk for bullying has focused on LGBT youth, overweight/obese youth, or youth with disabilities, some recent research has begun to identify other groups that may be at heightened risk.[22] Because this research is in its early stages, the evidence is not yet compelling on whether these groups do experience disparities in perpetrating or being targeted by bullying behavior. Consequently, the committee highlights the following groups as warranting further study to establish their risk status.

Socioeconomic Status

The literature on socioeconomic status and bullying contains conflicting results. Higher socioeconomic status has been associated with higher levels of perpetration (Barboza et al., 2009; Shetgiri et al., 2012) but so has lower socioeconomic status (Christie-Mizell et al., 2011; Garner and Hinton, 2010; Glew et al., 2005; Jansen et al., 2011, 2012; Nordhagen et al., 2005; Pereira et al., 2004; Schwartz et al., 1997). Other studies found that socioeconomic status was not associated with perpetration (Flouri and Buchanan, 2003; Zimmerman et al., 2005).

The evidence for an association between socioeconomic status and being bullied is similarly inconsistent. Specifically, some studies found that neither economic deprivation (Wilson et al., 2012), family income (Garner and Hinton, 2010), nor general socioeconomic status (Magklara et al., 2012) predicted greater risk of being targeted by bullying behavior. Other studies found that insufficient parental income (Lemstra et al., 2012) and low social class (Pereira et al., 2004) predicted increased rates of being the target in bullying incidents. These conflicting results may be due in part to different measures and conceptualizations of socioeconomic status. In addition, other environmental or social–ecological factors that are often not included in evaluative models may account for the differences in these findings. For example, Barboza and colleagues (2009) argued that perpetration emerges as a function of social climate deficits, where social supports may mediate perpetration regardless of demographic characteristics, including socioeconomic status. Thus, further research is warranted on the mediating and moderating variables in the association between socioeconomic status and either bullying perpetration or being targeted for bullying. (See Chapter 3 for a more detailed discussion of moderation.)

Immigration Status

The results to date from research on the association between immigration status and bullying involvement are inconsistent. For example, Lim and Hoot (2015) investigated the bullying involvement of third and sixth

---

[22] This section is adapted from a study (Rose, 2015) commissioned by the committee for this report.

grade students who were immigrants, refugees, or native born. The majority of these students who were refugees or immigrants came from Burma, Burundi, Iraq, Somalia, Thailand, and Yemen. The refugees and immigrants did not report higher levels of being bullied than the native-born American students. However, qualitative data suggested that youth with refugee status responded as "nonpassive victims," meaning they would try to defend themselves when physically attacked, whereas immigrants and native-born youth who were bullied responded to bullying more passively. The inconsistencies in the results may be associated with age of the respondents, total sample size, nationality of the immigrants/refugees, or other environmental or social–ecological factors (Hong et al., 2014), all of which require greater attention in future studies.

Minority Religious Affiliations

Few studies have specifically investigated the bullying involvement of youth from minority religious groups. However, evidence from other areas of violence suggests that youth from religious minorities may experience higher rates of being bullied than those who identify as Christians. For instance, the percentage of hate crimes in the United States that are grounded in religious affiliation has increased from 10 percent in 2004 to 28 percent in 2012 (Wilson, 2014). Since schools are reflective of society as a whole, and bullying involvement is grounded in a social–ecological context that includes community and societal factors (Hong and Espelage, 2012), this targeting of religious minorities may carry over into the school environment. However, this hypothesis requires empirical documentation.

Youth with Intersectional Identities

As noted in the earlier discussion of weight status as a factor in bullying, "intersectionality" refers to individuals with multiple stigmatized statuses (e.g., black lesbian youth). The majority of studies on bullying perpetration and targeting have examined identity groups in isolation, but there is increasing acknowledgement that multiple intersecting identities can exacerbate or attenuate health outcomes (e.g., Bowleg, 2008; McCall, 2005). An exception is the study by Garnett and colleagues (2014), which analyzed the intersectionality of weight-related bullying with bullying for other reasons. Among 965 Boston youth sampled in the 2006 Boston Youth Survey, participants had been discriminated against or bullied (or assaulted) for any of four attributes (race or ethnicity, immigration status, perceived sexual orientation, and weight). Participants who were bullied for their race and weight had higher rates of being targeted for bullying behavior, compared with students who had two or more of the other characteristics

(Garnett et al., 2014). As discussed earlier, the extent to which intersecting identities affect the prevalence of bullying perpetration and targeting remains largely unknown and therefore represents an important area for future study.

Children and adolescents have mostly stated that the differences in their physical appearance contribute to the possibility of their being bullied (Lunde et al., 2007). There is concern that students with characteristics, such as obesity, disabilities, food allergies, and gender issues could put them directly in the path of being more likely to be bullied (Schuster and Bogart, 2013). These categories may intersect at the micro level of individual experience to reflect multiple interlocking systems of privilege and oppression at the macro, social-structural level (Bowleg, 2012).

Urbanicity

Is bullying more prevalent in urban schools than in suburban or rural schools? Because large-city urban schools are often located in inner-city areas of concentrated poverty and exposure to violence, theories of social disorganization suggest that bullying might be more common in such contexts (Bradshaw et al., 2009). However, there is not much research in support of this hypothesis. Rural students have self-reported at least as much bullying in their schools as did urban youth (Dulmus et al., 2004; Stockdale et al., 2002). Moreover, data from large national studies in the United States indicate that students in rural schools report somewhat more bullying than those in urban and suburban schools (Nansel et al., 2001; Robers et al., 2013). In particular Robers and colleagues (2013) found, using 2011 National Center for Education Statistics data, that 25 percent of students in urban schools reported some bullying, compared with 29 percent in suburban schools and 30 percent in rural schools. One reason that has been suggested for this difference is that smaller rural schools, some of which have fewer school transitions (e.g., lacking a separate middle school between elementary and high school grades), may typically consolidate social reputations and provide fewer opportunities for targeted youth to redefine how they are perceived by peers (Farmer et al., 2011).

What may differ by urbanicity of schools are the reasons for targeting certain individuals in a pattern of bullying behavior. For example, Goldweber and colleagues (2013) documented that urban African American youth were more likely to report race-based bullying by peers than were rural or suburban youth. As noted above in the section on "Prevalence of Bullying by Race and Ethnicity," the connection between experiences of peer bullying and racial discrimination merits further study.

ISSUES IN DEVELOPING ESTIMATES OF
BULLYING IN THE UNITED STATES

Current efforts to estimate prevalence of bullying and cyberbullying behavior are characterized by disagreement and confusion. This chapter has pointed out the major challenges associated with generating accurate and reliable estimates of bullying and cyberbullying rates in the United States. The issues to be addressed are summarized here in terms of definitional issues and issues of measurement and sampling.

Definitional Issues

As attention to bullying behavior has grown in recent years, concerns have been raised that efforts to characterize bullying vary considerably and that a lack of a consistent definition "hinders our ability to understand the true magnitude, scope, and impact of bullying and track trends over time" (Gladden et al., 2014, p. 1). One such approach to measuring bullying includes providing an explicit definition or explanation of what is meant by bullying to study participants. In contrast, some approaches simply use the word "bullying" but do not define it, whereas others list specific behaviors that constitute bullying without using the term "bullying" (Gladden et al., 2014; Sawyer et al., 2008). Even if the definition is provided, researchers must assume that respondents (who are often children) fully understand the broad and difficult concept of bullying—including its elements of hostile intent, repetition, and power imbalance and its various forms—when answering. However, research has shown that this level of comprehension might not be uniformly present for children of all age groups and cultures (Monks and Smith, 2006; Smith et al., 2002; Strohmeier and Toda, 2008; Vaillancourt et al., 2008). For instance, 8-year-old children consider fewer negative behavior options to be bullying than do 14-year-old adolescents (Smith et al., 2002). Furthermore, children hold very different definitions of bullying from those held by researchers. Bullying may also be understood and defined differently in different languages and cultures (Arora, 1996). Smith and colleagues (2002) showed that terms used in different cultures differed remarkably in their meanings. For example, some terms captured verbal aggression, while others were connected instead with physically aggressive acts or with social exclusion. These definitional issues are also relevant to cyberbullying, as there is no uniform definition used across studies.

Perspectives from the Field

There is still a lot of variability when it comes to defining bullying: Parents, children, and schools or medical professionals can mean a wide range of different things when they use the term "bullying." Bullying varies in different developmental stages, and we should acknowledge that it is not always obvious. Even so, bullying can be characterized as the kind of behavior that would actually be considered harassment if the people involved were over age 18. However you look at it, a standardized definition would help us more precisely target bullying behavior and consequences while avoiding misunderstandings.

—Summary of themes from service providers/community-based providers focus group
(See Appendix B for additional highlights from interviews.)

Measurement and Sampling Issues

Measuring bullying and cyberbullying is very difficult. The variability in prevalence rates reflects a number of measurement and sampling issues. First, studies reporting prevalence rates of bullying problems may rely on different data sources, such as peer versus teacher nominations or ratings, observations by researchers, or self-report questionnaires. Particularly with children, the self-report strategy poses a unique problem in regard to possible underreporting or overreporting (Solberg, 2003). Some children who bully other students will choose not to respond honestly on the relevant questionnaire items for fear of retribution from adults. To date, a majority of information is gathered via self-reports, which have limitations; however, the committee does not believe that official reports are necessarily a better or more reliable source of information. The committee also acknowledges that for studies examining the prevalence of bullying by a certain demographic category, such as obesity or sexual orientation, it is not possible to say who is the "most bullied" by comparing students with one set of demographic characteristics with other students with different demographic characteristics.

Second, research suggests that the approach to measuring bullying does affect the pattern of responses and in turn may influence the prevalence rates. For example, a study of over 24,000 elementary, middle, and high school age youth found significantly higher prevalence rates for bullying when it was assessed using a behavior-based approach (i.e., asking about the experience of specific forms and acts of bullying) than when it was measured using a definition-based approach (Sawyer et al., 2008). A similar pattern occurs for cyberbullying, For example, one study used a definition that read "repeatedly [trying] to hurt you or make you feel bad by e-mailing/e-messaging you or posting a blog about you on the Internet (MySpace)." This study found the prevalence of cybervictimization to be 9 percent (Selkie et al., 2015). Another study asked about "the use of the Internet, cell phones and other technologies to bully, harass, threaten or embarrass someone" and found cybervictimization prevalence to be 31 percent (Pergolizzi et al., 2011).

Third, studies may differ with regard to the reference period used in measuring bullying. For example, a question may refer to a whole school year or one school term, the past couple of months, or over a lifetime. Response and rating categories may vary in both number and specificity as well. Such categories may consist of a simple yes or no dichotomy; of various applicability categories such as "does not apply at all" and "applies perfectly"; or of relatively vague frequency alternatives ranging from "seldom" to "very often" or from "not at all in the past couple of months" to "several times a week."

Fourth, some studies use different criteria for differentiating students who have been bullied and students who have not, as well as students who have and have not bullied others. This variation in identification makes prevalence rates difficult to compare (Solberg, 2003). A majority of studies do not ask questions about children who have bullied or children who have been bystanders, instead focusing on children who have been bullied. Taken together, these findings suggest that researchers need to be cautious about interpreting their findings in light of their measurement approach.

SUMMARY

Estimates of bullying inform an evidence-based understanding about the extent of the problem and bring attention to the need to address the problem and allocate the funding to do so. Prevalence estimates provide information for policy makers, identify where education is needed, identify vulnerable populations, and help direct assistance and resources. As this chapter has explained, generating reliable estimates for the number of children who have bullied and the number who have been bullied is not an easy task. In some cases, the task is extraordinarily difficult. For example, existing research suggests disparities in rates of bullying by a variety of characteristics, including sexual orientation, disability, and obesity, mostly due to the lack of nationally representative data on these and other vulnerable groups. Bullying must be understood as a social problem characterized by numerous challenges to estimating its prevalence and the conditions associated with it. In summary, based on its review of the available evidence, the committee maintains that, despite the current imperfect estimates, bullying and cyberbullying in the United States is clearly prevalent and therefore worthy of attention.

FINDINGS AND CONCLUSIONS

Findings

Finding 2.1: Estimates of bullying and cyberbullying prevalence reported by national surveys vary greatly, ranging from 17.9 percent to 30.9 percent of school-age children for the prevalence of bullying behavior at school and from 6.9 percent to 14.8 percent for the prevalence of cyberbullying. The prevalence of bullying among some groups of youth is even higher. For instance, the prevalence of bullying of lesbian, gay, bisexual, and transgender youth is approximately double that of heterosexual and cisgender youth.

Finding 2.2: The extent to which rates of bullying and cyberbullying have changed in recent years is unclear.

Finding 2.3: The four major national surveys that include bullying do not uniformly address all age groups and school levels.

Finding 2.4: A majority of prevalence data collection is done through self-reports or observation.

Finding 2.5: A majority of national studies do not ask questions about children who have bullied or children who have been bystanders.

Finding 2.6: Many studies differ with regard to the reference period used in measuring bullying behavior (e.g., last month versus last 12 months).

Finding 2.7: Studies use different definitional criteria for differentiating students who have been bullied and cyberbullied and students who have not, as well as students who bully and cyberbully and students who do not.

Finding 2.8: Existing research suggests that there are disparities in rates of bullying by a variety of characteristics, including sexual orientation, disability, and obesity. However, there is a lack of nationally representative data on these and other vulnerable groups. Future research is therefore needed to generate representative estimates of bullying, including bias-based and discriminatory bullying, to accurately identify disparity groups.

Conclusions

Conclusion 2.1: Definitional and measurement inconsistencies lead to a variation in estimates of bullying prevalence, especially across disparate samples of youth. Although there is a variation in numbers, the national surveys show bullying behavior is a real problem that affects a large number of youth.

Conclusion 2.2: The national datasets on the prevalence of bullying focus predominantly on the children who are bullied. Considerably less is known about perpetrators, and nothing is known about bystanders in that national data.

Conclusion 2.3: Cyberbullying should be considered within the context of bullying rather than as a separate entity. The Centers for Disease Control and Prevention definition should be evaluated for its application to cyberbullying. Although cyberbullying may already be included, it is not perceived that way by the public or by the youth population.

Conclusion 2.4: Different types of bullying behaviors—physical, relational, cyber—may emerge or be more salient at different stages of the developmental life course.

Conclusion 2.5: The online context where cyberbullying takes place is nearly universally accessed by adolescents. Social media sites are used by the majority of teens and are an influential and immersive medium in which cyberbullying occurs.

REFERENCES

Arora, C.M. (1996). Defining bullying towards a clearer general understanding and more effective intervention strategies. *School Psychology International, 17*(4), 317-329.
Barboza, G.E., Schiamberg, L.B., Oehmke, J., Korzeniewski, S.J., Post, L.A., and Heraux, C.G. (2009). Individual characteristics and the multiple contexts of adolescent bullying: An ecological perspective. *Journal of Youth and Adolescence, 38*(1), 101-121.
Berlan, E.D., Corliss, H.L., Field, A.E., Goodman, E., and Austin, S.B. (2010). Sexual orientation and bullying among adolescents in the Growing Up Today study. *Journal of Adolescent Health, 46*(4), 366-371.
Blake, J.J., Lund, E.M., Zhou, Q., Kwok, O.-m., and Benz, M.R. (2012). National prevalence rates of bully victimization among students with disabilities in the United States. *School Psychology Quarterly, 27*(4), 210.

Bowleg, L. (2008). When black + lesbian + woman ≠ black lesbian woman: The methodological challenges of qualitative and quantitative intersectionality research. *Sex Roles,* 59(5-6), 312-325.

Bowleg, L. (2012). The problem with the phrase women and minorities: Intersectionality— an important theoretical framework for public health. *American Journal of Public Health,* 102(7), 1267-1273.

Bradshaw, C.P., Sawyer, A.L., and O'Brennan, L.M. (2009). A social disorganization perspective on bullying-related attitudes and behaviors: The influence of school context. *American Journal of Community Psychology,* 43(3-4), 204-220.

Card, N.A., Stucky, B.D., Sawalani, G.M., and Little, T.D. (2008). Direct and indirect aggression during childhood and adolescence: A meta-analytic review of gender differences, intercorrelations, and relations to maladjustment. *Child Development,* 79(5), 1185-1229.

Centers for Disease Control and Prevention. (2010). Youth Risk Behavior Surveillance— United States, 2009. *Morbidity and Mortality Weekly Report,* 59(SS-5), 1-142.

Centers for Disease Control and Prevention. (2012). Youth Risk Behavior Surveillance— United States, 2009. *Morbidity and Mortality Weekly Report,* 61(4), 1-162.

Centers for Disease Control and Prevention. (2014a). *LGBTQ Youth Programs at a Glance.* Available: http://www.cdc.gov/lgbthealth/youth-programs.htm [December 2015].

Centers for Disease Control and Prevention. (2014b). Youth Risk Behavior Surveillance— United States *Morbidity and Mortality Weekly Report,* 63(4), 1-169.

Centers for Disease Control and Prevention. (2015a). *Childhood Obesity Facts.* Available: http://www.cdc.gov/healthyschools/obesity/facts.htm [November 2015].

Centers for Disease Control and Prevention. (2015b). *Defining Childhood Obesity.* Available: http://www.cdc.gov/obesity/childhood/defining.html [November 2015].

Christie-Mizell, C.A., Keil, J.M., Laske, M.T., and Stewart, J. (2011). Bullying behavior, parents' work hours, and early adolescents' perceptions of time spent with parents. *Youth & Society,* 43(4), 1570-1595.

Conron, K.J., Scout, N., and Austin, S.B. (2008). "Everyone has a right to, like, check their box": Findings on a measure of gender identity from a cognitive testing study with adolescents. *Journal of LGBT Health Research,* 4(1), 1-9. doi: 10.1080/15574090802412572.

Cook, C.R., Williams, K.R., Guerra, N.G., and Kim, T. (2010). Variability in the prevalence of bullying and victimization. In S.R. Jimerson, S.M. Swearer, and D.L. Espelage (Eds.), *Handbook of Bullying in Schools: An International Perspective* (pp. 347-362). New York: Routledge.

Cowie, H., Bauman, S., Coyne, I., Myers, C., Pörhölä, M., and Almeida, A. (2013). Cyberbullying amongst university students. In P.K. Smither and G. Steffgen (Eds.), *Cyberbullying Through the New Media: Findings from an International Network* (pp. 165-177). London, UK: Psychology Press.

DeVoe, J.F., and Bauer, L. (2010). *Student Victimization in U.S. Schools: Results from the 2007 School Crime Supplement to the National Crime Victimization Survey* (NCES 2010-319). Washington, DC: U.S. Government Printing Office.

DeVoe, J.F., and Bauer, L. (2011). *Student Victimization in U.S. Schools: Results from the 2009 School Crime Supplement to the National Crime Victimization Survey.* Washington, DC: U.S. Government Printing Office.

Dulmus, C.N., Theriot, M.T., Sowers, K.M., and Blackburn, J.A. (2004). Student reports of peer bullying victimization in a rural school. *Stress, Trauma, and Crisis,* 7(1), 1-16.

Eisenberg, M.E., and Aalsma, M.C. (2005). Bullying and peer victimization: Position paper of the Society for Adolescent Medicine. *Journal of Adolescent Health,* 36(1), 88-91.

Espelage, D.L., Aragon, S.R., Birkett, M., and Koenig, B.W. (2008). Homophobic teasing, psychological outcomes, and sexual orientation among high school students: What influence do parents and schools have? *School Psychology Review* 37(2), 202-216.

Farmer, T.W., Hamm, J.V., Leung, M.-C., Lambert, K., and Gravelle, M. (2011). Early adolescent peer ecologies in rural communities: Bullying in schools that do and do not have a transition during the middle grades. *Journal of Youth and Adolescence, 40*(9), 1106-1117.

Farmer, T.W., Petrin, R., Brooks, D.S., Hamm, J.V., Lambert, K., and Gravelle, M. (2012). Bullying involvement and the school adjustment of rural students with and without disabilities. *Journal of Emotional and Behavioral Disorders, 20*(1), 19-37.

Felix, E.D., and Green, J.G. (2010). Popular girls and brawny boys. In S.R. Jimerson, S.M. Swearer, and D.L. Espelage (Eds.), *Handbook of Bullying in Schools. An International Perspective* (pp. 173-185). New York: Routledge.

Finkelhor, D., Turner, H., Ormrod, R., Hamby, S., and Kracke, K. (2012). *Children's Exposure to Violence: A Comprehensive Survey.* U.S. Department of Justice, Office of Justice Programs, Office of Juvenile Justice and Delinquency Prevention. Available: https://www.ncjrs.gov/pdffiles1/ojjdp/grants/248444.pdf [June 2016].

Finkelhor, D., Turner, H.A., Shattuck, A., and Hamby, S.L. (2015). *Violence, Crime, and Abuse Exposure in a National Sample of Children and Youth: An Update.* U.S. Department of Justice, Office of Justice Programs, Office of Juvenile Justice and Delinquency Prevention. Available: http://www.ojjdp.gov/pubs/248547.pdf [June 2016].

Flouri, E., and Buchanan, A. (2003). The role of mother involvement and father involvement in adolescent bullying behavior. *Journal of Interpersonal Violence, 18*(6), 634-644.

Garner, P.W., and Hinton, T.S. (2010). Emotional display rules and emotion self-regulation: Associations with bullying and victimization in community-based after school programs. *Journal of Community & Applied Social Psychology, 20*(6), 480-496.

Garnett, B.R., Masyn, K.E., Austin, S.B., Miller, M., Williams, D.R., and Viswanath, K. (2014). The intersectionality of discrimination attributes and bullying among youth: An applied latent class analysis. *Journal of Youth and Adolescence, 43*(8), 1225-1239.

Garofalo, R., Wolf, R.C., Kessel, S., Palfrey, J., and DuRant, R.H. (1998). The association between health risk behaviors and sexual orientation among a school-based sample of adolescents. *Pediatrics, 101*(5), 895-902.

GenIUSS Group. (2013). *Gender-Related Measures Overview.* The Williams Institute. Available: http://williamsinstitute.law.ucla.edu/wp-content/uploads/GenIUSS-Gender-related-Question-Overview.pdf [April 2016].

Gladden, R.M., Vivolo-Kantor, A.M., Hamburger, M.E., and Lumpkin, C.D. (2014). *Bullying Surveillance among Youths: Uniform Definitions for Public Health and Recommended Data Elements, Version 1.0.* Atlanta, GA: Centers for Disease Control and Prevention and U.S. Department of Education.

Glew, G.M., Fan, M.-Y., Katon, W., Rivara, F.P., and Kernic, M.A. (2005). Bullying, psychosocial adjustment, and academic performance in elementary school. *Archives of Pediatrics & Adolescent Medicine, 159*(11), 1026-1031.

Goldweber, A., Waasdorp, T.E., and Bradshaw, C.P. (2013). Examining associations between race, urbanicity, and patterns of bullying involvement. *Journal of Youth and Adolescence, 42*(2), 206-219.

Grant, J.M., Mottet, L., Tanis, J.E., Harrison, J., Herman, J., and Keisling, M. (2011). *Injustice at Every Turn: A Report of the National Transgender Discrimination Survey.* National Center for Transgender Equality. Available: http://www.thetaskforce.org/static_html/downloads/reports/reports/ntds_full.pdf [October 2015].

Gray, W.N., Kahhan, N.A., and Janicke, D.M. (2009). Peer victimization and pediatric obesity: A review of the literature. *Psychology in the Schools, 46*(8), 720-727.

Griffiths, L.J., Wolke, D., Page, A.S., and Horwood, J. (2006). Obesity and bullying: Different effects for boys and girls. *Archives of Disease in Childhood, 91*(2), 121-125.

Hanlon, B.M. (2004). *2003 Massachusetts Youth Risk Behavior Survey Results.* Malden: Massachusetts Department of Education.

Hong, J.S., and Espelage, D.L. (2012). A review of research on bullying and peer victimization in school: An ecological system analysis. *Aggression and Violent Behavior, 17*(4), 311-322.

Hong, J.S., Peguero, A.A., Choi, S., Lanesskog, D., Espelage, D.L., and Lee, N.Y. (2014). Social ecology of bullying and peer victimization of Latino and Asian youth in the United States: A review of the literature. *Journal of School Violence, 13*(3), 315-338.

Iannotti, R.J. (2012). *Health Behavior in School-Aged Children (HBSC), 2005-2006.* Ann Arbor, MI: Inter-university Consortium for Political and Social Research.

Iannotti, R.J. (2013). *Health Behavior in School-Aged Children (HBSC), 2009-2010.* Ann Arbor, MI: Inter-university Consortium for Political and Social Research.

Jansen, D.E., Veenstra, R., Ormel, J., Verhulst, F.C., and Reijneveld, S.A. (2011). Early risk factors for being a bully, victim, or bully/victim in late elementary and early secondary education. The Longitudinal Trails Study. *BMC Public Health, 11*(1), 1-7.

Jansen, P.W., Verlinden, M., Dommisse-van Berkel, A., Mieloo, C., van der Ende, J., Veenstra, R., Verhulst, F.C., Jansen, W., and Tiemeier, H. (2012). Prevalence of bullying and victimization among children in early elementary school: Do family and school neighbourhood socioeconomic status matter? *BMC Public Health, 12*(1), 1-10.

Janssen, I., Craig, W.M., Boyce, W.F., and Pickett, W. (2004). Associations between overweight and obesity with bullying behaviors in school-aged children. *Pediatrics, 113*(5), 1187-1194.

Juvonen, J., and Gross, E.F. (2008). Extending the school grounds?—Bullying experiences in cyberspace. *Journal of School Health, 78*(9), 496-505.

Kosciw, J.G., Greytak, E.A., Bartkiewicz, M.J., Boesen, M.J., and Palmer, N.A. (2012). *The 2011 National School Climate Survey: The Experiences of Lesbian, Gay, Bisexual, and Transgender Youth in Our Nation's School.* Washington, DC: Education Resources Information Center, Institute of Education Sciences, U.S. Department of Education.

Kowalski, R.M., Limber, S.P., and Agatston, P.W. (2012). *Cyberbullying: Bullying in the Digital Age.* West Sussex, UK: Wiley-Blackwell.

Kraft, E., and Wang, J. (2010). An exploratory study of the cyberbullying and cyberstalking experiences and factors related to victimization of students at a public liberal arts college. *International Journal of Technoethics, 1*(4), 74-91.

Larochette, A.-C., Murphy, A.N., and Craig, W.M. (2010). Racial bullying and victimization in Canadian school-age children: Individual and school level effects. *School Psychology International, 31*(4), 389-408.

Lemstra, M.E., Nielsen, G., Rogers, M.R., Thompson, A.T., and Moraros, J.S. (2012). Risk indicators and outcomes associated with bullying in youth aged 9-15 years. *Canadian Journal of Public Health/Revue Canadienne de Santé Publique, 103*(1), 9-13.

Lenhart, A., Duggan, M., Perrin, A., Stepler, R., Rainie, H., and Parker, K. (2015). *Teens, Social Media & Technology Overview 2015.* Available: http://www.pewinternet.org/files/2015/04/PI_TeensandTech_Update2015_0409151.pdf [September 2015].

Lim, S.J.J., and Hoot, J.L. (2015). Bullying in an increasingly diverse school population: A socioecological model analysis. *School Psychology International.* doi: 0143034315571158.

Limber, S.B. (2014). *Bullying Among Children and Youth.* Unpublished manuscript of a study commissioned by the Planning Committee on Increasing Capacity for Reducing Bullying and Its Impact on the Lifecourse of Youth Involved. Department of Psychology and Institute on Family and Neighborhood Life, Clemson University, SC.

Limber, S.B, Olweus, D., and Luxenberg, H. (2013). *Bullying in U.S. Schools, 2012 Status Report.* Center City, MN: Hazelden Foundation.

Lunde, C., Frisén, A., and Hwang, C.P. (2007). Ten-year-old girls' and boys' body composition and peer victimization experiences: Prospective associations with body satisfaction. *Body Image, 4*(1), 11-28.

Magklara, K., Skapinakis, P., Gkatsa, T., Bellos, S., Araya, R., Stylianidis, S., and Mavreas, V. (2012). Bullying behaviour in schools, socioeconomic position, and psychiatric morbidity: A cross-sectional study in late adolescents in Greece. *Child and Adolescent Psychiatry and Mental Health, 6*(8), 2-13.

McCall, L. (2005). The complexity of intersectionality. *Signs: Journal of Women in Culture and Society. 30*(3), 1771-1800.

McGuire, J.K., Anderson, C.R., Toomey, R.B., and Russell, S.T. (2010). School climate for transgender youth: A mixed-method investigation of student experiences and school responses. *Journal of Youth and Adolescence, 39*(10), 1175-1188.

McLaughlin, C., Byers, R., and Vaughn, R. (2010). *Responding to Bullying among Children with Special Educational Needs and/or Disabilities.* London, UK: Anti-Bullying Alliance.

Monks, C.P., and Smith, P.K. (2006). Definitions of bullying: Age differences in understanding of the term and the role of experience. *British Journal of Developmental Psychology, 24*(4), 801-821.

Moreno, M.A., Kota, R., Schoohs, S., and Whitehill, J.M. (2013). The Facebook influence model: A concept mapping approach. *Cyberpsychology, Behavior, and Social Networking, 16*(7), 504-511.

Nansel, T.R., Overpeck, M., Pilla, R.S., Ruan, W.J., Simons-Morton, B., and Scheidt, P. (2001). Bullying behaviors among U.S. youth: Prevalence and association with psychosocial adjustment. *Journal of the American Medical Association, 285*(16), 2094-2100.

Neumark-Sztainer, D., Falner, N., Story, M., Perry, C., Hannan, P.J., and Mulert, S. (2002). Weight-teasing among adolescents: Correlations with weight status and disordered eating behaviors. *International Journal of Obesity and Related Metabolic Disorders. 26*(1), 123-131.

Nordhagen, R., Nielsen, A., Stigum, H., and Köhler, L. (2005). Parental reported bullying among Nordic children: A population-based study. *Child: Care, Health and Development, 31*(6), 693-701.

Ogden, C.L., Carroll, M.D., Kit, B.K., and Flegal, K.M. (2014). Prevalence of childhood and adult obesity in the United States, 2011-2012. *Journal of the American Medical Association, 311*(8), 806-814.

Olsen, E.O.M., Kann, L., Vivolo-Kantor, A., Kinchen, S., and McManus, T. (2014). School violence and bullying among sexual minority high school students, 2009-2011. *Journal of Adolescent Health, 55*(3), 432-438.

Olweus, D. (2013). School bullying: Development and some important challenges. *Annual Review of Clinical Psychology, 9*, 751-780.

Oppliger, P.A. (2013). *Bullies and Mean Girls in Popular Culture.* Jefferson, NC: McFarland & Company.

Pereira, B., Mendonca, D., Neto, C., Valente, L., and Smith, P.K. (2004). Bullying in Portuguese schools. *School Psychology International, 25*(2), 241-254.

Pergolizzi, F., Pergolizzi, J., Gan, Z., Macario, S., Pergolizzi, J.V., Ewin, T., and Gan, T.J. (2011). Bullying in middle school: Results from a 2008 survey. *International Journal of Adolescent Medicine and Health, 23*(1), 11-18.

Peskin, M., Tortolero, S.R., and Markham, C.M. (2006). Bullying and victimization among black and Hispanic adolescents. *Adolescence, 41*, 467-484.

Puhl, R.M., and Latner, J.D. (2007). Stigma, obesity, and the health of the nation's children. *Psychological Bulletin, 133*(4), 557.

Reisner, S.L., Greytak, E.A., Parsons, J.T., and Ybarra, M.L. (2015). Gender minority social stress in adolescence: Disparities in adolescent bullying and substance use by gender identity. *Journal of Sex Research, 52*(3), 243-256.

Rice, E., Petering, R., Rhoades, H., Winetrobe, H., Goldbach, J., Plant, A., Montoya, J., and Kordic, T. (2015). Cyberbullying perpetration and victimization among middle school students. *American Journal of Public Health, 105*(3), e66-e72.

Rivers, I. (2001). The bullying of sexual minorities at school: Its nature and long-term correlates. *Educational and Child Psychology, 18*(1), 32-46.

Robers, S., Kemp, J., and Truman, J. (2013). *Indicators of School Crime and Safety: 2012.* NCES 2013-036/NCJ 241446. Washington, DC: National Center for Education Statistics, U.S. Department of Education.

Rose, C.A. (2015). *Bullying and Vulnerable Populations: Exploring Predictive and Protective Factors Associated with Disproportionate Representation.* Unpublished manuscript of a study commissioned by the Committee on the Biological and Psychosocial Effects of Peer Victimization: Lessons for Bullying Prevention. Department of Special Education, University of Missouri, Columbia.

Rose, C.A., Espelage, D.L., and Monda-Amaya, L.E. (2009). Bullying and victimisation rates among students in general and special education: A comparative analysis. *Educational Psychology, 29*(7), 761-776.

Rose, C.A., Monda-Amaya, L.E., and Espelage, D.L. (2010). Bullying perpetration and victimization in special education: A review of the literature. *Remedial and Special Education, 32*, 114-130.

Rose, C.A., Simpson, C.G., and Moss, A. (2015). The bullying dynamic: Prevalence of involvement among a large-scale sample of middle and high school youth with and without disabilities. *Psychology in the Schools, 52*(5), 515-531.

Russell, S.T., Driscoll, A.K., and Truong, N. (2002). Adolescent same-sex romantic attractions and relationships: Implications for substance use and abuse. *American Journal of Public Health, 92*(2), 198-202.

Russell, S.T., Everett, B.G., Rosario, M., and Birkett, M. (2014). Indicators of victimization and sexual orientation among adolescents: Analyses from Youth Risk Behavior Surveys. *American Journal of Public Health, 104*(2), 255-261.

Sawyer, A.L., Bradshaw, C.P., and O'Brennan, L.M. (2008). Examining ethnic, gender, and developmental differences in the way children report being a victim of "bullying" on self-report measures. *Journal of Adolescent Health, 43*, 106-114. doi:10.1016/j.jadohealth.2007.12.011.

Schenk, A.M., and Fremouw, W.J. (2012). Prevalence, psychological impact, and coping of cyberbully victims among college students. *Journal of School Violence, 11*(1), 21-37.

Schuster, M.A., and Bogart, L.M. (2013). Did the ugly duckling have PTSD? Bullying, its effects, and the role of pediatricians. *Pediatrics, 131*(1), e288-e291.

Schwartz, D., Dodge, K.A., Pettit, G.S., and Bates, J.E. (1997). The early socialization of aggressive victims of bullying. *Child Development, 68*(4), 665-675.

Selkie, E.M., Fales, J.L., and Moreno, M.A. (2015). Cyberbullying prevalence among U.S. middle and high school age adolescents: A systematic review and quality assessment. *Journal of Adolescent Health, 58*(2), 125-133.

Shetgiri, R., Lin, H., and Flores, G. (2012). Identifying children at risk for being bullies in the United States. *Academic Pediatrics, 12*(6), 509-522.

Smith, P.K., Cowie, H., Olafsson, R.F., Liefooghe, A.P., Almeida, A., Araki, H., del Barrio, C., Costabile, A., Dekleva, B., and Houndoumadi, A. (2002). Definitions of bullying: A comparison of terms used, and age and gender differences, in a fourteen-country international comparison. *Child Development, 73*(4), 1119-1133.

Smith, P.K., Mahdavi, J., Carvalho, M., Fisher, S., Russell, S., and Tippett, N. (2008). Cyberbullying: Its nature and impact in secondary school pupils. *Journal of Child Psychology and Psychiatry, 49*(4), 376-385.

Solberg, M.E. (2003). Prevalence estimation of school bullying with the Olweus bully/victim questionnaire. *Aggressive Behavior, 29*(3), 239-268.

Son, E., Parish, S.L., and Peterson, N.A. (2012). National prevalence of peer victimization among young children with disabilities in the United States. *Children and Youth Services Review, 34*(8), 1540-1545.

Spriggs, A.L., Iannotti, R.J., Nansel, T.R., and Haynie, D.L. (2007). Adolescent bullying involvement and perceived family, peer, and school relations: Commonalities and differences across race/ethnicity. *Journal of Adolescent Health, 41*(3), 283-293.

Stockdale, M.S., Hangaduambo, S., Duys, D., Larson, K., and Sarvela, P.D. (2002). Rural elementary students', parents', and teachers' perceptions of bullying. *American Journal of Health Behavior, 26*(4), 266-277.

Strohmeier, D., and Toda, Y. (2008). *Cross-National Similarities and Differences. The Extent to Which Bullying and Victimisation Are Similar, or Show Differences, Across Cultures, Especially Western and Eastern Cultures.* Paper presented at the preconference "Victimisation in Children and Youth," 20th Biennial Meeting of the International Society for the Study of Behavioural Development, July, Wurzburg, Germany.

Twyman, K.A., Saylor, C.F., Saia, D., Macias, M.M., Taylor, L.A., and Spratt, E. (2010). Bullying and ostracism experiences in children with special health care needs. *Journal of Developmental & Behavioral Pediatrics, 31*(1), 1-8.

U.S. Department of Education. (2013). *Student Reports of Bullying and Cyber-Bullying: Results from the 2011 School Crime Supplement to the National Crime Victimization Survey.* Washington DC: Author.

U.S. Department of Education. (2015). *Student Reports of Bullying and Cyber-Bullying: Results from the 2013 School Crime Supplement to the National Crime Victimization Survey.* Washington DC: Author. Available: http://nces.ed.gov/pubs2015/2015056.pdf [April 2015].

U.S. Department of Health and Human Services. (2008). *Health Behavior in School-Aged Children (HBSC), 2001-2002.* Health Resources and Services Administration. Maternal and Child Health Bureau. Ann Arbor, MI: Inter-university Consortium for Political and Social Research.

U.S. Government Accountability Office. (2012). *School Bullying-Extent of Legal Protections for Vulnerable Groups Needs to Be More Fully Assessed.* Washington, DC: Author.

Vaillancourt, T., McDougall, P., Hymel, S., Krygsman, A., Miller, J., Stiver, K., and Davis, C. (2008). Bullying: Are researchers and children/youth talking about the same thing? *International Journal of Behavioral Development, 32*(6), 486-495.

Wensley, K., and Campbell, M. (2012). Heterosexual and nonheterosexual young university students' involvement in traditional and cyber forms of bullying. *Cyberpsychology, Behavior, and Social Networking, 15*(12), 649-654.

Wilson, M.L., Bovet, P., Viswanathan, B., and Suris, J.-C. (2012). Bullying among adolescents in a sub-Saharan middle-income setting. *Journal of Adolescent Health, 51*(1), 96-98.

Wilson, M.M. (2014). *Hate Crime Victimization 2004-2012 Statistics.* Washington, DC: U.S. Department of Justice. Available: http://www.bjs.gov/content/pub/pdf/hcv0412st.pdf [November 2015].

Wolak, J., Mitchell, K.J., and Finkelhor, D. (2007). Does online harassment constitute bullying? An exploration of online harassment by known peers and online-only contacts. *Journal of Adolescent Health, 41*(6), S51-S58.

World Health Organization. (2003). *Health Behavior in School-Aged Children (HBSC), 1997-1998.* Ann Arbor, MI: Inter-university Consortium for Political and Social Research.

Zimmerman, F.J., Glew, G.M., Christakis, D.A., and Katon, W. (2005). Early cognitive stimu-lation, emotional support, and television watching as predictors of subsequent bullying among grade-school children. *Archives of Pediatrics & Adolescent Medicine*, 159(4), 384-388.

3

Individuals within Social Contexts

To date, research on bullying has been largely descriptive. These descriptive data have provided essential insights into a variety of important factors on the topic of bullying, including prevalence, individual and contextual correlates, and adverse consequences. At the same time, the descriptive approach has often produced inconsistencies—for example, some descriptive studies on racial/ethnic differences in those who are bullied found that African Americans are more bullied than Latinos (Peskin et al., 2006), whereas others found no group differences (Storch et al., 2003). Such inconsistencies are due, in part, to lack of attention to contextual factors that render individual characteristics such as race/ethnicity more or less likely to be related to bullying experiences. Consequently, there has been a call to advance the field by moving from descriptive studies to an approach that identifies processes that can explain heterogeneity in bullying experiences by focusing on contextual factors that modulate the effect of individual characteristics (e.g., ethnicity, gender, age, sexual orientation) on bullying behavior (Hong et al., 2015; Swearer and Hymel, 2015).

Such an approach is not new. In fact, it has long been recognized that individuals are embedded within situations that themselves are embedded within broader social contexts (Bronfenbrenner, 1979). Whereas a situation refers to "a particular concrete physical and social setting in which a person is embedded at any one point in time," context is "the surround for situations (and individuals in situations). Context is the *general and continuing* multilayered and interwoven set of material realities, social structures, patterns of social relations, and shared belief systems that surround any given situation" (Ashmore et al., 2004, p. 103). This "person by situation by context" interaction has been applied to personality (Mischel and Shoda, 1995) and to social characteristics; for example, collective identities (Ashmore et al., 2004), but it also applies to bullying. For instance, a gay student may be bullied in the locker room following gym class. But this particular situation (i.e., locker room after gym class) occurs within a broader social context, such as whether anti-bullying laws include sexual orientation as an enumerated group and whether the surrounding community views homosexuality as a normal or deviant expression of sexuality. These contextual factors influence the manner in which this situation unfolds. Some of these social contexts are far more likely to prevent the bullying of the gay youth from occurring or to buffer the negative effects more effectively if the bullying occurs.

This chapter is organized around social contexts that can either attenuate or exacerbate (i.e., moderate) the effect of individual characteristics on bullying behavior. Thus, it moves beyond current descriptions of contextual correlates of bullying—which examine main effect relations between a contextual factor, such as schools, and a bullying outcome, such as perpetration—to identify contextual moderators of individual characteristics on bullying and related outcomes. Doing this requires analyses that specifically examine moderation (a moderator analysis), or effect modification. A moderator is defined as a "qualitative (e.g., sex, race, class) or quantitative (e.g., level of reward) variable that affects the direction and/or strength of the relation between an independent or predictor variable and a dependent or criterion variable" (Baron and Kenny, 1986, p. 1174).[1] Moderators can either magnify or diminish the association between the independent and dependent variables. For instance, if a study shows that adolescent girls develop depressive symptoms following interpersonal stressors, whereas adolescent boys do not, this would provide evidence that sex moderates the relationship between interpersonal stressors and depressive symptoms. Figure 3-1 illustrates a moderator model with three causal paths (a, b, c) that lead to an outcome variable of interest.

Why a focus on moderators? Prevention science is based on a fundamental assumption that a "careful scientific review of risk and protective factors for a given condition or impairment must be undertaken before the prevention trial is designed" (Cicchetti and Hinshaw, 2002, p. 669). Moderators help with specificity and precision in that they afford researchers the ability to "make precise predictions regarding the processes that guide behavior and, in particular, to specify explicitly the conditions under which

---

[1] A variable functions as a mediator "to the extent that it accounts for the relation between the predictor and the criterion" (Baron and Kenny, 1986, p. 1176). Mediators are distinguished from moderators as they address *how or why* certain effects occur, whereas moderators explain *when* certain effects hold (Baron and Kenny, 1986).

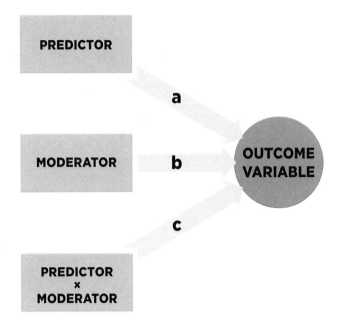

FIGURE 3-1 Moderator model.
SOURCE: Adapted from Baron and Kenny (1986, Fig. 1, p. 1174).

these processes operate" (Rothman, 2013, p. 190). In other words, before one can influence pathways in a positive direction, one must first understand the factors that increase the risk of poorer outcomes, as well as the factors that mitigate this risk.

The committee first discusses conceptual frameworks that underpin our approach. We then present illustrative examples across a variety of different social contexts—peers, families, schools, communities, and broad macrosystems—to demonstrate the utility of such an approach and to offer guidance for the field of bullying studies moving forward. The chapter ends with an outlining of areas that warrant greater attention in future research, as well as the committee's findings and conclusions.

CONCEPTUAL FRAMEWORKS

This chapter largely draws upon two theoretical and conceptual frameworks that have been frequently used in the bullying literature: the ecological theory of development and the concepts of equifinality and multifinality. Although these concepts and theories differ in focus, they share the overarching point that people are embedded in contexts that modulate the effect of individual characteristics on developmental, social, and health outcomes. This insight is key to understanding how different social contexts affect the extent to which youths' individual characteristics (e.g., gender, age, race/ ethnicity, and sexual orientation) are associated with bullying perpetration or being bullied. Later in this chapter, the committee draws on a third conceptual framework—namely, stigma[2]—that has received comparatively less attention in the bullying literature but that we believe provides an important framework for understanding both the disparities in rates of bullying and in types of bullying (i.e., bias-based bullying) that have been observed in the literature.

Ecological Theory of Development

Bronfenbrenner's (1979) bioecological model, which highlights the transactional nature of multiple levels of influence on human development, conceptualizes humans as nested within four levels (see Figure 3-2). The most proximal system is the *microsystem* (e.g., school, family), which includes immediate surroundings that more directly affect the individual. The next level of influence, the *mesosystem*, describes how the different parts of a child's microsystem interact together. The *exosystem* includes neighborhoods or school systems. The *macrosystem* includes the broad norms and trends in the culture and policies, which impact development and behavior.

This ecological model has been applied to bullying (Swearer and Espelage, 2004; Swearer and Hymel, 2015; Swearer et al., 2010), providing a comprehensive framework in which to understand bullying in particular and peer victimization more generally. This application illustrates the interaction of intrapersonal, family, school, peer, and community characteristics that may influence victimization and in turn modulate the risk for adjustment and behavioral problems.

For example, the microsystem of the classroom, the family, or the peer group has been correlated with experiences of bullying behavior (Card et al., 2007). Risk factors and protective factors within the mesosystem, which can act as moderators, may include interacting microsystems such as parent-teacher relationships; however, few studies have jointly examined the influence of such risk and protective factors (Card et al., 2008). Several studies have examined risk factors for bullying behavior within the exosystem, such as urbanicity of school setting or other school-level indicators

---

[2] As noted in the recent National Academies of Sciences, Engineering, and Medicine report, *Ending Discrimination Against People with Mental and Substance Use Disorders: The Evidence for Stigma Change* (2016), some stakeholder groups are targeting the word "stigma" itself and the Substance Abuse and Mental Health Services Administration (SAMHSA) is shifting away from the use of this term. The committee determined that the word stigma was currently widely accepted in the research community and uses this term in the report.

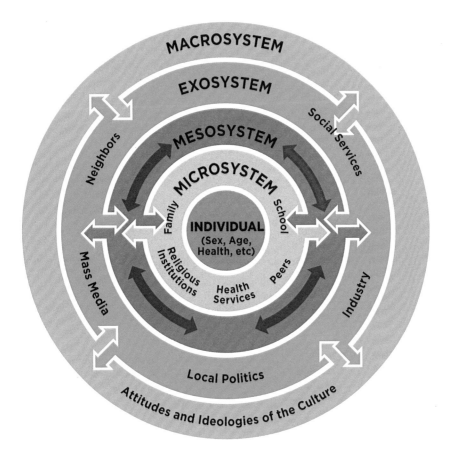

FIGURE 3-2 Bronfenbrenner's ecological theory of development.
SOURCE: Adapted from Bronfenbrenner (1979).

of concentrated disadvantage or school climate (Bradshaw and Waasdorp, 2009; Gregory et al., 2010; Wang and Degol, 2015). Others address the macrosystem, including a focus on anti-bullying legislation (Hatzenbuehler and Keyes, 2013; Hatzenbuehler et al., 2015a). More recent evolutions of the ecological model have now layered on the *chronosystem,* which characterizes the broader historical and temporal context in which an individual is embedded. For example, recent increases in the use of mobile technologies and the Internet (Lenhart et al., 2008) resulted in a novel contextual influence for today's youth, whereas previous generations of adolescents did not have such experiences (Espelage et al., 2013).

In summary, the ecological model provides a framework from which to further understand the influence that social contexts may have on both rates of bullying behavior and individuals' experiences of negative outcomes, including mental health outcomes. By incorporating multiple levels of influence to explain and predict individual outcomes, the ecological model allows for a broader conceptualization of the various contextual influences on youth bullying.

Equifinality and Multifinality

The complex interplay of risk, protection, and resilience resulting from different contextual influences explains why there is variation in the adjustment and developmental outcomes of children who are bullied, such as why not all youth who are bullied develop adjustment problems. This idea is highlighted in Cicchetti and Rogosch's (1996) equifinality and multifinality theory of developmental psychopathology. There is considerable variability in processes and outcomes, and this variability is linked to varied life experiences that contribute to adaptive and maladaptive outcomes. In the case of equifinality, the same outcome—such as being an individual who bullies or an individual who is bullied—may derive from different pathways. For example, Haltigan and Vaillancourt (2014) found that for some youth, the pathway to bullying others began with being targeted by peers, while for others the pathway was initiated with low levels of bullying others. But the end result of these two diverse trajectories is the same: bullying perpetration. In the case of multifinality, instances that start off on a similar trajectory of bullying perpetration or peer victimization can result in vastly different outcomes. Figure 3-3 provides a schematic representation of these two concepts.

As an example, Kretschmer and colleagues (2015) examined maladjustment patterns among children exposed to bullying in early and mid-adolescence and found evidence for multifinality. That is, bullied youth experienced a variety of mental health outcomes as a function of being bullied, including problems with withdrawal/depression, anxiety, somatic complaints, delinquency, and aggression. However, when these varied outcomes were considered together, internalizing problems (withdrawal and anxiety) were the most common outcome.

The idea that there is diversity in "individual patterns of adaptation and maladaptation" is consistent with the current state of knowledge concerning involvement with bullying (Cicchetti and Rogosch, 1996, p. 599). For instance, in the Haltigan and Vaillancourt (2014) study, joint trajectories of bullying perpetration and being targeted for bullying across elementary school and middle school were examined and four distinct trajectories of involvement were noted. In the first group, there was low-to-limited

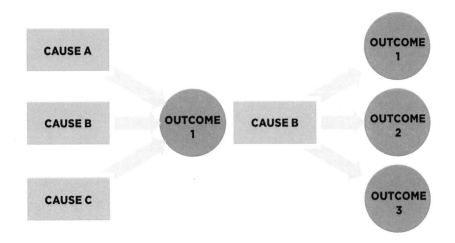

FIGURE 3-3 Conceptual diagram of equfinality and mutlifinality.
SOURCE: Illustration of concept proposed by Cicchetti and Rogosch (1996).

involvement in perpetration or in being a target for bullying.[3] In the second group, involvement in bullying perpetration increased over time, and in the third group, being a target of bullying decreased over time. In the fourth group, a target-to-bully trajectory was found, which was characterized by decreasing rates of being targeted and increasing perpetration rates. The mental health outcomes associated with these distinct trajectories of bullying involvement also varied. Mental health problems in high school were particularly pronounced for children who were bullied in elementary school but were not bullied in middle school and for those who started off as targets of bullying and became bullies over time (Haltigan and Vaillancourt, 2014). These findings are consistent with a growing body of literature demonstrating the enduring effects of being bullied, effects that seem to last well into adulthood (Kljakovic and Hunt, 2016; McDougall and Vaillancourt, 2015).

PEERS

Peers are a critical social context that affect many aspects of bullying in large part because peers influence group norms, attitudes, and behavior

---

[3]Haltigan and Vaillancourt (2014) used the terms "peer victimization" or "victimization" to refer to the role of being bullied in bullying incidents (in the terminology preferred for this report, the "target" role in the bullying dyad).

(Faris and Felmlee, 2014; Vaillancourt et al., 2010; Veenstra et al., 2013). This section discusses research related to peers as a social context.

Multiple Participant Roles in Bullying

To acknowledge this larger peer context, bullying can be conceptualized as a group phenomenon, with multiple peers taking on roles other than perpetrator and target (Olweus, 1993; Salmivalli, 2001, 2010, 2014). Acknowledging the group context is particularly important, given what is known about the causes of bullying. Contemporary theory and research suggest that individuals who bully others are largely motivated to gain (or maintain) high status among their peers (see review in Rodkin et al., 2015). Because status such as popularity, dominance, visibility, and respect are attributes assigned by the group, individuals who bully need spectators to confer that status (Salmivalli and Peets, 2009). Observational studies have documented that witnesses are present in about 85 percent of bullying episodes (Hawkins et al., 2001; Pepler et al., 2010).

Witnesses to bullying take on various roles. Based largely on observational studies and a peer nomination method developed by Salmivalli and colleagues (1996), a growing literature suggests that there are at least four major participant roles in typical bullying episodes in addition to the perpetrator-target dyad. Two participant roles support the individual who bullies (the perpetrator in a particular incident). They are *assistants*, or *henchmen*, who get involved to help the perpetrator once the episode has begun, and *reinforcers* who encourage the perpetrator by laughing or showing other signs of approval. Supporting a target are *defenders*, who actively come to his or her aid. In observational research, less than 20 percent of witnessed bullying episodes had defenders who intervened on the target's behalf, with defender actions successfully terminating the bullying about half the time (Hawkins et al., 2001). The presence of defenders in classrooms is associated with fewer instances of bullying behavior, whereas the presence of reinforcers is linked to increased incidence of bullying (Salmivalli et al., 2011).

The final participant role is *bystanders*, or onlookers, who are present during the bullying event but remain neutral (passive), helping neither the target nor the perpetrator. The low rate of observed defending indicates that bystanders coming to the aid of targets are relatively rare (Pepler et al., 2010). With increasing age from middle childhood to adolescence, bystanders become even more passive (Marsh et al., 2011; Pöyhönen et al., 2010; Trach et al., 2010). Passive bystander behavior reinforces the belief that targets of bullying are responsible for their plight and bring their problems on themselves (Gini et al., 2008). Bystanders doing nothing can also send a message that bullying is acceptable.

Given their potential to either counter or reinforce the acceptability of bullying behavior, bystanders have been the focus of most participant role research; the goal has been to examine what factors might tip the scales in favor of their assisting the perpetrator or the target (i.e., becoming either reinforcers of the bullying or defenders of those bullied). Self-enhancement and self-protective motives likely encourage bystanders to support the perpetrator (Juvonen and Galván, 2008). Children not only improve their own status by aligning themselves with powerful perpetrators; they can also lower their risk of becoming the perpetrator's next target.

Conversely, a number of personality and social status characteristics are associated with bystanders' willingness to defend the target of a bullying incident. The degree of empathy for the child who is being bullied and the strength of bystanders' sense of self-efficacy are predictors of the likelihood that witnesses become defenders (Gini et al., 2008; Pozzoli and Gini, 2010). Thus, it may not be enough to sympathize with the victim's plight; going from passive bystander to active defender requires that witnesses believe they have the skills to make a difference. Witnesses who themselves have high social status and feel a sense of moral responsibility to intervene are also more likely to help the victim (Pöyhönen et al., 2010; Pozzoli and Gini, 2010).

By way of summary, a useful schematic representation of the various participant roles in a bullying incident was offered by Olweus (2001) in what he labels the *Bullying Circle* (see Figure 3-4). These roles are depicted as a continuum that varies along two dimensions: the attitude of different participants toward perpetrator and target (positive, negative, or indifferent) and tendency to act (that is, to get involved or not).

Research indicates that attitudes and intentions that define these roles vary depending on individual variables such as age, gender, personality, and social status, as well as contexts such as classroom norms favoring the perpetrator or the target. Whether bystanders defend or rebuff the perpetrator or target, as opposed to remaining passive, seems to be especially moderated by peer group norms. Bystanders are less likely to stand up for the target of a bullying event in classrooms where bullying has high prestige (i.e., where frequent perpetrators are the most popular children (Peets et al., 2015), but they are more likely to help when injunctive norms (the expectation of what peers *should* do) and descriptive norms (what they *actually* do) favor the target (Pozzoli et al., 2012). In some peer groups, bullying behavior will be tolerated and encouraged, while in other groups, bullying behavior will be actively dissuaded. For example, Sentse and colleagues (2007) found that 13 year olds who bullied others were rejected by peers if such behavior was not normative within their class. Conversely, in classes where bullying behavior was more common, or normative, frequent perpetrators were liked by their peers.

While social norms about bullying may be powerful, they are not al-

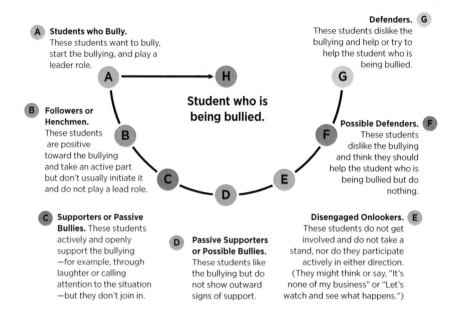

FIGURE 3-4 The Bullying Circle: Students' modes of reaction/roles in an acute bullying situation.
SOURCE: Adapted from Olweus (2001, Fig. 1.1, p. 15).

ways accurate. Studying perceived norms about bullying in middle school, Perkins and colleagues (2011) found that students overestimated the extent to which their peers engaged in bullying, were targets of bullying, and tolerated such behavior. An intervention that communicated accurate norms based on a schoolwide student survey indicating overwhelming disapproval of bullying resulted in less reported bullying over the course of a school year. When students were informed that their schoolmates did not approve of bullying, they were less likely to engage in the behavior themselves. This research illustrates the power of peer norms about the prevalence of and tolerance for bullying that can influence student participant roles, especially the willingness of bystanders to come to the aid of victims (Pozzoli et al., 2012).

Perspectives from the Field

Peer perceptions of what's going on are significant: Kids typically have a lot of pride and fear of what others might say about them if they seek help—they may not be as interested in mentors or student assistance programs, for example, because they fear being targeted more for seeking counseling or support. Even going into the counselor's office can mark students as "weak," which increases their likelihood of becoming bullying targets.

—Summary from community-based providers'
focus group discussing bullying
(See Appendix B for additional highlights from interviews.)

Friends as Protective Factors

Friendships are very important for children's development because they make it possible for children to acquire basic social skills. In the context of bullying, friendships represent a protective factor for children at risk of being bullied. Having friends, and particularly being liked by peers, is important in protecting against being targeted (Hodges et al., 1999; Pellegrini and Long, 2002). The number of friends seems to protect against being targeted; however, the protection is weaker when the friends are themselves targets of bullying incidents or have internalizing problems (Fox and Boulton, 2006; Hodges et al., 1999; Pellegrini et al., 1999). In a study to examine friendship quality as a possible moderator of risk factors in predicting peer bullying victimization, the findings of Bollmer and colleagues (2005) suggest that having a high-quality best friendship might function in different capacities to protect children from becoming targets of bullying and also to attenuate perpetration behavior.

FAMILY

The family context is perhaps one of the most influential on children's development. As a result, it is not surprising that families also play a role in bullying prevention. However, the majority of research on family influences, from both a risk and resiliency perspective, has been on psychopathology and children's adjustment (Collins et al., 2000), rather than on bullying specifically. These studies are further limited in that they are almost all cross-sectional correlational studies based on student self-report on the same instrument. Nevertheless, in this section the committee discusses some illustrative examples of how the family context can both exacerbate and attenuate the effect of individual characteristics on bullying outcomes.

Family functioning, typically assessed in terms of family involvement, expressiveness, conflict, organization, decision making to resolve problems, and confiding in each other (Cunningham et al., 2004), has been linked to perpetrator/target roles. For example, Stevens and colleagues (2002) found that Dutch children (ages 10-13) reported bullying others more when they also perceived their own family to be lower on family functioning. Rigby (1993) found that Australian girls, but not boys, were more likely to report being bullied if they also perceived their family to not be well functioning. Moreover, girls were more likely to report being bullied if they had a more negative relationship with their mother, whereas for boys, a negative relationship with an absent father predicted reports of being bullied (Rigby, 1993). Holt and colleagues (2008) examined the parent-child concordance of involvement with bullying and how family characteristics were related to bullying involvement. They found that American children (fifth grade) whose family life was characterized as less functional (i.e., higher levels of criticism, fewer rules, and more child maltreatment) were more likely to report being bullied. Involvement in bullying as a perpetrator was linked to poor supervision, child maltreatment, and greater exposure to intimate partner violence (Holt et al., 2008). In another moderator analysis of British adolescents ages 14-18, Flouri and Buchanan (2003) found that teens from single-parent families reported bullying others more than did teens from intact families. However, involvement in bullying was attenuated when the teens also reported that their mother and father were involved in their life—for example, by spending time with them, talking through their worries, taking an interest in school work, or helping with plans for the future (Flouri and Buchanan, 2003). Finally, Brittain (2010) found that fifth grade Canadian boys who reported being bullied but whose parents were unaware of their plight were less depressed if their parents reported higher family functioning. There are relatively few moderator analyses that address how family functioning affects prevalence of perpetrating behavior.

Whereas the findings from the above studies suggest that parental support can buffer youth against the negative effects of bullying behavior, other studies have shown that this effect is not consistent across all groups of youth. For example, using data from the Dane County Youth Assessment (DCYA), which included 15,923 youth in grades 7-12, Poteat and colleagues (2011) found that parental support was most consistent in moderating the effects of general and homophobic bullying behavior on risk of suicidality for heterosexual white and racial/ethnic minority youth who had been targeted in such incidents. However, in nearly all cases, parental support did not moderate these effects for lesbian, gay, bisexual, and transgender (LGBT) youth, nor did it moderate the effects of these types of being bullied on the targets' sense of school belonging. The authors speculate that one potential reason for these results is that LGBT students may be less likely to discuss homophobic bullying with their parents than do heterosexual youth because of the stigma of homosexuality (e.g., discussing homophobic bullying could necessitate coming out to parents, which could lead to parental rejection and/or victimization). Another possibility raised by the authors is that general parental support, which was the focus of this study, is not sufficient to protect LGBT youth from the negative consequences of homophobic bullying behavior and that more specific forms of support (e.g., explicitly affirming an LGBT identity) might be required. Although more research is needed to understand the mechanisms underlying this result, this study demonstrates that the broader macrosystem context (e.g., stigma at the cultural level) renders some protective factors, such as parental support, less available to certain groups of youth. This research also highlights the importance of identifying contexts that are uniquely protective for specific subgroups of youth.

SCHOOLS

Bullying has been most studied within the school context, and several school-level factors have been identified as positive correlates of more prevalent bullying behavior. These factors include poor teacher-student relationships (Richard et al., 2012), lack of engagement in school activities (e.g., Barboza et al., 2009), and perceptions of negative school climates (Unnever and Cornell, 2004). In this section, the committee considers several factors at the school level that have been shown to moderate the effect of individual characteristics on bullying outcomes.

Perspectives from the Field

Certain kids are much more vulnerable to bullying: Bullying behavior is not evenly distributed—certain kids take the brunt of it, including Asperger's kids and others with disabilities, as well as minorities, immigrants, refugees, goth types, nerdy kids, or any others who occupy the fringes and are already uncomfortable in their own skins. Though it can start in the first grade, the really challenging stuff often crops up in the fifth and sixth grades, especially among girls. The ones being bullied are the very kids already at risk for depression, bipolar disorder, and anxiety, which bullying can worsen. Social media can exacerbate this by making it less obvious and visible.

—Summary from community-based providers'
focus group discussing bullying
(See Appendix B for additional highlights from interviews.)

Organization of Instruction

School instructional practices can exacerbate the experience of bullying. In one recent study, Echols (2015) examined the role of academic teaming—the practice of grouping students together into smaller learning communities for instruction—in influencing middle school students' bullying experiences. Students in these teams often share the majority of their academic classes together, limiting their exposure to the larger school community (Echols, 2015). The social and academic benefits of small learning communities have been highlighted in the literature (Mertens and Flowers, 2003). However, Echols (2015) found that, for students who were not well liked by their peers, teaming *increased* the experience of being bullied by their peers[4] from the fall to spring of sixth grade. In other words, socially vulnerable adolescents who were traveling with the same classmates throughout most of the school day were found to have few opportunities to redefine their social identities or change their status among peers. Related to this work, research on classroom size has shown that smaller classrooms or learning communities (relative to large classrooms or learning environments) sometimes magnify the effects of being bullied on adjustment because the targets of bullying are more visible in these less populated settings (Klein and Cornell, 2010; Saarento et al., 2013).

Organization of Discipline

Fair discipline practices in schools can reduce the risks associated with bullying behavior as well as the amount of bullying that occurs. Disciplinary structure is the degree to which schools consistently and fairly enforce rules, while adult support is the degree to which teachers and other authority figures in schools are perceived as caring adults. Recent studies found that high schools with an authoritative discipline climate, characterized by high levels of both disciplinary structure and adult support for students, had fewer reported bullying incidents (Cornell et al., 2013; Gregory et al., 2010). In contrast, high schools with low structure and low support had the highest prevalence of bullying behavior. Rather than embracing zero tolerance policies that exclusively focus on structure (rule enforcement), more authoritative approaches to discipline view both structure and support as necessary and complementary. In a large study of several hundred high schools in Virginia that surveyed ninth graders and their teachers, Gregory and colleagues (2010) found that both students and teachers reported lower prevalence of bullying in schools that were rated by students as high on

---

[4] Self-reported victimization was measured by asking students how often someone engaged in aggression toward them (e.g., hitting, kicking, calling bad names, etc.) since the beginning of the school year.

structure regarding fair rule enforcement and high on warm supportive relationships with adults. Moderation was not explicitly tested in this study, but it raises the possibility that the organization of school discipline can serve as a contextual modifier of individual characteristics on bullying behavior, which should be explored in future research.

Classroom Norms

A specific type of research on school norms relates to deviation from classroom and school norms. As has been found in other analyses of person-context mismatch (Stormshak et al., 1999; Wright et al., 1986), children who have been bullied might feel especially bad when this role pattern is discrepant with the behaviors of most other students in their classroom or school. When bullying is a rare occurrence in classrooms or schools, children and youth who are bullied exhibit higher levels of anxiety and depression compared to children and youth who are bullied in classrooms or schools with higher prevalence of bullying (Bellmore et al., 2004; Leadbeater et al., 2003; Schacter and Juvonen, 2015). Four studies on bullying and classroom or school norms that are consistent with this mismatch hypothesis are described in more detail below.

Leadbeater and colleagues (2003) reported that first graders with higher baseline levels of emotional problems, compared to children with low baseline levels of emotional problems, experienced more instances of being bullied when they were in classrooms with a high level of social competence among students. To the extent that first graders' own ratings of bullying behavior and prosocial acts deviated from the classroom norm and they were high in perceiving themselves as targets of bullying, they were judged by their teachers to be depressed and sad (Leadbeater et al., 2003). Similarly, Bellmore and colleagues (2004) documented that the relation between being bullied and social anxiety was strongest when sixth grade students resided in classrooms that were judged by their teachers to be orderly rather than disorderly. In this case, the more orderly classrooms were those in which students on average scored low on teacher-rated aggression (Bellmore et al., 2004).

Most recently, Schacter and Juvonen (2015) examined victimization and characterological self-blame in the sixth grade of middle schools that were characterized as either high or low in overall prevalence of bullying behavior. Characterological self-blame refers to perceptions of self-blame that are internal, attributable to uncontrollable causes, and are stable. The authors found that characterological self-blame increased from the fall to spring for bullied students attending school with low (relative to high) overall prevalence of bullying, a result that suggests that a perception of deviating from the school norm increased students' endorsement of attributions for being bullied to factors that implicate one's core self. In all four studies, a positive classroom or school norm (prosocial conduct, high social order, low peer victimization) resulted in worse outcomes for bullied children who deviated from those norms than in contexts where the classroom or school norm was less positive.

Ethnic Composition of Classrooms and Schools

Today's multiethnic urban schools are products of the dramatic changes in the racial/ethnic composition of the school-age population in just a single generation (Orfield et al., 2012). For example, since 1970, the percentage of White non-Latino students in U.S. public schools has dropped from 80 percent to just over 50 percent, while Latinos have grown from 5 percent to 22.8 percent of the school-age (kindergarten through twelfth grade) population in U.S. public schools. As American public schools become more ethnically diverse, researchers have examined whether some ethnic groups are more vulnerable to peer bullying than others, in the context of varying levels of ethnic composition of classrooms and schools (Rubin et al., 2011). Rather than restricting analyses to comparisons between different racial/ethnic groups, these studies have examined whether students are in the numerical majority or minority in their school context. From this research, it is evident that bullied students are more likely to be members of numerical-minority ethnic groups than majority groups (see Graham, 2006; Graham and Bellmore, 2007). Such findings are consistent with theoretical analyses of bullying as involving an imbalance of power between perpetrator and target (Rubin et al., 2011). Numerical majority versus minority status is one form of asymmetric power relation.

As a further elaboration on the study of ethnic context, it has also been documented that members of the ethnic majority group who are bullied face their own unique challenges. For example, students with reputations as being bullied who are also members of the majority ethnic group feel especially anxious and lonely, in part because they deviate from what is perceived as normative for their numerically more powerful group (i.e., to be aggressive and dominant) (Graham et al., 2009). Deviation from the norm can then result in more self-blame ("it must be me").

If there are risks associated with being a member of either the minority or majority ethnic group, then this has implications for the kinds of ethnic configurations that limit both the amount and impact of bullying. Research indicates that the best configuration is an ethnically diverse context where no one group holds the numerical balance of power (Felix and You, 2011; Juvonen et al., 2006). According to Juvonen and her colleagues (2006), using a sample of 2,000 sixth graders from 11 middle schools in southern California, greater ethnic diversity within a classroom was associated with lower levels of self-reported experiences of being bullied. Similarly, using a sample of 161,838 ninth and eleventh grade students from 528 schools in California (drawn from the California Healthy Kids Survey's 2004-2005 data sample), Felix and You (2011) found that school diversity was related to less physical and verbal harassment from peers.

In summary, a great deal of American bullying research is conducted in urban schools where multiple ethnic groups are represented, but much of that research is just beginning to examine the role that ethnicity plays in the experience of bullying behavior (Graham and Bellmore, 2007). There is not enough evidence that ethnic group per se is the critical variable, for there is no consistent evidence in the literature that any one ethnic group is more or less likely to be the target of bullying (see the meta-analysis by Vitoroulis and Vaillancourt, 2014). Rather, the more important context variable is whether ethnic groups are the numerical majority or minority in their school. Numerical-minority group members appear to be at greater risk for being targets of bullying because they have fewer same-ethnicity peers to help ward off potential perpetrators; youth who are bullied but members of the majority ethnic group may suffer more than numerical-minority youth who are bullied because they deviate from the norms of their group to be powerful, and ethnically diverse schools may reduce actual rates of bullying behavior because the numerical balance of power is shared among many groups. These studies serve as a useful starting point for a much fuller exploration of the ways in which school ethnic diversity can be a protective factor.

Teachers

Teachers and school staff are in a unique and influential position to promote healthy relationships and to intervene in bullying situations (Pepler, 2006). They can play a critical role in creating a climate of support and empathy both inside and outside of the classroom. Although teachers are not considered a direct part of the peer ecology, they are believed to have considerable influence on the peer ecology by directly or indirectly shaping students' social behavior as well as by acting as bridging agents to other settings and other adults that influence the child's development (Gest and Rodkin, 2011). They are the one group of professionals in a child's life who have the opportunity to view the whole child in relation to the social ecology in which he or she is embedded (Farmer et al., 2011b).

Teachers vary in the behavior they identify as bullying, and they also perceive the various types of bullying differently (Blain-Arcaro et al., 2012). When teachers identify bullying situations, they are more likely to intervene if they perceive the incident to be serious, if they are highly empathic with the individual who is being bullied, or if they show high levels of self-efficacy (Yoon, 2004). Several studies have shown that teachers perceive physical bullying as more serious than verbal bullying and verbal bullying as more serious than relational bullying. Accordingly, they are more likely to intervene on behalf of students whom they believe are being physically bullied and/or who show distress (Bauman and Del Rio, 2006; Blain-Arcaro et al., 2012; Craig et al., 2011). Both teachers and education support professionals have said that they want more training related to bullying and cyberbullying related to sexual orientation, gender, and race (Bradshaw et al., 2013).

Teachers are unlikely to intervene if they do not have proper training (Bauman et al., 2008). Both students and teachers report that teachers do not know how to intervene effectively, which prevents students from seeking help and contributes to teachers ignoring bullying (Bauman and Del Rio, 2006; Salmivalli et al., 2005). More than one-half of bullied children do not report being bullied to a teacher, making it that much more important that teachers be trained in varied ways of identifying and dealing with bullying situations. Teachers who participated in a bullying prevention program that included teacher training felt more confident about handing bullying problems, had more supportive attitudes about students who were targets of bullying, and felt more positive about working with parents regarding bullying problems (Alsaker, 2004).

Teachers' beliefs, perceptions, attitudes, and thoughts affect how they normally interact with their students (Kochenderfer-Ladd and Pelletier, 2008; Oldenburg et al., 2015; Troop-Gordon and Ladd, 2015). Teachers who have been bullied in the past may have empathy for children who are bullied by their peers. For example, teachers who report having been bullied by peers in childhood tend to perceive bullying as a problem at their school (Bradshaw et al., 2007). Also, teachers who were more aggressive as children may be less empathetic toward targeted children and less inclined to address students' aggressive behavior, compared with teachers who were less aggressive as children (Oldenburg et al., 2015).

Connectedness to others has been shown to be a significant buffer for developing adjustment problems among bullied youth. Specifically, studies indicate that having at least one trusted and supportive adult at school, which in many cases is a teacher, can help buffer LGBT youth who are bullied from displaying suicidal behaviors (Duong and Bradshaw, 2014). Related research on peer connections and school connectedness also indicates that youth who are more connected are less likely to be bullied, and even when they are bullied, they are less likely to develop a range of adjustment problems (e.g., internalizing problems) (Morin et al., 2015).

This research has been largely descriptive, examining correlates associated with teachers' likelihood of intervening to address bullying. Consequently, understanding which contextual factors may be associated with whether teachers are more or less likely to intervene to address bullying that targets some groups of youth (and not others) is an important avenue for future inquiry.

COMMUNITIES

Although most research on contextual moderators on bullying outcomes has focused on factors at the peer, family, and school levels, research has also begun to examine ways in which contextual factors at the community level serve as important modifiers. Generally, these factors have focused on neighborhood correlates, such as neighborhood safety (Espelage et al., 2000) and poverty (Bradshaw et al., 2009), but broader cultural factors, including exposure to violent television (Barboza et al., 2009), have also received some attention in the literature. In this section, the committee reviews three such modifiers of bullying outcomes at the community level—community norms, neighborhood context, and acculturation context.

Community Norms

Community norms are contextual factors that can differentially shape the experience of bullying. In one illustrative example, researchers demonstrated that body weight norms (e.g., acceptance of heavier bodies) differ across racial/ethnic groups. For example, in one laboratory-based study, Hebl and Heatherton (1998) had black and white women rate photographs of thin, average, and large black and white women. Whereas white women rated large women (especially large white women) lower on a variety of dimensions (e.g., attractiveness, intelligence, happiness, relationship and job success) than average or thin women, these patterns were not observed among black women, especially when they were rating large black women (Hebl and Heatherton, 1998). Consistent with this finding, one nationally representative study of over 20,000 overweight/obese participants found that blacks were less likely than whites to perceive discrimination based on weight (Hatzenbuehler et al., 2009).

How might these community norms around body image and weight affect weight-based bullying among youth? Most studies on this topic have been conducted among samples of exclusively white youth. However, some studies that have stratified their analyses by race/ethnicity have shown differences in weight-based teasing and stigmatization (weight-based bullying as a distinct outcome has not been examined). For instance, in data from Project EAT (Eating Among Teens), a longitudinal study of 1,708 adolescent boys and girls, overweight black girls were significantly less likely than overweight white girls to report ever being teased about their weight by their peers. Further, among those who were teased, fewer black girls than white girls were bothered by peer teasing due to weight (Loth et al., 2008). This finding of moderation by race has been replicated in other studies with similar outcomes. For instance, in a study of 157 youth, ages 7-17, black girls reported significantly lower levels of weight-based stigmatization than white girls (Gray et al., 2011). Studies that explicitly model statistical interactions between race and community norms are needed to fully test this hypothesis, but the available evidence suggests that community norms can act as a contextual moderator of weight-based bullying.

Neighborhood Context

Neighborhood contexts may also serve as a contextual moderator of bullying outcomes. In one example of a study on neighborhood factors, researchers obtained data on LGBT hate crimes involving assaults or assaults with battery from the Boston Police Department; these crimes were then linked to individual-level data from a population-based sample of Boston high school students (n = 1,292). The results indicated that sexual-minority youth residing in neighborhoods with higher rates of LGBT assault hate crimes were significantly more likely to report being bullied, compared with sexual-minority youth residing in neighborhoods with lower rates of LGBT assault hate crimes (Hatzenbuehler et al., 2015b). No associations were found between overall neighborhood-level violent crimes and reports of being bullied among sexual-minority adolescents, which is evidence for the specificity of the results to LGBT assault hate crimes. Importantly, although moderation was not explicitly modeled in this study, no associations were found between LGBT assault hate crimes and reports of being bullied among heterosexual adolescents. This result suggests the effect of neighborhood climate on bullying outcomes was specific to the sexual minority adolescents.

Perspectives from the Field

Neighborhood culture matters: Sometimes a kid being bullied is instead seen as someone who just gets into a lot of fights, and since that's "normal" for that particular environment, the behavior is not being flagged as bullying, specifically. Neighborhood cultures may not want outsiders intervening, so they may not wish to consider bullying systematically and may not be as responsive to interventions unless they are culturally suitable.

Summary from community-based providers discussing bullying
(See Appendix B for additional highlights from interviews.)

Acculturation Context

Acculturation is defined as the "process of adapting to or incorporating values, behavior, and cultural artifacts from the predominant culture" (Sulkowski et al., 2014, p. 650). Berry (2006, p. 287) defined *acculturative stress* as stress reactions to "life events that are rooted in the experience of acculturation." He found that acculturative stress can take a variety of forms, ranging from individual (e.g., coping with a socially devalued identity) and familial (e.g., navigating pressures that emerge from potential conflicts between disparate cultural groups) to structural (e.g., difficulties resulting from restrictive immigration policies). Although there is a large literature on acculturation and acculturative stress as predictors of mental health outcomes among adolescent immigrant populations in the United States (Gonzales et al., 2002), less is known about how acculturation and acculturative stress may influence bullying outcomes among this population (Smokowski et al., 2009). However, preliminary evidence suggests that acculturation and acculturative stress are associated with being a target of bullying for Latino and Asian/Pacific Islander adolescents in the United States (Forrest et al., 2013; Stella et al., 2003) and for immigrant youths in Spain (Messinger et al., 2012).

These studies have begun to suggest important insights into associations between acculturation, acculturative stress, and bullying, but there is currently a dearth of literature explicating the mechanisms through which these factors might be related to bullying outcomes. For instance, some research indicates that parent-adolescent conflict and low parental investment might partially explain the relationship between acculturation and youth violence outcomes, especially among Latino adolescents, but this work is still in its initial stages, and the identification of other mediators is warranted (Smokowski et al., 2009). Moreover, few of these studies have explicitly examined acculturation and acculturative stress as contextual modifiers of bullying behaviors among adolescents. Thus, the identification of mediators and moderators that influence the association between acculturation, acculturative stress, and related factors (e.g., ethnic identity) and bullying outcomes remains an important direction for future research.

MACROSYSTEM

As discussed at the beginning of this chapter, the broadest level of Bronfenbrenner's bioecological model of development is the macrosystem, which includes societal norms, or "blueprints," that may be expressed through ideology and/or laws. The macrosystem has received less attention when compared to other contextual factors (e.g., peers, parents, schools) in the bullying literature. However, there is emerging evidence that the macrosystem is an important context that has implications for understanding the disproportionate rates of bullying among certain groups of youth, as well as the types of bullying (i.e., bias-based bullying) that some youth experience.

With respect to bullying, one important aspect of the macrosystem is the characteristics, identities, and/or statuses that a particular society devalues—that is, who and what is the target of stigma. Goffman (1963, p. 3) defined stigma as "an attribute that is deeply discrediting" and noted that there are three types of stigma: stigma related to physical attributes; stigma related to an individual's character; and stigma related to an "undesired difference from what we had anticipated" (Goffman, 1963, p. 5). In one of the most widely used definitions of stigma, Link and Phelan (2001, p. 367) stated that stigma exists when the following interrelated components converge:

> In the first component, people distinguish and label human differences. In the second, dominant cultural beliefs link labeled persons to undesirable characteristics—to negative stereotypes. In the third, labeled persons are placed in distinct categories so as to accomplish some degree of separation of "us" from "them." In the fourth, labeled persons experience status loss and discrimination that lead to unequal outcomes. Stigmatization is entirely contingent on access to social, economic and political power that allows the identification of differentness, the construction of stereotypes, the separation of labeled persons into distinct categories and the full execution of disapproval, rejection, exclusion and discrimination. Thus we apply the term stigma when elements of labeling, stereotyping, separation, status loss and discrimination co-occur in a power situation that allows them to unfold.

At the macrosystem level, stigma is promulgated through laws and policies that differentially target certain groups for social exclusion or that create conditions that disadvantage some groups over others (Burris, 2006; Corrigan et al., 2004). Examples include constitutional amendments that banned same-sex marriage for gays and lesbians, differential sentencing for crack as opposed to powdered cocaine for racial minorities, immigration policies that allow special scrutiny of people suspected of being undocumented for Latinos, and a lack of parity in medical treatment of mental illness for people with mental disorders. Stigma is also expressed at the level of the macrosystem through broad social norms that create and perpetuate negative stereotypes against certain groups (Herek and McLemore, 2013). There is emerging evidence that stigma at the macrosystem level contributes to adverse health outcomes among members of stigmatized groups and explains health disparities that exist between stigmatized and non-stigmatized populations (for reviews, see Hatzenbuehler, 2014; Link and Hatzenbuehler, 2016; Richman and Hatzenbuehler, 2014). Thus, stigma is manifested in the macrosystem through laws, policies, and social norms that in turn serve as a significant source of stress and disadvantage for members of stigmatized groups.

The role of stigma in bullying is evident in the groups of youth that are expressly targeted for bullying. As reviewed in Chapter 2, several groups of youth—including LGBT youth (Berlan et al., 2010), youth with disabilities (Rose et al., 2009), and overweight/obese youth (Janssen et al., 2004)—are at increased risk of being bullied, and each of these characteristics or identities (sexual orientation, disability status, obesity) is stigmatized within the current U.S. context, as is evident in laws and policies, institutional practices, and broad social/cultural attitudes surrounding these characteristics or identities (Herek and McLemore, 2013; Puhl and Latner, 2007; Susman, 1994).

Evidence for the role of stigma in bullying is also found in the particular types of bullying that some youth face—namely, bias-based bullying. Greene (2006) defined bias-based bullying as "attacks motivated by a victim's actual or perceived membership in a legally protected class" (p. 69) and distinguished this form of bullying from general (i.e., nonbias-based) bullying, which is motivated by student characteristics unrelated to group membership, such as personality (Greene, 2006). According to this definition, a student does not have to identify with a particular identity (e.g., gay) or be a member of a social group (e.g., Muslim) to be the target of bias-based bullying; if bullying occurs because the perpetrator merely perceives that the target is a member of a legally protected class, it is enough to warrant the label of bias-based bullying.

While early research on bullying largely neglected to consider youths' motivations for bullying behaviors, recent research has documented that some bullying and related forms of peer victimization, such as harassment, are due to bias and discrimination. In one example of this work, Russell and colleagues (2012) used data from two population-based surveys of adolescents: the 2008-2009 Dane County Youth Assessment (DCYA; n = 17,366) and the 2007-2008 California Healthy Kids Survey (CHKS; n = 602,612). In the DCYA, adolescents were asked how often they had been "bullied, threatened, or harassed" in the past 12 months because they were perceived as lesbian, gay, or bisexual or because of their race/ethnicity. In the CHKS, adolescents were asked about bias-based bullying/harassment due to sexual orientation, race/ethnicity, religion, gender, and physical or mental disability in the past 12 months. Respondents were also asked about general forms of bullying and harassment not due to any of these specific categories. Among adolescents who reported being bullied or harassed, over one-third (DCYA: 35.5%, CHKS: 40.3%) reported bias-based bullying/harassment, underscoring how prevalent this basis for bullying is among adolescents.

Researchers have also examined relationships between bias-based bullying/harassment and several adverse outcomes, including substance use, mental health, and school-related outcomes (e.g., grades, truancy), and recent evidence suggests that experiences of bias-based bullying may be related to more negative outcomes than general forms of bullying. For instance, in the aforementioned study by Russell and colleagues (2012), mental health status and substance use outcomes were worse among youth who experienced bias-based bullying/harassment than among those who experienced bullying/harassment that was unrelated to bias. Similar results were observed in a convenience sample of 251 ninth-to-eleventh grade students in an all-male college preparatory school; boys who reported bias-based bullying due to perceived sexual orientation ("because they say I'm gay") experienced more adverse outcomes (e.g., symptoms of anxiety and depression, negative perceptions of school climate) than boys who reported being bullied for reasons unrelated to perceived sexual orientation (Swearer et al., 2008). These findings are consistent with evidence that hate-crime victimization among lesbian, gay, and bisexual adults is associated with greater psychological distress than is crime victimization that is unrelated to bias (Herek et al., 1999).

Taken together, this research highlights the role of stigma and related constructs (bias, discrimination) in explaining disparities in responses to being bullied and in revealing motivations for some forms of bullying. However, the role of stigma and its deleterious consequences is more often discussed in research on discrimination than on bullying. In the committee's view, there needs to be more cross-fertilization between these two literatures. Moreover, this research suggests that interventions need to target stigma processes in order to address disparities in bullying and reduce bias-based bullying. However, as is evident in Chapter 5 (Preventive Interventions), bullying prevention programs currently do not incorporate theories or measures of stigma and therefore overlook one important mechanism underlying motivations for bullying. Thus, new intervention models are necessary to address the under-recognized role of stigma in bullying behaviors.

AREAS OF FUTURE RESEARCH

This chapter reviewed studies that examined social contexts that either reduce or exacerbate the influence of individual characteristics (e.g., weight status, sexual orientation, and race/ethnicity) on bullying outcomes. This approach explicitly required analyses of moderation in addition to analyses of contextual correlates. However, other studies have identified contextual correlates that may also serve as moderators but have thus far not been examined as such. In this section, the committee reviews contextual correlates at the school and community level that warrant greater attention in future studies that are explicitly attentive to moderation.

School Climate

There is a lack of consensus in the research literature on the definition of "school climate" and the parameters with which to measure it. Consequently, the term "school climate" has been used to encompass many different aspects of the school environment (Thapa et al., 2013; Zullig et al., 2011). For instance, perceptions of school climate have been linked to academic achievement (Brand et al., 2008); school attendance and school avoidance (Brand et al., 2003); depression (Loukas et al., 2006); and various behavior problems or indicators of such problems, including bullying (Bandyopadhyay et al., 2009), and school suspensions (Bear et al., 2011). Examining the possible link between school climate and bullying is an important component of the bullying literature, since demonstrating this link establishes bullying as a systemic problem that needs to be understood at the macro level, not just as a result of microlevel factors (Swearer and Espelage, 2004).

The available literature indicates that negative school climate is associated with greater aggression and victimization; additionally, positive school environment is associated with fewer aggressive and externalizing behaviors (Espelage et al., 2014; Goldweber et al., 2013; Johnson, 2009). Several studies have found a direct relation between school climate and the psychological adaptation of the individual (Kuperminc et al., 2001; Reis et al., 2007). It has been found, for example, that children attending a school in which behaviors such as bullying were acceptable by the adults were at greater risk of becoming involved in such behaviors (Swearer and Espelage, 2004). Schools that have less positive school climates may exhibit lower quality interactions between students, teachers, peers, and staff (Lee and Song, 2012).

Available literature on authoritative climate, a theory that posits that disciplinary structure and adult support of students are the two key dimensions of school climate (Gregory and Cornell, 2009), provides a conceptual framework for school climate that helps to specify and measure the features of a positive school climate (Cornell and Huang, 2016; Cornell et al., 2013; Gregory et al., 2010). Disciplinary structure refers to the idea that school rules are perceived as strict but fairly enforced. Adult support refers to student perceptions that their teachers and other school staff members treat them with respect and want them to be successful (Konold et al., 2014). A study to examine how authoritative school climate theory provides a framework for conceptualizing these two key features found that higher disciplinary structure and student support were associated with lower prevalence of teasing and bullying and of victimization in general. An authoritative school climate is conducive to lower peer victimization (Cornell et. al., 2015). Overall, schools with an authoritative school climate are associated with positive student outcomes (Cornell and Huang, 2016) and lower dropout rates (Cornell et al., 2013; Jia et. al., 2015).

School Transition

As children progress through the education system they often change schools. For some, the transition to a new school is positive, while for others the transition is linked to difficulties related to academic functioning, school connectedness and engagement, and self-esteem (Forrest et al., 2013; Wang et al., 2015; Wigfield et al., 1991). A number of factors may be associated with negative perceptions of school transition (Wang et al., 2015). These factors include students' social functioning (McDougall and Hymel, 1998), school environment (Barber and Olsen, 2004), mental health (Benner and Graham, 2009), students' academic attitudes and perceptions of academic control and importance (Benner, 2011), family characteristics (Barber and Olsen, 2004), and pubertal development (Forrest et al., 2013).

School transition has been associated with students' involvement in bullying. Most early work suggested that bullying perpetration was more common among children after the transition to a new school as part of the normal school transition process. (Pellegrini and Bartini, 2000; Pellegrini and Long, 2002; Pepler et al., 2006), and this increase in bullying perpetration was presumed to be driven by the changes in the peer group. That is, with a new change to the social landscape, children were presumed to bully others as a way of gaining social status within their new social environment. One issue with these studies, however, is that they had no comparison group: the group of transitioning students was not compared with a group of students who did not change schools. Thus, one cannot determine whether the reported differences in bullying rates were due to a change associated with typical development or if they resulted from a change in the social context.

In two more recent moderation studies, this well-accepted finding is challenged. Specifically, Farmer and colleagues (2011a) and Wang and colleagues (2015) found that students in schools without a transition reported higher rates of being bullied and bullying perpetration than did students in schools with a transition. These findings support a conclusion that context matters in understanding changes in patterns of bullying behavior over the school transition years.

Gay-Straight Alliances

Gay-Straight Alliances (GSAs) are typically student-led, school-based clubs existing in middle and high schools with goals involving improving school climate for LGBT youth and educating the school community about LGBT issues. GSAs typically serve four main roles: as a source of counseling and support for LGBT students; as a safe space for LGBT students and their friends; as a primary vehicle for education and awareness in schools; and as part of broader efforts to educate and raise awareness in schools (Greytak and Kosciw, 2014). Although studies have established GSAs as correlates of lower rates of victimization among LGBT youth (Goodenow et al., 2006), only one study of 15,965 students in 45 Wisconsin schools has examined interactions between GSAs and sexual orientation in predicting general or homophobic victimization (Poteat et al., 2013).[5] Although no statistically significant interaction was found between GSAs and sexual orientation in predicting these outcomes, there was a trend (i.e., lower levels of general and homophobic victimization among LGBT youth in schools with GSAs). Thus, future research is needed to examine whether school diversity clubs do moderate the impact of individual characteristics on bullying outcomes.

Extracurricular Activities and Out of School-time Programs

Eighty percent of American youth ages 6-17 participate in extracurricular activities, which include sports and clubs (Riese et al., 2015). Although most children and youth participate in out-of-school activities, most researchers have only examined bullying within the school context. Only a few studies have examined bullying outside of school, and their results have been mixed. For example, in one study examining the risk behavior of high school athletes, results indicated that 41 percent had engaged in bullying perpetration (Johnson and McRee, 2015). This result is consistent with other studies showing that the social elite of a school, which tends to be dominated by athletes, engage in a disproportionate amount of bullying perpetration (Vaillancourt et al., 2003). It is also consistent with studies showing an association between participation in contact school sports like football and the perpetration of violence (Kreager, 2007). However, a recent study using data from the National Survey of Children's Health (ages 6-17), suggests that involvement in extracurricular activities, which includes sports, is associated with less involvement in bullying perpetration (Riese et al., 2015).

The protective role of sports on children's well-being is well docu-

---

[5]Homophobic victimization was measured using the following item: "In the past twelve months, how often have you been bullied, threatened, or harassed about being perceived as gay, lesbian, or bisexual?" (Poteat et al., 2013, p. 4).

mented (Guest and McRee, 2009; Vella et al., 2015), although somewhat mixed depending on the outcome used by the study (see review by Farb and Matjasko, 2012). For example, Taylor and colleagues (2012) reported that among African American girls, participation in sports was associated with lower rates of bullying behavior and that this relation was mediated by self-esteem, which was also enhanced in sport-participating girls. However, in another study examining involvement with school sports and school-related extracurricular activities in a nationally representative sample of 7,990 American students from 578 public schools, results indicated that involvement in intramural sports and classroom-related extracurricular activities increased the likelihood of being bullied by peers, while participation in interscholastic sports was associated with a decreased likelihood of being a target of bullying (Peguero, 2008).

Virtual and Media Contexts

Outside of school, the online world is among the most common public "places" where today's adolescents spend time. Social media platforms, such as Facebook, Twitter, and Instagram are used by the majority of youth; most youth log into social media at least once daily, and most youth maintain more than one social media platform (Lenhart et al., 2015). Social media provides youth opportunities to stay connected to friends, develop an online identify, and seek information about peers. Studies have shown that peer interactions online can be just as important, in relation to self-esteem and friendships, as those expressed offline (Valkenburg and Peter, 2011). Other work has illustrated that social media has become a normative part of the friendship formation and maintenance process (Chou and Edge, 2012). Because of the popularity of these tools among youth, and their easy, anytime-access using mobile devices, they have become woven into the fabric of teens' lives and relationships. These technologies present both new opportunities and challenges to teens as they navigate relationships, social situations, and bullying behavior.

There is evidence to support a correlation between being bullied online and in person (Ybarra and Mitchell, 2004). Few studies have explored different online contexts as moderators of the bullying experience, but some factors that are present in the online world have been proposed to explain how the online context may moderate the experience of bullying. In contrast to school-based bullying, where a youth can seek respite at home, the online context is available 24/7 and may lead to a youth feeling that the bullying experience is inescapable (Agatston et al., 2007). A second factor is that in contrast to in-person bullying where the perpetrator's identity is easily known, the online context provides the potential for bullying to be anonymous. However, a recent study found that cases in which a perpetrator's identity is unknown to a target are relatively infrequent (Turner et al., 2015). A third factor differentiating the online context is that a single bullying event can be distributed widely (or "go viral"), which can lead to varied interpretations of what it means to have a bullying experience be repeated (Turner et al., 2015).

An area in which concern for bullying experiences exists but little research has been done is in the online gaming context. Studies have shown that video game play is nearly universal among youth, and approximately a third of males reported playing games every day (Olson et al., 2007). A salient feature of the online video game environment that may impact bullying rates or experiences are that many popular games promote aggressive behavior or violence to win the game; one study found that at least one-half of adolescents' listed favorite games were violent in nature (Olson et al., 2007). A recent study found positive associations between the time spent using online games, exposure to violent media, and cyberbullying experiences, suggesting that spending time in online or media contexts that promote aggression or violence may be associated with bullying experiences (Chang et al., 2015).

Policy Context

Although research on anti-bullying policies has explored main effects (see Chapter 6), it is also possible for the policy context to serve as a moderator of bullying outcomes. For instance, literature related to both homophobia and bullying (Chesir-Teran, 2003; Rutter and Leech, 2006) suggests that teachers often fail to intervene for a variety of reasons, such as a limited knowledge of how to intervene and homophobic attitudes. This research, however, has largely focused on individual attitudes of teachers. A contextual factor that affects the likelihood of effective teacher intervention in instances of homophobic bullying is broader social policies that place unique burdens on teachers, including "No Promo Homo" laws. These state laws have different scope and reach, and in some cases only apply to some grades or certain domains of instruction. However, these laws can be vaguely written and misapplied and, in extreme cases, can expressly forbid teachers from discussing LGBT issues in a positive light. Such policies are currently in place in eight states: Alabama, Arizona, Louisiana, Mississippi, Oklahoma, South Carolina, Texas, and Utah (Gay, Lesbian, and Straight Education Network, 2015; Movement Advancement Project, 2015). They represent one example of a policy context moderating the extent to which individual actors (i.e., teachers) can effectively respond to bullying behavior.

SUMMARY

In this chapter, the committee moved beyond descriptive data to consider social contexts that moderate the effect of individual characteristics on bullying behavior. The chapter drew upon two theoretical and conceptual frameworks, the ecological theory of development and the concepts of equifinality and multifinality, to inform its approach to this chapter. Evidence from the four social contexts, including peers, family, schools, and communities, was reviewed, with a specific focus on studies that examine moderation (for a visual representation of these contexts as conceptualized by the committee, see Figure 3-5). With regard to peers, the group context is important to consider, given what is known about factors associated with bullying. As noted earlier in this chapter, some peer groups will tolerate and encourage bullying behavior, whereas in other groups, bullying behavior will be actively discouraged. Having friends and being liked by peers can protect children against being bullied, and having a high-quality best friendship might function in different capacities to protect children from being targets of bullying behavior.

Families can play an important role in bullying prevention, and family functioning has been linked to whether a child is identified as one who engages in bullying perpetration or one who is the target of bullying behavior. Whereas parent support can buffer some children and youth against the negative effects of bullying, this is not true across all groups of youth.

Bullying behavior has most often been studied in the school context. The organization of instruction, organization of discipline, classroom norms, the ethnic composition of classrooms and schools, and teachers are several factors at the school level that have been shown to moderate the effect of individual characteristics on bullying outcomes. A school's instructional practices such as academic teaming can worsen the experience of bullying. Moreover, schools' discipline climate is associated with individuals' risk of being bullied as well as the amount of bullying that occurs. Further, positive classroom or social norms resulted in worse outcomes for children who were bullied and who deviated from those norms than for children with similar social experience but in contexts where the classroom or school norm was less positive.

With regard to the ethnic composition of schools, there is not sufficient evidence to indicate that ethnic group per se is the critical variable, as there is no consistent evidence that any one ethnic group is more or less likely to be the target of bullying. Numerical-minority group members appear to be at greater risk for being bullied because they have fewer same-ethnicity peers to help ward off potential perpetrators. Finally, teachers and school staff are in a position to promote healthy relationships and to intervene in

THE LANDSCAPE OF BULLYING

Composition of peer groups, shifting demographics, changing societal norms, and modern technology are contextual factors that must be considered to understand and effectively react to bullying in the United States. Youth are embedded in multiple contexts, and each of these contexts interacts with individual characteristics of youth in ways that either exacerbate or attenuate the association between these individual characteristics and bullying perpetration or victimization.

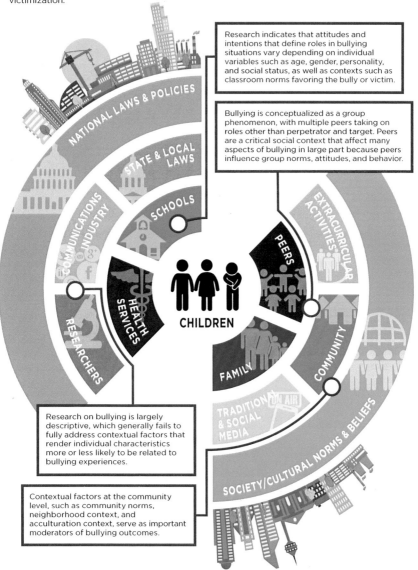

Research indicates that attitudes and intentions that define roles in bullying situations vary depending on individual variables such as age, gender, personality, and social status, as well as contexts such as classroom norms favoring the bully or victim.

Bullying is conceptualized as a group phenomenon, with multiple peers taking on roles other than perpetrator and target. Peers are a critical social context that affect many aspects of bullying in large part because peers influence group norms, attitudes, and behavior.

Research on bullying is largely descriptive, which generally fails to fully address contextual factors that render individual characteristics more or less likely to be related to bullying experiences.

Contextual factors at the community level, such as community norms, neighborhood context, and acculturation context, serve as important moderators of bullying outcomes.

FIGURE 3-5 The landscape of bullying.

bullying situations in schools. They can also create a climate of support and empathy.

Three modifiers of bullying outcomes at the community level—community norms, neighborhood context, and acculturation context—were reviewed in this chapter. Community norms can differentially shape the experience of bullying. Similarly, neighborhood contexts may also serve as contextual moderators of bullying outcomes. There is also evidence that acculturative stress and acculturation are associated with being a target of bullying for Latino and Asian/Pacific Islander adolescents in the United States. Finally, the committee identified several contextual correlates at the school and community level that need greater attention in future studies that explicitly attend to moderation. These include school climate, school transition, school diversity clubs, extracurricular activities and out-of-school time programs, virtual and media contexts, and the policy context.

FINDINGS AND CONCLUSIONS

Findings

Finding 3.1: Research on bullying is largely descriptive (i.e., focused on prevalence rates or correlates of bullying, rather than on identifying mediators and moderators), which generally fails to fully address contextual factors that render individual characteristics more or less likely to be related to bullying experiences.

Finding 3.2: The ecological model provides a framework from which to further understand the influence that social contexts may have on both rates of being bullied and experiences of negative mental health outcomes among those who are bullied.

Finding 3.3: Bullying is conceptualized as a group phenomenon, with multiple peers taking on roles other than perpetrator and target. Peers are a critical social context that affects many aspects of bullying—in large part because peers influence group norms, attitudes, and behavior.

Finding 3.4: The seemingly low rate of observed defending indicates that bystanders coming to the aid of targets of bullying are relatively rare. Bystanders become even more passive with age.

Finding 3.5: Research indicates that attitudes and intentions that define roles in bullying situations vary depending on individual variables such as age, gender, personality, and social status, as well as contexts such as classroom norms favoring the perpetrator or target.

Finding 3.6: The majority of research on family influences, both from risk and resiliency perspectives, has been on psychopathology and children's adjustment rather than on bullying specifically.

Finding 3.7: Teachers and school staff are in a unique and influential position to address bullying situations.

Finding 3.8: There is not enough consistent evidence that shows that one racial or ethnic group is more or less likely to be the target of bullying; rather, the more important contextual variable is whether racial or ethnic groups are the numerical majority or minority in their school.

Finding 3.9: Connectedness to others has been shown to be a significant buffer for the development of adjustment problems among bullied youth.

Finding 3.10: Contextual factors at the community level, such as community norms, neighborhood context, and acculturation context, serve as important moderators of bullying outcomes.

Finding 3.11: Contextual factors at the level of the macrosystem, such as stigma, contribute to bullying behaviors. In particular, several stigmatized groups of youth (e.g., lesbian, gay, bisexual, and transgender youth; youth with disabilities) are at heightened risk for being targets of bullying. Moreover, stigma is one mechanism underlying some motivations to bully, as in the case of bias-based bullying. Recent research has suggested that youth who are targets of bias-based bullying/harassment report more adverse psychosocial outcomes compared to youth who are targets of bullying/harassment that is unrelated to bias.

Finding 3.12: Some contextual factors at the school and community level have received less attention than others. For instance, there is comparatively less research on the extent to which school transition, extracurricular activities, and out-of-school-time programs serve as moderators that influence whether individual characteristics are associated with bullying involvement either as perpetrators, targets, or both.

Conclusions

Conclusion 3.1: Youth are embedded in multiple contexts, ranging from peer and family to school, community, and macrosystem. Each of these contexts can affect individual characteristics of youth (e.g., race/ethnicity, sexual orientation) in ways that either exacerbate or attenuate the association between these individual characteristics and perpetrating and/or being the target of bullying behavior.

Conclusion 3.2: Contextual factors operate differently across groups of youth, and therefore contexts that protect some youth against the negative effects of bullying are not generalizable to all youth. Consequently, research is needed to identify contextual factors that are protective for specific subgroups of youth that are most at risk of perpetrating or being targeted by bullying behavior.

Conclusion 3.3: The ecological model allows for a broad conceptualization of the various contextual influences on youth bullying.

Conclusion 3.4: Other conceptual models—particularly stigma—have been underutilized in the bullying literature and yet hold promise (1) for understanding the causes of disproportionate rates of bullying among certain groups of youth, (2) for identifying motivations for some types of bullying (i.e., bias-based bullying), and (3) for providing additional targets for preventive interventions.

Conclusion 3.5: Studying experiences of being bullied in particular vulnerable subgroups (e.g., those based on race/ethnicity or sexual orientation) cannot be completely disentangled from the study of discrimination or of unfair treatment based on a stigmatized identity. These are separate empirical literatures (school-based discrimination versus school-based bullying) although often they are studying the same phenomena. There should be much more cross-fertilization between the empirical literatures on school bullying and discrimination due to social stigma.

REFERENCES

Agatston, P.W., Kowalski, R., and Limber, S. (2007). Students' perspectives on cyber bullying. *Journal of Adolescent Health, 41*(6), S59-S60.

Alsaker, F.D. (2004). Bernese programme against victimisation in kindergarten and elementary school. In P.K. Smith, D. Pepler, and K. Rigby (Eds.), *Bullying in Schools: How Successful Can Interventions Be?* (pp. 289-306). Cambridge, UK: Cambridge University Press.

Ashmore, R.D., Deaux, K., and McLaughlin-Volpe, T. (2004). An organizing framework for collective identity: Articulation and significance of multidimensionality. *Psychological Bulletin, 130*(1), 80-114.

Bandyopadhyay, S., Cornell, D.G., and Konold, T.R. (2009). Validity of three school climate scales to assess bullying, aggressive attitudes, and help seeking. *School Psychology Review, 38*(3), 338.

Barber, B.K., and Olsen, J.A. (2004). Assessing the transitions to middle and high school. *Journal of Adolescent Research, 19*(1), 3-30.

Barboza, G.E., Schiamberg, L.B., Oehmke, J., Korzeniewski, S.J., Post, L.A., and Heraux, C.G. (2009). Individual characteristics and the multiple contexts of adolescent bullying: An ecological perspective. *Journal of Youth and Adolescence, 38*(1), 101-121.

Baron, R.M., and Kenny, D.A. (1986). The moderator–mediator variable distinction in social psychological research: Conceptual, strategic, and statistical considerations. *Journal of Personality and Social Psychology, 51*(6), 1173-1182.

Bauman, S., and Del Rio, A. (2006). Preservice teachers' responses to bullying scenarios: Comparing physical, verbal, and relational bullying. *Journal of Educational Psychology, 98*(1), 219-231.

Bauman, S., Rigby, K., and Hoppa, K. (2008). U.S. teachers' and school counsellors' strategies for handling school bullying incidents. *Educational Psychology, 28*(7), 837-856.

Bear, G.G., Gaskins, C., Blank, J., and Chen, F.F. (2011). Delaware School Climate Survey-Student: Its factor structure, concurrent validity, and reliability. *Journal of School Psychology, 49*(2), 157-174.

Bellmore, A.D., Witkow, M.R., Graham, S., and Juvonen, J. (2004). Beyond the individual: The impact of ethnic context and classroom behavioral norms on victims' adjustment. *Developmental Psychology, 40*(6), 1159-1172.

Benner, A.D. (2011). The transition to high school: Current knowledge, future directions. *Educational Psychology Review, 23*(3), 299-328.

Benner, A.D., and Graham, S. (2009). The transition to high school as a developmental process among multiethnic urban youth. *Child Development, 80*(2), 356-376.

Berlan, E.D., Corliss, H.L., Field, A.E., Goodman, E., and Austin, S.B. (2010). Sexual orientation and bullying among adolescents in the Growing up Today study. *Journal of Adolescent Health, 46*(4), 366-371.

Berry, J.W. (2006). Acculturated stress. In P.T.P. Wong and L.C.G. Wong (Eds.), *Handbook of Multicultural Perspectives on Stress and Coping* (pp. 287-298). New York: Springer.

Blain-Arcaro, C., Smith, J.D., Cunningham, C.E., Vaillancourt, T., and Rimas, H. (2012). Contextual attributes of indirect bullying situations that influence teachers' decisions to intervene. *Journal of School Violence, 11*(3), 226-245.

Bollmer, J.M., Milich, R., Harris, M.J., and Maras, M.A. (2005). A friend in need: The role of friendship quality as a protective factor in peer victimization and bullying. *Journal of Interpersonal Violence, 20*(6), 701-712.

Bradshaw, C.P., and Waasdorp, T.E. (2009). Measuring and changing a "culture of bullying." *School Psychology Review, 38*(3), 356-361.

Bradshaw, C.P., Sawyer, A.L., and O'Brennan, L.M. (2007). Bullying and peer victimization at school: Perceptual differences between students and school staff. *School Psychology Review, 36*(3), 361-382.

Bradshaw, C.P., Sawyer, A.L., and O'Brennan, L.M. (2009). A social disorganization perspective on bullying-related attitudes and behaviors: The influence of school context. *American Journal of Community Psychology, 43*(3-4), 204-220.

Bradshaw, C.P., Waasdorp, T.E., O'Brennan, L.M., and Gulemetova, M. (2013). Teachers' and education support professionals' perspectives on bullying and prevention: Findings from a National Education Association study. *School Psychology Review, 42*(3), 280-297.

Brand, S., Felner, R., Shim, M., Seitsinger, A., and Dumas, T. (2003). Middle school improvement and reform: Development and validation of a school-level assessment of climate, cultural pluralism, and school safety. *Journal of Educational Psychology, 95*(3), 570-588.

Brand, S., Felner, R.D., Seitsinger, A., Burns, A., and Bolton, N. (2008). A large-scale study of the assessment of the social environment of middle and secondary schools: The validity and utility of teachers' ratings of school climate, cultural pluralism, and safety problems for understanding school effects and school improvement. *Journal of School Psychology, 46*(5), 507-535.

Brittain, H. L. (2010). *A Multi-Informant Study of Peer Victimization, Children's Mental Health, and Academic Achievement: The Moderating Role of Family* (Master's thesis). University of Ottawa.

Bronfenbrenner, U. (1979). *The Ecology of Human Development: Experiments by Design and Nature*: Cambridge, MA: Harvard University Press.

Burris, S. (2006). Stigma and the law. *The Lancet, 367*(9509), 529-531.

Card, N.A., Isaacs, J., and Hodges, E.V. (2007). Correlates of school victimization: Implications for prevention and intervention. In J.E. Zins, M.K. Elias, and C.A. Maher (Eds.), *Bullying, Victimization, and Peer Harassment: A Handbook of Prevention and Intervention* (pp. 339-366). New York: Haworth Press.

Card, N.A., Stucky, B.D., Sawalani, G.M., and Little, T.D. (2008). Direct and indirect aggression during childhood and adolescence: A meta-analytic review of gender differences, intercorrelations, and relations to maladjustment. *Child Development, 79*(5), 1185-1229.

Chang, F.-C., Chiu, C.-H., Miao, N.-F., Chen, P.-H., Lee, C.-M., Chiang, J.-T., and Pan, Y.-C. (2015). The relationship between parental mediation and Internet addiction among adolescents and the association with cyberbullying and depression. *Comprehensive Psychiatry, 57*, 21-28.

Chesir-Teran, D. (2003). Conceptualizing and assessing heterosexism in high schools: A setting-level approach. *American Journal of Community Psychology, 31*(3-4), 267-279.

Chou, H.-T.G., and Edge, N. (2012). "They are happier and having better lives than I am": The impact of using Facebook on perceptions of others' lives. *Cyberpsychology, Behavior, and Social Networking, 15*(2), 117-121.

Cicchetti, D., and Hinshaw, S.P. (2002). Editorial: Prevention and intervention science: Contributions to developmental theory. *Development and Psychopathology, 14*(04), 667-671.

Cicchetti, D., and Rogosch, F.A. (1996). Equifinality and multifinality in developmental psychopathology. *Development and Psychopathology, 8*(04), 597-600.

Collins, W.A., Maccoby, E.E., Steinberg, L., Hetherington, E.M., and Bornstein, M.H. (2000). Contemporary research on parenting: The case for nature and nurture. *American Psychologist, 55*(2), 218-232.

Cornell, D., and Huang, F. (2016). Authoritative school climate and high school student risk behavior: A cross-sectional multi-level analysis of student self-reports. *Journal of Youth and Adolescence*. doi: 10.1007/s10964-016-0424-3.

Cornell, D., Gregory, A., Huang, F., and Fan, X. (2013). Perceived prevalence of teasing and bullying predicts high school dropout rates. *Journal of Educational Psychology, 105*(1), 138-149.

Cornell, D., Shukla, K., and Konold, T. (2015). Peer victimization and authoritative school climate: A multilevel approach. *Journal of Educational Psychology, 107*(4), 1186-1201.

Corrigan, P.W., Markowitz, F.E., and Watson, A.C. (2004). Structural levels of mental illness stigma and discrimination. *Schizophrenia Bulletin, 30*(3), 481-491.

Craig, K., Bell, D., and Leschied, A. (2011). Preservice teachers' knowledge and attitudes regarding school-based bullying. *Canadian Journal of Education/Revue Canadienne de l'Education, 34*(2), 21-33.

Cunningham, C.E., McHolm, A., Boyle, M.H., and Patel, S. (2004). Behavioral and emotional adjustment, family functioning, academic performance, and social relationships in children with selective mutism. *Journal of Child Psychology and Psychiatry, 45*(8), 1363-1372.

Duong, J., and Bradshaw, C. (2014). Associations between bullying and engaging in aggressive and suicidal behaviors among sexual minority youth: The moderating role of connectedness. *Journal of School Health, 84*(10), 636-645.

Echols, L. (2015). Social consequences of academic teaming in middle school: The influence of shared course taking on peer victimization. *Journal of Educational Psychology, 107*(1), 272-283.

Espelage, D.L., Bosworth, K., and Simon, T.R. (2000). Examining the social context of bullying behaviors in early adolescence. *Journal of Counseling and Development, 78*(3), 326-333.

Espelage, D.L., Rao, M.A., and Craven, R.G. (2013). Theories of cyberbullying. In S. Bauman, D. Cross, and J. Walker (Eds), *Principles of Cyberbullying Research: Definitions, Measures, and Methodology* (pp. 49-67). New York: Routledge.

Espelage, D.L., Polanin, J.R., and Low, S.K. (2014). Teacher and staff perceptions of school environment as predictors of student aggression, victimization, and willingness to intervene in bullying situations. *School Psychology Quarterly, 29*(3), 287-305.

Farb, A.F., and Matjasko, J.L. (2012). Recent advances in research on school-based extracurricular activities and adolescent development. *Developmental Review, 32*(1), 1-48.

Faris, R., and Felmlee, D. (2014). Casualties of social combat: School networks of peer victimization and their consequences. *American Sociological Review, 79*(2), 228-257.

Farmer, T.W., Hamm, J.V., Leung, M.-C., Lambert, K., and Gravelle, M. (2011a). Early adolescent peer ecologies in rural communities: Bullying in schools that do and do not have a transition during the middle grades. *Journal of Youth and Adolescence, 40*(9), 1106-1117.

Farmer, T.W., Lines, M.M., and Hamm, J.V. (2011b). Revealing the invisible hand: The role of teachers in children's peer experiences. *Journal of Applied Developmental Psychology, 32*(5), 247-256.

Felix, E.D., and You, S. (2011). Peer victimization within the ethnic context of high school. *Journal of Community Psychology, 39*(7), 860-875.

Flouri, E., and Buchanan, A. (2003). The role of mother involvement and father involvement in adolescent bullying behavior. *Journal of Interpersonal Violence, 18*(6), 634-644.

Forrest, C.B., Bevans, K.B., Riley, A.W., Crespo, R., and Louis, T.A. (2013). Health and school outcomes during children's transition into adolescence. *Journal of Adolescent Health, 52*(2), 186-194.

Fox, C.L., and Boulton, M.J. (2006). Friendship as a moderator of the relationship between social skills problems and peer victimisation. *Aggressive Behavior, 32*(2), 110-121.

Gay, Lesbian, and Straight Education Network. (2015). *State Maps.* Available: http://www.glsen.org/article/state-maps [September 2015].

Gest, S.D., and Rodkin, P.C. (2011). Teaching practices and elementary classroom peer ecologies. *Journal of Applied Developmental Psychology, 32*(5), 288-296.

Gini, G., Albiero, P., Benelli, B., and Altoe, G. (2008). Determinants of adolescents' active defending and passive bystanding behavior in bullying. *Journal of Adolescence, 31*(1), 93-105.

Goffman, E. (1963). *Stigma: Notes on Management of Spoiled Identity.* New York: Simon & Schuster.

Goldweber, A., Waasdorp, T.E., and Bradshaw, C.P. (2013). Examining the link between forms of bullying behaviors and perceptions of safety and belonging among secondary school students. *Journal of School Psychology, 51*(4), 469-485.

Gonzales, N.A., George P.K., Antonio, A., Morgan-Lopez, D.S., and Sirolli, A. (2002). Acculturation and the mental health of Latino youths: An Integration and critique of the literature. In J.M. Contreras, K.A. Kerns, and A.M. Neal-Barnett (Eds.), *Latino Children and Families in the United States* (pp. 45-76). Westport, CT: Praeger.

Goodenow, C., Szalacha, L., and Westheimer, K. (2006). School support groups, other school factors, and the safety of sexual minority adolescents. *Psychology in the Schools, 43*(5), 573-589.

Graham, S. (2006). Peer victimization in school: Exploring the ethnic context. *Current Directions in Psychological Science, 15*(6), 317-321.

Graham, S., and Bellmore, A.D. (2007). Peer victimization and mental health during early adolescence. *Theory Into Practice, 46*(2), 138-146.

Graham, S., Bellmore, A., Nishina, A., and Juvonen, J. (2009). "It must be me": Ethnic diversity and attributions for peer victimization in middle school. *Journal of Youth and Adolescence, 38*(4), 487-499.

Gray, W.N., Simon, S.L., Janicke, D.M., and Dumont-Driscoll, M. (2011). Moderators of weight-based stigmatization among youth who are overweight and non-overweight: The role of gender, race, and body dissatisfaction. *Journal of Developmental & Behavioral Pediatrics, 32*(2), 110-116.

Greene, M.B. (2006). Bullying in schools: A plea for measure of human rights. *Journal of Social Issues, 62*(1), 63-79.

Gregory, A. and Cornell, D. (2009). "Tolerating" adolescent needs: Moving beyond zero tolerance policies in high school. *Theory into Practice, 48*(20), 106-113.

Gregory, A., Cornell, D., Fan, X., Sheras, P., Shih, T.-H., and Huang, F. (2010). Authoritative school discipline: High school practices associated with lower bullying and victimization. *Journal of Educational Psychology, 102*(2), 483-496.

Greytak, E.A., and Kosciw, J.G. (2014). Predictors of U.S. teachers' intervention in anti-lesbian, gay, bisexual, and transgender bullying and harassment. *Teaching Education, 25*(4), 410-426.

Guest, A.M., and McRee, N. (2009). A school-level analysis of adolescent extracurricular activity, delinquency, and depression: The importance of situational context. *Journal of Youth and Adolescence, 38*(1), 51-62.

Haltigan, J.D., and Vaillancourt, T. (2014). Joint trajectories of bullying and peer victimization across elementary and middle school and associations with symptoms of psychopathology. *Developmental Psychology, 50*(11), 2426-2436.

Hatzenbuehler, M.L. (2014). Structural stigma and the health of lesbian, gay, and bisexual populations. *Current Directions in Psychological Science, 23,* 127-132.

Hatzenbuehler, M.L., and Keyes, K.M. (2013). Inclusive anti-bullying policies and reduced risk of suicide attempts in lesbian and gay youth. *Journal of Adolescent Health, 53*(1), S21-S26.

Hatzenbuehler, M.L., Keyes, K.M., and Hasin, D.S. (2009). Associations between perceived weight discrimination and the prevalence of psychiatric disorders in the general population. *Obesity, 17*(11), 2033-2039.

Hatzenbuehler, M.L., Schwab-Reese, L., Ranapurwala, S.I., Hertz, M.F., and Ramirez, M.R. (2015a). Associations between anti-bullying policies and bullying in 25 states. *Journal of the American Medical Association Pediatrics, 169*(10), e152411.

Hatzenbuehler, M.L., Duncan, D., and Johnson, R. (2015b). Neighborhood-level LGBT hate crimes and bullying among sexual minority youths: A geospatial analysis. *Violence and Victims, 30*(4), 663-675.

Hawkins, D., Pepler, D.J., and Craig, W.M. (2001). Naturalistic observations of peer interventions in bullying. *Social Development, 10*(4), 512-527.

Hebl, M.R., and Heatherton, T.F. (1998). The stigma of obesity in women: The difference is black and white. *Personality and Social Psychology Bulletin, 24,* 417-426.

Herek, G.M., and McLemore, K.A. (2013). Sexual prejudice. *Annual Review of Psychology, 64,* 309-333.

Herek, G.M., Gillis, J.R., and Cogan, J.C. (1999). Psychological sequelae of hate-crime victimization among lesbian, gay, and bisexual adults. *Journal of Consulting and Clinical Psychology, 67,* 945-951.

Hodges, E.V., Boivin, M., Vitaro, F., and Bukowski, W.M. (1999). The power of friendship: Protection against an escalating cycle of peer victimization. *Developmental Psychology, 35*(1), 94-101.

Holt, M.K., Kaufman Kantor, G., and Finkelhor, D. (2008). Parent/child concordance about bullying involvement and family characteristics related to bullying and peer victimization. *Journal of School Violence, 8*(1), 42-63.

Hong, J.S., Espelage, D.L., and Sterzing, P.R. (2015). Understanding the antecedents of adverse peer relationships among early adolescents in the United States: An ecological systems analysis. *Youth & Society*, 1-24. doi: 10.1177/0044118X15569215.

Janssen, I., Craig, W.M., Boyce, W.F., and Pickett, W. (2004). Associations between overweight and obesity with bullying behaviors in school-aged children. *Pediatrics, 113*(5), 1187-1194.

Jia, Y., Konold, T.R., and Cornell, D. (2015). Authoritative school climate and high school dropout rates. *School Psychology Quarterly, 2*, 289-303. doi: 10.1037/spq0000139.

Johnson, K.E., and McRee, A.-L. (2015). Health-risk behaviors among high school athletes and preventive services provided during sports physicals. *Journal of Pediatric Health Care, 29*(1), 17-27.

Johnson, S.L. (2009). Improving the school environment to reduce school violence: A review of the literature. *Journal of School Health, 79*(10), 451-465.

Juvonen, J., and Galván, A. (2008). Peer influence in involuntary social groups: Lessons from research on bullying. In M.J. Prinstein and K.A. Dodge (Eds.), *Understanding Peer Influence in Children and Adolescents* (pp. 225-244). New York: Guilford Press.

Juvonen, J., Nishina, A., and Graham, S. (2006). Ethnic diversity and perceptions of safety in urban middle schools. *Psychological Science, 17*(5), 393-400.

Kljakovic, M., and Hunt, C. (2016). A meta-analysis of predictors of bullying and victimization in adolescnece. *Journal of Adolescence, 49*(2016), 134-145.

Klein, J., and Cornell, D. (2010). Is the link between large high schools and student victimization an illusion? *Journal of Educational Psychology, 102*(4), 933.

Kochenderfer-Ladd, B., and Pelletier, M.E. (2008). Teachers' views and beliefs about bullying: Influences on classroom management strategies and students' coping with peer victimization. *Journal of School Psychology, 46*(4), 431-453.

Konold, T. Cornell, D., Huang, F., Meyer, P., Lacey, A., Nekvasil, E., Heilbrun, A., and Sukla, K. (2014). Multilevel multi-informant structure of the Authoritative School Climate Survey. *School Psychology Quarterly, 29*(3), 238-255.

Kreager, D.A. (2007). Unnecessary roughness? School sports, peer networks, and male adolescent violence. *American Sociological Review, 72*(5), 705-724.

Kretschmer, T., Barker, E.D., Dijkstra, J.K., Oldehinkel, A.J., and Veenstra, R. (2015). Multifinality of peer victimization: Maladjustment patterns and transitions from early to mid-adolescence. *European Child and Adolescent Psychiatry, 24*(10), 1169-1179.

Kuperminc, G.P., Leadbeater, B.J., and Blatt, S.J. (2001). School social climate and individual differences in vulnerability to psychopathology among middle school students. *Journal of School Psychology, 39*(2), 141-159.

Leadbeater, B., Hoglund, W., and Woods, T. (2003). Changing contexts? The effects of a primary prevention program on classroom levels of peer relational and physical victimization. *Journal of Community Psychology, 31*(4), 397-418.

Lee, C., and Song, J. (2012). Functions of parental involvement and effects of school climate on bullying behaviors among South Korean middle school students. *Journal of Interpersonal Violence*, 1-28. doi: 0886260511433508.

Lenhart, A., Arafeh, S., and Smith, A. (2008). *Writing, Technology, and Teens.* Available: http://www.pewinternet.org/files/old-media/Files/Reports/2008/PIP_Writing_Report_FINAL3.pdf.pdf [September 2015].

Lenhart, A., Duggan, M., Perrin, A., Stepler, R., Rainie, H., and Parker, K. (2015). *Teens, Social Media & Technology Overview 2015*. Available: http://www.pewinternet. org/2015/04/09/teens-social-media-technology-2015/ [September 2015].

Link, B.G., and Hatzenbuehler, M.L. (2016). Stigma as an unrecognized determinant of population health: Research and policy implications. *Journal of Health Politics, Policy, and Law*. doi: 10.1215/03616878-3620869.

Link, B.G., and Phelan, J.C. (2001). Conceptualizing stigma. *Annual Review of Sociology, 27*, 363-385.

Loth, K., van den Berg, P., Eisenberg, M.E., and Neumark-Sztainer, D. (2008). Stressful life events and disordered eating behaviors: Findings from Project Eat. *Journal of Adolescent Health, 43*(5), 514-516.

Loukas, A., Suzuki, R., and Horton, K.D. (2006). Examining school connectedness as a mediator of school climate effects. *Journal of Research on Adolescence, 16*(3), 491-502.

Marsh, H.W., Nagengast, B., Morin, A.J., Parada, R.H., Craven, R.G., and Hamilton, L.R. (2011). Construct validity of the multidimensional structure of bullying and victimization: An application of exploratory structural equation modeling. *Journal of Educational Psychology, 103*(3), 701-732.

McDougall, P., and Hymel, S. (1998). Moving into middle school: Individual differences in the transition experience. *Canadian Journal of Behavioural Science/Revue Canadienne des Sciences du Comportement, 30*(2), 108-120.

McDougall, P., and Vaillancourt, T. (2015). Long-term adult outcomes of peer victimization in childhood and adolescence: Pathways to adjustment and maladjustment. *American Psychologist, 70*(4), 300-310.

Mertens, S.B., and Flowers, N. (2003). Middle school practices improve student achievement in high poverty schools. *Middle School Journal, 35*(1), 33-45.

Messinger, A.M., Nieri, T.A., Villar, P., and Luengo, M.A. (2012). Acculturation stress and bullying among immigrant youths in Spain. *Journal of School Violence, 11*(4), 306-322.

Mischel, W., and Shoda, Y. (1995). A cognitive-affective system theory of personality: Reconceptualizing situations, dispositions, dynamics, and invariance in personality structure. *Psychological Review, 102*(2), 246-268.

Morin, H.K., Bradshaw, C.P., and Berg, J.K. (2015). Examining the link between peer victimization and adjustment problems in adolescents: The role of connectedness and parent engagement. *Psychology of Violence, 5*(4), 422-432.

Movement Advancement Project. (2015). *Safe Schools Laws*. Available: http://www.lgbtmap. org/equality-maps/safe_school_laws [September 2015].

National Acadmies of Sciences, Engineering, and Medicine. (2016). *Ending Discriminiation Against People with Mental and Substance Use Disorders: The Evidence for Stigma Change*. Washington, DC: The National Academies Press.

Oldenburg, B., van Duijn, M., Sentse, M., Huitsing, G., van der Ploeg, R., Salmivalli, C., and Veenstra, R. (2015). Teacher characteristics and peer victimization in elementary schools: A classroom-level perspective. *Journal of Abnormal Child Psychology, 43*(1), 33-44.

Olson, C.K., Kutner, L.A., Warner, D.E., Almerigi, J.B., Baer, L., Nicholi, A.M., and Beresin, E.V. (2007). Factors correlated with violent video game use by adolescent boys and girls. *Journal of Adolescent Health, 41*(1), 77-83.

Olweus, D. (1993). Victimization by peers: Antecedents and long-term outcomes. In K.H. Rubin and J.B. Asendorpf (Eds.), *Social Withdrawal, Inhibition, and Shyness in Childhood* (pp. 315-341). New York: Psychology Press.

Olweus, D. (2001). Peer harassment: A critical analysis and some important issues. In J. Juvonen and S. Graham (Eds.), *Peer Harassment in School: The Plight of the Vulnerable and Victimized* (pp. 3-20). New York: Guilford Press.

Orfield, G., Kucsera, J., and Siegel-Hawley, G. (2012). *E Pluribus . . . Separation: Deepening Double Segregation for More Students*. Los Angeles: University of California, The Civil Rights Project. Available: http://escholarship.org/uc/item/8g58m2v9 [November 2015].

Peets, K., Pöyhönen, V., Juvonen, J., and Salmivalli, C. (2015). Classroom norms of bullying alter the degree to which children defend in response to their affective empathy and power. *Developmental Psychology, 51*(7), 913-920.

Peguero, A.A. (2008). Bullying victimization and extracurricular activity. *Journal of School Violence, 7*(3), 71-85.

Pellegrini, A.D., and Bartini, M. (2000). A longitudinal study of bullying, victimization, and peer affiliation during the transition from primary school to middle school. *American Educational Research Journal, 37*(3), 699-725.

Pellegrini, A., and Long, J.D. (2002). A longitudinal study of bullying, dominance, and victimization during the transition from primary school through secondary school. *British Journal of Developmental Psychology, 20*(2), 259-280.

Pellegrini, A.D., Bartini, M., and Brooks, F. (1999). School bullies, victims, and aggressive victims: Factors relating to group affiliation and victimization in early adolescence. *Journal of Educational Psychology, 91*(2), 216.

Pepler, D.J. (2006). Bullying interventions: A binocular perspective. *Journal of the Canadian Academy of Child and Adolescent Psychiatry, 15*(1), 16-20.

Pepler, D.J., Craig, W.M., Connolly, J.A., Yuile, A., McMaster, L., and Jiang, D. (2006). A developmental perspective on bullying. *Aggressive Behavior, 32*(4), 376-384.

Pepler, D.J., Craig, W.M., and O'Connell, P. (2010). Peer processes in bullying: Informing prevention and intervention strategies. In S.R. Jimerson, S.M. Swearer, and D.L. Espelage (Eds.), *Handbook of Bullying in Schools: An International Perpective* (pp. 469-479). New York: Routledge.

Peskin, M.F., Tortolero, S.R., and Markham, C.M. (2006). Bullying and victimization among black and Hispanic adolescents. *Adolescence, 41*(163), 467-484.

Perkins, H.W., Craig, D.W., and Perkins, J.M. (2011). Using social norms to reduce bullying: A research intervention among adolescents in five middle schools. *Group Processes and Intergroup Relations. 14*(5), 703-722.

Poteat, V.P., Mereish, E.H., DiGiovanni, C.D., and Koenig, B.W. (2011). The effects of general and homophobic victimization on adolescents' psychosocial and educational concerns: The importance of intersecting identities and parent support. *Journal of Counseling Psychology, 58*(4), 597-609.

Poteat, V.P., Sinclair, K.O., DiGiovanni, C.D., Koenig, B.W., and Russell, S.T. (2013). Gay–straight alliances are associated with student health: A multischool comparison of LGBTQ and heterosexual youth. *Journal of Research on Adolescence, 23*(2), 319-330.

Pöyhönen, V., Juvonen, J., and Salmivalli, C. (2010). What does it take to stand up for the victim of bullying? The interplay between personal and social factors. *Merrill-Palmer Quarterly, 56*(2), 143-163.

Pozzoli, T., and Gini, G. (2010). Active defending and passive bystanding behavior in bullying: The role of personal characteristics and perceived peer pressure. *Journal of Abnormal Child Psychology, 38*(6), 815-827.

Pozzoli, T., Gini, G., and Vieno, A. (2012). The role of individual correlates and class norms in defending and passive bystanding behavior in bullying: A multilevel analysis. *Child Development, 83*(6), 1917-1931.

Puhl, R.M., and Latner, J.D. (2007). Stigma, obesity, and the health of the nation's children. *Psychological Bulletin, 133*(4), 557.

Reis, J., Trockel, M., and Mulhall, P. (2007). Individual and school predictors of middle school aggression. *Youth & Society, 38*(3), 322-347.

Richard, J.F., Schneider, B.H., and Mallet, P. (2012). Revisiting the whole-school approach to bullying: Really looking at the whole school. *School Psychology International, 33*(3), 263-284.

Richman, L.S., and Hatzenbuehler, M.L. (2014). A multi-level analysis of stigma and health: Implications for research and policy. *Policy Insights from Behavioral and Brain Sciences, 1*(1), 213-221.

Riese, A., Gjelsvik, A., and Ranney, M.L. (2015). Extracurricular activities and bullying perpetration: Results from a nationally representative sample. *Journal of School Health, 85*(8), 544-551.

Rigby, K. (1993). School children's perceptions of their families and parents as a function of peer relations. *Journal of Genetic Psychology, 154*(4), 501-513.

Rodkin, P.C., Espelage, D.L., and Hanish, L.D. (2015). A relational framework for understanding bullying: Developmental antecedents and outcomes. *American Psychologist, 70*(4), 311.

Rose, C.A., Espelage, D.L., and Monda-Amaya, L.E. (2009). Bullying and victimization rates among students in general and special education: A comparative analysis. *Educational Psychology, 29*(7), 761-776.

Rothman, A.J. (2013) Exploring connections between moderators and mediators: Commentary on subgroup analyses in intervention research. *Prevention Science, 14*(2), 189-192.

Rubin, K.H., Bukowski, W.M., and Laursen, B. (Eds.) (2011). *Handbook of Peer Interactions, Relationships, and Groups.* New York: Guilford Press.

Russell, S.T., Sinclair, K.O., Poteat, V.P., and Koenig, B. (2012). Adolescent health and harassment based on discriminatory bias. *American Journal of Public Health, 102*(3), 493-495.

Rutter, P.A., and Leech, N.L. (2006). Sexual minority youth perspectives on the school environment and suicide risk interventions: A qualitative study. *Journal of Gay & Lesbian Issues in Education, 4*(1), 77-91.

Saarento, S., Kärnä, A., Hodges, E.V., and Salmivalli, C. (2013). Student-, classroom-, and school-level risk factors for victimization. *Journal of School Psychology, 51*(3), 421-434.

Salmivalli, C. (2001). Group view on victimization. In J. Juvonen and S. Graham (Eds.), *Peer Harassment in School* (pp. 398-419). New York: Guilford Press.

Salmivalli, C. (2010). Bullying and the peer group: A review. *Aggression and Violent Behavior, 15*(2), 112-120.

Salmivalli, C. (2014). Participant roles in bullying: How can peer bystanders be utilized in interventions? *Theory Into Practice, 53*(4), 286-292.

Salmivalli, C., and Peets, K. (2009). Bullies, victims, and bully-victim relationships in middle childhood and early adolescence. In K.H. Rubin, W.M. Bukowski, and B. Laursen (Eds.), *Handbook of Peer Interactions, Relationships, and Groups* (pp. 322-340). New York: Guilford Press.

Salmivalli, C., Lagerspetz, K., Björkqvist, K., Österman, K., and Kaukiainen, A. (1996). Bullying as a group process: Participant roles and their relations to social status within the group. *Aggressive Behavior, 22*(1), 1-15.

Salmivalli, C., Kaukiainen, A., and Voeten, M. (2005). Anti-bullying intervention: Implementation and outcome. *British Journal of Educational Psychology, 75*(3), 465-487.

Salmivalli, C., Voeten, M., and Poskiparta, E. (2011). Bystanders matter: Associations between reinforcing, defending, and the frequency of bullying behavior in classrooms. *Journal of Clinical Child & Adolescent Psychology, 40*(5), 668-676.

Schacter, H.L., and Juvonen, J. (2015). The effects of school-level victimization on self-blame: Evidence for contextualized social cognitions. *Developmental Psychology, 51*(6), 841-847.

Sentse, M., Scholte, R., Salmivalli, C., and Voeten, M. (2007). Person–group dissimilarity in involvement in bullying and its relation with social status. *Journal of Abnormal Child Psychology, 35*(6), 1009-1019.

Smokowski, P.R., David-Ferdon, C., and Stroupe, N. (2009). Acculturation and violence in minority adolescents: A review of the empirical literature. *Journal of Primary Prevention, 30*(3-4), 215-263.

Stella, M.Y., Huang, Z.J., Schwalberg, R.H., Overpeck, M., and Kogan, M.D. (2003). Acculturation and the health and well-being of U.S. immigrant adolescents. *Journal of Adolescent Health, 33*(6), 479-488.

Stevens, V., De Bourdeaudhuij, I., and Van Oost, P. (2002). Relationship of the family environment to children's involvement in bully/victim problems at school. *Journal of Youth and Adolescence, 31*(6), 419-428.

Storch, E.A., Nock, M.K., Masia-Warner, C., and Barlas, M.E. (2003). Peer victimization and social-psychological adjustment in Hispanic and African American children. *Journal of Child and Family Studies, 12*(4), 439-452.

Stormshak, E.A., Bierman, K.L., Bruschi, C., Dodge, K.A., and Coie, J.D. (1999). The relation between behavior problems and peer preference in different classroom contexts. *Child Development, 70*(1), 169-182.

Sulkowski, M.L., Bauman, S., Wright, S., Nixon, C., and Davis, S. (2014). Peer victimization in youth from immigrant and non-immigrant U.S. families. *School Psychology International, 35*(6), 649-669.

Susman, J. (1994). Disability, stigma, and deviance. *Social Science & Medicine, 38*, 15-22.

Swearer, S.M., and Espelage, D.L. (2004). Introduction: A social-ecological framework of bullying among youth. In D.L. Espelage and S.M. Swearer (Eds.), *Bullying in Schools: A Social-Ecological Perspective on Prevention and Intervention* (pp. 1-12). Mahwah, NJ: Lawrence Erlbaum.

Swearer, S.M., and Hymel, S. (2015). Understanding the psychology of bullying: Moving toward a social-ecological diathesis–stress model. *American Psychologist, 70*(4), 344-353.

Swearer, S.M., Turner, R.K., Givens, J.E., and Pollack, W.S. (2008). "You're so gay!" Do different forms of bullying matter for adolescent males? *School Psychology Review, 37,* 160-173.

Swearer, S.M., Espelage, D.L., Vaillancourt, T., and Hymel, S. (2010). What can be done about school bullying? Linking research to educational practice. *Educational Researcher, 39*(1), 38-47.

Taylor, M.J., Wamser, R.A., Welch, D.Z., and Nanney, J.T. (2012). Multidimensional self-esteem as a mediator of the relationship between sports participation and victimization: A study of African American girls. *Violence and Victims, 27*(3), 434-452.

Thapa, A., Cohen, J., Guffey, S., and Higgins-D'Alessandro, A. (2013). A review of school climate research. *Review of Educational Research, 83*(3), 357-385.

Trach, J., Hymel, S., Waterhouse, T., and Neale, K. (2010). Bystander responses to school bullying: A cross-sectional investigation of grade and sex differences. *Canadian Journal of School Psychology, 25*(1), 114-130.

Troop-Gordon, W., and Ladd, G.W. (2015). Teachers' victimization-related beliefs and strategies: Associations with students' aggressive behavior and peer victimization. *Journal of Abnormal Child Psychology, 43*(1), 45-60.

Turner, H.A., Finkelhor, D., Shattuck, A., Hamby, S., and Mitchell, K. (2015). Beyond bullying: Aggravating elements of peer victimization episodes. *School Psychology Quarterly, 30*(3), 366-384.

Unnever, J.D., and Cornell, D.G. (2004). Middle school victims of bullying: Who reports being bullied? *Aggressive Behavior, 30*(5), 373-388.

Vaillancourt, T., Hymel, S., and McDougall, P. (2003). Bullying is power: Implications for school-based intervention strategies. *Journal of Applied School Psychology, 19*(2), 157-176.

Vaillancourt, T., McDougall, P., Hymel, S., and Sunderani, S. (2010). The relationship between power and bullying behavior. In S.R. Jimerson, S.M. Swearer, and D.L. Espelage (Eds.), *Handbook of Bullying in Schools: An International Perspective* (pp. 211-222). New York: Routledge.

Valkenburg, P.M., and Peter, J. (2011). Online communication among adolescents: An integrated model of its attraction, opportunities, and risks. *Journal of Adolescent Health, 48*(2), 121-127.

Veenstra, R., Dijkstra, J.K., Steglich, C., and Van Zalk, M.H. (2013). Network–behavior dynamics. *Journal of Research on Adolescence, 23*(3), 399-412.

Vella, S.A., Cliff, D.P., Magee, C.A., and Okely, A.D. (2015). Associations between sports participation and psychological difficulties during childhood: A two-year follow up. *Journal of Science and Medicine in Sport, 18*(3), 304-309.

Vitoroulis, I., and Vaillancourt, T. (2014). Meta-analytic results of ethnic group differences in peer victimization. *Aggressive Behavior, 41*, 149-170.

Wang, M.-T., and Degol, J.L. (2015). School climate: A review of the construct, measurement, and impact on student outcomes. *Educational Psychology Review, 17*(2), 1-38.

Wang, W., Brittain, H., McDougall, P., and Vaillancourt, T. (2015). Bullying and school transition: Context or development? *Child Abuse & Neglect, 51*, 237-248.

Wigfield, A., Eccles, J.S., Mac Iver, D., Reuman, D.A., and Midgley, C. (1991). Transitions during early adolescence: Changes in children's domain-specific self-perceptions and general self-esteem across the transition to junior high school. *Developmental Psychology, 27*(4), 552-565.

Wright, J.C., Giammarino, M., and Parad, H.W. (1986). Social status in small groups: Individual–group similarity and the social "misfit." *Journal of Personality and Social Psychology, 50*(3), 523-536.

Ybarra, M.L., and Mitchell, K.L. (2004). Online aggressor/targets, aggressors, and targets: A comparison of associated youth characteristics. *Journal of Child Psychology and Psychiatry, 45*(7), 1308-1316.

Yoon, J.S. (2004). Predicting teacher interventions in bullying situations. *Education and Treatment of Children, 27*(1), 37-45.

Zullig, K.J., Huebner, E.S., and Patton, J.M. (2011). Relationships among school climate domains and school satisfaction. *Psychology in the Schools, 48*(2), 133-145.

4

Consequences of Bullying Behavior

Bullying behavior is a serious problem among school-age children and adolescents; it has short- and long-term effects on the individual who is bullied, the individual who bullies, the individual who is bullied and bullies others, and the bystander present during the bullying event. In this chapter, the committee presents the consequences of bullying behavior for children and youth. As referenced in Chapter 1, bullying can be either direct or indirect, and children and youth may experience different types of bullying. Specifically the committee examines physical (including neurobiological), mental, and behavioral health consequences. The committee also examines consequences for academic performance and achievement and explores evidence for some of the mechanisms proposed for the psychological effects of bullying. When applicable, we note the limited, correlational nature of much of the available research on the consequences of bullying.

CONSEQUENCES FOR INDIVIDUALS WHO ARE BULLIED

Mounting evidence on bullying has highlighted the detrimental effects of being bullied on children's health and behavior (Gini and Pozzoli, 2009; Lereya et al., 2015; Reijntjes et al., 2010; Ttofi et al., 2011). In this section, the committee reviews the research on physical, psychosocial, and academic achievement consequences for those children and youth who are bullied.

Perspectives from the Field

Being bullied makes young people incredibly insecure: When you're being bullied, you can feel constantly insecure and on guard. Even if you're not actively being bullied, you're aware it could start anytime. It has a big mental and emotional impact—you feel unaccepted, isolated, angry, and withdrawn. You're always wondering how you can do better and how you can escape a bully's notice. You're also stunted because of the constant tension and because maybe you forego making certain friendships or miss out on taking certain chances that could actually help your development.

—Summary of themes from young adults focus group
(See Appendix B for additional highlights from interviews.)

Physical Health Consequences

The physical health consequences of bullying can be immediate, such as physical injury, or they can involve long-term effects, such as headaches, sleep disturbances, or somatization.[1] However, the long-term physical consequences of bullying can be difficult to identify and link with past bullying behavior versus being the result of other causes such as anxiety or other adverse childhood events that can also have physical effects into adulthood (Hager and Leadbeater, 2016). In one of the few longitudinal studies on the physical and mental effects of bullying, Bogart and colleagues (2014) studied 4,297 children and their parents from three urban locales: Birmingham, Alabama; 25 contiguous school districts in Los Angeles County, California; and one of the largest school districts in Houston, Texas. Bogart and her team were interested in the cumulative effects of bullying on an individual. They collected data when the cohort was in fifth grade (2004 to 2006), seventh grade (2006 to 2008), and tenth grade (2008 to 2010). Data consisted of responses to the Peer Experience Questionnaire, the Pediatric Quality of Life Inventory with its Psychosocial Subscale and Physical Health Subscale, and a Self-Perception Profile. The Physical Health Subscale measured perceptions of physical quality of life.

Bogart and colleagues (2014) found that children who were bullied experienced negative physical health compared to non-involved peers. Among seventh grade students with the worst-decile physical health, 6.4 percent were not bullied, 14.8 percent had been bullied in the past only, 23.9 per-

---

[1] Somatization is "a syndrome of physical symptoms that are distressing and may not be fully explained by a known medical condition after appropriate investigation. In addition, the symptoms may be caused or exacerbated by anxiety, depression, and interpersonal conflicts, and it is common for somatization, depression, and anxiety to all occur together" (Greenberg, 2016).

cent had been bullied in the present only, and nearly a third (30.2%) had been bullied in both the past and present. These effects were not as strong when students were in tenth grade. Limitations to this study were that physical health was measured by participants' perceptions of their health-related quality of life, rather than by objectively defined physical symptoms. It is critical to understand that this study, or other studies assessing correlations between behavior and events, cannot state that the events caused the behavior. Future research might build on this large multisite longitudinal study and obtain more in-depth evidence on individuals' physical health as a consequence of bullying.

In their study of 2,232 twins reared together and separately as a part of the Environmental Risk (E-Risk) Longitudinal Twin Study, Baldwin and colleagues (2015) found that children who had experienced chronic bullying showed greater adiposity subsequently, but not at the time of victimization. The study revealed that at age 18, these children had a higher body mass index (b = 1.11, CI [0.33, 1.88]), waist-hip ratio (b = 0.017, CI [0.008, 0.026]), and were at a higher risk of being overweight (OR = 1.80, CI [1.28, 2.53]) than their nonbullied counterparts (Baldwin et al., 2015).

An important future direction for research is to gather more information on physical consequences such as elevated blood pressure, inflammatory markers, and obesity in light of work showing effects on these outcome of harsh language by parents and other types of early life adversity (Danese and Tan, 2014; Danese et al., 2007; Evans et al., 2007; Miller and Chen, 2010).

Somatic Symptoms

Most of the extant evidence on the physical consequences—somatic symptoms in particular—of bullying pertains to the individual who is bullied. The emotional effects of being bullied can be expressed through somatic disturbances, which, similar to somatization, are physical symptoms that originate from stress or an emotional condition. Common stress or anxiety-related symptoms include sleep disorders, gastrointestinal concerns, headaches, palpitations, and chronic pain. The relationship between peer victimization and sleep disturbances has been well documented (Hunter et al., 2014; van Geel et al., 2014).

For instance, Hunter and colleagues (2014) examined sleep difficulties (feeling too tired to do things, had trouble getting to sleep, and had trouble staying asleep) among a sample of 5,420 Scottish adolescents. The researchers found that youth who were bullied (OR = 1.72, 95% CI [1.07, 2.75]) and youth who bully (OR = 1.80, CI [1.16, 2.81]) were nearly twice as likely as youth who were not involved in bullying to experience sleep difficulties. One limitation of this study is that it was based on self-reports, which have sometimes been criticized as being subject to specific biases. Patients with insomnia may overestimate how long it takes them to fall asleep (Harvey and Tang, 2012). Another limitation is that the study included young people at different stages of adolescence. Sleep patterns and sleep requirements vary across the different stages of adolescence.

A recent meta-analysis based on 21 studies involving an international sample of 363,539 children and adolescents examined the association between peer victimization and sleeping problems. A broader focus on peer victimization was used because of the definitional issues related to bullying. The authors defined peer victimization as "being the victim of relational, verbal or physical aggression by peers" (van Geel et al., 2015, p. 89). Children and youth who were victimized reported more sleeping problems than children who did not report victimization ($OR = 2.21$, 95% CI [2.01, 2.44]). Moreover, the relationship between peer victimization and sleeping problems was stronger for younger children than it was for older children (van Geel et al., 2015). This study was based on cross-sectional studies that varied widely in how peer victimization and sleeping problems were operationalized and thus cannot make any claims about causal relations between peer victimization and sleeping problems.

Knack and colleagues (2011a) posited that bullying results in meaningful biological alterations that may result in changes in one's sensitivity to pain responses. A recent meta-analysis by Gini and Pozzoli (2013) concluded that children and adolescents who are bullied were at least twice as likely to have psychosomatic disturbances (headache, stomachache, dizziness, bedwetting, etc.) than nonbullied children and adolescents ($OR = 2.39$, 95% CI [1.76, 3.24] for longitudinal studies; $OR = 2.17$, 95% CI [1.91, 2.46] for cross-sectional studies). Although the use of self-report measures are very common in bullying research and are usually considered to be valid and reliable (Ladd and Kochenderfer-Ladd, 2002), their use requires adequate self-awareness on the part of the respondent, and some children who are bullied may be in denial about their experience of having been bullied.

There is also evidence of gender differences in the physical effects of being bullied. For example, Kowalski and Limber (2013) examined the relation between experiences with cyberbullying or traditional bullying (i.e., bullying that does not involve digital electronic means of communication) and psychological and physical health, as well as academic performance, of 931 students in grades 6 through 12 living in rural Pennsylvania. Students were asked how often in the past 4 weeks they experienced 10 physical health symptoms, with scores across these 10 symptoms averaged to provide an overall health index (higher scores equal more health problems). Traditional bullying was defined as "aggressive acts that are meant to hurt another person, that happen repeatedly, and that involve an imbalance of power" (Kowalski and Limber, 2013, p. S15). The authors found that girls who were traditionally bullied reported more anxiety and overall health problems than boys who were bullied (females: $M = 1.65$, $SD = 0.41$; males: $M = 1.42$, $SD = 0.38$). A limitation of this study is that it is correlational in nature and the authors cannot conclude that being a victim of traditional bullying caused the psychological or physical problems.

In summary, it is clear that children and youth who have been bullied also experience a range of somatic disturbances. There are also gender differences in the physical health consequences of being bullied.

Neuroendocrinology of Stress

Psychological and physical stressors, such as being the target of bullying, activate the stress system centered on the hypothalamic-pituitary-adrenal (HPA) axis (Dallman et al., 2003; McEwen and McEwen, 2015). The role of HPA and other hormones is to promote adaptation and survival, but chronically elevated hormones can also cause problems. Stress has ubiquitous effects on physiology and the brain, alters levels of many hormones and other biomarkers, and ultimately affects behavior. Therefore, both a general understanding of stress during early adolescence and, where known, specific links between stress and bullying can provide insight into the enduring effects of bullying.

The levels of the stress hormone cortisol have been shown to change in targets of repeated bullying, with being bullied associated with a blunted cortisol response (Booth et al., 2008; Kliewer, 2006; Knack et al., 2011b; Ouellet-Morin et al., 2011; Vaillancourt et al., 2008). To the committee's knowledge, no study has examined bidirectional changes in cortisol, although there is evidence to suggest that cortisol is typically elevated immediately following many types of stress and trauma but blunted after prolonged stress (Judd et al., 2014; Miller et al., 2007). Kliewer (2006) did find that cortisol increased from pre-task to post-task (i.e., watching a video clip from the film *Boyz 'n the Hood* followed by a discussion) among youth who had been bullied, and in a more recent study, Kliewer and colleagues (2012) reported, among African American urban adolescents, that peer victimization was associated with greater sympathetic nervous system (fight or flight reaction) reactivity to a stress task (measured using salivary α-amylase, an enzyme that increases in saliva when the sympathetic nervous system is activated). However, in these studies, the immediate effect of being bullied on stress reactivity was not examined. In contrast, Ouellet-Morin and colleagues (2011) and Knack and colleagues (2011b) did not find an increase in cortisol in bullied youth following a psychosocial stress test but rather found a blunted pattern of response after the test had concluded (see Figures 4-1 and 4-2). In order to test whether, in the short-term, bullying

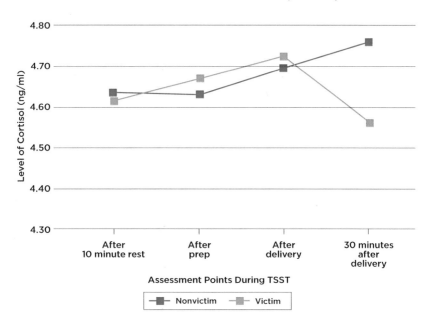

FIGURE 4-1 Cortisol reactivity for victimized and nonvictimized adolescents during the Trier Social Stress Test.
SOURCE: Adapted from Knack et al. (2011b, Fig. 3, p. 5).

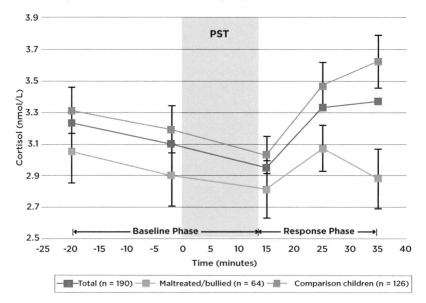

FIGURE 4-2 Cortisol responses to a psychosocial stress test (PST) in the total sample and according to maltreatment/bullying victimization.
SOURCE: Adapted from Ovellet-Morin et al. (2011, Fig. 1, p. 14).

produces an increase in cortisol, whereas in the long-term it is associated with a blunted cortisol response (as seen with other types of psychosocial stressors; Judd et al., 2014; Miller et al., 2007), a longitudinal study is needed to examine bullying chronicity and regulation of the HPA axis. The importance of this future work notwithstanding, there is evidence to support a finding that when stress becomes prolonged, the stress hormone system becomes hypofunctional and a blunted stress response results (McEwen, 2014).

When stress becomes prolonged, the stress hormone system becomes hypofunctional and a blunted stress response results (Knack et al., 2012a; McEwen, 2014; Vaillancourt et al., 2013a). That is, the elevation in cortisol in response to stress fails to occur. Scientists are not exactly sure how this happens, but evidence suggests that the stress system has shut itself down through "negative feedback." Although on the surface this may seem to be beneficial, it is not. Cortisol has many functions and serves to regulate myriad biological systems; a blunted stress response compromises the orchestration of cortisol's biological functions. The critical importance of the massive over-activation of the stress system producing a blunted stress response is clinically relevant since it is associated with posttraumatic stress disorder and other psychiatric disorders (Heim et al., 1997). It is also relevant for understanding an individual's inability to self-regulate and cope with stress.

Prolonged stress also disrupts the circadian or daily rhythm of cortisol, which is normally elevated in the morning and slowly decreases over the day to result in low levels at bedtime (Barra et al., 2015). An altered circadian rhythm results not only in difficulty awaking in the morning but also in difficulty falling asleep at night. It can cause profound disruption in sleep patterns that can initiate myriad additional problems; sleep deficits are associated with problems with emotional regulation, learning, mood disorders, and a heightened social threat detection and response system (McEwen and Karatsoreos, 2015). Recent research suggests that the consolidation of memories[2] one learns each day continues during sleep (Barnes and Wilson, 2014; Shen et al., 1998). Sleep disturbances disrupt memory consolidation, and studies in animals suggest stress during learning engages unique neurochemical and molecular events that cause memory to be encoded by some unique mechanism (Baratta et al., 2015; Belujon and Grace, 2015; McGaugh, 2015; Rau and Fanselow, 2009). Although victims of bullying have sleep problems (Miller-Graff et al., 2015), causal relations between bullying, sleep disorders, learning/memory consolidation, and cortisol dysregulation have not been established. Indeed, these correla-

---

[2] Consolidation of memory is a biological process where the information one learns is stabilized within neural circuits and placed into long-term memory through a complex orchestration of molecular-level change and gene activation within neurons.

tions between being a target of bullying and physiological problems may highlight important interactions between events and outcome, but it is also likely that unidentified variables might be the critical causal factors.

It is also noteworthy that the HPA axis showed heightened responsiveness during the peak ages of bullying (Blakemore, 2012; Dahl and Gunnar, 2009; Romeo, 2010; Spear, 2010). For example, cortisol response characteristics in children are such that, when cortisol is activated, the hormonal response is protracted and takes almost twice as much time to leave the blood and brain compared to adults (Romeo, 2010, 2015).The circadian rhythm of cortisol also seems altered during early adolescence, most notably associated with morning cortisol levels, with levels increasing with age and pubertal development (Barra et al., 2015). Animal models suggest that the extended cortisol response begins in pre-puberty and indicate that recovery from stressful events is more challenging during this age range (Romeo, 2015).

Emotional regulation, including a person's ability to recover from a traumatic or stressful event, involves being able to regulate or normalize stress hormone levels. Before adolescence, children's ability to regulate their stress response can be greatly assisted by parents or other significant caregivers—a process referred to as "social buffering" (Hostinar et al., 2014; Ouellet-Morin et al., 2011, 2013). Specifically, it is well documented in the human and animal research literature that a sensitive caregiver or a strong support system can greatly dampen the stress system's response and actually reduce the amount of stress hormone released, as well as shorten the amount of time the stress hormones circulate within the body and brain. This results in dramatic decreases in stress-related behavior (Gee et al., 2014; Hostinar et al., 2014).The social cues actually reduce stress by reducing the activation of the stress system, or HPA axis, at the level of the hypothalamus (Hennessy et al., 2009, 2015; Moriceau and Sullivan, 2006). The social stimuli that buffer children as they transition into adolescence appear to begin to have greater reliance on peers rather than on the caregiver (Hostinar et al., 2015).

Other physiological effects of stress include the activation of the immune system by bullying-induced stress (Copeland et al., 2014; McCormick and Mathews, 2007), and a cardiovascular blunting among individuals with a history of being bullied (Newman, 2014). Other hormones and physiological mechanisms are also involved in the stress activation response. For example, cortisol is associated with an increase in testosterone, the male sex hormone associated with aggression in nonhuman animals and with dominance and social challenge in humans, particularly among boys and men (Archer, 2004). In fact, in rodents the combined assessment of testosterone and cortisol provides more predictive value of behavioral variability (McCormick and Mathews, 2007) compared to controls (Márquez et al., 2013). In humans, there is increasing evidence supporting an interaction between testosterone and cortisol in the prediction of social aggression (see Montoya et al., 2012). In a study of 12-year-olds, Vaillancourt and colleagues (2009) found that testosterone levels were higher among bullied boys than nonbullied boys, but lower among bullied girls than nonbullied girls. The authors speculated that the androgen dynamics were possibly adrenocortical in origin, highlighting the need to examine testosterone and cortisol in consort. To date, researchers have only investigated cortisol response to being bullied (Kliewer, 2006; Knack et al., 2011b; Ouellet-Morin et al., 2011; Vaillancourt et al., 2008), and only one study has examined testosterone and peer victimization (Vaillancourt et al., 2009). There are no studies examining these two important hormones together in relation to bullying perpetration or to being bullied.

Together, the research on both humans and animals suggests that stress is beneficial when it is experienced at low-to-moderate levels, whereas prolonged or repeated stress becomes toxic by engaging a unique neural and molecular cascade within the brain that is thought to initiate a different developmental pathway. Indeed, from animal models, brain architecture is altered by chronic stress, with amygdala activity being enhanced, hippocampal function impaired, and medial prefrontal cortex function being reduced, leading to increased anxiety and aggression and decreased capacity for self-regulation, as well as a more labile mood (Chattarji et al., 2015; McEwen and Morrison, 2013; McEwen et al., 2015). This stress effect on the brain is particularly strong when experienced during adolescence, but it is even more pronounced if combined with early life adversity (Gee et al., 2014; Hanson et al., 2015; Richter-Levin et al., 2015; Romeo, 2015; Sandi and Haller 2015). This could produce behavioral responses that become maladaptive by compromising emotional and cognitive functioning or perhaps it could produce adaptive behavior for a dangerous environment that results in socially inappropriate behavior.

Consequences of Bullying on Brain Function

Being a child or youth who is bullied changes behavior, and neuroscience research suggests this experience may also change the brain (Bradshaw et al., 2012; Vaillancourt et al., 2013a). The major technique used to monitor brain function in humans is functional magnetic resonance imaging (fMRI), which works by monitoring blood flow to indirectly assess the functioning of thousands of brain cells over an area of the brain. This technique has rarely been used on either the perpetrator or target of a bullying incident during this very particular social interaction, and for that reason little is known about whether or not the brain of a child who bullies or of a child who has been bullied is different before these experiences or is changed by them. These very specific studies are required before one can make definitive statements about the brain for this topic or for how this information might help develop novel interventions or prevention.

Additionally, it is important to consider two limitations for understanding fMRI. First, one cannot scan the brain of a child during the action of bullying or being a target of bullying. Instead, one must rely on the child staying perfectly still as the investigator tries to approximate one or two aspects of the complex experience that occur in this complicated behavioral interaction. For example, the fMRI task used during a brain imaging session might mimic social exclusion as one facet of bullying, without the full social and emotional context of the real bullying process. Although this is an important methodology, these results need to be assessed with caution at this time and not directly applied as an accepted scientific interpretation of bullying. Therefore, the examples used below to assess brain function rely not on monitoring actual instances of bullying behavior but on monitoring components of behaviors that are thought to occur during a bullying incident.

Second, fMRI monitors a large brain area, which is composed of many smaller brain areas, each of which is involved in many, many behaviors, many of which are not yet fully understood. Thus, it is difficult to determine why the brain area one is examining changed, since that brain area is involved in hundreds of diverse behaviors. For this reason, the results reviewed below need to be viewed as preliminary and should not be misinterpreted as explaining any aspect of the experience of bullying. Rather, these preliminary results highlight the importance of brain assessment before and after bullying experiences, including developing monitorable tasks that more closely approximate the bullying experience within the physical constraints of an immobile subject during an fMRI brain scan. The value of neuroscience is that it enables exploration of brain mechanisms controlling behavior that are not obvious from behavioral assessment.

Social Pain

Whereas there are no studies directly examining bullying using neural imaging techniques, there are several studies examining how the brain processes social pain. Social pain describes the "feelings of pain that follow the experiences of peer rejection, ostracism, or loss" (Vaillancourt et al., 2013a, p. 242). Social pain is consistent with how people describe their feeling about being bullied. For example, one victim of bullying described the emotional toll of his experience by saying, "I feel like, emotionally, they [his bullies] have been beating me with a stick for 42 years" (Vaillancourt et al., 2013a, p. 242).

Researchers have demonstrated that when people experience social pain, they activate regions in their brain similar to those activated when they experience physical pain (Eisenberger, 2012; Eisenberger and Lieberman, 2004; Eisenberger et al., 2003; Kross et al., 2011; Vaillancourt et al., 2010a). Specifically, the dorsal anterior cingulate cortex, which is part of the prefrontal cortex, seems to be implicated in the processing of both physical and social pain. The fact that physical and social pain have overlapping neural systems might explain why people tend to use physical pain metaphors (e.g., "It broke my heart when she called me ugly.") when describing their experiences with being humiliated, oppressed, or rejected (Eisenberger, 2012). Eisenberger and Leiberman (2004) noted that these fMRI results are correlations between pain and the anterior cingulate cortex and could reflect other functions of that brain region, such as detecting conflict or errors, different ideas or goals about the task, or individual differences in the task difficulty. In a recent fMRI study by Rudolph and colleagues (2016), adolescent girls were socially excluded during a laboratory task (i.e., cyberball; Williams et al., 2000). Results indicated that activation of the social pain network—the dorsal anterior cingulate cortex, subgenual anterior cingulate cortex, and anterior insula—was associated with internalizing symptoms. Of note, this effect was particularly pronounced among adolescent girls with a history of peer victimization.[3]

In addition to studies on social pain, there are some studies examining how the brains of children who had been bullied reacted subsequently to different stimuli. Experiences of being bullied can alter an individual's view of the world. While no brain imaging study has directly addressed this issue, a longitudinal study investigating the risk factors of depression found that being a child who was bullied at ages 11 and 12 was associated with a decreased response to reward in the medial prefrontal cortex at age 16, although it was unclear if these brain differences were present before the bullying experiences or developed after them (Casement et al., 2014). The medial prefrontal cortex, which is a brain area involved in memory and learning, was found to be disrupted in children who have been bullied (Vaillancourt et al., 2011). Because it also has countless other functions including decision making, risk taking, and conflict monitoring, disruption of this region compromises one's ability to interpret results with respect to bullying (Euston et al., 2012; Vaillancourt et al., 2011).

In another fMRI study involving children, 10-12 years old, who were presented with a task that examined their response to negative feedback stimuli of emotional faces, greater and more extensive brain activation was found in the amygdala, orbitofrontal cortex, and ventrolateral prefrontal cortex of children who had been rejected by their peers, compared with

---

[3] Peer victimization was measured with a 21-item revised version of the Social Experiences Questionnaire. The measure assesses overt and relational victimization and frequency of different acts of victimization (Rudolph et al., 2016).

children in a control group who had not been rejected by peers (Lee et al., 2014), a condition that is highly correlated with being bullied by peers ($r = .57$; Knack et al., 2012a).The prefrontal cortex is a very large brain area with many subareas, all of which serve diverse functions in many different behaviors, not just executive function. Indeed, the prefrontal cortex processes pain, self-regulation, stress integration, and safety signals and has been implicated in psychiatric disorders, higher order learning, extinction (active process to suppress a memory), personality, social behavior, planning, decision making, and many other behaviors and percepts including social exclusion, social/physical pain, and empathy (Casey and Jones, 2010; Spear, 2013).These few studies are consistent with other imaging studies demonstrating functional brain differences among individuals who were maltreated in childhood (Lim et al., 2014, 2015). Taken together, this work supports a finding that being exposed to such adversity during maturation has enduring effects on brain function, although additional research is needed to establish the parameters controlling these effects (and qualifying the generalization).

There is also evidence that stressful events, such as might occur with bullying experiences, impact emotional brain circuits, an inference that is supported by changes in amygdala architecture and function described earlier in animal models in adulthood but more robust changes in brain structure are produced by stress during early life and around adolescence (Chattarji et al., 2015; McEwen and Morrison, 2013; McEwen et al., 2015). This point is critical because the stress system of adolescents seems to have a heightened sensitivity, and experiencing bullying can increase stress hormones (Romeo, 2010, 2015; Spear, 2013; Vaillancourt et al., 2011). Human brain scanning experiments suggest the prefrontal cortex is affected by stress through attenuating the connectivity to the hippocampus and amygdala, which are brain areas critical for emotional regulation and emotional memories (Ganzel et al., 2008; Liston et al., 2009). Animal research shows that this connectivity loss is caused by stress-induced atrophy of the prefrontal cortex (Radley et al., 2006), although this brain region does show the ability to recover once the stress has terminated (Liston et al., 2009). One aspect of being a target of bullying is that the memory of the experience seems to be enduring; the unique function of the prefrontal cortex and emotional circuits during preadolescence and adolescence may provide insight into the enduring memories of being bullied. Specifically, one function of the prefrontal cortex is to help suppress memories that are no longer important or true. Typically, memories are not simply forgotten or unlearned. Rather, as we update information in our brain, the old memory is suppressed by overlaying a new memory to attenuate the old memory, an active brain process called extinction (Milaid and Quirk, 2012). With respect to memories of trauma, of being bullied, or of experiencing a threat, the prefrontal cortex is important for attenuating (extinguishing) memories in emotional brain areas, such as the amygdala. Importantly, dramatic changes occur in the extinction system during adolescence, where fear extinction learning is attenuated relative to children and adults (Pattwell et al., 2012, 2013). This learning mode has been modeled in animals to understand how the process occurs in the adolescent brain (Kim and Richardson, 2010; Nair and Gonzalez-Lima, 1999; Pattwell et al., 2012). The research suggests that around the time of adolescence, it is more difficult to decrease emotionally aversive memories, such as experiences of being bullied, than at other times in the life cycle. Furthermore, anxious teens (anxiety is sometimes comorbid with experience of being bullied) show even greater difficulties with processing extinction of fear memory (Jovanovic et al., 2013).

In conclusion, the available evidence indicates that the brain functioning of individuals who are bullied is altered (see reviews by Bradshaw et al., 2012; Vaillancourt et al., 2013a). However, it is difficult to ascertain fully what it means when fMRI scans detect an alteration in brain activity. In terms of understanding the prolonged and repeated stress associated with bullying, this research suggests that greater experience with being bullied and repeated exposure as a target of bullying produces a neural signature in the brain that could underlie some of the behavioral outcomes associated with being bullied.

Psychosocial Consequences

In this section, the committee examines what is known about the psychosocial consequences of being bullied. A common method of examining mental health issues separates internalizing and externalizing problems (Sigurdson et al., 2015). Internalizing symptoms include problems directed within the individual, such as depression, anxiety, fear, and withdrawal from social contacts. Externalizing symptoms reflect behavior that is typically directed outwards toward others, such as anger, aggression, and conduct problems, including a tendency to engage in risky and impulsive behavior, as well as criminal behavior. Externalizing problems also include the use and abuse of substances.

Psychological problems are common after being bullied (see review by Hawker and Boulton, 2000) and include internalizing problems, such as depression, anxiety, and, especially for girls, self-harming behavior (Kidger et al., 2015; Klomek et al., 2009, 2015). There can also be subsequent externalizing problems, especially for boys (see review by McDougall and Vaillancourt, 2015). Rueger and colleagues (2011) found consistent concurrent association with timing of peer victimization and maladjustment. Both psychological and academic outcomes were particularly strong for students who experienced sustained victimization over the school year.

Perspectives from the Field

"And these are the kids that are at risk for anxiety and depression and bipolar disorder to begin with, and it almost seems like it's a cycle that makes it worse. So they are isolated and they are angry, they are fearful. Many of them end up severely depressed, attempting suicide, utilizing NSSIs [nonsuicidal self-injuries] for comfort. Some turn to gangs because that is the group that would accept them. So that's when we get involved and we have to start working backwards."

—Quote from community-based provider discussing bullying during focus group
(See Appendix B for additional highlights from interviews.)

Internalizing Problems

A robust literature documents that youth who are bullied often have low self-esteem and feel depressed, anxious, and lonely (Juvonen and Graham, 2014). Data from developmental psychopathology research indicate that stressful life events can lead to the onset and maintenance of depression, anxiety, and other psychiatric symptoms and that for many youth, being bullied is a major life stressor (Swearer and Hymel, 2015). Based on sociometric nominations, targets of bullying also are disliked by the general peer group (Knack et al., 2012b).

Several meta-analyses have specifically explored the relation between depression and being bullied at school (Ttofi et al., 2011) and victimized by peers[4] (Hawker and Boulton, 2000; Reijntjes et al., 2010). Individuals who had been cyberbullied reported higher levels of depression and suicidal ideation, as well as increased emotional distress, externalized hostility, and delinquency, compared with peers who were not bullied (Patchin, 2006; Ybarra et al., 2006). Furthermore, severity of depression in youth who have been cyberbullied has been shown to correlate with the degree and severity of cyberbullying (Didden et al., 2009).

Two meta-analyses found that across several different longitudinal studies using different study populations, internalizing emotional problems increases both the risk and the harmful consequences of being bullied (Cook et al., 2010; Reijntjes et al., 2010). Internalizing problems can thus function

---

[4]Reijntjes and colleagues (2010, p. 244) defined peer victimization as taking "various forms, including direct bullying behaviors (e.g., teasing, physical aggression) as well as more indirect manifestations such as group exclusion or malicious gossip." Hawker and Boulton (2000, p. 441) defined peer victimization as "the experience among children of being a target of the aggressive behavior of other children, who are not siblings and not necessarily age-mates."

as both antecedents and consequences of bullying (Reijntjes et al., 2010; Vaillancourt et al., 2013b). Although most longitudinal studies suggest that psychological problems result from being bullied (see review by McDougall and Vaillancourt, 2015) and meta-analyses (Reijntjes et al., 2010; Ttofi et al., 2011) support this directionality, there is some evidence that for some youth, the temporal pattern begins with mental health problems (Kochel et al., 2012; Vaillancourt et al., 2013b).

In a large cohort of Canadian children followed every year from grade 5 to grade 8, Vaillancourt and colleagues (2013b) found that internalizing problems in grades 5 and 7 predicted increased self-reported bullying behavior the following year. They noted that these findings provide evidence for the "symptom-driven pathway" across time with increased internalizing problems predicting greater self-reported peer victimization. This "symptom-drive pathway" was noted from grade 5 to grade 6 and again from grade 7 to grade 8 and was consistent with other published work. For instance, Kochel et al. (2012) reported a symptom-driven pathway in which depressive symptoms predicted peer victimization[5] 1 year later (grade 4 to grade 5 and grade 5 to grade 6) and argued that this pathway may result from depressed youth displaying "social deficits," selecting "maladaptive relationships," and/or displaying a behavioral style that is perceived poorly by the peer group (Kochel et al., 2012, p. 638). Vaillancourt and colleagues (2013b) have also argued that depressed youth could be more "treat sensitive." That is, these youth may select information from their environment that is consistent with their negative self-opinion. The idea that certain individuals may be more sensitive to environmental cues or make more hostile interpretation of ambiguous social data has been well documented in the literature (Crick and Dodge, 1994; Dodge, 1986). This work is consistent with studies showing that social information processing differs in children based on their experience with being bullied and that hypersensitivity can impact their interpretation of social behavior and their self-reports of subsequent incidents of being bullied (Camodeca et al., 2003; Smalley and Banerjee, 2013).

Most longitudinal studies to date are of relatively short duration (i.e., less than 2 years) and focus on a narrow developmental period such as childhood or adolescence (McDougall and Vaillancourt, 2015). Nevertheless, there are several recently published studies examining the long-term adult outcomes of childhood bullying. These studies indicate that being bullied does affect future mental health functioning, as reviewed in the following paragraphs.

---

[5] Peer victimization was measured using peer, self-, and teacher reports, including peer nominations, a four-item self-report victimization scale, and a six-item teacher report victimization scale (Kochel et al., 2012).

Most long-term studies of childhood bullying have focused on links to internalizing problems in adulthood, demonstrating robust long-standing effects (Gibb et al., 2011; Olweus, 1993b; Sourander et al., 2007; Stapinski et al., 2014). For example, Bowes and colleagues (2015) examined depression in a large sample of participants who reported being the target of bullying at age 13 and found higher rates of depression at age 18 compared to peers who had not been bullied. Specifically, they reported that 14.8 percent of participants who reported being frequently bullied in childhood at age 13 were clinically depressed at age 18 ($OR = 2.96$, 95% CI [2.21, 3.97]) and that the population attributable fraction was 29.2 percent, suggesting that close to a third of the variance in depression could be explained by being bullied in childhood (Bowes et al., 2015).

In another longitudinal study using two large population-based cohorts from the United Kingdom (the ALSPAC Cohort) and the United States (the GSMS Cohort), Lereya and colleagues (2015) reported that the effects of childhood bullying on adult mental health were stronger in magnitude than the effects of being maltreated by a caregiver in childhood. Being bullied only (and not maltreated) placed individuals at higher risk for mental health difficulties than being maltreated only (and not bullied) ($OR = 1.6$, 95% CI [1.1, 2.2] for ALSPAC cohort; $OR = 3.8$, 95% CI [1.8, 7.9] for GSMS cohort). Children who were bullied were more likely than maltreated children to be anxious ($OR = 4.9$, 95% CI [2.0, 12.0] for GSMS cohort), depressed ($OR = 1.7$, 95% CI [1.1, 2.7] for ALSPAC cohort), and to engage in self-harming behavior ($OR = 1.7$, 95% CI [1.1-2.6] for ALSPAC cohort) in adulthood (Lereya et al., 2015).

Similarly, Stapinski and colleagues (2014) found that adolescents who experienced frequent peer victimization[6] were two to three times more likely to develop an anxiety disorder 5 years later at age 18 than nonvictimized adolescents ($OR = 2.49$, 95% CI [1.62, 3.85]). The association remained after adjusting for potentially confounding individual and family factors and was not attributable to diagnostic overlap with depression. Frequently victimized adolescents were also more likely to develop multiple internalizing problems in adulthood (Stapinski et al., 2014). After controlling for childhood psychiatric problems or family hardship, Copeland and colleagues (2013) found that individuals who were bullied continued to have higher prevalence of generalized anxiety ($OR = 2.7$, 95% CI [1.1, 6.3]).

These findings suggest that being bullied and internalizing problems such as depression are mutually reinforcing, with the experience of one increasing the risk of the other in a harmful cycle that contributes to the

---

[6]Stapinski et al. (2014) used a modified version of the Bullying and Friendship Interview Schedule to assess self-reported peer victimization. This measure includes items on overt victimization, such as threats, physical violence, and relational victimization.

high stability of being both bullied and experiencing other internalizing problems. These studies also suggest that the long-term consequences of being bullied, which extend into adulthood, can be more severe than being maltreated as a child by a caregiver.

Externalizing Problems

Alcohol and drug abuse and dependence have been associated with being bullied as a child (Radliff et al., 2012). A longitudinal study of adolescents found that those who reported being bullied were more likely to report use of alcohol, cigarettes, and inhalants 12 months later (Tharp-Taylor et al., 2009), compared to those who did not report being bullied. More longitudinal research that tracks children through adulthood is needed to fully understand the link between being bullied and substance abuse (see review by McDougall and Vaillancourt, 2015).

Several studies show links between being bullied and violence or crime, especially for men (Gibb et al., 2011; McGee et al., 2011; Sourander et al., 2007, 2011). A meta-analysis by Reijntjes and colleagues (2011) that included studies with data on 5,825 participants showed that after controlling for externalizing symptoms at baseline, peer victimization—under which they included being the target of teasing, deliberate exclusion, and being the target of physical threats and malicious gossip—was associated over time with exhibiting externalizing problems such as aggression, truancy, and delinquency ($r = .14$, 95% CI [.09, .19]). This research team also found that externalizing problems predicted changes in peer victimization over time ($r = .13$, 95% CI [.04, .21]) and concluded that there is a bidirectional relationship between peer victimization and externalizing problems.

Psychotic Symptoms

Evidence from the broader research on childhood trauma and stress indicates that earlier adverse life experiences, such as child abuse, are associated with the development of psychotic symptoms later in life (Institute of Medicine and National Research Council, 2014b). Until recently, the association between bullying and psychotic symptoms has been understudied (van Dam et al., 2012). Two recent meta-analyses support the association between bullying and the development of psychotic symptoms later in life (Cunningham et al., 2015; van Dam et al., 2012). van Dam and colleagues (2012) conducted a meta-analysis of 14 studies to assess whether being bullied in childhood is related to the development of psychotic (either clinical or nonclinical) symptoms. (Nonclinical psychotic symptoms[7] place individuals at risk for the development of psychotic disorders (Cougnard et al., 2007).) Results from the analyses of studies that examined the association between bullying and nonclinical symptoms (six studies) were more definitive (adjusted $OR = 2.3$; 95% CI [1.5, 3.4]), with stronger associations when there was an increased frequency, severity, and persistence of bullying (Cougnard et al., 2007). Although some research has found this association, a recent longitudinal study from New Zealand found that the link between bullying and the development of psychosis later in life is likely not causal but instead reflects the fact that individuals who display disordered behaviors across childhood and adolescences are more likely to become bullying targets (Boden et al., 2016) An analysis of studies that examined the association between bullying and psychosis in clinical samples was inconclusive (van Dam et al., 2012).

A recent meta-analysis conducted by Cunningham and colleagues (2015) examined ten European prospective studies, four from the Avon Longitudinal Study of Parents and Children. This analysis found that individuals who were bullied were more than twice as likely to develop later psychotic symptoms, compared to those who were not bullied ($OR = 2.1$, 95% CI [1.1, 4.0]). These results were consistent in all but one of the studies included in the meta-analysis. More longitudinal research is needed to more fully understand the mechanisms through which trauma such as bullying may lead to the development of psychotic symptoms (Cunningham et al., 2015; van Dam et al., 2012). Importantly, this research will need to be prospective and examine the development of bullying *and* psychotic symptoms in order to truly identify the temporal priority. The inclusion criteria for the Cunningham and colleagues (2015) meta-analysis included that the study had to be prospective and had to include a measure of psychosis and that bullying needed to be reported before the age of 18. Although the authors stated that "bullying appears to cause later development of psychosis," such a conclusion requires that mental health functioning be assessed early and over time, as it is possible that premorbid characteristics may make individuals targets for poor peer treatment (see Kochel et al., 2012; Vaillancourt et al., 2013b, regarding depression leading to peer victimization).

Academic Performance Consequences

A growing literature has documented that targets of bullying suffer diminished academic achievement whether measured by grades or standard-

---

[7]Nonclinical psychotic symptoms are symptoms that do not meet the clinical definition for those psychotic disorders associated with such symptoms.

ized test scores (Espelage et al., 2013; Nakamoto and Schwartz, 2010). Cross-sectional research indicates that children who are bullied are at increased risk for poor academic achievement (Beran, 2009; Beran and Lupart, 2009; Beran et al., 2008; Glew et al., 2005; Neary and Joseph, 1994; see also meta-analysis by Nakamoto and Schwartz, 2010) and increased absenteeism (Juvonen et al., 2000; Kochenderfer and Ladd, 1996; Vaillancourt et al., 2013b).

The negative relation between being bullied and academic achievement is evident as early as kindergarten (Kochenderfer and Ladd, 1996) and continues into high school (Espinoza et al., 2013; Glew et al., 2008). In a 2-week daily diary study with ninth and tenth grade Latino students, Espinoza and colleagues (2013) reported that on days when adolescents' reports of being bullied were greater than what was typical for them, they also reported more academic challenges such as doing poorly on a quiz, test, or homework and felt like less of a good student. Thus, even episodic encounters of being bullied can interfere with a student's ability to concentrate on any given day. In a cross-sectional study of more than 5,000 students in grades 7, 9, and 11, Glew and colleagues (2008) found that for every 1-point increase in grade point average (GPA), the odds of being a child who was bullied (versus a bystander) decreased by 10 percent. However, due to the cross-sectional nature of this study, this association does not establish whether lower academic achievement among children who were bullied was a consequence of having been bullied.

Several short-term (one academic year) longitudinal studies indicate that being bullied predicts academic problems rather than academic problems predicting being a target of bullying (Kochenderfer and Ladd, 1996; Schwartz et al., 2005). Given the impairments in brain architecture associated with self-regulation and memory in animal models and the currently limited imaging data in human subjects, this is a reasonable inference, although reverse causation is possible. For instance, early life abuse and neglect impair these same abilities, lower self-esteem, and may make an individual more likely to be a target of bullying. In one of the few longitudinal studies to extend beyond one year, Juvonen and colleagues (2011) examined the relation between victimization[8] and academic achievement across the three years of middle school. Academic adjustment was measured by both year-end grades and teacher reports of engagement. These authors found that more self-reported victimization was related to lower school achievement from sixth to eighth grade. For every 1-unit increase in victimization (on a 1-4 scale), GPA declined by 0.3 points.

---

[8] Peer victimization was measured using a modified six-item version of the Peer Victimization Scale, which asks students to select a statement that is most like them. Higher scores indicated higher levels of peer victimization (Juvonen et al., 2011).

Other short-term longitudinal studies found similar results. For example, Nansel and colleagues (2003) found that being bullied in a given year (grade 6 or 7) predicted poor academic outcomes the following year, after controlling for prior school adjustment and if they were previously targets of bullying or not. Similarly, Schwartz and colleagues (2005) reported a negative association for third and fourth grade children between victimization[9] and achievement 1 year later. In addition, Baly and colleagues (2014) found that the cumulative impact of being bullied over 3 years from sixth grade to eighth grade had a negative impact on GPA and standardized test scores.

However, other studies have not found such associations. For instance, Kochenderfer and Ladd (1996) found no relation between being bullied and subsequent academic achievement in their study of students assessed in the fall and spring of kindergarten, nor did Rueger and Jenkins (2014) in their study of seventh and eighth graders assessed in the fall and spring of one academic year. Feldman and colleagues (2014) also reported no association between being a target of bullying and academic achievement in their 5-year longitudinal study of youth ages 11-14. Poor academic performance can also be a predictor of peer victimization (Vaillancourt et al., 2013b). The authors found that poor writing performance in third grade predicted increased bullying behavior in fifth grade that was stable until the end of eighth grade.

The longitudinal associations between peer victimization and school attendance are also equivocal, with some showing positive associations (Baly et al., 2014; Buhs et al., 2006; Gastic, 2008; Kochenderfer and Ladd, 1996; Smith et al., 2004) and others not finding a statistically significant association (Forero et al., 1999; Glew et al., 2008; Rueger et al., 2011; Vaillancourt et al., 2013b).[10]

In summary, there have been a number of cross-sectional and longitudinal studies that have provided support for a relation between being bullied and increased risk for poor academic achievement. However, given the inconsistent results found with longitudinal studies, more research is warranted in this area to more fully ascertain the relation between being bullied and academic achievement over time.

---

[9] Peer victimization was measured using a 16-item peer nomination interview and a teacher-completed Social Behavior Rating Scale (Schwartz et al., 2005).

[10] Peer victimization is used here to include the broader category of bullying, peer victimization, and bullying behavior.

CONSEQUENCES FOR INDIVIDUALS WHO BULLY

There is evidence that supports a finding that individuals who bully others have contradictory attributes (Institute of Medicine and National Research Council, 2014a; Vaillancourt et al., 2010b). Research suggests that there are children and adolescents who bully others because they have some form of maladjustment (Olweus, 1993a) or, as mentioned in Chapter 3, are motivated by establishing their status in a social network (Faris and Ennett, 2012; Rodkin et al., 2015; Sijtsema et al., 2009; Vaillancourt et al., 2003). Consequently, the relation between bullying, being bullied, acceptance, and rejection is complex (Veenstra et al., 2010). This complexity is also linked to a stereotype held by the general public about individuals who bully. This stereotype casts children and youth who bully others as being high on psychopathology, low on social skills, and possessing few assets and competencies that the peer group values (Vaillancourt et al., 2010b). Although some occurrence of this "stereotypical bully" or "classic bully" is supported by research (Kumpulainen et al., 2001; Olweus, 1993a; Sourander et al., 2007), when researchers consider social status in relation to perpetration of bullying behavior, a different profile emerges. These studies suggest that most children and youth who bully others wield considerable power within their peer network and that high-status perpetrators tend to be perceived by peers as being popular, socially skilled, and leaders (de Bruyn et al., 2010; Dijkstra et al., 2008; Peeters et al., 2010; Thunfors and Cornell, 2008; Vaillancourt et al., 2003). High-status bullies have also been found to rank high on assets and competencies that the peer group values such as being attractive or being good athletes (Farmer et al., 2003; Vaillancourt et al., 2003); they have also been found to rank low on psychopathology and to use aggression instrumentally to achieve and maintain hegemony (for reviews, see Rodkin et al., 2015, and Vaillancourt et al., 2010b). Considering these findings of contrasting characteristics of perpetrators of bullying behavior, it makes sense that the research on outcomes of perpetrating is mixed. Unfortunately, most research on the short- and long-term outcomes of perpetrating bullying behavior has not taken into account this heterogeneity when considering the impact to children and youth who have bullied their peers.

Psychosomatic Consequences

Findings from cross-sectional studies that reported data on individuals who bullied others have shown that these individuals are at risk of developing psychosomatic problems (Gini, 2008; Srabstein et al., 2006). Gini and Pozzoli (2009) conducted a meta-analysis to test whether children involved in bullying behavior in any role are at risk for psychosomatic problems. They included studies (n = 11) that examined the association between bullying involvement and psychosomatic complaints in children and adolescents between the ages of 7 and 16. The studies included in the meta-analysis used self-report questionnaires; reports from peers, parents, or teachers; and clinical interviews that resulted in a clinical rating of the subject's behaviors and health problems. The included studies also had enough information to calculate effect sizes. An analysis of six studies that met the selection criteria revealed that children who bully had a higher risk (OR = 1.65, 95% CI [1.34, 2.04]) of exhibiting psychosomatic problems than their uninvolved peers.

This meta-analysis was limited because of its inclusion of cross-sectional and observational studies. Such studies do not allow firm conclusions on cause and effect; hence, the association between bullying perpetration and psychosomatic problems may be difficult to interpret. The methodologies used in the studies make them susceptible to bias and misclassification due to the reluctance of individuals who bully to identify themselves as perpetrators of bullying behavior. Also, the different forms of victimization included in the underlying studies were not reported in this meta-analysis. Additional research is needed to examine the involvement in perpetrating bullying behavior and its short- and long-term psychosomatic consequences.

Psychotic Problems

Using a population-based cohort study, Wolke and colleagues (2014) examined whether bullying perpetration and being a target of bullying in elementary school predicted psychotic experiences[11] in adolescence. The authors assessed 4,720 individuals between the ages of 8 and 11 who were involved in bullying either as perpetrators or targets. At age 18, suspected or definite psychotic experiences were assessed using semistructured interviews. After controlling for the child's gender, intelligence quotient at age 8, and childhood behavioral and emotional problems, the researchers found that both individuals who are bullied (child report at age 10: OR = 2.4, 95% CI [1.6, 3.4]; mother report: OR = 1.6, 95% CI [1.1, 2.3]) and individuals who bullied others (child report at age 10: OR = 4.9, 95% CI [1.3, 17.7]; mother report: OR = 1.2, 95% CI [0.46, 3.1]) had a higher prevalence of psychotic experiences at age 18. The authors concluded that "involvement in any role in bullying may increase the risk of developing psychotic experiences in adolescence" (Wolke et al., 2014, p. 2208).

In summary, several studies have focused on the consequences of bully-

---

[11]Psychotic experiences included hallucinations (visual and auditory), delusions (spied on, persecution, thoughts read, reference, control, grandiosity), and experiences of thought interference (broadcasting, insertion, and withdrawal), and any unspecified delusions.

ing for individuals who are bullied and have also reported more broadly on consequences for perpetrators of aggressive behavior (see Gini and Pozzoli, 2009; Lereya et al., 2015; Reijntjes et al., 2010; Ttofi et al., 2011), but the consequences of bullying involvement for individuals who perpetrate bullying behavior have been rarely studied to date. That is, although there is a rich literature on aggressors and the outcomes of being aggressive, there are few studies examining *bullying* perpetration specifically, taking into account the power imbalance, repetition, and intentionality that differentiates aggression from bullying from other forms of peer aggression. As discussed in Chapter 2, the available research on the prevalence of bullying behavior focuses almost entirely on the children who are bullied. More research, in particular longitudinal research, is needed to understand the short- and long-term physical health, psychosocial, and academic consequences of bullying involvement on the individuals who have a pattern of bullying others, when those individuals are distinguished from children who engage in general aggressive behavior.

CONSEQUENCES FOR INDIVIDUALS WHO BULLY AND ARE ALSO BULLIED

Individuals who bully and are also bullied experience a particular combination of consequences that both children who are only perpetrators and children who are only targets also experience, such as comorbidity of both externalizing and internalizing problems, negative perception of self and others, poor social skills, and rejection by the peer group. However, at the same time this combination of roles in bullying is negatively influenced by the peers with whom they are interacting (Cook et al., 2010). After controlling for adjustment problems existing prior to incidents of bullying others or being bullied, a nationally representative cohort study found that young children who have been both perpetrators and targets of bullying tended to develop more pervasive and severe psychological and behavioral outcomes than individuals who were only bullied (Arseneault et al., 2006).

Adolescents who were involved in cyberbullying as both perpetrators and targets have been found to be most at risk for negative mental and physical health consequences, compared to those who were only perpetrators, those who were only targets, or those who only witnessed bullying (Kowalski and Limber, 2013; Nixon, 2014). For example, the results from a study by Kowalski and Limber (2013) that examined the relation between children's and adolescents' experiences with cyberbullying or traditional bullying and outcomes of psychological health, physical health, and academic performance showed that students who were both perpetrators and targets had the most negative scores on most measures of psychological health, physical health, and academic performance, when compared to those who were only perpetrators, only targets, or only witnesses of bullying incidents.

Physical Health Consequences

Wolke and colleagues (2001) examined the association of direct and relational bullying experience with common health problems and found that students ages 6-9 who bullied others and were also bullied by others had more physical health symptoms than children who were only perpetrators or were not involved in bullying behavior. Hunter and colleagues (2014) evaluated whether adolescents who were involved in bullying experienced sleep difficulties more than adolescents who were not involved. They analyzed surveys that were originally collected on behalf of the UK National Health Service and had been completed by adolescents ages 11-17. Controlling for gender, school-stage, socioeconomic status, ethnicity, and other factors known to be associated with sleep difficulties—alcohol consumption, tea or coffee consumption, and illegal drug use—the authors found that individuals who were both perpetrators and targets in bullying incidents were almost three times more likely ($OR = 2.90$, 95% CI [1.17, 4.92]) to experience these sleep difficulties, compared to uninvolved young people. Additional research is needed to identify the mechanisms underlying short- and long-term physical health outcomes of individuals who bully and are also bullied.

Psychosocial Consequences

There is evidence that individuals who are both perpetrators and targets of bullying have the poorest psychosocial profile among individuals with any involvement in bullying behavior; their psychosocial maladjustment, peer relationships, and health problems are similar to individuals who are only bullied, while their school bonding and substance use is similar to individuals who are only perpetrators (Graham et al., 2006; Nansel et al., 2001, 2004). Individuals who both bully and are also bullied by others experience a greater variety of both internalizing and externalizing symptoms than those who only bully or those who are only bullied (Kim et al., 2006).

Internalizing Problems

Some meta-analyses have examined the association between involvement in bullying and internalizing problems in the school-age population and concluded that that individuals who are both perpetrators and targets of bullying had a significantly higher risk for psychosomatic problems than individuals who were only perpetrators or who were only targets (Gini and Pozzoli, 2009; Reijntjes et al., 2010). In their meta-analysis, Gini and Pozzoli (2009) reviewed studies that examined the association between involvement in bullying and psychosomatic complaints in children and adolescents. Analysis of a subgroup of studies ($N = 5$) that reported analyses for individuals who bully and are also bullied by others showed that these individuals have a significantly higher risk for psychosomatic problems than uninvolved peers ($OR = 2.22$, 95% CI [1.77, 2.77]).

Studies suggest that individuals who bully and who are also bullied by others are especially at risk for suicidal ideation and behavior, due to increased mental health problems (see Holt et al., 2015, and Box 4-1).

Externalizing Problems

Similar to individuals who bully, individuals who bully and are also bullied by others often demonstrate heightened aggression compared with non-involved peers. Compared to these other groups, they are by far the most socially ostracized by their peers, most likely to display conduct problems, and least engaged in school, compared with those who are either just perpetrators or just targets; they also report elevated levels of depression and loneliness (Juvonen et al., 2003). Additional research is needed that examines the unique consequences of those children and youth characterized as "bully-victims" because often they are not separated out from "pure victims" (those who are bullied only) in studies. School shootings are a violent externalizing behavior that has been associated with consequences of bullying behavior in the popular media (see Box 4-2 for additional detail).

Psychotic Symptoms

Several studies have examined the associations between bullying involvement in adolescence and mental health problems in adulthood and have found that individuals who have bullied others and have also been bullied had increased risk of high levels of critical symptoms of psychosis compared to non-involved peers (Gini, 2008; Sigurdson et al., 2015). Research is limited in this area, and the topic warrants further investigation.

CONSEQUENCES OF BULLYING FOR BYSTANDERS

Bullying cannot be viewed as an isolated phenomenon; it is intertwined within the particular peer ecology that emerges, an ecology constituted of social processes that serve particular functions for the individual and for the group (Rodkin, 2004). Bullying frequently occurs in the presence of children and youth who are bystanders or witnesses. Research indicates that

---

BOX 4-1
Suicidality: A Summary of the Available Meta-Analyses

A number of studies have estimated the association between bullying involvement and suicidal ideation and behaviors. (See meta-analyses by Holt et al., 2015 and by van Geel et al., 2014; also see reviews by Kim and Leventhal, 2008, and by Klomek et al., 2010) For example, the review of cross-sectional and longitudinal studies ($n = 31$) by Klomek and colleagues (2010) found that the increased risk (odds ratios) of suicidal ideation and (or) suicide attempts associated with bullying behavior (both perpetration and being a target) in cross-sectional studies ranged from 1.4 to 10.0 and in longitudinal studies ranged from 1.7 to 11.8. The authors noted that from cross-sectional studies, individuals who are bullied have high levels of suicidal ideation and are more likely to attempt suicide compared with uninvolved peers.

The most recent meta-analysis, conducted by Holt and colleagues (2015), used multilevel meta-analytic modeling to review 47 cross-sectional and longitudinal studies[a] (38.3% from the United States, 61.7% in non-U.S. samples). These studies measured being a target of bullying ($n = 46$), bullying perpetration ($n = 25$), and bully-victim status ($n = 11$). Across all studies, Holt and colleagues (2015) found a statistically significant odds ratio for being a target of bullying and suicidal ideation ($OR = 2.34$, 95% CI [2.03, 2.69]). The results of the meta-analysis indicated a significant association between bullying perpetration and suicidal ideation ($OR = 2.12$, 95% CI [1.67, 2.69]). The association with suicidal ideation was stronger among those who were both perpetrators and targets in bullying incidents ($OR = 3.81$, 95% CI [2.13, 6.80]). These results are consistent with other studies (Kim and Leventhal, 2008; Klomek et al., 2010).

---

bullying can have significant adverse effects on these bystanders (Polanin et al., 2012).

Bystanders have reported feelings of anxiety and insecurity (Rigby and Slee, 1993) which stemmed, in part, from fears of retaliation (Musher-Eizenman et al., 2004) and which often prevented bystanders from seeking help (Unnever and Cornell, 2003). In a study to explore the impact of bullying on the mental health of students who witness it, Rivers and colleagues (2009) surveyed 2,002 students, ages 12-16 and attending 14 schools in the United Kingdom, using a questionnaire that included measures of bullying at school, substance abuse, and mental health risk. They found that witnessing bullying significantly predicted elevated mental health risks even after controlling for the effect of also being a perpetrator or victim (range of = .07 to .15). They also found that being a witness to the bullying predicted elevated levels (= .06) of substance use. Rivers and Noret (2013) found van Geel and colleagues (2014) also conducted a meta-analysis[b] to examine the relationship between peer victimization, cyberbullying, and suicidal ideation or suicide attempts. A total of 34 studies that included participants between the ages 9 and 12 and focused on the relation between peer victimization and suicidal ideation were included in the meta-analysis. They found a significant association between peer victimization and suicidal ideation (OR = 2.23, 95% CI [2.10, 2.37]). They found this association to hold for individuals who were only targets of bullying (OR = 1.75, 95% CI [1.42, 2.14]) and for individuals who were both targets and perpetrators (OR = 2.35, 95% CI [1.75, 3.15]). There was also a significant association between peer victimization and suicide attempts (OR = 2.55, 95% CI [1.95, 3.34]).

These findings taken together support an overarching conclusion that individuals who are involved in bullying, whether as perpetrators, targets, or both, are significantly more likely to contemplate or attempt suicide, compared with children who are not involved in bullying (Klomek et al., 2007). Further, there is not enough evidence to date to conclude that bullying is a causal factor for youth suicides. Focusing solely on bullying as a causal factor would ignore the many other influences that contribute to youth suicides.

[a]Longitudinal studies were included in this meta-analysis, but only if the association between bullying involvement and suicidal ideation/behaviors was captured at the same time point" (Holt et al., 2015, p. e498).
[b]Authors searched for articles containing one or more of the character strings "bully," "tease," "victim," "mobbing," "ragging," or "harassment" in conjunction with the string "suicide". The authors only included studies that were focused on bullying by peers and excluded other kinds of victimization.

that, compared to students who were not involved in bullying, those who observed bullying reported more symptoms of interpersonal sensitivity (e.g., feelings of being hurt or inferior), helplessness, and potential suicide ideation.

In conclusion, there is very limited research available on the consequences of witnessing bullying for those children and youth who are the bystanders. Studies of bystander behavior have traditionally sought to understand their motives for participation in bullying (Salmivalli, 2010), their roles (Lodge and Frydenberg, 2005; Salmivalli et al., 1996), their behavior (either reinforcing the bully or defending the victim) in bullying situations (Salmivalli et al., 2011), and why observers intervene or do not intervene (Thornberg et al., 2012) from a social dynamic perspective, without exploring the emotional and psychological impact of witnessing bullying. More research is needed to understand these consequences.

BOX 4-2
Bullying and School Shootings

School shootings, particularly multiple homicide incidents, have generated great public concern and fostered the widespread impression that schools are no longer safe places for students (Borum et al., 2010). When a school shooting occurs, media coverage and anecdotal reports often point to bullying as a main factor that drives the perpetrators of the incident (the "shooters") to act (Kimmel and Mahler, 2003; Rocque, 2012). It is important to examine the evidence on the role bullying may play in motivating these high-profile incidents.

Several characteristics of the research that has been conducted on school shootings bear mentioning. First, to date, research has not been able to establish a reliable profile or set of risk factors that predicts who will become a school shooter (Langman, 2015; Vossekuil et al., 2002) Second, it is important to keep in mind that multiple-victim school shootings are low base rate events, and thus caution should be used in generalizing findings from these rare events to broad populations of students (Mulvey and Cauffman, 2001). There is also a lack of reliable evidence of school shootings that were successfully prevented or averted (but see Madfis, 2014). Given that school shootings are rare events, most of what is known about them comes from studies that aggregate events over many years. These studies mostly employ qualitative methods, including descriptive post-incident psychological autopsies of the shooters (Langman, 2015), analysis of media accounts (Kimmel and Mahler, 2003), or in-depth interviews of a small subset of surviving shooters (Flannery et al., 2013; Vossekuil et al., 2002).

When examining these cases to assess the role that being a target or perpetrator of bullying may have played, this research has the same definitional challenges characteristic of other studies of bullying. Specifically, in studies of school shooters many terms are used to describe bullying or bullying-related behaviors. These include characterizations of the shooters as tormented, being rejected by peers, victimized, harassed, or bullied or depiction of the incident as being related to the shooters' social isolation, disconnection, or feeling marginalized (O'Toole et al., 2014). Many of these terms and characterizations of the individual or the incident are then referred to as bullying. Few studies or reviews have specifically examined incidents of school shootings related to any formal definition of bullying or bullying-related behavior.

Given the limited number of cases and the reliance on qualitative post-hoc investigations of shootings, the association between mental health issues and how these contribute to the behavior of shooters are not yet fully understood, particularly issues that may be related to bullying behavior (as victim or perpetrator) such as depression, anger, or suicidal intent (Flannery et al., 2013; Langman, 2009; Shultz et al., 2014). Rampage shootings[a] (at schools and in public places) also receive significant media attention, and there may be overlap in the characteristics of these events with targeted school shootings. While school-shooting incidents in higher education settings appear to be increasing in frequency, the most systematic research to date has been done on shootings that occurred in kindergarten through grade 12 (K-12) settings that resulted in multiple homicide victims, so that is the committee's focus here unless otherwise noted.

Finally, it is important to note that not all school shootings are the same, and that there are significantly more shootings involving one victim than multiple-victim incidents. Shootings can occur for a variety of reasons including, but not limited to, gang-related violence, drug activity, suicide, shootings to settle interpersonal disputes, or homicides abated by suicide. The motivation of the shooter can be very different across incidents, and there is not always the opportunity to discover or study these variations of intent (Flannery et al., 2013).

One of the most comprehensive studies of targeted K-12 multiple-victim school shootings was conducted by the U.S. Department of Education and the U.S. Secret Service (Vossekuil et al., 2002). As part of the Safe School Initiative, Vossekuil and colleagues examined 37 separate incidents that occurred over a 25-year period between 1974 and 2000, carried out by 41 adolescent shooters. Similar to studies that have been conducted since then, they examined primary source materials related to the shooting, including investigative reports and school, court, and mental health records. In addition, they conducted individual interviews with 10 surviving shooters, so they were able to delve deeper into the "process of the attack," understood from the perspective of the shooter, from the incident's conceptualization to its execution (Vossekuil et al., 2002).

Related to the issue of bullying, Vossekuil and colleagues (2002, p. 35) concluded that "many attackers (71%; $n = 29$ of 41) felt bullied, persecuted or injured by others prior to the attack." With respect to the implications related to this observation, they further stated that "Bullying was not a factor in every case, and clearly not every child who is bullied in school will pose a risk for targeted violence in school. Nevertheless, in a number of the incidents of targeted school violence studied, attackers described being bullied in terms that suggested that these experiences approached torment."

These findings about the potential role of bullying in school shootings are generally consistent with examinations of shootings conducted at that time by the Federal Bureau of Investigation (O'Toole, 2000) and with an in-depth review of incidents of lethal school violence by the National Research Council and Institute of Medicine (2003). In a case study of 15 school shootings, Leary and colleagues (2003) found that social rejection, including bullying, was a key factor in 13 of the incidents. In an analysis of secondary media reports on 28 random school shootings from 1982 to 2001, Kimmel and Mahler (2003) concluded that most of the shooters, who were almost all white males, acted violently as a retaliatory response to being bullied and teased, particularly with respect to threats made about their manhood. These qualitative analyses of cases and media accounts suggest prior experiences of being the target of bullying have been an important factor in school shootings, but a clear causal link between being the target of bullying and becoming a school shooter has not yet been established. Other factors such as experiencing a prior traumatic event, family factors, mental health, hyper-masculinity, or school climate have been postulated as additional contributors to school shooting incidents (Borum et al., 2010; Flannery et al., 2013; Klein, 2012; Langman, 2009, 2015; O'Toole et al., 2014; Reuter-Rice, 2008; Vossekuil et al., 2002). Further, risk of school shooting is not just a result of having been bullied; in some cases school shooters were identified as the perpetrators of bullying (Langman, 2009; Newman et al., 2004).

continued

BOX 4-2 Continued

It is important to note that while the study for the Safe School Initiative is one of the most comprehensive to date on K-12 school shooters, its findings are still based on a small sample of incidents. There have been many more school shootings since 2000, including an increase in the number of incidents on college campuses (Flannery et al., 2013).

More recent detailed descriptions, reviews, and analyses of school shooting incidents have resulted in less definitive conclusions about the potential role of bullying (Flannery et al., 2013; Langman, 2015). For example, Langman (2015) conducted a detailed case study review of 48 school shooters who were of high school, college, or adult age (and a few cases that occurred outside the United States) and concluded that "most school shooters were not victims of bullying" (p. 195). He further explained, "Despite the widespread belief that school shooters are virtually always victims of bullying, this does not appear to be true. The connection between bullying and school shootings is, however, difficult to untangle" (p. 195). Langman concluded, "The fact that some shooters were harassed does not account for their attacks. After all, the vast majority of students who are harassed never commit murder. This does not mean that bullying was never a factor in school shootings. For some shooters, it was one more problem on top of many others. It was never, however, the only problem. *There were always other issues*" (Langman, 2015, p. 19 [emphasis added]).

In summary, the evidence to date is based mostly on intensive post-incident psychological autopsies and qualitative case study analyses of investigative reports in the popular media and limited interviews with surviving shooters. Most investigations have concluded that prior bullying, with an emphasis on the shooter being the target of bullying, may play a role in many school shootings but not all. It is a factor, and perhaps an important one, but it does not appear to be the main factor influencing a decision to carry out these violent acts. Further, there is not enough evidence to date (qualitative or quantitative) to conclude that bullying is a causal factor for multiple-homicide targeted school shootings nor is there clear evidence on how bullying or related mental health and behavior issues contribute to school shootings. While there is clear consensus that no reliable profile or set of risk factors exists for predicting who will become a school shooter, there is as yet no such consensus on the role that prior bullying experience plays in these incidents. While being the target of bullying may play an important contributing role in the motivation for many school shooters, focusing solely on bullying as a causal factor would ignore the many other influences that contribute to school shootings. Effective preventive intervention of school shootings is much more likely to occur via the use of a comprehensive threat assessment approach, rather than a focus on any singular risk factor (Borum et al., 2010; Cornell, 2006; Fein et al., 2002; Flannery et al., 2013). This area of research requires additional empirical and systematic study of the role of bullying in all types of school shootings—including single-victim incidents, those that result in injury but not death, and shootings that are successfully averted.

---

[a]Researchers use the terms "rampage" or "spree" shootings to identify cases with multiple victims, either unknown or known to the assailant.

MULTIPLE EXPOSURES TO VIOLENCE[12]

One subpopulation of school-aged youth that may be at increased risk for detrimental short- and long-term outcomes associated with bullying victimization is poly-victims. Finkelhor and colleagues (2007) coined the terms "poly-victim" and "poly-victimization" to represent a subset of youth who experience multiple victimizations of different kinds—such as exposure to (1) violent and property crimes (e.g., assault, sexual assault, theft, burglary), (2) child welfare violations (child abuse, family abduction), (3) the violence of warfare and civil disturbances, and (4) being targets of bullying behavior—and who manifest high levels of traumatic symptomatology. The identification of a poly-victim is grounded not only in the frequency of the victimization but also in victimization across multiple contexts and perpetrators (Finkelhor et al., 2007, 2009).

Ford and colleagues (2010) determined that poly-victims were more likely to meet criteria for psychiatric disorder, including being two times more likely to report depressive symptoms, three times more likely to report posttraumatic stress disorder, up to five times more likely to use alcohol or drugs, and up to eight times more likely to have comorbid disorders, compared to youth that did not meet criteria for poly-victimization. Poly-victims often engaged in delinquent behavior, associated with deviant peers (Ford et al., 2010), and were entrenched within the juvenile justice system (Ford et al., 2013). Students who were poly-victims in the juvenile justice system reported higher levels of traumatic symptomatology (Finkelhor et al., 2005). However, it is currently unclear whether being bullied plays a major or minor role in poly-victimization.

MECHANISMS FOR THE PSYCHOLOGICAL
EFFECTS OF BULLYING

In the following sections, the committee describes five potential mechanisms for the psychological effects of bullying behavior for both the children who are bullied and children who bully. These include self-blame, social cognition, emotional dysregulation, genetic predisposition to mental health outcomes and bullying, and telomere erosion.[13]

---

[12] This section is adapted from Rose (2015, pp. 18-21).

[13] A telomere is the "segment at the end of each chromosome arm which consists of a series of repeated DNA sequences that regulate chromosomal replication at each cell division." See http://ghr.nlm.nih.gov/glossary=telomere [December 2015]. Telomeres are associated with "chromosomal stability" and the regulation of "cells' cellular replicative lifespan" (Kiecolt-Glaser et al., 2011, p. 16).

Self-Blame

One important mechanism for the psychological effects of bullying is how the targets of bullying construe the reason for their plight (Graham, 2006). For example, a history of bullying and the perception of being singled out as a target might lead an individual to ask "Why *me*?" In the absence of disconfirming evidence, some might come to blame themselves for their peer relationship problems. Self-blame and accompanying negative affect can then lead to many negative outcomes, including low self-esteem, anxiety, and depression (Graham and Juvonen, 1998).

The adult rape literature (another form of victimization) highlights a correlation between experiencing rape and self-attributions that imply personal deservingness, labeled characterological self-blame, since they may lead to the person thinking of themselves as chronic victims (Janoff-Bulman, 1979). From an attributional perspective, characterological self-blame is internal and therefore reflects on the self; it is stable and therefore leads to an expectation that harassment will be chronic; and it is uncontrollable, suggesting an inability to prevent future harassment. Attributing negative outcomes to internal, stable, and uncontrollable causes leads individuals to feel both hopeless and helpless (Weiner, 1986). In contrast, behavioral self-blame (e.g., "I was in the wrong place at the wrong time") implies a cause that is both unstable (the harassment is not expected to occur again) and controllable (there are responses in one's repertoire to prevent future harassment). Several researchers in the adult literature have documented that individuals who make characterological self-blaming attributions for negative outcomes cope more poorly, feel worse about themselves, and are more depressed than individuals who make attributions to their behavior (see Anderson et al., 1994). Research with early adolescents also revealed that characterological self-blame for academic and social failure resulted in heightened depression (Cole et al., 1996; Tilghman-Osborne et al., 2008).

In the first attribution study focused specifically on bullying, Graham and Juvonen (1998) documented that sixth grade students with reputations as targets made more characterological self-blaming attributions for harassment than behavioral self-blaming attributions. Characterological self-blame, in turn, partly mediated the relationship between victim status and psychological maladjustment as measured by depression and social anxiety. Many studies since then have documented the relation between being targets of bullying, characterological self-blame, and maladjustment (Graham et al., 2006, 2009; Perren et al., 2012; Prinstein et al., 2005). Furthermore, bullied youth who endorsed characterological self-blame were likely to develop negative expectations about the future, which may also increase risk for continued bullying. For example, Schacter and colleagues (2014) reported that characterological self-blame endorsed in the fall of sixth grade predicted increases in reports of being bullied in the spring of sixth grade. Self-blame can then instigate psychological distress over time as well as increases in experiences of being bullied.

Such findings have implications for interventions targeted at bullied youth. The goal would be to change targets' maladaptive thoughts about the causes of their plight. For example, one could seek more adaptive attributions that could replace characterological self-blame. In some cases, change efforts might target behavioral explanations for being bullied (e.g., "I was in the wrong place at the wrong time"). In such cases, the goal would be to help targeted youth recognize that they have responses in their repertoire to prevent future encounters with harassing peers—that is, the cause is unstable and controllable (Graham and Bellmore, 2007). External attributions also can be adaptive because they protect self-esteem (Weiner, 1986). Knowing that others are also victims or that there are some aggressive youth who randomly single out unsuspecting targets can help lessen the tendency to self-blame (Graham and Bellmore, 2007; Nishina and Juvonen, 2005). This approach of altering dysfunctional thoughts about oneself to produce changes in affect and behavior has produced a rich empirical literature on attribution therapy in educational and clinical settings (see Wilson et al., 2002). The guiding assumption of that research can be applied to alleviating the plight of targets of bullying.

Social Cognition

The most commonly cited models of social cognitive processes often connect back to work by Bandura (1973), as well as to more recent conceptualizations by Crick and Dodge (1994). These models have been applied to understanding aggressive behavior, but there has been less research applying these models to bullying behavior specifically. Related research by Anderson and Bushman (2002) on their general aggression model allows for a more focused understanding of the thoughts, feelings, and behaviors that contribute to the development of the negative outcome. This framework characterizes the inputs, the routes, the proximal processes, and the outcomes associated with aggressive behavior and either being targeted by or perpetrating bullying behavior (Kowalski and Limber, 2013; Vannucci et al., 2012). Although these theories pertain to aggressive behavior more broadly, given that bullying is considered by most researchers to be a specific form of aggressive behavior, these broader theories may also improve understanding of the etiology and development of bullying. For example, research on hostile attribution bias suggests that aggressive youth are particularly sensitive to ambiguous and potentially hostile peer behaviors. Similar hypersensitivity to threat is also likely present in youth who bully.

Another particular element of social cognitive processes that has been linked with aggressive behavior is normative beliefs about aggressive retaliation (Crick and Dodge, 1994; Huesmann and Guerra, 1997). Such beliefs include the belief that aggressive retaliation is normative, acceptable, or justified, given the context of provocation. There has been exploration of links between these beliefs and both reactive and proactive aggression. However, there has been relatively limited research specifically focused on bullying behavior. Yet, the available literature suggests that although it may seem as if targets of bullying would most likely endorse such attitudes, it is the perpetrators of bullying, including those who are involved in bullying as both a perpetrator and a target, who are mostly likely to support aggressive retaliation (Bradshaw et al., 2009, 2013; O'Brennan et al., 2009).

Emotion Dysregulation

Attempts to identify mechanisms linking bullying to adverse outcomes have largely focused on social-cognitive processes (Dodge et al., 1990) as described above. More recently, researchers have begun to examine emotion dysregulation as an additional mechanism that explains associations between peer victimization and adverse outcomes. Emotion regulation refers to the strategies that people use to "increase, maintain, or decrease one or more components of an emotional response" (Gross, 2001, p. 215). One's choices among such strategies have implications not only for how robustly one responds to a stressor but also for how quickly one can recover from a stressful experience. Several studies have shown that emotion regulation difficulties—also called *emotion dysregulation*—increase youths' risk of exposure to peer victimization (Hanish et al., 2004[14]) and to bullying (Mahady Wilton et al., 2000). However, it is important to understand whether peer victimization itself causes emotion regulation difficulties, which in turn predict the adverse outcomes that result from peer victimization (e.g., depression, aggressive behaviors).

Several lines of evidence support the hypothesis that emotion dysregulation may account for the relationship between peer victimization and adverse outcomes among adolescents. First, constructs that are related to peer victimization—including social exclusion (Baumeister et al., 2005) and stigma (Inzlicht et al., 2006)—impair self-regulation. Second, chronic stress during childhood and adolescence leads to deficits in emotion regulation (Repetti et al., 2002). Bullying has been conceptualized as a chronic stressor for children who are the perpetrators and the targets (Swearer and Hymel, 2015), which in turn may disrupt emotion regulation processes. Third, laboratory-based studies have indicated that peer victimization is associated

---

[14]Peer victimization was measured by a teacher-reported seven-item measure with items measuring broader peer victimization (Hanish et al., 2004).

with emotion dysregulation (e.g., self-directed negative emotion, emotional arousal and reactivity) in the context of a novel peer interaction (Rudolph et al., 2009) and in a contrived play-group procedure (Schwartz et al., 1993). Over time, the effort required to manage the increased arousal and negative affect associated with peer victimization[15] may eventually diminish individuals' coping resources and therefore their ability to understand and adaptively manage their emotions, leaving them more vulnerable to adverse outcomes (McLaughlin et al., 2009).

Several studies have provided empirical support for emotion dysregulation as a mediator of the association between peer victimization and adverse outcomes among adolescents. In one of the first longitudinal demonstrations of mediation, McLaughlin and colleagues (2009), using data from a large, prospective study of adolescents (ages 11-14), showed that peer victimization at baseline predicted increases in emotion dysregulation four months later, controlling for initial levels of emotion dysregulation. In turn, emotion dysregulation predicted subsequent psychological distress (depressive and anxious symptoms), thereby mediating the prospective relationship between peer victimization (relational and reputational forms) and internalizing symptoms (McLaughlin et al., 2009). Subsequent research from this same sample of adolescents showed that emotion dysregulation also mediated the prospective relationship between peer victimization and subsequent aggressive behavior (Herts et al., 2012).

There is also emerging evidence that emotion regulation mediates relationships between bullying and adverse outcomes. In one example of this work, Cosma et al. (2012) examined associations between bullying and several emotion regulation strategies, including rumination, catastrophizing, and other-blaming, in a sample of adolescents. Although bullying was predictive for each of these emotion regulation strategies, only one (catastrophizing) mediated the relationship between being a target of bullying and subsequent emotional problems. Thus, while more research is needed, existing evidence suggests that both social-cognitive and emotion regulation processes may be important targets for preventive interventions among youths exposed to peer victimization and bullying.

Genetic Predisposition to Mental Health Outcomes and Bullying

Longitudinal research suggests that being the victim or perpetrator of bullying does not lead to the same pathological or nonpathological outcomes in every person (McDougall and Vaillancourt, 2015). There are many factors that contribute to how a person responds to the experience

---

[15]Peer victimization was measured using the Revised Peer Experiences Questionnaire, which assesses overt, relational, and reputational victimization by peers (McLaughlin et al., 2009).

of being victimized, with very strong links already established with life experiences, as reviewed above. Most studies examining heterogeneity in outcomes associated with bullying have focused on environmental characteristics, such as individual, family, and school-level features to explain why some individuals fare better or worse when involved with bullying (Vaillancourt et al., in press). For example, the moderating role of the family has been examined with results indicating that bullied children and youth with better home environments tend to fare better than those living with more complicated families (Flouri and Buchanan, 2003; also see Chapter 3 of this report). Far fewer studies have examined the role of potential genetic influences as mediators between life experiences such as bullying and mental health outcomes. Identifying potential genetic influences is critical for improving understanding of the rich behavioral and epidemiological data already gathered. At the present time, evidence-based understanding of physiology and neuroscience is very limited, and insufficient data have been gathered to produce informed hypothesis testing.

There is a growing body of literature examining the relative role of genes' interaction with the environment in relation to experiences with trauma. However, there are fewer studies exploring potential relations between genes and being the target or perpetrator of bullying. At first glance these studies may appear to suggest that a person's involvement with bullying is predetermined based on his/her genetic profile. Yet, it is important to bear in mind that heritable factors are also associated with specific environments—meaning it is difficult to separate genetic effects from environmental effects. This is a phenomenon termed *gene-environment correlations*, abbreviated as rGE (Brendgen, 2012; Plomin et al., 1977; Scarr and McCartney, 1983). For example, aggression, which is highly heritable (Niv et al., 2013), can be linked to the selection of environments in different ways (for review, see Brendgen, 2012). Aggressive children may choose friends who are similar in their genetically influenced behavioral characteristic of being aggressive, and this type of selection influences the characteristics of their peer group (Brendgen, 2012, p. 420). This is an example of selective rGE. A child's genetically influenced characteristic to be aggressive can also produce a negative reaction from others, such as being disliked. This environmental variable of being rejected now "becomes correlated with the aggressive genotype" (Brendgen, 2012, p. 421). This is an example of evocative rGE. Another way that a person's genetic predisposition can be correlated with their environment is through a more passive process, called a passive rGE (Brendgen, 2012). For example, aggressive parents may be more likely to live in high-crime neighborhoods, which influence the probability that their child will be associating with antisocial peers. These important rGE processes and confounds of interaction notwithstanding, it is worth mentioning that the research on the genetics of being a target or perpetrator of bullying is still in its infancy, and caution is needed when evaluating the results, as replication is much needed in this area. Before considering these studies, the committee first reviews the concept of how genetic differences influence behavior because it is important to clarify new concepts in this burgeoning area of science (see Box 4-3).

With this backdrop in mind, the committee focused on twin studies of familial (family environment) versus genetic influence, gene by environment interaction, and a newer area of inquiry, epigenetics: the study of cellular

---

BOX 4-3
How Do Genes Influence Behavior?

Genes control development to determine our basic physical characteristics, such as eye color, which has a varied phenotypic expression (i.e., there are many different eye colors), and characteristics determined by multiple genes, in a far more complicated manner than is often assumed. At birth, the brain looks very similar to an adult brain in gross morphology, but it is smaller and careful analysis of details of the brain, particularly its neural circuitry, shows that it is far from mature. Brain development continues through adolescence into emerging adulthood (Giedd et al., 1999; Spear, 2010, Ch. 3), and genes continue to play an important role in determining its development. This very prolonged period of brain development means that the type of environment one lives in can interact with genetic factors to produce a brain that is better suited to living in certain conditions, such as the cold climate of Alaska, the heat of Florida, or an arid desert. This interaction between brain development and the environment has enabled humans to expand their geographic territory.

Similarly, cultural and family experiences interact with a developing child's genome to produce individual differences in temperament, personality, cognition, and emotion, but these experiences also prepare the individual for that particular environment. For example, growing up in a harsh environment of reduced economic or nutritional resources or in a hostile environment due to war or living in an unsafe neighborhood can influence brain development so that an individual is better prepared, or adapted to be better prepared, to cope with their environment throughout the life span (Kalmakis and Chandler, 2015; Perry and Sullivan, 2014; Sanchez and Pollak, 2009). This research points to the importance of social relationships and the ability of strong nurturing caregivers and a strong, dependable support system in buffering the stress response and preventing stress from becoming "toxic stress" (Shonkoff et al., 2009). Throughout life, but particularly during development, experiences within intimate social relationships have a very profound effect on individuals' brain development (Perry and Sullivan, 2014; Shonkoff et al., 2009). Trauma experienced without being buffered by social support (which reduces stress responses) leaves children particularly vulnerable to the effects of toxic stress (Hostinar et al., 2014; Yang and McLoyd, 2015).

and physiological phenotypic trait variations caused by external or environmental factors.

Twin Studies

Twin studies are routinely used to examine the relative influence of genetics and the environment on a particular phenomenon, such as being the target or perpetrator of bullying. In these studies, the causes of phenotypic variation (for example the variation in being a target or perpetrator of bullying) is separated into three components: (1) the additive genetic component or the heritable factor; (2) the shared environment component or the aspect of the environment twins share such as poor family functioning; and (3) the nonshared environment component or the aspect of the environment that is unique to each twin, such as the classroom if twins are in different classes.

Studies that decompose the unique effects of the environment and genetics on bullying behavior are best illustrated by two examples. Using data from the Environmental Risk (E-Risk) Longitudinal Twin Study, a study of high-risk[16] British twins reared together and apart, Ball and colleagues (2008) examined children's involvement in bullying and the genetic versus environmental contributions associated with their involvement. The twins in this study were assessed at ages 7 and 10 on their experiences with bullying, using teacher and parent reports. Results indicated that 73 percent of the variation in being the target of bullying and 61 percent of the variation in bullying perpetration were accounted for by genetic factors. In another study of Canadian twins reared together and assessed at age 7, using teacher and peer reports to assess peer victimization and aggression, Brendgen and colleagues (2008) found that for girls, 60 percent of the variation in aggression was accounted for by genetic factors and for boys, the variation estimate was 66 percent. For peer victimization, the Canadian study found that genetics did not play a role in the prediction of being targeted by peers. In fact, almost all of the variance was accounted for by environmental factors—29 percent of the variance in peer victimization was from the shared environment and 71 percent from the nonshared environment. The authors concluded that "genetic modeling showed that peer victimization is an environmentally driven variable that is unrelated to children's genetic disposition" (Brendgen et al., 2008, p. 455).

These two studies address the role genetics might play in the expression of aggressive behavior but conflict on the heritability of being a target of bullying. Most studies examining the heritability of externalizing problems,

---

[16]High risk was defined as a mother who had her first child at age 20 or younger (Moffitt, 2002).

which includes studies on perpetrating aggression and bullying, report high heritability estimates. In fact, a recent meta-analysis found that aggression and rule-breaking were highly influenced by genetics, estimating the heritability rate at 41 percent (Niv et al., 2013). Moreover, studies have found that the heritability estimates tend to be higher for more serious forms of antisocial behavior. For example, the heritability of psychopathy in 7-year-old British twin children reared together and apart and studied in the Twins Early Development Study was reported to be 81 percent (Viding et al., 2005). However, estimates of the heritability of peer victimization vary across studies, as illustrated by the above results from Ball and colleagues (2008) contrasted with those from Brendgen and colleagues (2008), and even within studies (Brendgen et al., 2008, 2013).

Brendgen and colleagues have since revised their assessment about the role genetics play in the prediction of being the target of bullying. In a more recent study, following the same children highlighted in the 2008 paper (Brendgen et al., 2008) across three assessment periods (kindergarten, grade 1, and grade 4), Boivin and colleagues (2013) reported that at each grade, among twins who were reared together and apart, genetic factors accounted for a notable percentage of the variance in children's difficulties with peers. Peer difficulties were assessed as a latent factor derived from self-, teacher-, and peer-reports of peer victimization[17] and peer rejection. Specifically, in kindergarten and grade 1, 73 percent of the variance was accounted by genetic factors and in grade 4, genetic factors account for 94 percent of the variance in peer rejection and victimization.

There are several reasons for discrepancies between and within studies of the genetic contribution to bullying behavior. One reason is related to how peer victimization is assessed. Parent-, teacher-, peer-, and self-reports of bullying victimization have been shown to vary considerably across reporters (Ostrov and Kamper, 2015; Patton et al., 2015; Shakoor et al., 2011); thus, the method used to assess involvement with bullying may lead to different results. Another reason for the differences may be related to development. The influence of the environment is expected to change as children age. Young children are particularly sensitive to family influences, while the influence of peers tends to matter more during adolescence (Harris, 1995). Moreover, the type of environment a person is exposed to (i.e., harsh or nurturing) interacts with genes to produce a brain that is tailored to deal with the particular demands of that environment.

Taken together, the genetic studies reviewed suggest that aggression, which characterizes the perpetrator role in bullying (Vaillancourt et al.,

---

[17]Peer victimization was assessed through teacher, peer, and self-ratings. Children were asked to circle photographs of two classmates who get called names by other children and who are often pushed or hit by other children.

2008), might have heritable components, but the findings on being the target of bullying or other aggressive behavior are mixed. Thus, the role of genetic influences on both perpetrating and being a target of bullying requires more empirical attention before conclusions can be drawn.

Gene-by-Environment Interactions

Researchers also question whether specific genotypic markers of vulnerability (e.g., candidate genes) influence developmental outcomes in the face of adversity (i.e., environment). Importantly, there is some indication that genetics influences the mental health issues related to bullying highlighted above, such as depression and heightened aggression. For example, in gene-environment studies, candidate genes have been examined as moderators of the exposure to a toxic stressor such as child maltreatment and health outcomes such as depression. When the body experiences repeated bouts of stress that fail to resolve quickly, the heightened state of vigilance and preparedness depletes it of resources and the stress hormone cortisol begins to produce adverse effects. Specifically, prolonged stress disrupts brain functions and results in compromised decision making, faulty cognitive assessment, compromised learning and memory, and a heightened sense of threat that alters behavior (Lupien et al., 2005; McEwen, 2014). There is evidence that the impact of changes in cortisol (either too high or too low) on learning may contribute, in part, to bullied children's decline in academic performance (Vaillancourt et al., 2011), overeating/metabolic disorder, or emotional dysregulation, but this research is relatively new and needs to be explicitly explored within the context of bullying (McEwen, 2014).

A paradigmatic example of this type of study is one by Caspi and colleagues (2003), in which the moderating role of a functional polymorphism in the promoter region of the serotonin transporter gene 5-HTTLPR was examined in relation to exposure to maltreatment in childhood and depression in adulthood. Results indicated that depression rates were far greater among abused individuals if they had two copies of the short allele.[18] Among individuals with a long allele, depression rates were lower, suggesting that the long allele was protective, while the short allele was a risk factor for depression in the face of adversity. Although the exact role of this serotonin-related gene has been a subject of controversy, a meta-analysis concluded that overall, the results are consistent across studies (Karg et al., 2011). Nevertheless, skepticism and controversy remain regarding studies of gene-environment interactions (Dick et al., 2015; Duncan, 2013; Duncan and Keller, 2011; Duncan et al., 2014). This important debate notwith-

---

[18] An allele is an alternate form of the same gene. Except for the XY chromosomes in males, human chromosomes are paired, so a cell's genome usually has two alleles for each gene.

standing, there is evidence that variations in genotype might moderate the relation between exposure to being bullied and health outcomes. For example, Sugden and colleagues (2010) found that bullied children who carried two short versions of the 5-HTTLPR gene were more likely to develop emotional problems than bullied children who carried the long allele. Importantly, this moderating effect was present even when pre-victimization emotional problems were accounted for statistically. In addition to this study, three other studies have demonstrated the moderating effect of the 5-HTTLPR gene in the bullying-health link (Banny et al., 2013; Benjet et al., 2010; Iyer et al., 2013), with depression being worse for carriers of the short/short genotype (both alleles are the short version) than carriers of the short/long and long/long genotypes.

Although the evidence suggests that genotypes moderate the relation between being a target of bullying and poorer mental health functioning like depression, it is important to acknowledge that this relation is more complex. Indeed, some individuals may be particularly biologically sensitive to negative environmental influences such as being bullied, but this genetic vulnerability can also be linked to better outcomes in the context of a more supportive and enriched environment (see Vaillancourt et al., in press). This phenomenon is termed *differential susceptibility* (Belsky and Pluess, 2009; Boyce and Ellis, 2005). For example, in their study of 5 and 6-year old children, Obradovic and colleagues (2010) found that high stress reactivity as measured using respiratory sinus arrhythmia and salivary cortisol was linked to poorer socioemotional behavior in the context of being in an environment that was high in family adversity. In a context characterized by lower adversity, high stress-reactive children had more adaptive outcomes.

To the committee's knowledge, there are no studies that have examined bullying perpetration in relation to serotonin transporter polymorphisms, although there are studies that have examined this polymorphism in aggressive and non-aggressive children. For example, Beitchman et al. (2006) examined 5-HTTLPR in clinically referred children between the ages of 5 and 15 and found a positive association between the short/short genotype and aggression. In other studies, the short allele has been associated with problems with impulse control that includes the use of aggression (Retz et al., 2004).

The moderating role of different candidate genes has also been examined in relation to exposure to childhood adversity and poorer developmental outcomes (see review by Vaillancourt et al., in press). With respect to bullying, only a few studies have examined gene-environment interactions. In one study by Whelan and colleagues (2014), harsh parenting was associated with increased peer victimization and perpetration, but this effect was not moderated by the Monoamine Oxidase A (MAOA) genotype.[19] In another longitudinal study, Kretschmer and colleagues (2013) found that carriers of the 4-repeat homozygous variant of the dopamine receptor D4 gene were more susceptible to the effects of peer victimization[20] on delinquency later in adolescence than noncarriers of this allele. Finally, in a large sample of post-institutionalized children from 25 countries, VanZomeren-Dohm and colleagues (2015) examined the moderating role of FKBP5 rs1360780[21] in the relation between peer victimization[22] and depression symptoms. In this study, gender was also found to be a moderator. Specifically, girls who had the minor genotype (TT or CT) were more depressed at higher levels of peer victimization, but less depressed at lower level of peer victimization than girls who had CC genotype. For boys, the CC genotype was associated with more symptoms of depression than girls with the same CC genotype who had been bullied.

It is clear that genetics influences how experiences contribute to mental and physical well-being, although the specifics of these gene-environment interactions are complex and not completely understood. Even though genes appear to modulate humans' response to being a target or a perpetrator of bullying behavior, it is still unclear what aspects of these experiences are interacting with genes and which genes are implicated to produce the variability in outcomes. Human genes and environment interact in a very complex manner: what biological events a particular gene influences can change at different stages of development. That gene therefore interacts with the environment in unique ways across the development timeline. These gene-environment interactions can be subtle and are under constant flux (Lake and Chan, 2015). Knowing both the genes involved and the specific environment conditions is critically important to understanding these interactions; a simplistic view of either the genetic or environmental component, especially when considered in isolation from the behavioral literature, is unlikely to be productive.

---

[19] The MAOA genotype has been called the "warrior" gene because of its association with aggression in studies using surveys and observations (McDermott et al., 2009).

[20] Peer victimization was measured using a teacher-report 3-item scale that assessed relational victimization in the classroom (Kretschmer et al., 2013).

[21] The FKBP5 rs1360780 gene is associated with a number of different psychological disorders (Wilker et al., 2014).

[22] VanZomeren-Dohm and colleagues (2015 measured peer victimization using the MacArthur Health and Behavior Questionnaire Parent-Form, version 2.1, in which parents reported on their children's experiences of overt peer victimization.

Epigenetic Consequences

It is clear from the research reviewed here that there are a variety of pathways leading to adaptive and maladaptive endpoints and that these pathways can also vary within the "system" along with other conditions and attributes (McDougall and Vaillancourt, 2015, p. 300), *including a person's genetic susceptibility.* In this section, the committee focuses on studies examining how genetic susceptibility can make certain individuals more sensitive to negative environmental influences.

Although a person's DNA is fixed at conception (i.e., nonmalleable), environment can have a strong effect on how some genes are used at each of the stages of development. One way such changes in gene use and expression can occur is through an *epigenetic* effect, in which environmental events alter the portions of the genome that control when gene replication is turned on or off and what parts of a gene get transcribed (McGowan et al., 2009; Roth, 2014). That is, while an individual's genetic information is critically important, the environment can help to increase or decrease how some genetic information is used by indirectly turning on or off some genes based on input received by somatic cells from the environment. Such epigenetic alterations have been empirically validated in several animal studies. For example, in one line of epigenetic studies, infant rat pups are raised with either low- or high-nurturing mothers or with mothers that treated the pups harshly. The researchers found that the type of maternal care received in infancy had a notable effect on the rats' subsequent ability to deal with stress (McGowan et al., 2011; Roth and Sweatt, 2011; Weaver et al., 2004). The behavioral effects were correlated with changes in DNA methylation.[23] Epigenetic changes associated with gene-environment interactions is a new and exciting research area that provide a direct link between how our genes are read and is thought to enable us to pass our experiences to the next generations. It is helpful to think of genes as books in a library and epigenetics as placing a barrier in front of a book to decrease the chances it is read or providing easy access to the book. Thus far, research has found that certain epigenetic mechanisms are strongly correlated with different neurobehavioral developmental trajectories, including changes in vulnerability and resilience to psychopathology. How epigenetics relates to individual responses to being a target or perpetrator of bullying is not clear, but the research in related areas of behavior highlights an important emerging area for investigation.

Various epigenetic processes appear to interact with many changes in

---

[23]DNA methylation is a heritable epigenetic mark involving the covalent transfer of a methyl group to the C-5 position of the cytosine ring by DNA methyltransferases (a family of enzymes that act on DNA). Cytosine is one of the four bases that occur in varying sequences to form the "code" carried by strands of DNA (Robertson, 2005).

the brain produced by early life experiences, including not only the number and shape of brain cells but also how these cells connect to one another at synapses (Hanson et al., 2015).

Regarding bullying, the committee identified only one study that has examined epigenetic changes. Specifically, Ouellet-Morin and colleagues (2013) found an increase in DNA methylation of the serotonin transporter gene for children who had been bullied by their peers but not in children who had not been bullied. These researchers also found that children with higher serotonin DNA methylation had a blunted cortisol response to stress, which they had previously shown changes as a consequence of poor treatment by peers (Ouellet-Morin et al., 2011). That is, their 2011 study of twin children assessed at ages 5 and 10 found that being bullied was correlated with a change in how the body responds to stress. Bullied children displayed a blunted cortisol response to a psychosocial stress test. Because the design of the study involved an examination of identical twins who were discordant with respect to their experiences of being bullied (one twin was bullied while the other one was not), Ouellet-Morin and colleagues (2011) concluded that the effect could not be attributed to "variations in either genetic makeup, family environment, or other concomitant factors, nor could they be attributed to the twins' perceptions of the degree of stress experienced during the task" (Vaillancourt et al., 2013a, p. 243).

In summary, it is important to note that there is no gene for being a perpetrator or a target of bullying behavior. Based on current knowledge of the genetics of complex social behavior, such as bullying, the genetic component of individual response is likely to involve multiple genes that interact with the environment in a complex manner. The current understanding of genetics and complex behaviors is that genes do not *cause* a behavior; gene-by-environment studies do not use the word "environment" the same way it is used in everyday language or even in traditional social psychology (as in Chapter 3). Rather, it is a construct used in a model to estimate how much variability exists in a given environment. This means that the same gene placed in different environments would yield very different percentages for gene-environment interactions. It is unclear how this information would inform our understanding of bullying.

Telomere Erosion Consequences

Epigenetic research has found that negative life experiences can alter the expression of a gene, which in turn, can confer a risk for poor outcomes. Research also suggests that the experience of being bullied is associated with telomere erosion. The end of each chromatid has been found to shorten as people age; this telomere "tail" also erodes as a function of engaging in unhealthy behavior such as smoking or being obese. Telomere erosion is also associated with certain illnesses such as cancer, diabetes, and heart disease (Blackburn and Epel, 2012; Kiecolt-Glaser et al., 2011; Vaillancourt et al., 2013a). Given these associations, scientists are now examining telomere erosion as a biomarker of stress exposure (Epel et al., 2004), including the stress of being bullied by peers.

A recent longitudinal study by Shalev and colleagues (2013) examined telomere erosion in relation to children's exposure to violence,[24] a significant early-life stressor that is known to have long-term consequences for health. They found that exposure to violence, including being a target of bullying, was associated with telomere erosion for children assessed at age 5 and again at age 10. The sample for this study included 236 children recruited from the Environmental-Risk Longitudinal Twin Study (Moffitt, 2002), 42 percent of whom had one or more exposures to violence. The study found that cumulative exposure to violence[25] is positively associated with accelerated telomere erosion in children, from baseline to follow-up, with potential impact for life-long health (Shalev et al., 2013).

SUMMARY

In this chapter, the committee reviewed and critically analyzed the available research on the physical health, psychosocial, and academic achievement consequences for children and youth who are bullied, for those who bully, for those who are both bullied and bullies, and for those who are bystanders to events of bullying. It also examined the potential mediating mechanisms of, and the genetic predisposition to, mental health outcomes associated with childhood and youth experiences of bullying behavior. Most studies are cross-sectional and thus provide only associations suggestive of a possible causal effect. This problem is most acute for studies based on anonymous self-report, in which both the independent variable (experience of bullying in one or more roles) and dependent variables (such as emotional adjustment) are data collected at the same time from sources subject to various forms of bias.

The limited amount of data from longitudinal and experimental research designs limits the ability to draw conclusions with respect to causality. Additional longitudinal studies, for example, could help establish that the negative consequences attributed to bullying were not present before the bullying occurred. But even this does not prove a causal effect, since bullying and the associated impairments might be products of some third

---

[24]Exposure to violence included domestic violence, bullying victimization, and physical abuse by an adult.

[25]Cumulative violence exposure was measured by an index that summed each type of violence exposure.

factor. Below, the committee summarizes what is known about associations and consequences and identifies key conclusions that can be drawn from this evidence base.

FINDINGS AND CONCLUSIONS

Findings

Finding 4.1: Individuals who both bully and are also bullied by others experience a greater variety of both internalizing and externalizing symptoms than those who only bully or are only bullied.

Finding 4.2: Individuals who bully others are likely to experience negative emotional, behavioral, and mental health outcomes, though most research has not distinguished perpetration of bullying from other forms of peer aggression.

Finding 4.3: A large body of research indicates that individuals who have been bullied are at increased risk of subsequent mental, emotional, and behavioral problems, especially internalizing problems.

Finding 4.4: Studies of bystander behavior in bullying have rarely examined the emotional and psychological impact of witnessing bullying.

Finding 4.5: Children and youth who are bullied subsequently experience a range of somatic disturbances.

Finding 4.6: Social-cognitive factors (e.g., self-blame) and unsuccessful emotion regulation (i.e., emotion dysregulation) mediate relationships between bullying and adverse outcomes.

Finding 4.7: There is evidence that stressful events, such as might occur with experiences of being bullied, alter emotional brain circuits. This potential outcome is critically in need of further investigation.

Finding 4.8: Genetics influences how experiences contribute to mental and physical well-being, although the nature of this relationship is complex and not completely understood.

Finding 4.9: Emerging evidence suggests that repeated exposure to bullying may produce a neural signature that could underlie some of the behavioral outcomes associated with being bullied.

Finding 4.10: There are limited data on the physical health consequence of bullying for those individuals who are involved in bullying as targets, perpetrators, as both targets and perpetrators, and as bystanders.

Finding 4.11: Poly-victims (individuals who are targets of multiple types of aggression) are more likely to experience negative emotional, behavioral, and mental health outcomes than individuals targeted with only one form of aggression.

Finding 4.12: The long-term consequences of being bullied extend into adulthood and the effects can be more severe than other forms of being maltreated as a child.

Finding 4.13: Individuals who are involved in bullying (as perpetrators, targets, or both) in any capacity are significantly more likely to contemplate or attempt suicide, compared to children who are not involved in bullying. It is not known whether bystanders are at increased risk of suicidal ideation or suicide attempts.

Finding 4.14: There is not enough evidence to date to conclude that being the target of bullying is a causal factor for multiple-homicide targeted school shootings, nor is there clear evidence on how experience as a target or perpetrator of bullying, or the mental health and behavior issues related to such experiences, contribute to school shootings.

Conclusions

Conclusion 4.1: Further research is needed to obtain more in-depth evidence on the physical health consequences of being the target of bullying including neural consequences.

Conclusion 4.2: Additional research is needed to examine mediators of short- and long-term physical health outcomes of individuals who are bullied. Evidence is also needed regarding how these outcomes vary over time for different groups of children and youth, why individuals with similar experiences of being bullied might have different physical health outcomes, and how physical and emotional health outcomes intersect over time.

Conclusion 4.3: Although the effects of being bullied on the brain are not yet fully understood, there are changes in the stress response systems and in the brain that are associated with increased risk for mental health problems, cognitive function, self-regulation, and other physical health problems.

Conclusion 4.4: Bullying has significant short- and long-term internalizing and externalizing psychological consequences for the children who are involved in bullying behavior.

Conclusion 4.5: The data are unclear on the role of bullying as one of or a precipitating cause of school shootings.

Conclusion 4.6: Individuals who both bully others and are themselves bullied appear to be at greatest risk for poor psychosocial outcomes, compared to those who only bully or are only bullied and to those who are not bullied.

Conclusion 4.7: While cross-sectional studies indicate that children who are bullied are at increased risk for poor academic achievement relative to those who are not bullied, the results from longitudinal studies are inconsistent and warrant more research.

Conclusion 4.8: Existing evidence suggests that both social-cognitive and emotion regulation processes may mediate the relation between being bullied and adverse mental health outcomes.

Conclusion 4.9: Although genes appear to modulate humans' response to being either a target or a perpetrator of bullying behavior, it is still unclear what aspects of these experiences are interacting with genes and which genes are implicated to produce the variability in outcomes. Examining the role of genes in bullying in the context of the environment is essential to providing meaningful information on the genetic component of individual differences in outcomes from being a target or a perpetrator of bullying behavior.

REFERENCES

Anderson, C.A., and Bushman, B.J. (2002). Human aggression. *Annual Review of Psychology, 53*(1), 27-51.

Anderson, C.A., Miller, R.S., Riger, A.L., Dill, J.C., and Sedikides, C. (1994). Behavioral and characterological attributional styles as predictors of depression and loneliness: Review, refinement, and test. *Journal of Personality and Social Psychology, 66*(3), 549-558.

Archer, J. (2004). Testosterone and human aggression: An evaluation of the challenge hypothesis. *Neuroscience and Biobehavioral Reviews, 30*(3), 319-345.

Arseneault, L., Walsh, E., Trzesniewski,K., Newcombe, R., Caspi, A., and Moffitt, T. (2006). Bullying victimization uniquely contributes to adjustment problems in young children: A nationally representative cohort study. *Pediatrics, 118*(1), 130-138.

Baldwin, J., Arseneault, L., and Danese, A. (2015). Childhood bullying and adiposity in young adulthood: Findings from the E-Risk Longitudinal Twin Study. *Psychoneuroendocrinology, 61*, 16.

Ball, H.A., Arseneault, L., Taylor, A., Maughan, B., Caspi, A., and Moffitt, T.E. (2008). Genetic and environmental influences on victims, bullies and bully-victims in childhood. *Journal of Child Psychology and Psychiatry, 49*(1), 104-112.

Baly, M.W., Cornell, D.G., and Lovegrove, P. (2014). A longitudinal investigation of self- and peer reports of bullying victimization across middle school. *Psychology in the Schools, 51*(3), 217-240.

Bandura, A. (1973). *Aggression: A Social Learning Analysis.* Englewood Cliffes, NJ: Prentice-Hall.

Banny, A.M., Cicchetti, D., Rogosch, F.A., Oshri, A., and Crick, N.R. (2013). Vulnerability to depression: A moderated mediation model of the roles of child maltreatment, peer victimization, and serotonin transporter linked polymorphic region genetic variation among children from low socioeconomic status backgrounds. *Development and Psychopathology, 25*(03), 599-614.

Baratta, M.V., Kodandaramaiah, S.B., Monahan, P.E., Yao, J., Weber, M.D., Lin, P.-A., Gisabella, B., Petrossian, N., Amat, J., and Kim, K. (2015). Stress enables reinforcement-elicited serotonergic consolidation of fear memory. *Biological Psychiatry, 79*(10), 814-822.

Barnes, D.C., and Wilson, D.A. (2014). Slow-wave sleep-imposed replay modulates both strength and precision of memory. *Journal of Neuroscience, 34*(15), 5134-5142.

Barra, C.B., Silva, I.N., Rodrigues, T.M.B., Santos, J.L.S., and Colosimo, E.A. (2015). Morning serum basal cortisol levels are affected by age and pubertal maturation in school-aged children and adolescents. *Hormone Research in Paediatrics, 83*(1), 55-61.

Baumeister, R.F., DeWall, C.N., Ciarocco, N.J., and Twenge, J.M. (2005). Social exclusion impairs self-regulation. *Journal of Personality and Social Psychology, 88*(4), 589-604.

Beitchman, J.H., Baldassarra, L., Mik, H., Hons, B., Vincenzo De Luca, M., King, N., Bender, D., Ehtesham, S., and Kennedy, J.L. (2006). Serotonin transporter polymorphisms and persistent, pervasive childhood aggression. *American Journal of Psychiatry, 163*(6), 1103-1105.

Belsky, J., and Pluess, M. (2009). Beyond diathesis stress: Differential susceptibility to environmental influences. *Psychological Bulletin, 135*(6), 885-908.

Belujon, P., and Grace, A.A. (2015). Regulation of dopamine system responsivity and its adaptive and pathological response to stress. *Proceedings of the Royal Society of London B: Biological Sciences, 282*(1805),1-10.

Benjet, C., Thompson, R.J., and Gotlib, I.H. (2010). 5-HTTLPR moderates the effect of relational peer victimization on depressive symptoms in adolescent girls. *Journal of Child Psychology and Psychiatry, 51*(2), 173-179.

Beran, T. (2009). Correlates of peer victimization and achievement: An exploratory model. *Psychology in the Schools, 46*(4), 348-361.

Beran, T.N., and Lupart, J. (2009). The relationship between school achievement and peer harassment in Canadian adolescents: The importance of mediating factors. *School Psychology International, 30*(1), 75-91.

Beran, T.N., Hughes, G., and Lupart, J. (2008). A model of achievement and bullying: Analyses of the Canadian National Longitudinal Survey of Children and Youth data. *Educational Research, 50*(1), 25-39.

Blackburn, E.H., and Epel, E.S. (2012). *Nature, 490*(7419), 169-171.

Blakemore, S.-J. (2012). Development of the social brain in adolescence. *Journal of the Royal Society of Medicine, 105*(3), 111-116.

Boden, J.M., van Stockum, S., Horwood, L.J., and Fergusson, D.M. (2016). Bullying victimization in adolescence and psychotic symptomatology in adulthood: Evidence from a 35-year study. *Psychological Medicine, 46*(6), 1311-1320.

Bogart, L.M., Elliott, M.N., Klein, D.J., Tortolero, S.R., Mrug, S., Peskin, M.F., Davies, S.L., Schink, E.T., and Schuster, M.A. (2014). Peer victimization in fifth grade and health in tenth grade. *Pediatrics, 133*(3), 440-447.

Boivin, M., Brendgen, M., Vitaro, F., Dionne, G., Girard, A., Perusse, D., and Tremblay, R.E. (2013). Strong genetic contribution to peer relationship difficulties at school entry: Findings from a longitudinal twin study. *Child Development, 84*(3), 1098-1114.

Booth, A., Granger, D.A., and Shirtcliff, E.A. (2008). Gender- and age-related differences in the association between social relationship quality and trait levels of salivary cortisol. *Journal of Research on Adolescence, 18*(2), 239-260.

Borum, R., Cornell, D.G., Modzeleski, W., and Jimerson, S.R. (2010). What can be done about school shootings? A review of the evidence. *Educational Researcher, 39*(1), 27-37.

Bowes, L., Joinson, C., Wolke, D., and Lewis, G. (2015). Peer victimisation during adolescence and its impact on depression in early adulthood: Prospective cohort study in the United Kingdom. *The BMJ, 350*, 1-9.

Boyce, W.T., and Ellis, B.J. (2005) Biological sensitivity to context: I. An evolutionary-developmental theory of the origins and functions of stress reactivity. *Development and Psychopathology, 17*(2), 271-301.

Bradshaw, C.P., Sawyer, A.L., and O'Brennan, L.M. (2009). A social disorganization perspective on bullying-related attitudes and behaviors: The influence of school context. *American Journal of Community Psychology, 43*(3-4), 204-220.

Bradshaw, C.P., Goldweber, A., Fishbein, D., and Greenberg, M.T. (2012). Infusing developmental neuroscience into school-based preventive interventions: Implications and future directions. *Journal of Adolescent Health, 51*(2), S41-S47.

Brendgen, M. (2012). Genetics and peer relations: A review. *Journal of Research on Adolescence, 22*(3), 419-437.

Bradshaw, C.P., Goldweber, A., and Garbarino, J. (2013). Linking social-environmental risk factors with aggression in suburban adolescents: The role of social-cognitive mediators. *Psychology in Schools, 50*(5), 433-450.

Brendgen, M., Boivin, M., Vitaro, F., Bukowski, W.M., Dionne, G., Tremblay, R.E., and Pérusse, D. (2008). Linkages between children's and their friends' social and physical aggression: Evidence for a gene–environment interaction? *Child Development, 79*(1), 13-29.

Brendgen, M., Girard, A., Vitaro, F., Dionne, G., and Boivin, M. (2013). Do peer group norms moderate the expression of genetic risk for aggression? *Journal of Criminal Justice, 41*(5), 324-330.

Buhs, E.S., Ladd, G.W., and Herald, S.L. (2006). Peer exclusion and victimization: Processes that mediate the relation between peer group rejection and children's classroom engagement and achievement? *Journal of Educational Psychology, 98*(1), 1-13.

Camodeca, M., Goossens, F.A., Schuengel, C., and Terwogt, M.M. (2003). Links between social information processing in middle childhood and involvement in bullying. *Aggressive Behavior, 29*(2), 116-127.

Casement, M.D., Guyer, A.E., Hipwell, A.E., McAloon, R.L., Hoffmann, A.M., Keenan, K.E., and Forbes, E.E. (2014). Girls' challenging social experiences in early adolescence predict neural response to rewards and depressive symptoms. *Developmental Cognitive Neuroscience, 8*, 18-27.

Casey, B., and Jones, R.M. (2010). Neurobiology of the adolescent brain and behavior: Implications for substance use disorders. *Journal of the American Academy of Child & Adolescent Psychiatry, 49*(12), 1189-1201.

Caspi, A., Sugden, K., Moffitt, T.E., Taylor, A., Craig, I.W., Harrington, H., McClay, J., Mill, J., Martin, J., and Braithwaite, A. (2003). Influence of life stress on depression: Moderation by a polymorphism in the 5-HTT gene. *Science, 301*(5631), 386-389.

Chattarji, S., Tomar, A., Suvrathan, A., Ghosh, S., and Rahman, M.M. (2015). Neighborhood matters: Divergent patterns of stress-induced plasticity across the brain. *Nature Neuroscience, 18*(10), 1364-1375.

Cole, D.A., Peeke, L.G., and Ingold, C. (1996). Characterological and behavioral self-blame in children: Assessment and development considerations. *Development and Psychopathology, 8*(02), 381-397.

Cook, C.R., Williams, K.R., Guerra, N.G., Kim, T.E., and Sadek, S. (2010). Predictors of bullying and victimization in childhood and adolescence: A meta-analytic investigation. *School Psychology Quarterly, 25*(2), 65-83.

Copeland, W.E., Wolke, D., Angold, A., and Costello, E.J. (2013). Adult psychiatric outcomes of bullying and being bullied by peers in childhood and adolescence. *Journal of the American Medical Association Psychiatry, 70*(4), 419-426.

Copeland, W.E., Wolke, D., Lereya, S.T., Shanahan, L., Worthman, C., and Costello, E.J. (2014). Childhood bullying involvement predicts low-grade systemic inflammation into adulthood. *Proceedings of the National Academy of Sciences of the United States of America, 111*(21), 7570-7575.

Cornell, D. (2006). *School Violence: Fears vs. Facts*. New York: Routledge.

Cosma, A., Balazsi, R., Dobrean, A., and Baban, A. (2012). Bullying victimization, emotional problems and cognitive emotion regulation in adolescence. *Psychology & Health, 27*, 185-188.

Cougnard, A., Marcelis, M., Myin-Germeys, I., De Graaf, R., Vollebergh, W., Krabbendam, L., Lieb, R., Wittchen, H.-U., Henquet, C., and Spauwen, J. (2007). Does normal developmental expression of psychosis combine with environmental risk to cause persistence of psychosis? A psychosis proneness–persistence model. *Psychological Medicine, 37*(04), 513-527.

Crick, N.R., and Dodge, K.A. (1994). A review and reformulation of social information-processing mechanisms in children's social adjustment. *Psychological Bulletin, 115*(1), 74-101.

Cunningham, T., Hoy, K., and Shannon, C. (2015). Does childhood bullying lead to the development of psychotic symptoms? A meta-analysis and review of prospective studies. *Psychosis 8*(1), 1-12.

Dahl, R.E., and Gunnar, M.R. (2009). Heightened stress responsiveness and emotional reactivity during pubertal maturation: Implications for psychopathology. *Development and Psychopathology, 21*(01), 1-6.

Dallman, M.F., Pecoraro, N., Akana, S.F., La Fleur, S.E., Gomez, F., Houshyar, H., Bell, M., Bhatnagar, S., Laugero, K.D., and Manalo, S. (2003). Chronic stress and obesity: A new view of "comfort food." *Proceedings of the National Academy of Sciences of the United States of America, 100*(20), 11696-11701.

Danese, A., and Tan, M. (2014). Childhood maltreatment and obesity: Systematic review and meta-analysis. *Molecular Psychiatry, 19*(5), 544-554.

Danese, A., Pariante, C. M., Caspi, A., Taylor, A., and Poulton, R. (2007). Childhood maltreatment predicts adult inflammation in a life-course study. *Proceedings of the National Academy of Sciences of the United States of America, 104*(4), 1319-1324.

de Bruyn, E., Cillessen, A., and Wissink, I. (2010). Associations of peer acceptance and perceived popularity with bullying and victimization in early adolescence. *Journal of Early Adolescence, 30*(4), 543-566.

Dick, D.M., Agrawal, A., Keller, M.C., Adkins, A., Aliev, F., Monroe, S., Hewitt, J.K., Kendler, K.S., and Sher, K.J. (2015). Candidate gene–environment interaction research: Reflections and recommendations. *Perspectives on Psychological Science, 10*(1), 37-59.

Didden, R., Scholte, R.H.J., Korzilius, H., de Moor, J.M.H., Vermeulen, A., O'Reilly, M., Lang, R., and Lancioni, G.E. (2009). Cyberbullying among students with intellectual and developmental disability in special education settings. *Developmental Neurorehabilitation, 12*(3), 146-151.

Dijkstra, J.K., Lindenberg, S., and Veenstra, R. (2008). Beyond the class norm: Bullying behavior of popular adolescents and its relation to peer acceptance and rejection. *Journal of Abnormal Child Psychology, 36*(8), 1289-1299.

Dodge, K.A. (1986). A social information processing model of social competence in children. In M. Perlmutter (Ed.), *Cognitive Perspectives on Children's Social and Behavioral Development: The Minnesota Symposia on Child Psychology, Volume 18* (pp. 77-125). New York: Psychology Press.

Dodge, K.A., Bates, J.E., and Pettit, G.S. (1990). Mechanisms in the cycle of violence. *Science, 250*(4988), 1678-1683.

Duncan, L.E. (2013). Paying attention to all results, positive and negative. *Journal of the American Academy of Child & Adolescent Psychiatry, 52*(5), 462-465.

Duncan, L.E., and Keller, M.C. (2011). A critical review of the first 10 years of candidate gene-by-environment interaction research in psychiatry. *Perspectives, 168*(10), 1041-1049.

Duncan, L.E., Pollastri, A.R., and Smoller, J.W. (2014). Mind the gap: Why many geneticists and psychological scientists have discrepant views about gene–environment interaction (G × E) research. *American Psychologist, 69*(3), 249-268.

Eisenberger, N.I. (2012). The neural bases of social pain: Evidence for shared representations with physical pain. *Psychosomatic Medicine, 74*(2), 126-135.

Eisenberger, N.I., and Lieberman, M.D. (2004). Why rejection hurts: A common neural alarm system for physical and social pain. *Trends in Cognitive Sciences, 8*(7), 294-300.

Eisenberger, N.I., Lieberman, M.D., and Williams, K.D. (2003). Does rejection hurt? An fMRI study of social exclusion. *Science, 302*(5643), 290-292.

Epel, E.S., Blackburn, E.H., Lin, J., Dhabhar, F.S., Adler, N.E., Morrow, J.D., and Cawthon, R.M. (2004). Accelerated telomere shortening in response to life stress. *Proceedings of the National Academy of Sciences of the United States of America, 101*(49), 17312-17315.

Espelage, D.L., and Swearer, S.M. (Eds.). (2004). *Bullying in American Schools: A Social-Ecological Perspective on Prevention and Intervention*. Mahwah, NJ: Lawrence Erlbaum Associates.

Espelage, D.L., Hong, J.S., Rao, M.A., and Low, S. (2013). Associations between peer victimization and academic performance. *Theory Into Practice, 52*(4), 233-240.

Espinoza, G., Gonzales, N.A., and Fuligni, A.J. (2013). Daily school peer victimization experiences among Mexican-American adolescents: Associations with psychosocial, physical, and school adjustment. *Journal of Youth and Adolescence, 42*(12), 1775-1788.

Euston, D.R., Gruber, A.J., and McNaughton, B.L. (2012). The role of medial prefrontal cortex in memory and decision making. *Neuron, 76*(6), 1057-1070.

Evans, G.W., Kim, P., Ting, A.H., Tesher, H.B., and Shannis, D. (2007). Cumulative risk, maternal responsiveness, and allostatic load among young adolescents. *Developmental Psychology, 43*(2), 341.

Faris, R., and Ennett, S. (2012). Adolescent aggression: The role of peer group status motives, peer aggression, and group characteristics. *Social Networks, 34*(4), 371-378.

Farmer, T.W., Estell, D.B., Bishop, J.L., O'Neal, K.K., and Cairns, B.D. (2003). Rejected bullies or popular leaders? The social relations of aggressive subtypes of rural African American early adolescents. *Developmental Psychology, 39*(6), 992-1004.

Fein, R.A., Vossekuil, B., Pollack, W.S., Borum, R., Modzeleski, W., and Reddy, M. (2002). *Threat Assessment in Schools: A Guide to Managing Threatening Situations and Creating Safe School Climates.* Washington, DC: U.S. Department of Education, Office of Elementary and Secondary Education, Safe and Drug-Free Schools Program and U.S. Secret Service, National Threat Assessment Center.

Feldman, M.A., Ojanen, T., Gesten, E.L., Smith-Schrandt, H., Brannick, M., Totura, C.M.W., Alexander, L., Scanga, D., and Brown, K. (2014). The effects of middle school bullying and victimization on adjustment through high school: Growth modeling of achievement, school attendance, and disciplinary trajectories. *Psychology in the Schools, 51*(10), 1046-1062.

Finkelhor, D., Ormrod, R.K., Turner, H.A., and Hamby, S.L. (2005). Measuring poly-victimization using the juvenile victimization questionnaire. *Child Abuse & Neglect, 29*(11), 1297-1312.

Finkelhor, D., Ormrod, R.K., and Turner, H.A. (2007). Poly-victimization: A neglected component in child victimization. *Child Abuse & Neglect, 31*(1), 7-26.

Finkelhor, D., Ormrod, R.K., and Turner, H.A. (2009). Lifetime assessment of poly-victimization in a national sample of children and youth. *Child Abuse & Neglect, 33*(7), 403-411.

Flannery, D.J., Modzeleski, W., and Kretschmar, J.M. (2013). Violence and school shootings. *Current Psychiatry Reports, 15*(1), 1-7.

Flouri, E., and Buchanan, A. (2003). The role of mother involvement and father involvement in adolescent bullying behavior. *Journal of Interpersonal Violence, 18*(6), 634-644.

Ford, J.D., Elhai, J.D., Connor, D.F., and Frueh, B.C. (2010). Poly-victimization and risk of posttraumatic, depressive, and substance use disorders and involvement in delinquency in a national sample of adolescents. *Journal of Adolescent Health, 46*(6), 545-552.

Ford, J.D., Grasso, D.J., Hawke, J., and Chapman, J.F. (2013). Poly-victimization among juvenile justice-involved youths. *Child Abuse & Neglect, 37*(10), 788-800.

Forero, R., McLellan, L., Rissel, C., and Bauman, A. (1999). Bullying behaviour and psychosocial health among school students in New South Wales, Australia, Cross-Sectional Survey. *BMJ, 319*(7206), 344-348.

Ganzel, B.L., Kim, P., Glover, G.H., and Temple, E. (2008). Resilience after 9/11: Multimodal neuroimaging evidence for stress-related change in the healthy adult brain. *Neuroimage, 40*(2), 788-795.

Gastic, B. (2008). School truancy and the disciplinary problems of bullying victims. *Educational Review, 60*(4), 391-404.

Gee, D.G., Gabard-Durnam, L., Telzer, E.H., Humphreys, K.L., Goff, B., Shapiro, M., Flannery, J., Lumian, D.S., Fareri, D.S., and Caldera, C. (2014). Maternal buffering of human amygdala-prefrontal circuitry during childhood but not during adolescence. *Psychological Science.* doi: 10.1177/0956797614550878.

Gibb, S.J., Horwood, L.J., and Fergusson, D.M. (2011). Bullying victimization/perpetration in childhood and later adjustment: Findings from a 30-year longitudinal study. *Journal of Aggression, Conflict and Peace Research, 3*(2), 82-88.

Giedd, J.N., Blumenthal, J., Jeffries, N.O., Castellanos, F.X., Liu, H., Zijdenbos, A., Paus, T., Evans, A.C., and Rapoport, J.L. (1999). Brain development during childhood and adolescence: A longitudinal MRI study. *Nature Neuroscience, 2*(10), 861-863.

Gini, G. (2008). Associations between bullying behaviour, psychosomatic complaints, emotional and behavioural problems. *Journal of Paediatrics and Child Health, 44*(9), 492-497.

Gini, G., and Pozzoli, T. (2009). Association between bullying and psychosomatic problems: A meta-analysis. *Pediatrics, 123*(3), 1059-1065.

Gini, G., and Pozzoli, T. (2013). Bullied children and psychosomatic problems: A meta-analysis. *Pediatrics, 132*(4), 720-729.

Glew, G.M., Fan, M.-Y., Katon, W., Rivara, F.P., and Kernic, M.A. (2005). Bullying, psychosocial adjustment, and academic performance in elementary school. *Archives of Pediatrics and Adolescent Medicine, 159*(11), 1026-1031.

Glew, G.M., Fan, M.-Y., Katon, W., and Rivara, F.P. (2008). Bullying and school safety. *Journal of Pediatrics, 152*(1), 123-128.

Graham, S. (2006). Peer victimization in school: Exploring the ethnic context. *Current Directions in Psychological Science, 15*(6), 317-321.

Graham, S., and Bellmore, A.D. (2007). Peer victimization and mental health during early adolescence. *Theory into Practice, 46*(2), 138-146.

Graham, S., and Juvonen, J. (1998). Self-blame and peer victimization in middle school: An attributional analysis. *Developmental Psychology, 34*(3), 587-599.

Graham, S., Bellmore, A.D., and Mize, J. (2006). Peer victimization, aggression, and their co-occurrence in middle school: Pathways to adjustment problems. *Journal of Abnormal Child Psychology, 34*(3), 349-364.

Graham, S., Bellmore, A., Nishina, A., and Juvonen, J. (2009). "It must be me": Ethnic diversity and attributions for peer victimization in middle school. *Journal of Youth and Adolescence, 38*(4), 487-499.

Greenberg, D.B. (2016). *Somatization: Epidemiology, Pathogenesis, Clinical Features, Medical Evaluation, and Diagnosis.* Available: http://www.uptodate.com/contents/somatization-treatment-and-prognosis?source=see_link [June 2016].

Gross, J.J. (2001). Emotion regulation in adulthood: Timing is everything. *Current Directions in Psychological Science, 10*(6), 214-219.

Hager, A.D., and Leadbeater, B.J. (2016). The longitudinal effects of peer victimization on physical health from adolescence to young adulthood. *Journal of Adolescent Health, 58*(3), 330-336.

Hanish, L.D., Eisenberg, N., Fabes, R.A., Spinrad, T.L., Ryan, P., and Schmidt, S. (2004). The expression and regulation of negative emotions: Risk factors for young children's peer victimization. *Development and Psychopathology, 16*(02), 335-353.

Hanson, J.L., Nacewicz, B.M., Sutterer, M.J., Cayo, A.A., Schaefer, S.M., Rudolph, K.D., Shirtcliff, E.A., Pollak, S.D., and Davidson, R.J. (2015). Behavioral problems after early life stress: Contributions of the hippocampus and amygdala. *Biological Psychiatry, 77*(4), 314-323.

Harris, J.R. (1995). Where is the child's environment? A group socialization theory of development. *Psychological Review, 102*(3), 458-489.

Harvey, A.G., and Tang, N.K. (2012). (Mis) perception of sleep in insomnia: A puzzle and a resolution. *Psychological Bulletin, 138*(1), 77-101.

Hawker, D.S., and Boulton, M.J. (2000). Twenty years' research on peer victimization and psychosocial maladjustment: A meta-analytic review of cross-sectional studies. *Journal of Child Psychology and Psychiatry, 41*(4), 441-455.

Heim, C., Owens, M.J., Plotsky, P.M., and Nemeroff, C.B. (1997). Persistent changes in corticotropin-releasing factor systems due to early life stress: Relationship to the pathophysiology of major depression and post-traumatic stress disorder. *Psychopharmacology Bulletin, 33*(2), 185-192.

Hennessy, M.B., Kaiser, S., and Sachser, N. (2009). Social buffering of the stress response: Diversity, mechanisms, and functions. *Frontiers in Neuroendocrinology, 30*(4), 470-482.

Hennessy, M.B., Schiml, P.A., Willen, R., Watanasriyakul, W., Johnson, J., and Garrett, T. (2015). Selective social buffering of behavioral and endocrine responses and Fos induction in the prelimbic cortex of infants exposed to a novel environment. *Developmental Psychobiology, 57*(1), 50-62.

Herts, K.L., McLaughlin, K.A., and Hatzenbuehler, M.L. (2012). Emotion dysregulation as a mechanism linking stress exposure to adolescent aggressive behavior. *Journal of Abnormal Child Psychology, 40*(7), 1111-1122.

Holt, M.K., Vivolo-Kantor, A.M., Polanin, J.R., Holland, K.M., DeGue, S., Matjasko, J.L., Wolfe, M., and Reid, G. (2015). Bullying and suicidal ideation and behaviors: A meta-analysis. *Pediatrics, 135*(2), e496-e509.

Hostinar, C.E., Sullivan, R.M., and Gunnar, M.R. (2014). Psychobiological mechanisms underlying the social buffering of the hypothalamic–pituitary–adrenocortical axis: A review of animal models and human studies across development. *Psychological Bulletin, 140*(1), 256-282.

Hostinar, C.E., Johnson, A.E., and Gunnar, M.R. (2015). Parent support is less effective in buffering cortisol stress reactivity for adolescents compared to children. *Developmental Science, 18*(2), 281-297.

Huesmann, L.R., and Guerra, N.G. (1997). Children's normative beliefs about aggression and aggressive behavior. *Journal of Personality and Social Psychology, 72*(2), 408-419.

Hunter, S.C., Durkin, K., Boyle, J.M., Booth, J.N., and Rasmussen, S. (2014). Adolescent bullying and sleep difficulties. *Europe's Journal of Psychology, 10*(4), 740-755.

Institute of Medicine and National Research Council. (2014a). *Building Capacity to Reduce Bullying: Workshop Summary.* Washington, DC: The National Academies Press.

Institute of Medicine and National Research Council. (2014b). *New Directions in Child Abuse and Neglect Research.* Washington, DC: The National Academies Press.

Inzlicht, M., McKay, L., and Aronson, J. (2006). Stigma as ego depletion: How being the target of prejudice affects self-control. *Psychological Science, 17*(3), 262-269.

Iyer, P.A., Dougall, A.L., and Jensen-Campbell, L.A. (2013). Are some adolescents differentially susceptible to the influence of bullying on depression? *Journal of Research in Personality, 47*(4), 272-281.

Janoff-Bulman, R. (1979). Characterological versus behavioral self-blame: Inquiries into depression and rape. *Journal of Personality and Social Psychology, 37*(10), 1798-1809.

Jovanovic, T., Smith, A., Gamwell, K., Nylocks, M., Norrholm, S.D., Ressler, K.J., and Bradley, B. (2013). Psychophysiological biomarkers of anxiety in children at high risk for trauma exposure. *Biological Psychiatry, 73*(9), 17S-17S.

Judd, L.L., Schettler, P.J., Brown, E.S., Wolkowitz, O.M., Sternberg, E.M., Bender, B.G., Bulloch, K., Cidlowski, J.A., de Kloet, E.R., and Fardet, L. (2014). Adverse consequences of glucocorticoid medication: Psychological, cognitive, and behavioral effects. *American Journal of Psychiatry, 171*(10), 1045-1051.

Juvonen, J., and Graham, S. (2014). Bullying in schools: The power of bullies and the plight of victims. *Annual Review of Psychology, 65*(1), 159-185.

Juvonen, J., Nishina, A., and Graham, S. (2000). Peer harassment, psychological adjustment, and school functioning in early adolescence. *Journal of Educational Psychology, 92*(2), 349-359.

Juvonen, J., Graham, S., and Schuster, M.A. (2003). Bullying among young adolescents: The strong, the weak, and the troubled. *Pediatrics, 112*(6), 1231-1237.

Juvonen, J., Wang, Y., and Espinoza, G. (2011). Bullying experiences and compromised academic performance across middle school grades. *Journal of Early Adolescence, 31*(1), 152-173.

Kalmakis, K.A., and Chandler, G.E. (2015). Health consequences of adverse childhood experiences: A systematic review. *Journal of the American Association of Nurse Practitioners, 27*(8), 457-465.

Karg, K., Burmeister, M., Shedden, K., and Sen, S. (2011). The serotonin transporter promoter variant (5-HTTLPR), stress, and depression meta-analysis revisited: Evidence of genetic moderation. *Archives of General Psychiatry, 68*(5), 444-454.

Kidger, J., Heron, J., Leon, D.A., Tilling, K., Lewis, G., and Gunnell, D. (2015). Self-reported school experience as a predictor of self-harm during adolescence: A prospective cohort study in the south west of England (ALSPAC). *Journal of Affective Disorders, 173,* 163-169.

Kiecolt-Glaser, J.K., Gouin, J.-P., Weng, N.-p., Malarkey, W.B., Beversdorf, D.Q., and Glaser, R. (2011). Childhood adversity heightens the impact of later-life caregiving stress on telomere length and inflammation. *Psychosomatic Medicine, 73*(1), 16-22.

Kim, Y.S., and Leventhal, B. (2008). Bullying and suicide. A review. *International Journal of Adolescent Medicine and Health, 20*(2), 133-154.

Kim, J.H., and Richardson, R. (2010). New findings on extinction of conditioned fear early in development: Theoretical and clinical implications. *Biological Psychiatry, 67*(4), 297-303.

Kim, Y.S., Leventhal, B.L., Koh, Y.-J., Hubbard, A., and Boyce, W.T. (2006). School bullying and youth violence: Causes or consequences of psychopathologic behavior? *Archives of General Psychiatry, 63*(9), 1035-1041.

Kimmel, M.S., and Mahler, M. (2003). Adolescent masculinity, homophobia, and violence: Random school shootings, 1982-2001. *American Behavioral Scientist, 46*(10), 1439-1458.

Klein, J. (2012). *The Bully Society: School Shootings and the Crisis of Bullying in America's Schools*: New York: New York University Press.

Kliewer, W. (2006). Violence exposure and cortisol responses in urban youth. *International Journal of Behavioral Medicine, 13*(2), 109-120.

Kliewer, W., Dibble, A.E., Goodman, K.L, and Sullivan, T.N. (2012). Physiological correlates of peer victimization and aggression in African American urban adolescents. *Development and Psychopathology, 24*(2), 637-650.

Klomek, A.B., Marrocco, F., Kleinman, M., Schonfeld, I.S., and Gould, M.S. (2007). Bullying, depression, and suicidality in adolescents. *Journal of the American Academy of Child & Adolescent Psychiatry, 46*(1), 40-49.

Klomek, A.B., Sourander, A., Niemelä, S., Kumpulainen, K., Piha, J., Tamminen, T., Almqvist, F., and Gould, M.S. (2009). Childhood bullying behaviors as a risk for suicide attempts and completed suicides: A population-based birth cohort study. *Journal of the American Academy of Child & Adolescent Psychiatry, 48*(3), 254-261.

Klomek, A.B., Sourander, A., and Gould, M. (2010). The association of suicide and bullying in childhood to young adulthood: A review of cross-sectional and longitudinal research findings. *Canadian Journal of Psychiatry, 55*(5), 282-288.

Klomek, A.B., Sourander, A., and Elonheimo, H. (2015). Bullying by peers in childhood and effects on psychopathology, suicidality, and criminality in adulthood. *The Lancet Psychiatry, 2*(10), 930-941.

Knack, J.M., Gomez, H.L., and Jensen-Campbell, L.A. (2011a). Bullying and its long-term health implications. In G. MacDonald and L.A, Jensen-Campbell (Eds.), *Social Pain: Neuropsychological and Health Implications of Loss and Exclusion* (pp. 215-236). Washington, DC: American Psychological Association.

Knack, J.M., Jensen-Campbell, L.A., and Baum, A. (2011b). Worse than sticks and stones? Bullying is associated with altered HPA axis functioning and poorer health. *Brain and Cognition, 77*(2), 183-190.

Knack, J., Vaillancourt, T., and Hutcherson, A. (2012a). Evidence of altered cortisol levels across child maltreatment, intimate partner abuse, and peer victimization. In A.N. Hutcherson (Ed.), *Psychology of Victimization* (pp. 205-218). New York: Nova Science. Available: https://www.novapublishers.com/catalog/product_info.php?products_ id=27225 [June 2016].

Knack, J.M., Tsar, V., Vaillancourt, T., Hymel, S., and McDougall, P. (2012b). What protects rejected adolescents from also being bullied by their peers? The moderating role of peer-valued characteristics. *Journal of Research on Adolescence, 22*(3), 467-479.

Kochel, K.P., Ladd, G.W., and Rudolph, K.D. (2012). Longitudinal associations among youth depressive symptoms, peer victimization, and low peer acceptance: An interpersonal process perspective. *Child Development, 83*(2), 637-650.

Kochenderfer, B.J., and Ladd, G.W. (1996). Peer victimization: Cause or consequence of school maladjustment? *Child Development, 67*(4), 1305-1317.

Kowalski, R.M., and Limber, S.P. (2013). Psychological, physical, and academic correlates of cyberbullying and traditional bullying. *Journal of Adolescent Health, 53*(1), S13-S20.

Kretschmer, T., Dijkstra, J.K., Ormel, J., Verhulst, F.C., and Veenstra, R. (2013). Dopamine receptor D4 gene moderates the effect of positive and negative peer experiences on later delinquency: The Tracking Adolescents' Individual Lives Survey study. *Development and Psychopathology, 25*(4 pt. 1), 1107-1117.

Kross, E., Berman, M.G., Mischel, W., Smith, E.E., and Wager, T.D. (2011). Social rejection shares somatosensory representations with physical pain. *Proceedings of the National Academy of Sciences of the United States of America, 108*(15), 6270-6275.

Kumpulainen, K., Räsänen, E., and Puura, K. (2001). Psychiatric disorders and the use of mental health services among children involved in bullying. *Aggressive Behavior, 27*(2), 102-110.

Ladd, G.W., and Kochenderfer-Ladd, B. (2002). Identifying victims of peer aggression from early to middle childhood: Analysis of cross-informant data for concordance, estimation of relational adjustment, prevalence of victimization, and characteristics of identified victims. *Psychological Assessment, 14*(1), 74-96.

Lake, A., and Chan, M. (2015). Putting science into practice for early child development. *The Lancet, 385*(9980), 1816-1817.

Langman, P. (2009). Rampage school shooters: A typology. *Aggression and Violent Behavior, 14*(1), 79-86.

Langman, P. (2015). *School Shooters: Understanding High School, College, and Adult Perpetrators.* Lanham, MD: Rowman & Littlefield.

Leary, M., Kowalski, R., Smith, L., and Phillips, S. (2003). Teasing, rejection, and violence: Case studies of the school shootings. *Aggressive Behavior, 29*(3), 202-214.

Lee, H.-S., Lee, J.-E., Lee, K.-U., and Kim, Y.-H. (2014). Neural changes associated with emotion processing in children experiencing peer rejection: A functional MRI study. *Journal of Korean Medical Science, 29*(9), 1293-1300.

Lereya, S.T., Copeland, W.E., Costello, E.J., and Wolke, D. (2015). Adult mental health consequences of peer bullying and maltreatment in childhood: Two cohorts in two countries. *The Lancet Psychiatry, 2*(6), 524-531.

Lim, L., Radua, J., and Rubia, K. (2014). Gray matter abnormalities in childhood maltreatment: A voxel-wise meta-analysis. *American Journal of Psychiatry, 171*(8), 854-863.

Lim, L., Hart, H., Mehta, M.A., Simmons, A., Mirza, K., and Rubia, K. (2015). Neural correlates of error processing in young people with a history of severe childhood abuse: An fMRI study. *American Journal of Psychiatry, 172*(9), 892-900.

Liston, C., McEwen, B., and Casey, B. (2009). Psychosocial stress reversibly disrupts prefrontal processing and attentional control. *Proceedings of the National Academy of Sciences of the United States of America, 106*(3), 912-917.

Lodge, J., and Frydenberg, E. (2005). The role of peer bystanders in school bullying: Positive steps toward promoting peaceful schools. *Theory Into Practice, 44*(4), 329-336.

Lupien, S.J., Fiocco, A., Wan, N., Maheu, F., Lord, C., Schramek, T., and Tu, M.T. (2005). Stress hormones and human memory function across the lifespan. *Psychoneuroendocrinology, 30*(3), 225-242.

Madfis, E. (2014). *The Risk of School Rampage: Assessing and Preventing Threats of School Violence.* New York: Polgrave MacMillan.

Mahady Wilton, M.M., Craig, W.M., and Pepler, D.J. (2000). Emotional regulation and display in classroom victims of bullying: Characteristic expressions of affect, coping styles, and relevant contextual factors. *Social Development, 9*(2), 227-245.

Márquez, C., Poirier, G.L., Cordero, M.I., Larsen, M.H., Groner, A., Marquis, J., Magistretti, P.J., Trono, D., and Sandi, C. (2013). Peripuberty stress leads to abnormal aggression, altered amygdala and orbitofrontal reactivity and increased prefrontal MAOA gene expression. *Translational Psychiatry, 3*(1), 1-12.

McCormick, C.M., and Mathews, I.Z. (2007). HPA function in adolescence: Role of sex hormones in its regulation and the enduring consequences of exposure to stressors. *Pharmacology Biochemistry and Behavior, 86*(2), 220-233.

McDermott, R., Tingley, D., Cowden, J., Frazzetto, G., and Johnson, D.D. (2009). Monoamine oxidase A gene (MAOA) predicts behavioral aggression following provocation. *Proceedings of the National Academy of Sciences of the United States of America, 106*(7), 2118-2123.

McDougall, P., and Vaillancourt, T. (2015). Long-term adult outcomes of peer victimization in childhood and adolescence: Pathways to adjustment and maladjustment. *American Psychologist, 70*(4), 300-310.

McEwen, B.S. (2014). The brain on stress: The good and the bad. In M. Popoli, D. Diamond, and G. Sanacora (Eds.), *Synaptic Stress and Pathogenesis of Neuropsychiatric Disorders* (pp. 1-18). New York: Springer.

McEwen, B.S., and Karatsoreos, I.N. (2015). Sleep deprivation and circadian disruption: Stress, allostasis, and allostatic load. *Sleep Medicine Clinics, 10*(1), 1-10.

McEwen, B.S., and McEwen, C.A. (2015). Social, psychological, and physiological reactions to stress. In R.A. Scott, S.M. Kosslyn, and N. Pinkerton (Eds.), *Emerging Trends in the Social and Behavioral Sciences: An Interdisciplinary, Searchable, and Linkable Resource* (pp. 1-15). New York: J. Wiley.

McEwen, B.S., and Morrison, J.H. (2013). The brain on stress: Vulnerability and plasticity of the prefrontal context over the life course. *Neuron, 79*(1), 16-29.

McEwen, B.S., Gray, J.D., and Nasca, C. (2015). Recognizing resilience: Learning from the effects of stress on the brain. *Neurobiology of Stress, 1*, 1-11.

McGaugh, J.L. (2015). Consolidating memories. *Annual Review of Psychology, 66*, 1-24.

McGee, T.R., Scott, J.G., McGrath, J.J., Williams, G.M., O'Callaghan, M., Bor, W., and Najman, J.M. (2011). Young adult problem behaviour outcomes of adolescent bullying. *Journal of Aggression, Conflict and Peace Research, 3*(2), 110-114.

McGowan, P.O., Sasaki, A., D'Alessio, A.C., Dymov, S., Labonté, B., Szyf, M., Turecki, G., and Meaney, M.J. (2009). Epigenetic regulation of the glucocorticoid receptor in human brain associates with childhood abuse. *Nature Neuroscience, 12*(3), 342-348.

McGowan, P.O., Suderman, M., Sasaki, A., Huang, T., Hallett, M., Meaney, M.J., and Szyf, M. (2011). Broad epigenetic signature of maternal care in the brain of adult rats. *PLoS One, 6*(2). Available: http://journals.plos.org/plosone/article?id=10.1371/journal.pone.0014739 [August 2016].

McLaughlin, K.A., Hatzenbuehler, M.L., and Hilt, L.M. (2009). Emotion dysregulation as a mechanism linking peer victimization to internalizing symptoms in adolescents. *Journal of Consulting and Clinical Psychology, 77*(5), 894-904.

Milaid, M.R., and Quirk, G.J. (2012). Fear extinction as a model for translational neuroscience: Ten years of progress. *Annual Review of Psychology, 63*, 129-151.

Miller, G.E., Chen, E., and Zhou, E.S. (2007). If it goes up, must it come down? Chronic stress and the hypothalamic-pituitary-adrenocortical axis in humans. *Psychological Bulletin, 133*(1), 25-45.

Miller, G. E., and Chen, E. (2010). Harsh family climate in early life presages the emergence of a proinflammatory phenotype in adolescence. *Psychological Science, 21*(6), 848-856.

Miller-Graff, L.E., Cater, Å.K., Howell, K.H., and Graham-Bermann, S.A. (2015). Victimization in childhood: General and specific associations with physical health problems in young adulthood. *Journal of Psychosomatic Research, 70*(4), 269-271.

Moffitt, T.E. (2002). Teen-aged mothers in contemporary Britain. *Journal of Child Psychology and Psychiatry, 43*(6), 727-742.

Montoya, E.R., Terburg, D., Bos, P.A., and Van Honk, J. (2012). Testosterone, cortisol, and serotonin as key regulators of social aggression: A review and theoretical perspective. *Motivation and Emotion, 36*(1), 65-73.

Moriceau, S., and Sullivan, R.M. (2006). Maternal presence serves as a switch between learning fear and attraction in infancy. *Nature Neuroscience, 9*(8), 1004-1006.

Mulvey, E., and Cauffman, E. (2001). The inherent limits of predicting school violence. *American Psychologist, 56*(10), 797-802.

Musher-Eizenman, D.R., Boxer, P., Danner, S., Dubow, E.F., Goldstein, S.E., and Heretick, D.M.L. (2004). Social-cognitive mediators of the relation of environmental and emotion regulation factors to children's aggression. *Aggressive Behavior, 30*(5), 389-408.

Nair, H.P., and Gonzalez-Lima, F. (1999). Extinction of behavior in infant rats: Development of functional coupling between septal hippocampal and vental tegmental regions. *The Journal of Neuroscience, 19*(19), 8646-8655.

Nakamoto, J., and Schwartz, D. (2010). Is peer victimization associated with academic achievement? A meta-analytic review. *Social Development, 19*(2), 221-242.

Nansel, T.R., Overpeck, M., Pilla, R.S., Ruan, W.J., Simons-Morton, B., and Scheidt, P. (2001). Bullying behaviors among U.S. youth: Prevalence and association with psychosocial adjustment. *Journal of the American Medical Association, 285*(16), 2094-2100.

Nansel, T.R., Haynie, D.L., and Simonsmorton, B.G. (2003). The association of bullying and victimization with middle school adjustment. *Journal of Applied School Psychology, 19*(2), 45-61.

Nansel, T.R., Craig, W., Overpeck, M.D., Saluja, G., and Ruan, W.J. (2004). Cross-national consistency in the relationship between bullying behaviors and psychosocial adjustment. *Archives of Pediatrics and Adolescent Medicine, 158*(8), 730-736.

National Research Council and Institute of Medicine. (2003). *Deadly Lessons: Understanding Lethal School Violence.* Case Studies of School Violence Committee. M.H. Moore, C.V. Petrie, A.A. Braga, and B.L. McLaughlin, Editors. Division of Behavioral and Social Sciences and Education. Washington, DC: The National Academies Press.

Neary, A., and Joseph, S. (1994). Peer victimization and its relationship to self-concept and depression among schoolgirls. *Personality and Individual Differences, 16*(1), 183-186.

Newman, K.S., Fox, C., Harding, D., Mehta, J., and Roth, W. (2004). *Rampage: The Social Roots of School Shootings.* New York: Basic Books.

Newman, M.L. (2014). Here we go again: Bullying history and cardiovascular responses to social exclusion. *Physiology & Behavior, 133*, 76-80.

Nishina, A., and Juvonen, J. (2005). Daily reports of witnessing and experiencing peer harassment in middle school. *Child Development, 76*(2), 435-450.

Niv, S., Tuvblad, C., Raine, A., and Baker, L.A. (2013). Aggression and rule-breaking: Heritability and stability of antisocial behavior problems in childhood and adolescence. *Journal of Criminal Justice, 41*(5), 285-291.

Nixon, C. (2014). Current perspectives: The impact of cyberbullying on adolescent health. *Adolescent Health, Medicine and Therapeutics*, 143-158.

O'Brennan, L.M., Bradshaw, C.P., and Sawyer, A.L. (2009). Examining developmental differences in the social-emotional problems among frequent bullies, victims, and bully/victims. *Psychology in the Schools*, 46(2), 100-115.

Obradovic, J., Bush, N.R., Stamperdahl, J., Adler, N.E., and Boyce, W.T. (2010). Biological sensitivity to context: The interactive effects of stress reactivity and family adversity on socioemotional behavior and school readiness. *Child Development*, 81(1), 270-289.

Olweus, D. (1993a). *Bullying at School. What We Know and What We Can Do*. Oxford, UK: Blackwell.

Olweus, D. (1993b). Victimization by peers: Antecedents and long-term outcomes. In K.H. Rubin and J.B. Asendorpf (Eds.), *Social Withdrawal, Inhibition, and Shyness in Childhood* (pp. 315-341). New York: Psychology Press.

Ostrov, J.M., and Kamper, K.E. (2015). Future directions for research on the development of relational and physical peer victimization. *Journal of Clinical Child & Adolescent Psychology*, 44(3), 509-519.

O'Toole, M.E. (2000). *The School Shooter: A Threat Assessment Perspective*. Quantico, VA: US Department of Justice, Federal Bureau of Investigation.

O'Toole, M.E., Folino, P.J., Garbarino, J., Gorelick, S.M., Häkkänen-Nyholm, H., Meloy, J.R., Samenow, S.E., and Nishimura, Y.S. (2014). Why do young males attack schools? Seven discipline leaders share their perspectives. *Violence and Gender*, 1(1), 13-18.

Ouellet-Morin, I., Odgers, C.L., Danese, A., Bowes, L., Shakoor, S., Papadopoulos, A.S., Caspi, A., Moffitt, T.E., and Arseneault, L. (2011). Blunted cortisol responses to stress signal social and behavioral problems among maltreated/bullied 12-year-old children. *Biological Psychiatry*, 70(11), 1016-1023.

Ouellet-Morin, I., Wong, C., Danese, A., Pariante, C., Papadopoulos, A., Mill, J., and Arseneault, L. (2013). Increased serotonin transporter gene (SERT) DNA methylation is associated with bullying victimization and blunted cortisol response to stress in childhood: A longitudinal study of discordant monozygotic twins. *Psychological Medicine*, 43(09), 1813-1823.

Patchin, J.W. (2006). Bullies move beyond the schoolyard: A preliminary look at cyberbullying. *Youth Violence and Juvenile Justice*, 4(2), 148-169.

Patton, D.U., Hong, J.S., Patel, S., and Kral, M.J. (2015). A systematic review of research strategies used in qualitative studies on school bullying and victimization. *Trauma, Violence, & Abuse*, 1-14. doi: 10.1177/1524838015588502.

Pattwell, S.S., Duhoux, S., Hartley, C.A., Johnson, D.C., Jing, D., Elliott, M.D., Ruberry, E.J., Powers, A., Mehta, N., Yand, R.R., Soliman, F., Glatt, C.E., Casey, B.J., Ninan, I, and Lee, F.S. (2012). Altered fear learning across development in both mouse and human. *Proceedings of the National Academy of Sciences of the United States of America*, 109(40), 16318-16323.

Pattwell, S.S., Lee, F.S., and Casey, B.J. (2013). Fear learning and memory across adolescent development: Hormones and behavior special issue: Puberty and adolescence. *Hormones and Behavior*, 64(2), 380-389.

Peeters, M., Cillessen, A.H., and Scholte, R.H. (2010). Clueless or powerful? Identifying subtypes of bullies in adolescence. *Journal of Youth and Adolescence*, 39(9), 1041-1052.

Perren, S., Ettekal, I., and Ladd, G. (2012). The impact of peer victimization on later maladjustment: Mediating and moderating effects of hostile and self-blaming attributions. *Journal of Child Psychology and Psychiatry*, 54(1), 46-55.

Perry, R., and Sullivan, R.M. (2014). Neurobiology of attachment to an abusive caregiver: Short-term benefits and long-term costs. *Developmental Psychobiology*, 56(8), 1626-1634.

Plomin, R., DeFries, J.C., and Loehlin, J.C. (1977). Genotype-environment interaction and correlation in the analysis of human behavior. *Psychological Bulletin*, 84(2), 309-322.

Polanin, J.R., Espelage, D.L., and Pigott, T.D. (2012). A meta-analysis of school-based bullying prevention programs' effects on bystander intervention behavior. *School Psychology Review*, 41(1), 47-65.

Prinstein, M.J., Cheah, C.S.L., and Guyer, A.E. (2005). Peer victimization, cue interpretation, and internalizing symptoms: Preliminary concurrent and longitudinal findings for children and adolescents. *Journal of Clinical Child & Adolescent Psychology*, 34(1), 11-24.

Radley, J.J., Rocher, A.B., Miller, M., Janssen, W.G., Liston, C., Hof, P.R., McEwen, B.S., and Morrison, J.H. (2006). Repeated stress induces dendritic spine loss in the rat medial prefrontal cortex. *Cerebral Cortex*, 16(3), 313-320.

Radliff, K.M., Wheaton, J.E., Robinson, K., and Morris, J. (2012). Illuminating the relationship between bullying and substance use among middle and high school youth. *Addictive Behaviors*, 37(4), 569-572.

Rau, V., and Fanselow, M.S. (2009). Exposure to a stressor produces a long lasting enhancement of fear learning in rats: Original research report. *Stress*, 12(2), 125-133.

Reijntjes, A., Kamphuis, J.H., Prinzie, P., and Telch, M.J. (2010). Peer victimization and internalizing problems in children: A meta-analysis of longitudinal studies. *Child Abuse & Neglect*, 34(4), 244-252.

Reijntjes, A., Kamphuis, J.H., Prinzie, P., Boelen, P.A., Van der Schoot, M., and Telch, M.J. (2011). Prospective linkages between peer victimization and externalizing problems in children: A meta-analysis. *Aggressive Behavior*, 37(3), 215-222.

Repetti, R.L., Taylor, S.E., and Seeman, T.E. (2002). Risky families: Family social environments and the mental and physical health of offspring. *Psychological Bulletin*, 128(2), 330-366.

Retz, W., Retz-Junginger, P., Supprian, T., Thome, J., and Rösler, M. (2004). Association of serotonin transporter promoter gene polymorphism with violence: Relation with personality disorders, impulsivity, and childhood adhd psychopathology. *Behavioral Sciences & the Law*, 22(3), 415-425.

Reuter-Rice, K. (2008). Male adolescent bullying and the school shooter. *Journal of School Nursing*, 24(6), 350-359.

Richter-Levin, G., Horovitz, O., and Tsoory, M.M. (2015). The early adolescent of "juvenile stress" translational animal model of posttraumatic stress disorder. In M.P. Safir, H.S. Wallach, and A. Rizzo (Eds.), *Future Directions in Post-Traumatic Stress Disorder: Prevention Diagnosis, and Treatment*. New York: Springer.

Rigby, K., and Slee, P.T. (1993). Dimensions of interpersonal relation among Australian children and implications for psychological well-being. *Journal of Social Psychology*, 133(1), 33-42.

Rivers, I., and Noret, N. (2013). Potential suicide ideation and its association with observing bullying at school. *Journal of Adolescent Health*, 53(1), S32-S36.

Rivers, I., Poteat, V.P., Noret, N., and Ashurst, N. (2009). Observing bullying at school: The mental health implications of witness status. *School Psychology Quarterly*, 24(4), 211-223.

Robertson, K.D. (2005). DNA methylation and human disease. *Nature Reviews: Genetics*, 6(8), 597-610.

Rocque, M. (2012). Exploring school rampage shootings: Research, theory, and policy. *Social Science Journal*, 49(3), 304-313.

Rodkin, P.C. (2004). Peer ecologies of aggression and bullying. In D.L. Espelage and S.M. Swearer (Eds.), *Bullying in American Schools: A Social-Ecological Perspective on Prevention and Intervention* (pp. 87-106). Mahwah, NJ: Lawrence Erlbaum Associates.

Rodkin, P.C., Espelage, D.L., and Hanish, L.D. (2015). A relational framework for understanding bullying: Developmental antecedents and outcomes. *American Psychologist, 70*(4), 311-321.

Romeo, R.D. (2010). Pubertal maturation and programming of hypothalamic–pituitary–adrenal reactivity. *Frontiers in Neuroendocrinology, 31*(2), 232-240.

Romeo, R.D. (2015). Perspectives on stress resilience and adolescent neurobehavioral function. *Neurobiology of Stress, 1*, 128-133.

Roth, T.L. (2014). How traumatic experiences leave their signature on the genome: An overview of epigenetic pathways in PTSD. *Frontiers in Psychiatry, 5*(93), 1-2.

Roth, T.L., and Sweatt, J.D. (2011). Epigenetic marking of the BDNF gene by early-life adverse experiences. *Hormones and Behavior, 59*(3), 315-320.

Rudolph, K.D., Troop-Gordon, W., and Flynn, M. (2009). Relational victimization predicts children's social-cognitive and self-regulatory responses in a challenging peer context. *Developmental Psychology, 45*(5), 1444-1454.

Rudolph, K.D., Miernicki, M.E., Troop-Gordon, W., Davis, M.M., and Telzer, E.H. (2016). Adding insult to injury: Neural sensitivity to social exclusion is associated with internalizing symptoms in chronically peer-victimized girls. *Social Cognitive and Affective Neuroscience.* doi: 10.1093/scan/nsw021.

Rueger, S.Y., and Jenkins, L.N. (2014). Effects of peer victimization on psychological and academic adjustment in early adolescence. *School Psychology Quarterly, 29*(1), 77-88.

Rueger, S.Y., Malecki, C.K., and Demaray, M.K. (2011). Stability of peer victimization in early adolescence: Effects of timing and duration. *Journal of School Psychology, 49*(4), 443-464.

Salmivalli, C. (2010). Bullying and the peer group: A review. *Aggression and Violent Behavior, 15*(2), 112-120.

Salmivalli, C., Lagerspetz, K., Björkqvist, K., Österman, K., and Kaukiainen, A. (1996). Bullying as a group process: Participant roles and their relations to social status within the group. *Aggressive Behavior, 22*(1), 1-15.

Salmivalli, C., Voeten, M., and Poskiparta, E. (2011). Bystanders matter: Associations between reinforcing, defending, and the frequency of bullying behavior in classrooms. *Journal of Clinical Child & Adolescent Psychology, 40*(5), 668-676.

Sanchez, M., and Pollak, S. (2009). Socio-emotional development following early abuse and neglect: Challenges and insights from translational research. In M. de Haan and M.R. Gunnar (Eds.), *Handbook of Developmental Social Neuroscience* (pp. 497-520). New York: Guilford Press.

Sandi, C., and Haller, J. (2015). Stress and the social brain: Behavioural effects and neurobiological mechanisms. *Nature Reviews Neuroscience, 16*, 290-304.

Scarr, S., and McCartney, K. (1983). How people make their own environments: A theory of genotype→ environment effects. *Child Development, 52*(2), 424-435.

Schacter, H.L., White, S.J., Chang, V.Y., and Juvonen, J. (2014). "Why me?": Characterological self-blame and continued victimization in the first year of middle school. *Journal of Clinical Child & Adolescent Psychology, 44*(3), 446-455.

Schwartz, D., Dodge, K.A., and Coie, J.D. (1993). The emergence of chronic peer victimization in boys' play groups. *Child Development, 64*(6), 1755-1772.

Schwartz, D., Gorman, A.H., Nakamoto, J., and Toblin, R.L. (2005). Victimization in the peer group and children's academic functioning. *Journal of Educational Psychology, 97*(3), 425-435.

Shakoor, S., Jaffee, S.R., Andreou, P., Bowes, L., Ambler, A.P., Caspi, A., Moffitt, T.E., and Arseneault, L. (2011). Mothers and children as informants of bullying victimization: Results from an epidemiological cohort of children. *Journal of Abnormal Child Psychology, 39*(3), 379-387.

Shalev, I., Moffitt, T.E., Sugden, K., Williams, B., Houts, R.M., Danese, A., Mill, J., Arseneault, L., and Caspi, A. (2013). Exposure to violence during childhood is associated with telomere erosion from 5 to 10 years of age: A longitudinal study. *Molecular Psychiatry, 18*(5), 576-581.

Shen, J., Kudrimoti, H., McNaughton, B., and Barnes, C. (1998). Reactivation of neuronal ensembles in hippocampal dentate gyrus during sleep after spatial experience. *Journal of Sleep Research, 7*(S1), 6-16.

Shonkoff, J.P., Boyce, W.T., and McEwen, B.S. (2009). Neuroscience, molecular biology, and the childhood roots of health disparities: Building a new framework for health promotion and disease prevention. *Journal of the American Medical Association, 301*(21), 2252-2259.

Shultz, J.M., Thoresen, S., Flynn, B.W., Muschert, G.W., Shaw, J.A., Espinel, Z., Walter, F.G., Gaither, J.B., Garcia-Barcena, Y., and O'Keefe, K. (2014). Multiple vantage points on the mental health effects of mass shootings. *Current Psychiatry Reports, 16*(9), 1-17.

Sigurdson, J.F., Undheim, A.M., Wallander, J.L., Lydersen, S., and Sund, A.M. (2015). The long-term effects of being bullied or a bully in adolescence on externalizing and internalizing mental health problems in adulthood. *Child and Adolescent Psychiatry and Mental Health, 9*(1), 1-13.

Sijtsema, J.J., Veenstra, R., Lindenberg, S., and Salmivalli, C. (2009). Empirical test of bullies' status goals: Assessing direct goals, aggression, and prestige. *Aggressive Behavior, 35*, 57-67.

Smalley, D., and Banerjee, R. (2013). The role of social goals in bullies' and victims' social information processing in response to ambiguous and overtly hostile provocation. *Social Development, 23*(3), 593-610.

Smith, P.K., Talamelli, L., Cowie, H., Naylor, P., and Chauhan, P. (2004). Profiles of non-victims, escaped victims, continuing victims and new victims of school bullying. *British Journal of Educational Psychology, 74*, 565-581.

Sourander, A., Jensen, P., Rönning, J.A., Elonheimo, H., Niemelä, S., Helenius, H., Kumpulainen, K., Piha, J., Tamminen, T., Moilanen, I., and Almqvist, F. (2007). Childhood bullies and victims and their risk of criminality in late adolescence. *Archives of Pediatrics and Adolescent Medicine, 161*(6), 546-552.

Sourander, A., Brunstein, K.A., Kumpulainen, K., Puustjärvi, A., Elonheimo, H., Ristkari, T., Tamminen, T., Moilanen, I., Piha, J., and Ronning, J. (2011). Bullying at age eight and criminality in adulthood: Findings from the Finnish Nationwide 1981 Birth Cohort Study. *Social Psychiatry and Psychiatric Epidemiology, 46*(12), 1211-1219.

Spear, L. (2010). *The Behavioral Neuroscience of Adolescence.* New York: WW Norton & Company.

Spear, L.P. (2013). Adolescent neurodevelopment. *Journal of Adolescent Health, 52*(2), S7-S13.

Srabstein, J.C., McCarter, R.J., Shao, C., and Huang, Z.J. (2006). Morbidities associated with bullying behaviors in adolescents. School based study of American adolescents. *International Journal of Adolescent Medicine and Health, 18*(4), 587-596.

Stapinski, L.A., Bowes, L., Wolke, D., Pearson, R.M., Mahedy, L., Button, K.S., Lewis, G., and Araya, R. (2014). Peer victimization during adolescence and risk for anxiety disorders in adulthood: A prospective cohort study. *Depression and anxiety, 31*(7), 574-582.

Sugden, K., Arseneault, L., Harrington, H., Moffitt, T.E., Williams, B., and Caspi, A. (2010). Serotonin transporter gene moderates the development of emotional problems among children following bullying victimization. *Journal of the American Academy of Child & Adolescent Psychiatry, 49*(8), 830-840.

Swearer, S.M., and Hymel, S. (2015). Understanding the psychology of bullying: Moving toward a social-ecological diathesis–stress model. *American Psychologist, 70*(4), 344-353.

Tharp-Taylor, S., Haviland, A., and D'Amico, E.J. (2009). Victimization from mental and physical bullying and substance use in early adolescence. *Addictive Behaviors, 34*(6), 561-567.

Thornberg, R., Tenenbaum, L., Varjas, K., Meyers, J., Jungert, T., and Vanegas, G. (2012). Bystander motivation in bullying incidents: To intervene or not to intervene? *Western Journal of Emergency Medicine, 13*(3), 247-252.

Thunfors, P., and Cornell, D. (2008). The popularity of middle school bullies. *Journal of School Violence, 7*(1), 65-82.

Tilghman-Osborne, C., Cole, D.A., Felton, J.W., and Ciesla, J.A. (2008). Relation of guilt, shame, behavioral and characterological self-blame to depressive symptoms in adolescents over time. *Journal of Social and Clinical Psychology, 27*(8), 809-842.

Ttofi, M.M., Farrington, D.P., Lösel, F., and Loeber, R. (2011). Do the victims of school bullies tend to become depressed later in life? A systematic review and meta-analysis of longitudinal studies. *Journal of Aggression, Conflict and Peace Research, 3*(2), 63-73.

Unnever, J.D., and Cornell, D.G. (2003). The culture of bullying in middle school. *Journal of School Violence, 2*(2), 5-27.

Vaillancourt, T., Hymel, S., and McDougall, P. (2003). Bullying is power: Implications for school-based intervention strategies. *Journal of Applied School Psychology, 19*(2), 157-176.

Vaillancourt, T., Duku, E., Decatanzaro, D., Macmillan, H., Muir, C., and Schmidt, L.A. (2008). Variation in hypothalamic–pituitary–adrenal axis activity among bullied and non-bullied children. *Aggressive Behavior, 34*(3), 294-305.

Vaillancourt, T., Decatanzaro, D., Duku, E., and Muir, C. (2009). Androgen dynamics in the context of children's peer relations: An examination of the links between testosterone and peer victimization. *Aggressive Behavior, 35*(1), 103-113.

Vaillancourt, T., Hymel, S., and McDougall, P. (2010a). Why does bullying hurt so much? Insights from neuroscience. In D. Espelage and S. Swearer (Eds.), *Bullying in North American Schools* (pp. 23-33). New York: Taylor & Francis.

Vaillancourt, T., McDougall, P., Hymel, S., and Sunderani, S. (2010b). The relationship between power and bullying behavior. In S.R. Jimerson, S.M. Swearer, and D.L. Espelage (Eds.), *Handbook of Bullying in Schools: An International Perspective* (pp. 211-222). New York: Routledge.

Vaillancourt, T., Duku, E., Becker, S., Schmidt, L.A., Nicol, J., Muir, C., and MacMillan, H. (2011). Peer victimization, depressive symptoms, and high salivary cortisol predict poorer memory in children. *Brain and Cognition, 77*(2), 191-199.

Vaillancourt, T., Hymel, S., and McDougall, P. (2013a). The biological underpinnings of peer victimization: Understanding why and how the effects of bullying can last a lifetime. *Theory Into Practice, 52*(4), 241-248.

Vaillancourt, T., Brittain, H.L., McDougall, P., and Duku, E. (2013b). Longitudinal links between childhood peer victimization, internalizing and externalizing problems, and academic functioning: Developmental cascades. *Journal of Abnormal Child Psychology, 41*(8), 1203-1215.

Vaillancourt, T., Sanderson, C., Arnold, P., and McDougall, P. (in press). The neurobiology of peer victimization: Longitudinal links to health, genetic risk, and epigenetic mechanisms. In C.P. Bradshaw (Ed.), *Handbook of Bullying Prevention: A Life Course Perspective*: National Association of Social Workers Press.

van Dam, D.S., van der Ven, E., Velthorst, E., Selten, J.P., Morgan, C., and de Haan, L. (2012). Childhood bullying and the association with psychosis in non-clinical and clinical samples: A review and meta-analysis. *Psychological Medicine, 42*(12), 2463-2474.

van Geel, M., Vedder, P., and Tanilon, J. (2014). Relationship between peer victimization, cyberbullying, and suicide in children and adolescents. *Journal of American Medical Association Pediatrics, 168*(5), 435-442.

van Geel, M., Goemans, A., and Vedder, P.H. (2015). The relation between peer victimization and sleeping problems: A meta-analysis. *Sleep Medicine Reviews, 27*, 89-95.

Vannucci, M., Nocentini, A., Mazzoni, G., and Menesini, E. (2012). Recalling unpresented hostile words: False memories predictors of traditional and cyberbullying. *European Journal of Developmental Psychology, 9*(2), 182-194.

VanZomeren-Dohm, A.A., Pitula, C.E., Koss, K.J., Thomas, K., and Gunnar, M.R. (2015). FKBP5 moderation of depressive symptoms in peer victimized, post-institutionalized children. *Psychoneuroendocrinology, 51*, 426-430.

Veenstra, R., Lindenberg, S., Munniksma, A., and Dijkstra, J.K. (2010). The complex relation between bullying, victimization, acceptance, and rejection: Giving special attention to status, affection, and sex differences. *Child Development, 81*(2), 480-486.

Viding, E., Blair, R.J.R., Moffitt, T.E., and Plomin, R. (2005). Evidence for substantial genetic risk for psychopathy in 7-year-olds. *Journal of Child Psychology and Psychiatry, 46*(6), 592-597.

Vossekuil, B., Fein, R.A., Reddy, M., Borum, R., and Modzeleski, W. (2002). *The Final Report and Findings of the Safe School Initiative: Implications for the Prevention of the Safe School Initiative.* Washington, DC: U.S. Secret Service and Department of Education.

Weaver, I.C., Cervoni, N., Champagne, F.A., D'Alessio, A.C., Sharma, S., Seckl, J.R., Dymov, S., Szyf, M., and Meaney, M.J. (2004). Epigenetic programming by maternal behavior. *Nature Neuroscience, 7*(8), 847-854.

Weiner, B. (1986). *An Attributional Theory of Motivation and Emotion.* New York: Springer-Verlag.

Whelan, Y.M., Kretschmer, T., and Barker, E.D. (2014). MAOA, early experiences of harsh parenting, irritable opposition, and bullying–victimization: A moderated indirect-effects analysis. *Merrill-Palmer Quarterly, 60*(2), 217-237.

Wilker, S., Pfeiffer, A., Kolassa, S., Elbert, T., Lingenfelder, B., Ovuga, E., Papassotiropoulos, A., de Quervain, D., and Kolassa, I.-T. (2014). The role of FKBP5 genotype in moderating long-term effectiveness of exposure-based psychotherapy for posttraumatic stress disorder. *Translational Psychiatry, 4*(6), 1-7.

Williams, K.D., Bernieri, F.J., Faulkner, S.L., Gada-Jain, N., and Grahe, J.E. (2000). The Scarlet Letter Study: Five days of social ostracism. *Journal of Personal & Interpersonal Loss, 5*(1), 19-63.

Wilson, T.D., Damiani, M., and Shelton, N. (2002). Improving the academic performance of college students with brief attributional interventions. In T.D. Wilson (Ed.), *Improving Academic Achievement: Impact of Psychological Factors on Education* (pp. 89-108). San Diego, CA: Elsevier BV.

Wolke, D., Woods, S., Bloomfield, L., and Karstadt, L. (2001). Bullying involvement in primary school and common health problems. *Archives of Disease in Childhood, 85*(3), 197-201.

Wolke, D., Lereya, S.T., Fisher, H., Lewis, G., and Zammit, S. (2014). Bullying in elementary school and psychotic experiences at 18 years: A longitudinal, population-based cohort study. *Psychological Medicine, 44*(10), 2199-2211.

Yang, G.S., and McLoyd, V.C. (2015). Do parenting and family characteristics moderate the relation between peer victimization and antisocial behavior? A 5-year longitudinal study. *Social Development, 24*, 748-765.

Ybarra, M.L., Mitchell, K.J., Wolak, J., and Finkelhor, D. (2006). Examining characteristics and associated distress related to Internet harassment: Findings from the second Youth Internet Safety Survey. *Pediatrics, 118*(4), e1169-e1177.

5

Preventive Interventions

The research on bullying prevention programming has increased considerably over the past 2 decades, which is likely due in part to the growing awareness of bullying as a public health problem that impacts individual youth as well as the broader social environment. Furthermore, the enactment of bullying-related laws and policies in all 50 states has drawn increased focus on prevention programming. In fact, many state policies require some type of professional development for staff or prevention programming related to bullying (Hatzenbuehler et al., 2015; Stuart-Cassel et al., 2011). Despite this growing interest in and demand for bullying prevention programming, there have been relatively few randomized controlled trials (RCTs) testing the efficacy or effectiveness of programs specifically designed to reduce or prevent the onset of bullying or offset its consequences on children and youth (Bradshaw, 2015; Jiménez-Barbero et al. 2016). Moreover, the much larger body and longer line of research focused on aggression, violence, and delinquency prevention has only recently begun to explore program impacts specific to bullying. The focus of that research has typically been on broader concepts, such as aggression, violence, delinquency, externalizing problems, etc. Therefore, it is quite possible that there are several violence or aggression prevention programs that have substantial effects on bullying, but there is currently too little data available from most violence prevention studies that employ RCT designs to formulate a conclusion regarding impacts on bullying specifically (Bradshaw, 2015).

In this chapter, the committee summarizes the current status of bullying prevention programming, while acknowledging both gaps in the extant literature and opportunities for future research. The committee first focuses

179

more narrowly on bullying prevention and intervention programming for which there are data specifically on bullying behaviors; greater emphasis is placed on RCTs, as compared to nonexperimental, correlational, or descriptive studies. The committee then considers the broader literature on other youth-focused violence prevention and intervention programming, with particular attention to potential conceptual or measurement overlap with bullying, since such models may hold promise for reducing rates or effects of bullying (Bradshaw, 2015; Hawkins et al. 2015). Although the committee was intentionally inclusive of the larger body of prevention programming literature, it acknowledges the caveats of such a broad focus, as findings from other violence prevention programs may not always generalize to bullying-specific outcomes (e.g., Espelage et al., 2013). Nevertheless, this review is not intended to be an exhaustive list of all evidence-based approaches to bullying or youth violence prevention; rather, the committee highlights particular models and frameworks for which there is a strong or emerging line of RCT studies suggesting promise for preventing or offsetting the consequences of bullying.

In an effort to organize the vast and somewhat disparate lines of prevention literature, the committee adopted the National Research Council's public health model of mental health intervention (Institute of Medicine, 1994) as a framework for conceptualizing the various programs and models across increasing levels of intensity (see Figure 5-1).

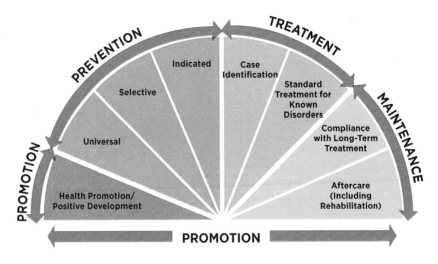

FIGURE 5-1 Mental health intervention spectrum.
SOURCE: Adapted from Institute of Medicine (1994, Fig. 2.1, p. 23).

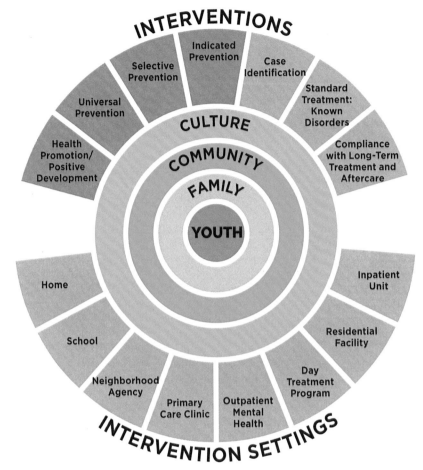

FIGURE 5-2 An ecodevelopmental model of prevention.
SOURCE: Adapted from National Research Council and Institute of Medicine (2009, Fig. 4-1, p. 73).

This model includes three levels of prevention programming (i.e., universal, selective, and indicated), which are preceded by promotion-focused programming and followed by treatment and maintenance (National Research Council and Institute of Medicine, 2009). Mental health promotion has been recognized as a key component of the mental health intervention continuum (National Research Council and Institute of Medicine, 2009). Although prevention programming can occur in multiple settings and ecological contexts (see Figure 5-2; also Espelage and Swearer, 2004; Swearer et al., 2010; Weisz et al., 2005), the majority of research has been conducted within schools. As a result, the committee made an effort to also provide examples of programs that occur in settings other than school, even when the literature base was thinner as it relates to bullying-specific programming and/or outcomes. After summarizing various research-based prevention frameworks and programs, the committee concludes by highlighting lessons learned from the extant research as it relates to critical features of bullying prevention programming and identifying future research directions related to bullying prevention programming.

MULTI-TIERED PREVENTION FRAMEWORK

An increasingly common approach to the prevention of emotional and behavioral disorders is the three-tiered public health model that includes universal, selective, and indicated preventive interventions, as illustrated in Figure 5-1 (Institute of Medicine, 1994; National Research Council and Institute of Medicine, 2009; Weisz et al., 2005). Similar frameworks have been proposed or articulated to conceptualize a multi-tiered system of supports (for a review, see Batsche, 2014). Although this continuum of preventive interventions can be applied to many behavioral, educational, mental health, and physical health problems, this report considers it primarily through the lens of bullying prevention among youth.

The Three Tiers

Specifically, *universal* prevention programs are aimed at reducing risks and strengthening skills for all youth within a defined community or school setting. Through universal programs, all members of the target population are exposed to the intervention regardless of risk for bullying. Using universal prevention approaches, a set of activities may be established that offers benefits to all individuals within that setting (e.g., school). Examples of universal or Tier 1 preventive interventions include social-emotional lessons that are used in the classroom, behavioral expectations taught by teachers, counselors coming into the classroom to model strategies for responding to or reporting bullying, and holding classroom meetings among students and teachers to discuss emotionally relevant issues related to bullying or equity. Universal interventions could also include guidelines for the use of digital media, such as youth's use of social network sites.

Most of the bullying prevention programs that have been evaluated with RCT designs have employed a universal approach to prevention (Ttofi and Farrington, 2011; Jiménez Barbero et al., 2016). Although universal bullying prevention programs are typically aimed at having effects on youth, they may also yield benefits for the individuals implementing the programs. For example, recent findings from a RCT of a social–emotional learning and behavior management program indicated that the program substantially affected the teachers who implemented the program, as well as affecting the students (Domitrovich et al., 2016). Similarly positive effects were observed in a randomized trial of a schoolwide Positive Behavior Support model, where implementation of the model demonstrated significant impacts on the staff members' perceptions of school climate (Bradshaw et al., 2009a). Consistent with the social-ecological model, these effects may be either direct—through the professional development provided to the teachers—or indirect through the improved behavior and enhanced organizational context of the setting in which the program is implemented. These types of secondary impacts on the broader school or community environment also likely occur in universal bullying prevention programs, many of which are intended to reduce bullying in conjunction with improving school climate (Bradshaw, 2013).

Most school-based bullying prevention programs would fall under the universal category of largely preventive interventions, with limited articulation of specific programs, activities, or supports for students not responding adequately to the universal model. Even if the programs focus on the whole school or climate/culture changes, they often take the perspective that a universal approach is the most important and potentially most effective intervention because all children can benefit from attempts to enhance school climate, change attitudes or awareness about bullying, reduce aggressive behavior, or improve related social skills or behavior. Furthermore, some universal programs follow the assumption that all students are considered to be at risk at some level for bullying behavior, either as perpetrators, targets, or bystanders (Rigby and Slee, 2008). In fact, there is a growing recognition that universal prevention programs do not equally benefit all individuals; rather, evidence is emerging that universal prevention programs may actually be more effective for higher risk students than those traditionally conceptualized as low risk (Bradshaw et al., 2015; Eron et al., 2002; Kellam et al., 1994). As a result, there is a growing trend in prevention research to explicitly examine variation in responsiveness to universal prevention programs in order to better understand which youth may be most affected by a particular model (Kellam et al., 1994; Lanza and Rhoades, 2013). This may also improve understanding of why some effect sizes of universal prevention programs are relatively modest when they are averaged across a large population, as a broader population may have a relatively low base rate for engaging in the behavior (Biglan et al., 2015). On the other hand, investing in prevention on a national level has the potential to produce significant and meaningful behavior change for larger populations of youth across a broad array of outcomes, not just outcomes related to bullying behavior (Biglan et al., 2015; Institute of Medicine and National Research Council, 2015).

The next level of the tiered prevention model is referred to as *selective preventive interventions*. These may either target youth who are at risk for engaging in bullying or target youth at risk of being bullied. Such programs may include more intensive social-emotional skills training, coping skills, or de-escalation approaches for youth who are involved in bullying. Consistent with a response-to-intervention framework, these Tier 2 approaches are employed to meet the needs of youth who have not responded adequately to the universal preventive intervention (National Research Council and Institute of Medicine, 2009).

The third tier includes *indicated preventive interventions*, which are typically tailored to meet the youth's needs and are of greater intensity as compared to the two previous levels of prevention. Indicated interventions incorporate more intensive supports and activities for those who are already displaying bullying behavior or have a history of being bullied and are showing early signs of behavioral, academic, or mental health consequences. The supports are usually tailored to meet the needs of the students demonstrating negative effects of bullying (Espelage and Swearer, 2008); they typically address mental and behavioral health concerns, often by including the youth's family. Such programs may also leverage expertise and involvement of teachers, education support professionals, school resource officers, families, health care professionals, and community members, thereby attempting to support the participating youth across multiple ecological levels. While a number of selective and indicated programs have demonstrated efficacy for a range of youth behavioral and mental health problems (for a review see National Research Council and Institute of Medicine, 2009), there has been considerably less research on selective and indicated prevention programs specific to bullying (Swearer et al., 2014).

Integrating Prevention Programs across the Tiers

Consistent with the public health approach to prevention (National Research Council and Institute of Medicine, 2009) and calls for multi-tier or multidisciplinary approaches to prevention, there is an increasing interest in layering components "on top of" or in combination with the universal intervention to address factors that may place youth at risk for being targets or perpetrators of bullying (universal plus targeted interventions). These combined programs often attempt to address at the universal level such factors as social skill development, social-emotional learning or self-regulation, which are intended to also reduce the chances that youth would engage in bullying or reduce the risk of further being bullied (Bradshaw, 2013, 2015; Merrell et al., 2008; Ttofi and Farrington, 2011; Vreeman and

Carroll, 2007). These combined programs are often characterized as universal, whole school, or climate/culture changing programs that may have additional "benefits" for perpetrators or targets (e.g., help them be more effective in coping with the stress of bullying). However, few have easily identifiable components that specifically target youth at risk for involvement in bullying behavior or those already identified as perpetrators or targets. Therefore much of what is currently known about bullying prevention derives from studies of universal programs, with limited research on selective and indicated models for prevention.

Current research is limited in its ability to specifically tease out the effects of targeted elements embedded in whole-school universal programs (Bradshaw, 2015; Ttofi and Farrington, 2011). For example, evaluators have not been able to assess whether it is the universal or targeted components (or the combination of the two) that leads to reductions in bullying behavior or improvements in social-emotional skills (Ttofi and Farrington, 2011). In fact, few of the truly multi-tiered programs have been evaluated using randomized, controlled esperimental designs to determine whether they are effective or lead to sustained behavior change. Moreover, once a child or youth is identified as a target or a perpetrator of bullying, the individual is often referred to mental health or behavioral health services providers in the community—in part because few school-based mental health professionals are available to provide these specialized services (Swearer et al., 2014).

In summary, despite calls for a layered public health approach to bullying prevention or calls for multicomponent, multilevel programs (Leff and Waasdorp, 2013), few studies of school-based bullying prevention programs have simultaneously evaluated both universal and targeted components (Bradshaw, 2015). Although many researchers encourage the use of a multi-tiered approach to address bullying, and there is conceptual research supporting the full integration of preventive interventions (Bradshaw, 2013, 2015; Espelage and Swearer, 2008; Hawley and Williford, 2015; Hong and Espelage, 2012; Swearer et al., 2012), relatively few large-scale RCT studies have examined the combined and tier-specific effects of multi-tiered programs on bullying. Yet, integrating the nested levels of support into a coherent, tiered framework could also reduce burden and increase efficiency of implementation (Bradshaw et al., 2014a; Domitrovich et al., 2010; Sugai and Horner, 2006).

Perspectives from the Field

Treatments could be better integrated: We could be doing more to integrate social services in schools with medical treatments, and we could also foster stronger relationships with varying organizations so we can make better referrals. Behavioral health counselors embedded in the school district as satellite offices could be helpful, particularly when they can work with pediatricians. Access to care is immensely important, as is supporting people in getting that access (particularly in seeking access without having to worry about stigma). Everyone needs to work together as a team with their own place on the pathway to preventing bullying. Another thing we've thought of is having mental health professionals in the room during pediatric visits to talk to the parent and conduct pre-screening.

—Summary from community-based providers focus group
(See Appendix B for additional highlights from interviews.)

PREVENTION PROGRAMS SPECIFICALLY IMPLEMENTED TO REDUCE BULLYING AND RELATED BEHAVIOR PROBLEMS

The sections that follow focus on the available efficacy and effectiveness research that has examined different bullying prevention programs, the vast majority of which have been implemented at the universal level and within schools. The committee first considers the evidence for the effectiveness of universal programs, many of which are whole-school efforts that may include some elements directed to youth at risk for bullying or those already engaged in bullying behaviors.[1] The committee also reviews the effectiveness of specific selective or indicated prevention programs, many of which were designed more broadly for youth with behavioral or mental health problems, rather than specifically for bullying.

The committee considered the broader literature on programs aimed at reducing youth aggressive behavior and those aimed at improving emotional and behavioral problems among youth. While most of these programs were not originally developed to address bullying behavior specifically, one may still learn much from them about means to reduce bullying-related behavior, or they may provide clues about how to improve resilience, social competence, or problem-solving skills that may lead to reductions in bullying perpetration or being bullied. In some instances, the committee has drawn

---

[1] Clinicians and policy makers define efficacy trials as trials that determine whether "an intervention produces expected results under ideal circumstances" and effectiveness trials as trials that "measure the degree of beneficial effect under 'real world' clinical settings" (Gartlehner et al., 2006).

upon literature from related fields, such as trauma exposure or research on how families can promote emotional resilience to being a target of bullying (Bowes et al., 2010). Few of these studies, however, have assessed or examined the impact of these interventions on behaviors specific to bullying. Rather, they may assess behaviors such as fighting, threats, violence, aggressive, or delinquent behavior. If one takes the position that most bullying can be characterized as aggressive behavior but not all aggressive or violent behavior meets the narrower definition of bullying (Farrington and Ttofi, 2011; Finkelhor et al., 2012; Leff and Waasdorp, 2013), then perhaps there are lessons to learn from interventions that have shown reductions in aggression and violence or improvements in social skills, even if bullying behavior was not the primary focus of the intervention. The same thinking applies to studies of peer victimization in that while being bullied may be characterized as a form of victimization, not all victimization by peers would be characterized as bullying, particularly with respect to the criteria of repeated targeting or a power imbalance (Finkelhor et al., 2012).

Perspectives from the Field

We should pay attention to the bully, too: Appropriate consequences for bullying should happen, including punishment, but we also need to ask what kids are going through that makes them want to bully. We need to actually talk to everyone, not accepting bullying but accepting that everyone is going through their own challenges and has their own needs. Bullies should be part of the solution and should not be isolated or ignored.

—Summary from community-based providers and young adults
focus groups discussing bullying

"Before you get angry, before you think of all the mean things you could say, just take time, take a breath, and think about what they're thinking. And that's how you solve it, that's how you help the bully. You ask them about it."

—Quote from a young adult in a focus group discussing bullying
(See Appendix B for additional highlights from interviews.)

Another reason the committee has considered the broader violence-prevention literature is that bullying often co-occurs with other behavioral and mental health problems, including aggression and delinquent behaviors (Bradshaw et al., 2013a; Swearer et al., 2012), and the risk factors targeted through preventive interventions are often interrelated. For example, aggressive youth are more likely to be rejected by their peers, to have associated academic problems (Nansel et al., 2003), or to experience higher rates of family discord or maltreatment (Shields and Cicchetti, 2001). Further, many preventive interventions seek to enhance positive or prosocial behaviors or improve social competence, in addition to reducing negative behaviors such as aggression and fighting (Embry et al., 1996; Flannery et al., 2003).

For example, a meta-analysis of school-based mental health promotion programs found that they can improve social-emotional skills, prosocial norms, school bonding, and positive social behavior, as well as result in reduced problem behaviors, such as aggression, substance use, and internalizing symptoms (Durlak et al., 2007; Durlak et al., 2011). An improvement in competence and social problem-solving skills may lead to reductions in bullying perpetration even if that was not the intended outcome of the intervention. Other studies have demonstrated improvements in youth coping skills and stress management (Kraag et al., 2006), which can be helpful to children who are bullied even if such children were not the original population targeted by the intervention. In summary, many school and community-based programs were not originally designed to specifically reduce bullying, but because they target related behaviors, they may provide valuable lessons that can inform efforts related to bullying prevention.

Summary of the Available Meta-Analyses

A number of recent meta-analyses have been conducted in an effort to identify the most effective and promising approaches within the field of bullying prevention; for a review of the meta-analyses see Ttofi and colleagues (2014). The most comprehensive review conducted to date was by Ttofi and Farrington (2011), who applied the Campbell Systematic Review procedures in reviewing 44 rigorous program evaluations and RCTs. The majority of these studies were conducted outside the United States or Canada (66%), and over a third of the programs were based in part on the work of Olweus (1993). Ttofi and Farrington (2011) found that the programs, on average, were associated with a 20-23 percent decrease in perpetration of bullying, and a 17-20 percent decrease in being bullied, as illustrated in Figures 5-3 and 5-4.[2]

As in other reviews and meta-analyses (Bradshaw, 2015; Leff and Waasdorp, 2013), Farrington and Ttofi (2009) concluded that in general the

---

[2]The committee includes details of studies where possible, in particular if the study employed a RCT design and where effect sizes are reported or control groups were used. We encourage the reader to refer to the original studies for additional details about study design, population, measurement, variables included in analyses, etc.

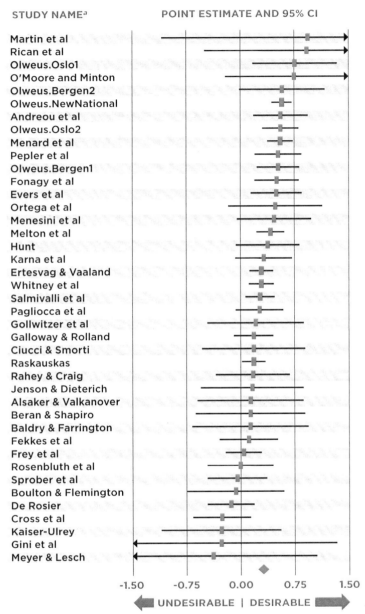

FIGURE 5-3 Forest graph showing the measure of program effect sizes in logarithm of odds ratio (LOR) for bullying perpetration.
SOURCE: Ttofi and Farrington (2011, Fig. 1, p. 38).

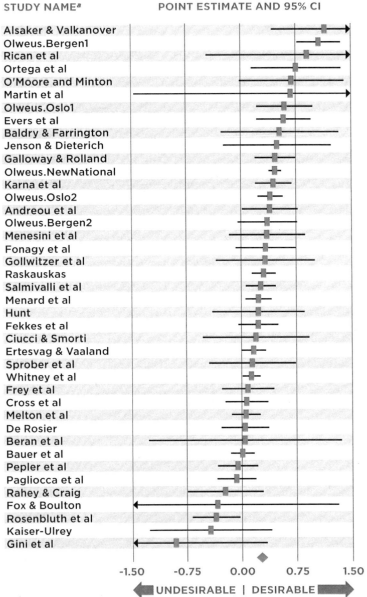

a For additional details about study design, population, measurement, variables included in analyses, etc., please refer to the original studies.

FIGURE 5-4 Forest graph showing the measure of program effect sizes in logarithm of odds ratio (LOR) for victimization.
SOURCE: Ttofi and Farrington (2011, Fig. 2, p. 39).

most effective programs are multicomponent, schoolwide programs that re-duce bullying and aggression across a variety of settings. However, as noted previously, these multicomponent programs are not always multi-tiered in the context of the public health model; rather, they may have multiple complementary program elements that all focus on universal prevention, such as a combination of a whole-school climate strategy coupled with a curriculum to prevent bullying or related behaviors. Furthermore, the de-signs of the studies precluded the researchers from isolating which program elements accounted for the program impacts. Nevertheless, Farrington and Ttofi (2009) concluded that parent training, improved playground super-vision, disciplinary methods, school conferences, videos, information for parents, classroom rules, and classroom management were program com-ponents associated with a decrease in students being bullied.

The whole-school bullying prevention programs (mostly based on or modeled after the extensively studied Olweus Bullying Prevention Program model, which aims at reducing bullying through components at multiple levels) also generally demonstrated positive effects, particularly in schools with more positive student-teacher relationships (Richard et al., 2012). In general, significant intervention effects have been demonstrated more often for programs implemented in Europe (Richard et al., 2012) and Scandina-vian countries (Farrington and Ttofi, 2009; Salmivalli, 2010) than in the United States (also see Bradshaw, 2015). Some researchers and practitioners have suggested that interventions implemented outside the United States may be more successful because they involve more homogeneous student samples in schools that are more committed to implementing programs as intended (Evans et al., 2014), compared with student samples and schools' commitment in the United States. Competing demands on student and teacher time, such as standardized testing, also limit U.S. teachers' perceived ability to focus on social-emotional and behavioral activities, as compared with traditional academic content. The challenges in designing and deliver-ing effective bullying prevention programs in the United States may also include the greater social and economic complexities of U.S. school popula-tions, including greater income disparities and racial/ethnic heterogeneity.

The meta-analyses, most notably the Ttofi and Farrington (2011) re-view, noted variation in program effects based on study design, as has been shown for most such intervention programs. For example, large-scale ef-fectiveness studies (i.e., studies of taking an intervention program to scale) did not produce effects as strong as those in more tightly controlled efficacy studies, where the program is often administered with greater support and researcher influence (Bradshaw, 2015; Ttofi and Farrington, 2011). Simi-larly, the effects generally were stronger in the non-RCT designs than in the RCTs, suggesting that the more rigorous the study design, the smaller the effect sizes (Farrington and Ttofi, 2009). Moreover, as has been shown in several other studies across multiple fields (e.g., Domitrovich et al., 2008), poor implementation fidelity has been linked with weaker program out- comes (also see Durlak et al., 2011).

Another important finding from the Ttofi and Farrington review was that, generally speaking, there are more school-based bullying prevention programs that involve middle-school youth than those that target youth of high school age. Of the programs that have been evaluated with RCT designs, the observed effects were generally larger for older youth (ages 11-14) than for younger children (younger than age 10) (Farrington and Ttofi, 2009; Ttofi and Farrington, 2011). However, this effect has not been consistent across all programs and all studies, as there is compelling de- velopmental research suggesting that the earlier one intervenes to prevent behavior problems, the more effective the intervention is (Kellam et al., 1994; Waasdorp et al., 2012). Unpacking this finding is likely to be com- plicated because different programs are often used at different age ranges, thereby confounding the child's age with the program used. However, more recently, some programs that were originally developed for a particular age group have been adapted for youth of a different age range (e.g., Promot- ing Alternative Thinking Strategies, Second Step, Coping Power; Olweus Bullying Prevention Program). Implementations of these programs span multiple age groups, with specific curricular or program activities that are developmentally appropriate for the target population (e.g., to address dif- ferent developmental needs for a third grader than for an eighth grader).

Other meta-analyses of school-based bullying intervention programs have not been as positive as the Ttofi and Farrington (2011) review (e.g., Merrell et al., 2008; Vreeman and Carroll, 2007). Some of these mixed findings may be due to different inclusion criteria, such as where the study was conducted (e.g., in the United States or Europe) or who conducted it (i.e., the program developer or an external evaluator). For example, Merrell and colleagues (2008) reviewed 16 studies of over 15,386 kindergarten through grade 12 (K-12) students in six different countries from 1980 through 2004. They concluded that the majority of outcomes were neither positive nor negative and generally lacked statistical significance one way or the other (they found a meaningful positive average effect on bullying for about one-third of all outcomes). They further concluded that programs are much more likely to show effects on attitudes, self-perceptions, and knowledge than on bullying behavior. Only one of the reviewed studies specifically included an intervention for at-risk students; a program that as- signed social workers to the primary school building to work with students at risk for perpetrating or being targets of bullying (Bagley and Pritchard, 1998). Bagley and Pritchard (1998) assessed student self-reports of bullying incidents and showed significant declines in bullying among students who received intervention services from social workers. Merrell and his colleagues (2008) did not weight the 16 studies in the meta-analysis for sample size, degree of experimental rigor, or threats to validity when they computed effect sizes within the individual research studies. Overall, however, they concluded that while some intervention studies had positive outcomes, these were mostly for attitudes and knowledge rather than improving (lessening the frequency of) youth self-reports of being perpetrators or targets of bullying (Merrell et al., 2008; Smith et al., 2004).

Vreeman and Carroll (2007) also conducted a systematic review of bullying preventive interventions, some of which combined programs across the tiers. They found that whole-school approaches with teacher training or individual counseling did better than curricular-only approaches. Of the 26 studies that met their inclusion criteria, only four included targeted interventions involving social and behavioral skills groups for children involved in bullying as perpetrators (Fast et al., 2003; Meyer and Lesch, 2000) and two targeted youth who were victims of bullying (DeRosier, 2004; Tierney and Dowd, 2000). According to Vreeman and Carroll (2007), three of the four studies focused on youth in middle school (sixth through eighth grade) and one examined third grade students. The only social skills training intervention that showed clear reductions in bullying was the study of third grade students. The other three studies of older youth produced mixed results.

Another more recent meta-analysis of bullying prevention programs by Jiménez-Barbero and colleagues (2016) examined a range of effects of 14 "anti-bullying" programs tested through RCTs, comprising 30,934 adolescents ages 10-16. All studies were published between 2000 and 2013. They examined not only bullying frequency (ES = 0.12) and victimization frequency (ES = 0.09), but also attitudes favoring bullying or school violence (ES = 0.18), attitudes against bullying or school violence (ES = 0.06), and school climate (ES = 0.03). See details of the individual studies below in Figure 5-5. This study was considerably smaller in scale than the Ttofi and Farrington (2011) meta-analysis, in large part because of stricter inclusion criteria. Furthermore, on average, these effect sizes were smaller than observed in the Ttofi and Farrington (2011) study. Because of the smaller sample size, it is difficult to formulate conclusions based on specific components (e.g., family, teacher) or youth subgroups (e.g., age of students). Taken together, the meta-analyses provide evidence that the effect sizes of universal programs are relatively modest. Yet these effects are averaged across a full population of youth; selective and indicated prevention approaches, which focus on youth more directly involved in bullying, will likely yield larger effect sizes, as has been seen in other studies of violence prevention programming (discussed later in this chapter).

In contrast to the somewhat mixed findings on interventions specifically for bullying prevention, the larger body of universal youth violence preven-

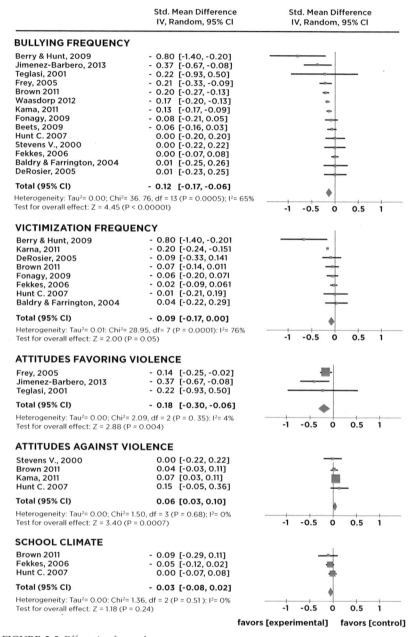

FIGURE 5-5 Effect size for each outcome measurement.
NOTE: For additional details about study design, population, measurement, variables included in analyses, etc., please refer to the original studies.
SOURCE: Adapted from Jiménez-Barbero et al. (2016, Fig. 2, p. 171).

tion programming has generally had more favorable results, particularly for preschool and elementary school children (Sawyer et al., 2015; Wilson and Lipsey, 2007). Systematic reviews and meta-analyses of school-based violence prevention programs (most that did not specifically address bullying behaviors) have shown many to be effective at reducing aggressive behavior and violence (Botvin et al., 2006; Durlak et al., 2011; Hahn et al., 2007; Mytton et al., 2002). Whereas some of the reviews of programs focused on bullying have reported greater effects for older students in middle or secondary schools versus students in primary schools (Mytton et al., 2002; Ttofi and Farrington, 2011), the programs focused on aggression and social competence have shown greater effects for younger children (Kärnä et al., 2011a). One factor may be variations in focus, such as reviews that cover secondary prevention trials for those at risk for aggression and violence (Mytton et al., 2002) versus reviews that include universal and whole school violence prevention programs (Hahn et al., 2007). For example, a review of violence prevention programs by Limbos and colleagues (2007) found that about one-half of 41 intervention studies showed positive effects, with indicated interventions for youth already engaged in violent behavior being more effective than universal or selective interventions.

Another comprehensive meta-review of 25 years of meta-analyses and systematic reviews of youth violence prevention programs concluded that most interventions demonstrate moderate program effects, with programs targeting family factors showing marginally larger effects compared to those that did not (Matjasko et al., 2012). Strength of evidence was rated as small, moderate, or strong by the authors using data on reported effect sizes. This meta-review suggested that studies consistently reported larger effect sizes for reduction of youth violent behavior for programs that targeted selected and indicated populations of youth versus universal prevention. The authors also found that programs with a cognitive-behavioral component tended to have larger effect sizes than those without that component or with only a behavioral component (Matjasko et al., 2012). These findings are generally consistent with a recent meta-analysis by Barnes and colleagues (2014), who found that school-based cognitive behavioral interventions were effective (mean ES = −0.23) on reducing aggressive behavior, especially those delivered universally compared with those provided in small group settings (Barnes et al., 2014).

Examples of Universal Multicomponent Prevention Programs to Address Bullying or Related Behavior

As noted above, many schoolwide bullying prevention programs include multiple components, both within and across the three prevention tiers. One such program is the Olweus Bullying Prevention Program (Olweus,

2005), which is also the most extensively studied bullying prevention program. It aims to reduce bullying through components at multiple levels, including schoolwide components; classroom activities and meetings; targeted interventions for individuals identified as perpetrators or targets; and activities aimed to increase involvement by parents, mental health workers, and others. Some studies of the Olweus Bullying Prevention Program have reported significant reductions in students' reports of bullying and antisocial behaviors (e.g., fighting, truancy) and improvements in school climate (Olweus et al., 1999). However, some smaller-scale studies of this model produced mixed results (e.g., Hanewinkel, 2004). Although other derivations of Olweus's model also have demonstrated promise at reducing bullying in North America (e.g., Pepler et al., 2004), these programs were generally more effective in Europe. Farrington and Ttofi (2009) found that programs that were conceptually based on the Olweus Bullying Prevention Program were the most effective, compared to the other programs examined ($OR = 1.50$ versus $OR = 1.31$, $p = .011$).

Another multicomponent and multi-tiered prevention model is Positive Behavioral Interventions and Supports (PBIS) (Sugai and Horner, 2006; see also Walker et al., 1996). PBIS aims to prevent disruptive behaviors and promote a positive school climate through setting-level change, in order to prevent student behavior problems systematically and consistently. The model draws upon behavioral, social learning, organizational, and positive youth development theories and promotes strategies that can be used by all staff consistently across all school contexts (Lewis and Sugai, 1999; Lindsley, 1992; Sugai et al., 2002). Through PBIS, staff and students work together to create a schoolwide program that clearly articulates positive behavioral expectations, provides incentives to students meeting these expectations, promotes positive student-staff interactions, and encourages data-based decision making by staff and administrators. The model aims to alter the school environment by creating both improved systems (e.g., discipline, reinforcement, and data management systems) and procedures (e.g., collection of office referral data, training, data-based decision making) in order to promote positive change in student and teacher behaviors (Kutash et al., 2006; Sugai and Horner, 2006). The PBIS model also emphasizes coaching to tailor the implementation process to fit the culture and context of the school. The PBIS framework acknowledges that there is no one-size-fits-all program or model, therefore, coaches work with the schools to collect data in order to identify needs and both local challenges and resources. They subsequently help the school choose the most suitable program to be integrated within the PBIS framework, and they provide support to staff to optimize implementation fidelity.

The PBIS model follows a multi-tiered prevention approach (Institute of Medicine, 1994; National Research Council and Institute of Medicine,

2009), whereby Tier 2 (selective/targeted) and Tier 3 (indicated) programs and supports are implemented to complement the Tier 1 (universal) components (Sugai and Horner, 2006; Walker et al., 1996). Recent randomized effectiveness trials of PBIS, largely focused on the universal, Tier 1 elements, have reported significant effects on bullying and peer rejection (effect sizes ranging from 0.11 to 0.14; see Bradshaw, 2015; Waasdorp et al., 2012), as well as school climate (effect sizes from 0.16 to 0.29; see Bradshaw et al., 2008; Horner et al., 2009), and discipline problems (effect sizes from 0.11 to 0.27; see Bradshaw et al., 2010, 2012, 2015). Other significant effects have been reductions in suspensions and office referrals (ES = 0.27; see Bradshaw et al., 2008, 2009a, 2010; Horner et al., 2009; Waasdorp et al., 2012). Another randomized trial of PBIS combining Tier 1 and 2 supports in elementary schools also demonstrated significant improvements, relative to Tier 1 only, on teacher and student behaviors such as special education usage, need for advanced tier supports, and teacher efficacy to manage student behavior problems (Bradshaw et. al., 2012). An ongoing RCT of PBIS in 58 high schools, which combines other programs at Tiers 2 and 3, is currently under way; the preliminary findings from this trial suggest positive effects on bullying, violence, school climate, and substance use (Bradshaw et al., 2014b).

The KiVa Antibullying Program is another schoolwide, multicomponent program that has demonstrated promising effects. It has been implemented nationally in Finland for students in grades 1 through 9. Its universal elements include activities designed to increase bystander empathy and efficacy, teacher training, and more-targeted strategies for students at risk for or engaged in bullying as perpetrators or victims. It provides classroom training and materials to promote open discussions between teachers and students, peer support for students who are bullied, training for school staff in disciplinary strategies, and informational materials for families to prevent and appropriately respond to bullying. Computer games are also used to help students practice bullying prevention skills.

In their nonrandomized national trial, Kärnä and colleagues (2011a, 2011b) showed that after 9 months of implementation, students in KiVa schools reported lower rates of bullying behavior compared to students in non-intervention control schools. Specifically, victimization rates decreased with age from grade 1 (25.9%) to grade 9 (9.3%), with the largest decrease occurring between grades 1 and 6. Compared to controls, students in the KiVa program reported lower rates of being targeted for bullying (OR = 1.22; 95% CI [1.19, 1.24]) and perpetration of bullying (OR = 1.18; 95% CI [1.15, 1.21]).

Previous evaluations of the KiVa Program have also found the greatest program effects for younger elementary age students (grades 1-6) and smaller effects for middle-school age children (grades 7-9). Generally, program effects increased through grade 4 but steadily declined from that point forward. Specifically, KiVa has demonstrated significant impacts on being a perpetrator or a target of bullying behavior among students in grades 4-6 (effect sizes from 0.03 to 0.33; see Kärnä, et al., 2011a, 2011b), as well as for youth in grades 1-9 (odds ratios from 0.46 to 0.79; see Garandeau et al., 2014). In one evaluation of the KiVa Program, Veenstra and colleagues (2014) showed that for fourth to sixth grade students, their perception of teacher efficacy in decreasing bullying was associated with lower levels of peer-reported bullying. They argued that teachers play an important role in anti-bullying programs and should be included as targets of intervention. Ahtola et al., (2012) also found in their evaluation of the KiVa Program that teacher support of the program was positively related to implementation adherence, which in turn contributes to the potential for enhanced program effects. KiVa has only been tested in Europe, although there are currently efforts under way to adapt the model for use in other countries such as the United States.

A recent meta-analysis examining developmental differences in the effectiveness of anti-bullying programs provides some supportive evidence for significant declines in program effectiveness for students in eighth grade and beyond (Yeager et al., 2015). Specifically, Yeager and colleagues examined hierarchical within-study moderation of program effects by age as compared to more typical meta-analytic approaches that examine between-study tests of moderation. Their findings are inconsistent with the findings of Ttofi and Farrington (2009), in which larger program effect sizes (reductions in perpetrating and being a target of bullying) were found for programs implemented with older students (typically defined as students over age 11) compared to younger students.

A number of social-emotional learning programs have also been developed and tested to determine impacts on a range of student outcomes (Durlak et al., 2007, 2011). Some of these models have shown promising effects on aggression and bullying-related outcomes. One such model is Second Step: A Violence Prevention Curriculum. This classroom-based curriculum for children of ages 4-14 aims to reduce impulsive, high-risk, and aggressive behaviors while increasing social-emotional competence and protective factors. The curriculum teaches three core competencies: empathy, impulse control and problem solving, and anger management (Flannery et al., 2005; Baughman Sladky et al., 2015). Students participate in 20-50-minute sessions two to three times per week, in which they practice social skills. Parents can participate in a six-session training that familiarizes them with the content in the children's curriculum. Teachers also learn how to deal with disruptions and behavior management issues. (Flannery et al., 2005). In one study, children in the Second Step Program showed a greater drop in antisocial behavior compared to those who did not receive the program, behaved less aggressively, and were more likely to prefer prosocial goals

(Flannery et al., 2005; Frey et al., 2005). Other studies of Second Step have demonstrated significant reductions in reactive aggression scores for children in kindergarten through second grade and significant reductions in teacher-rated aggression for the children rated highest on aggression at baseline (Hussey and Flannery, 2007).

In a RCT of 36 middle schools, Espelage et al. (2013) found that students in Second Step intervention schools were 42 percent less likely to self-report physical aggression than students in control schools, with aggression measured as incidents of fighting, but the authors reported that the program had no effect on verbal/relational bullying perpetration, peer victimization,[3] homophobic teasing, or sexual violence. In one of the first school-level RCTs of a violence prevention curriculum, Grossman and colleagues (1997) examined, via parent and teacher reports and investigator observation, the effects of the Second Step preventive intervention program on elementary student (second and third grade) aggressive and prosocial behavior. While they did not find changes over time in parent or teacher reports, behavioral observations of students in various school settings showed an overall decrease 2 weeks after the curriculum in physical aggression (−0.46 events per hour, $p = .03$) and an increase in neutral/prosocial behavior (+3.96 events per hour, $p = .04$) in the intervention group compared with the control group. One of the recurrent limitations faced by school-level analyses is that measures that have been validated as school-level constructs may not use measures that have only been validated for individual assessment. Similarly, analyses in many studies do not account for the nesting of students within classrooms or schools.

The Good Behavior Game is an elementary school-based prevention program that targets antecedents of youth delinquency and violence. It uses classroom behavior management as a primary strategy to improve on-task behavior and decrease aggressive behavior (Baughman Sladky et al., 2015). Evaluations of the Good Behavior Game in early elementary school have shown it results in reduced disruptive behavior, increased academic engagement time, and statistically significant reductions in the likelihood of highly aggressive children receiving a diagnosis of a conduct disorder by sixth grade, as well as a range of positive academic outcomes (Bradshaw et al., 2009a; Wilcox et al., 2008). The effects were generally strongest among the most aggressive boys, who, when exposed to the program starting in the first grade, had lower rates of antisocial personality disorder when diagnosed as young adults (Petras et al., 2008) and reduced rates of mental health service use, compared to those in the control group (Poduska et al., 2008).

Good Behavior Game has also been tested in combination with other

---

[3] Peer victimization was assessed using the three-item University of Illinois Victimization Scale (Espelage et al., 2013).

programs, such as Linking the Interests of Families and Teachers (LIFT), which combines school-based skills training with parent training for first and fifth graders. This program is implemented over the course of 21 one-hour sessions delivered across 10 weeks. LIFT uses a playground peer component to encourage positive social behavior and a 6-week group parent-training component. The Good Behavior Game is the classroom-based component of LIFT. LIFT also reduced playground aggression, reduced overall rates of aggression, and increased family problem solving (Eddy et al., 2000; Baughman Sladky et al., 2015).

Raising Healthy Children (Catalano et al., 2003), formerly known as the Seattle Social Development Project (Hawkins et al., 1999), is a multidimensional intervention that targets both universal populations and high-risk youth in elementary and middle school. The program uses teacher and parent training, emphasizing classroom management for teachers and conflict management, problem-solving, and refusal skills for children. Parents receive optional training programs that target rules, communication, and strategies to support their child's academic success. Follow-up at age 18 showed that the program significantly improved long-term attachment and commitment to school and school achievement and reduced rates of self-reported violent acts and heavy alcohol use (Hawkins et al., 1999). At age 21, students who had received the full intervention when young were also less likely to be involved in crime, to have sold illegal drugs in the past year, or to have received a court charge (Hawkins et al., 2005).

Steps to Respect is another multicomponent program that includes activities led by school counselors for youth involved in bullying, along with schoolwide prevention, parent activities and classroom management. (Frey et al., 2005, 2009; Baughman Sladky et al., 2015). One RCT of Steps to Respect showed a reduction of 31 percent in the likelihood of perpetrating physical bullying in intervention schools relative to control schools (adjusted odds ratio = 0.609) based on teacher reports of student behaviors (Brown et al., 2011). Brown and colleagues (2011) also showed significant improvements in student self-reports of positive school climate, increases in student and teacher/staff bullying prevention and intervention, and increases in positive bystander behavior for students in intervention schools compared to students in control schools (effect sizes ranged from 0.115 for student bullying intervention to 0.187 for student climate). They found no effects for student attitudes about bullying.

In a separate RCT of Steps to Respect, Frey and colleagues (2009) found, using teacher observations of student playground behaviors, statistically significant declines over 18 months in bullying ($d = 2.11, p < .01$), victimization ($d = 1.24, p < .01$) and destructive bystander behavior ($d = 2.26, p < .01$) for students in intervention schools compared to students in control schools. While student self-reports of victimization declined across 18 months, student self-reports of aggressive behavior did not change.

One of the most comprehensive, long-term school-based programs that has been developed to prevent chronic and severe conduct problems in high-risk children is Fast Track. Fast Track is based on the view that antisocial behavior stems from the interaction of influences across multiple contexts such as school, home, and the individual (Conduct Problems Prevention Research Group, 1999). The main goals of the program are to increase communication and bonds between and among these three domains; to enhance children's social, cognitive, and problem-solving skills; to improve peer relationships; and ultimately to decrease disruptive behavior at home and in school. Fast Track provides a continuum of developmentally sequenced preventive intervention spanning grades 1 through 10. It includes some of the program elements and frameworks mentioned above, such as a social-emotional learning curriculum developed in elementary school called Promoting Alternative Thinking Strategies, as well as a version of the Coping Power program for higher-risk students. Other elements include support to parents, which is tailored to meet the unique needs of the family and youth.

Thus, Fast Track is a combination of multiple programs across the tiers. It has demonstrated effectiveness in reducing aggression and conduct problems, as well as reducing associations with deviant peers, for students of diverse demographic backgrounds, including sex, ethnicity, social class, and family composition differences (Conduct Problems Prevention Research Group, 2002, 2010; National Center for Health Statistics and National Center for Health Services Research, 2001). In an examination of the longitudinal outcomes of high-risk children who were randomly assigned by matched sets of schools to intervention and control conditions, the Conduct Problems Prevention Research Group (2011) showed that 10 years of exposure to Fast Track intervention prevented lifetime prevalence (assessed in grades 3, 6, 9, and 12) of psychiatric diagnoses for conduct disorder, oppositional defiant disorder, externalizing disorder, and attention deficit hyperactivity disorder.

In addition, a recent RCT of Fast Track showed that early exposure to the intervention substantially reduced adult psychopathology at age 25 among high-risk early-starting conduct-problem children (Dodge et al., 2015). Specifically, intent-to-treat logistic regression analyses showed that 69 percent of participants in the control condition displayed at least one externalizing, internalizing, or substance use psychiatric problem (assessed via self-report or peer interview) at age 25, compared to 59 percent of those assigned to intervention ($OR = 0.59$, 95% CI [0.43, 0.81]; number needed to treat = 8). Intervention participants also received lower severity-weighted violent crime conviction scores (standardized estimate = -0.37). This study was a random assignment of nearly 10,000 kindergartners in three cohorts, who were followed through a 10-year intervention and then assessed at age 25 via arrest records, condition-blinded psychiatrically interviewed participants, and interview of a peer knowledgeable about the participant.

The above descriptions of the selected universal multicomponent programs that address bullying or related behavior and their tiered levels of prevention are summarized in Table 5-1. The ecological contexts in which these programs operate are summarized in Table 5-2.

TABLE 5-1 Summary of Selected Universal Multicomponent Prevention Programs that Address Bullying or Related Behavior

Program	Origin	Program Type	Typical Delivery Setting
Olweus Bullying Prevention Program	Norway	Bullying prevention, school, school climate, environmental strategies	School
Positive Behavioral Interventions and Supports (PBIS)		School climate, academic engagement, behavioral support, interpersonal skills, school/ classroom environment	School
KiVa Antibullying Program	Finland	Classroom curricula, school/classroom environment, bullying prevention/intervention, children exposed to violence	School
Second Step: A Violence Prevention Curriculum	U.S.	Social-emotional curricula, conflict resolution/interpersonal skills, school/classroom environment, bullying prevention/intervention	School

Examples of School-Based Selective and Indicated Prevention Programs to Address Bullying or Related Behaviors

As noted above, many of the schoolwide and universal prevention models included elements across the tiers, but here the committee considers programs that are largely focused at the selective and indicated level. Within schools, it is common for students who are involved in bullying to

Targeted Population	Age Range of Children Served	Program Goals
Children in kindergarten and elementary, middle, and high schools	5-18	• To reduce existing bullying problems among students. • To prevent the development of new bullying problems. • To achieve better peer relations at school.
Children in preschool, kindergarten, and elementary, middle, and high schools	4-18	• To prevent disruptive behaviors and promote a positive school climate through setting-level change.
All children	5-14	• To raise awareness of the role that a group plays in maintaining bullying. • To increase empathy toward the child who is the target of bullying. • To promote strategies to support the target of bullying and to support children's self-efficacy to use those strategies. • To increase children's skills in coping when they are bullied.
Children in preschool/ kindergarten, elementary school, and middle school	5-12	• To reduce impulsive, high-risk, and aggressive behaviors while increasing social-emotional competence and protective factors.

continued

TABLE 5-1 Continued

Program	Origin	Program Type	Typical Delivery Setting
Steps to Respect	U.S.	Bullying prevention, teacher training, social-emotional curricula, conflict resolution/interpersonal skills, school/classroom environment	School
Good Behavior Game	U.S.	Classroom management, classroom environment	School
Linking the Interests of Families and Teachers (LIFT)	U.S.	Academic engagement, classroom curricula, conflict resolution/interpersonal skills, parent training, school/classroom environment, children exposed to violence, alcohol and drug abuse prevention	School
Raising Healthy Children	U.S.	Academic engagement, conflict resolution/interpersonal skills, parent training, school/classroom environment, alcohol and drug abuse prevention	Home, School
Fast Track	U.S.	Academic engagement, social-emotional curricula, classroom curricula, conflict resolution/interpersonal skills, parent training, school/classroom environment	School

SOURCE: Program information was obtained from Blueprints for Healthy Youth Development at http://www.blueprintsprograms.com/programs [June 2016] and CrimeSolutons.gov at http://www.crimesolutions.gov/ [June 2016].

Targeted Population	Age Range of Children Served	Program Goals
Students in elementary and middle schools	8-12	• To increase staff awareness and responsiveness to bullying prevention. • To foster socially responsible beliefs. • To teach social-emotional skills to counter bullying and to promote healthy relationships.
Children in kindergarten, elementary school	6-10	• To improve on-task behavior and decrease aggressive behavior.
Children in elementary school and their families	6-11	• To prevent the development of aggressive and antisocial behaviors in elementary school children.
Children and their families	7-16	• To increase school commitment, academic performance, and social competency. • To reduce antisocial behavior.
Children identified for disruptive behavior and poor peer relations.	5-15	• To increase communication and bonds between and among these three domains. • To enhance children's social, cognitive, and problem-solving skills. • To improve peer relationships and ultimately to decrease disruptive behavior at home and in school.

NOTE: The information provided in Table 5-1 is meant to illustrate core features of program elements and focus rather than provide a detailed assessment of all aspects of a program or its demonstrated effects. The table is not intended to be an exhaustive list of all prevention pograms.

TABLE 5-2 Summary of Ecological Contexts in which Selected Universal Multicomponent Prevention Programs Operate

| ● INDIVIDUAL ● PEERS ● FAMILY ● SCHOOL ● COMMUNITY ● HEALTHCARE |

PROGRAM	INDIVIDUAL	PEERS	FAMILY	SCHOOL	COMMUNITY	HEALTHCARE
Olweus Bullying Prevention Program	●	●	●	●		
Positive Behavioral Interventions and Supports	●	●		●		
KiVa Antibullying Program	●	●		●		
Second Step: A Violence Prevention Curriculum	●	●		●		
Steps to Respect	●	●		●		
Good Behavior Game	●	●		●		
Linking the Interests of Families and Teachers	●		●	●		
Raising Healthy Children			●	●		
Fast Track	●	●	●	●		

NOTE: The information provided in Table 5-2 is meant to illustrate core features of program elements and focus rather than provide a detailed assessment of all aspects of a program or its demonstrated effects. The table is not intended to be an exhaustive list of all prevention programs.

SOURCE: Program information was obtained from Blueprints for Healthy Youth Development at http://www.blueprintsprograms.com/programs and CrimeSolutons.gov at http://www.crimesolutions.gov/ [June 2016].

be referred for some type of school-based or community counseling services (Swearer et al., 2014).

McElearney and colleagues (2013) reported that school counseling was an effective intervention for middle school students who had been bullied when the counseling focused on improving peer relationships. In their study, they collected longitudinal data from 202 students (mean age = 12.5) using the self-rated Strengths and Difficulties Questionnaire (SDQ).[4] In total, 27.2 percent of the student referrals to the intervention related to being bullied. Students who had been bullied had significantly higher initial status scores (LGC initial score = 1.40, $p < .001$) on the Peer Problems subscale of the SDQ and experienced a significantly more rapid rate of decrease on this subscale (LGC rate of change score = –0.25, $p < .001$) with each successive session of school counseling, compared with those students who had accessed the intervention for another reason. However, counseling sessions probably vary considerably in the services provided and the extent to which they employ evidence-based models.

A few studies have examined social workers or school mental health staff who provide intervention for youth involved in bullying, but the research in this area is rather weak, with relatively few systematic studies focused on assessing the impacts of selective and indicated programs on bullying (Swearer et al., 2014). Moreover, given the difficulty of determining the efficacy of counseling as an intervention per se, the committee focuses here more specifically on particular structured preventive intervention models that have been more formally articulated in a curriculum, many of which are delivered by school-based counselors, social workers, or psychologists.

For example, Berry and Hunt (2009) found preliminary support for a cognitive-behavioral intervention for anxious adolescent boys in grades 7-10 (mean age of 13.04 years) who had experienced bullying at school. Fung (2012) assessed a group treatment for youth ages 11-16, provided by social workers in Hong Kong using a social information processing model. Students were selected for intervention based on their high levels of aggressive behavior rather than bullying specifically, but the author did find that after 2 years of the intervention, students reported a decrease in reactive aggression but not proactive aggression. Fung (2012) also found that cognitive-behavioral group therapy was effective in reducing anxious and depressed emotions in children who are both the perperator and target of bullying.

One of the few evidence-based targeted intervention programs for late preadolescent children is the Coping Power Program (Lochman et al., 2013). Coping Power targets aggressive youth and their parents and is delivered by counselors in small groups over the course of a school year. Additional supports are provided to teachers to promote generalization of skills into nongroup settings. The program has demonstrated significant improvements in aggressive-disruptive behaviors and social interactions, many of which were maintained at 3-year follow-up for children from fourth through sixth grade (Lochman et al., 2013).

---

[4]The SDQ is a brief behavioral screening questionnaire that asks about 25 attributes, some positive and others negative (Goodman, 1997).

Having available strategies to cope with stress has also been shown to reduce depression among older adolescents who were bullied (Hemphill et al., 2014). Although originally developed for students in grades 4-6, there is currently an ongoing 40-school randomized trial testing a middle school version of this model; the trial has a particular focus on assessing outcomes related to bullying (Bradshaw et al., in press); a high school model of Coping Power is also currently in development and will soon be tested on 600 urban high school students (Bradshaw et al., in press).

DeRosier (2004) and DeRosier and Marcus (2005) evaluated the effects of a social-skills group intervention for children experiencing peer dislike, bullying, or social anxiety. In their study of third graders randomly assigned to treatment or to no-treatment control, DeRosier and Marcus (2005) showed that aggressive children exposed to the program reported greater declines in aggression and bullying behavior and fewer antisocial affiliations than aggressive children in the no-intervention control condition. The intervention resulted in decreased aggression on peer reports (Cohen's $d = 0.26$), decreased targets of bullying on self-reports (Cohen's $d = 0.10$) and fewer antisocial affiliations on self-reports (Cohen's $d = 0.11$) for the previously aggressive children (DeRosier and Marcus, 2005).

A study of elementary school students exposed to the FearNot! virtual learning intervention to enhance coping skills of children who were bullied showed a short-term improvement on escaping being bullied (Sapouna et al., 2010). In a separate evaluation of the FearNot! Program in the UK and German schools, exposure to the intervention was found to help non-involved primary grade children to become defenders of the target in virtual bullying situations, at least for youth in the German sample (Vannini et al., 2011).

There are also a number of preventive interventions that aim to address mental health problems but may also prove to be helpful for youth who are involved in bullying. For example, a school-based version of cognitive-behavioral therapy is. Cognitive Behavioral Intervention for Trauma in Schools (CBITS). This evidence-based treatment program is for youth ages 10-15 who have had substantial exposure to violence or other traumatic events and who have symptoms of posttraumatic stress disorder (PTSD) in the clinical range. The CBITS Program has three main goals: (1) to reduce symptoms related to trauma, (2) to build resilience, and (3) to increase peer and parent support. Based on a model of trauma-informed care, CBITS was developed to reduce symptoms of distress and build skills to improve children's abilities to handle stress and trauma in the future. The intervention incorporates cognitive-behavioral therapy skills in a small group format to address symptoms of PTSD, anxiety, and depression related to exposure to violence. CBITS was found to be more accessible to families who may not have been able or willing to participate outside of schools. CBITS was also found to significantly improve depressive symptoms in students with PTSD (Jaycox et al., 2010).

Examples of Family-Focused Preventive Interventions to Address Bullying

A few family-focused preventive interventions have been developed that may also demonstrate promising effects on bullying. For example, the Incredible Years Program aims to reduce aggressive and problem behaviors in children, largely through supports to parents, as well as students and teachers. It focuses on social skills training components (Webster-Stratton, 1999) and targets elementary school students with the aim of preventing further aggression and related behavior problems for youth with conduct problems but whose behavior would not yet be considered in the clinical range requiring treatment. Barrera and colleagues (2002) showed that high-risk elementary school children in the Incredible Years Program displayed lower levels of negative social behavior, including aggression, compared to control youth who did not receive the intervention. In another study, Webster-Stratton and colleagues (2008) showed that teacher training in combination with Dinosaur School in Head Start and first grade classrooms with at-risk students resulted in improved social competence and self-regulation and in fewer youth conduct problems. There is also a universal version of the Incredible Years Program delivered by teachers, which is currently being tested in two separate randomized trials. To the committee's knowledge, bullying has not been assessed as an outcome in prior studies of Incredible Years, although several impacts on other discipline and behavior problems have been observed in prior RCTs.

Another family-focused program is The Family Check-Up (also known as the Adolescent Transitions Program). This multilevel, family-centered intervention targets children at risk for problem behaviors or substance use. The Family Check-Up had historically been delivered in middle school settings, but more recent studies have extended the model to younger populations (e.g., 2-5 year olds in Dishion et al., 2014). Parent-focused elements of The Family Check-Up concentrate on developing family management skills such as using rewards, monitoring, making rules, providing reasonable consequences for rule violations, problem solving, and active listening (Dishion and Kavanagh, 2003). Connell and colleagues (2007) found that The Family Check-Up resulted in significantly fewer arrests; less use of tobacco, alcohol, and marijuana; and less antisocial behavior for intervention youth, compared with control group youth.

Another targeted program that includes supports for families is the Triple P intervention. A RCT of Resilience Triple P for Australian youth 6 to 12 years old found significant improvements for intervention youth compared to controls on teacher reports of overt victimization ($d = 0.56$), and child overt aggression toward peers ($d = 0.51$) as well as improvements in related mental health such as internalized feelings and depressive symptoms. The intervention that combined facilitative parenting with social and emotional skills training worked best (Healy and Sanders, 2014). An earlier study of Triple P for preschoolers at risk for conduct problems found that a version delivered by practitioners (clinical psychologists, psychologists, and psychiatrists) trained and supervised in the delivery of the interventions was more effective in reducing problem behaviors compared to a wait-list condition and a Triple P program that was self-directed (Sanders et al., 2000).

In addition to the largely school- and family-based programs summarized above, there are several evidence-based interventions that are more typically provided in the community (Baughman Sladky et al., 2015). Although these programs focus more generally on violence and aggression prevention, they may also produce effects on bullying related behaviors, such as conduct problems for perpetrators or those at risk for perpetration, or they may address the behavioral and mental health consequences of being bullied.

For example, a widely utilized intervention to address mental health issues for children and adolescents is Trauma Focused Cognitive Behavioral Therapy (TF-CBT) which has been shown to be effective in reducing mental health symptoms related to violence exposure (Cohen et al., 2006). TF-CBT has been particularly effective in treating children who are victims of sexual abuse (Cohen et al., 2005). While not specifically used to address being a target of bullying, TF-CBT can be used to treat complex trauma and has been shown to result in improvements to mental health issues related to peer victimization including PTSD symptoms, depression, anxiety, and externalizing behavior problems (Cohen et al., 2004; Deblinger et al., 2011).

Programs that are delivered in the community often include supports for parents as well as the youth. For example, Functional Family Therapy (FFT) is a family-based intervention program that targets youth between the ages of 11 and 18 who are at risk for and/or presenting with delinquency, violent or disruptive behavior, or substance use (Baughman Sladky et al., 2015). It is time-limited, averaging 8-12 sessions for referred youth and their families, with generally no more than 30 hours of direct service time for more difficult cases. FFT is multisystemic and multilevel in nature, addressing individual, family, and treatment system dynamics. It integrates behavioral (e.g., communication training) and cognitive-behavioral interventions (e.g., a relational focus). Assessment is an ongoing and multifaceted part of each phase (Henggeler and Sheidow, 2012). Evaluations of FFT have shown significant improvements in delinquent behavior and recidivism (Aos et al., 2011; Sexton and Alexander, 2000).

Brief Strategic Family Therapy (BSFT) is a short-term (approximately 12-15 sessions over 3 months) family-based intervention for children and youth ages 6-17 who are at risk for substance abuse and behavior problems (Robbins et al., 2002, 2007; Szapocznik and Williams, 2000). BSFT employs a structural family framework and focuses on improving family interactions. Evaluation results demonstrate decreases in substance abuse, conduct problems, associating with antisocial peers, and improvements in family functioning. In a small randomized trial of girls who were perpetrators of bullying, Nickel and colleagues (2006) found a decrease in bullying behavior (and expressive aggression) in the BSFT group, with improvements maintained at 1-year follow-up. Similar findings were observed in a separate study of BSFT for boys who were involved in bullying behavior. (Nickel et al., 2006).

Wraparound/Case Management is a multifaceted intervention designed to keep delinquent youth at home and out of institutions by "wrapping" a comprehensive array of individualized services and support networks "around" young people, rather than forcing them to enroll in predetermined, inflexible treatment programs (Bruns et al., 1995; Miles et al., 2006). Evaluations of Wraparound have found marked improvement in behavior and socialization, and youth in the intervention group were significantly less likely to reoffend compared to graduates of conventional programs (Carney and Buttell, 2003; Miles et al., 2006).

Multisystemic Therapy (MST) targets chronic, violent, or substance-abusing male or female juvenile offenders, ages 12-17, at risk of out-of-home placement, along with their families. MST is a family-based model that addresses multiple factors related to delinquency across key socio-ecological settings. It promotes behavior change in the youth's natural environment, using a strengths-based approach (Henggeler, 2011). Critical service characteristics include low caseloads (5:1 family-to-clinician ratio), intensive and comprehensive services (2-15 hours per week) and time-limited treatment duration (4-6 months) (Henggeler et al., 1999). Treatment adherence and fidelity are key ingredients for achieving long-term, sustained effects and decreasing drug use. Evaluations of MST that examined delinquency rates for serious juvenile offenders demonstrated a reduction in long-term rates of re-arrest, reductions in out-of home placements, and improvements in family functioning, and decreased mental health problems for serious juvenile offenders (Greenwood and Welsh, 2012; Schaeffer and Borduin, 2005). A recent meta-analysis of the effectiveness of MST across 22 studies containing 322 effect sizes found small but statistically significant treatment effects for its primary outcome of delinquent behavior, but the meta-analysis also found secondary outcomes such as psychopathology, substance use, family factors, out-of-home placements, and peer factors. For example, considering MST as an intervention that may affect bullying related behaviors, eight studies assessing peer relations showed improvements for aggressive youth treated with MST compared to youth treated via other modalities (mean effect size d = 0.213) (van der Stouwe et al., 2014).

Another communitywide prevention model that holds promise for reducing violence and related behavior problems is the Communities That Care (CTC) framework. CTC is a system for planning and organizing community resources to address adolescent problematic behavior such as aggression or drug use. It has five phases to help communities work toward their goals. The CTC system includes training events and guides for community leaders and organizations. The main goal is to create a "community prevention board" comprising public officials and community leaders to identify and reduce risk factors while promoting protective factors by selecting and implementing tested interventions throughout the community. Based on communitywide data on risk and protective factors, schools may select from a menu of evidence-based programs, which includes some of

TABLE 5-3 Summary of Selective and Indicated Prevention Programs that Address Bullying or Related Behavior

Program	Origin	Program Type	Typical Delivery Setting
Coping Power Program	U.S.	Cognitive behavioral treatment, parent training, social-emotional learning	School
Incredible Years	U.S.	Academic engagement, cognitive behavioral treatment, social-emotional curricula, conflict resolution/ interpersonal skills, family therapy, group therapy, parent training, school/classroom environment	Home, school, community
The Family Check-Up (formerly Adolescent Transitions)	U.S.	Academic engagement, crisis intervention/response, family therapy, parent training, school/classroom environment, motivational interviewing	School
Triple P	Australia	Parent training	School, community, home, hospital/ medical center, mental health/ treatment center

the models listed above. Thus, CTC is more of a data-informed process for selecting and implementing multiple evidence-based programs. As a result, it is difficult to attribute significant improvements in youth behavior to any one specific program. However, randomized studies testing the CTC model have shown statistically significant positive effects on delinquency, alcohol use, and cigarette use, all of which were lower by grade 10 among students in CTC communities, compared to students in control communities (Hawkins et al., 2011).

Descriptions of a subset of selective and indicated prevention programs that address bullying or related behavior and their tiered level of prevention are summarized in Table 5-3. The ecological contexts in which these programs operate are summarized in Table 5-4.

Targeted Population	Age Range of Children Served	Program Goals
Aggressive youth and their parents	8-15	• To increase competence, study skills, social skills, and self-control in aggressive children, as well as to improve parental involvement in their child's education.
Children at high risk for problem behaviors or substance use, along with their parents and teachers	2-8	• To reduce challenging behaviors in children and increase their social and self-control skills.
Families	2-7	• To assist families with high-risk adolescents by targeting parental engagement and motivating parents to improve their parenting practices.
Parents with a child in the age range between birth and 12 years	0-12	• To enhance parental competence and prevent or alter dysfunctional parenting practices, thereby reducing family risk factors both for child maltreatment and for children's behavioral and emotional problems.

continued

TABLE 5-3 Continued

Program	Origin	Program Type	Typical Delivery Setting
Cognitive Behavioral Intervention for Trauma in Schools (CBITS)		Cognitive behavioral treatment, group therapy, individual therapy, school/ classroom environment, trauma-informed	School, high crime neighborhood/hot spots
Trauma Focused Cognitive Behavioral Therapy (TF-CBT)		Cognitive behavioral treatment, family therapy, parent training, trauma-informed	Inpatient/ out-patient
Functional Family Therapy (FFT)	U.S.	Family therapy, individual therapy, probation/parole services	Inpatient/out-patient, home, community
Brief Strategic Family Therapy (BSFT)	U.S.	Alcohol and drug therapy/ treatment, conflict resolution/ interpersonal skills, family therapy, parent training, alcohol and drug prevention	Home, workplace, community
Wraparound/Case Management	U.S.	Individualized case management via team planning that is family-driven, culturally competent, and community-based	Home, community
Multisystemic Therapy (MST)	U.S.	Alternatives to detention, cognitive behavioral treatment, conflict resolution/ interpersonal skills, family therapy, individual therapy, parent training	Home, community, school
Communities That Care (CTC)	U.S.	Classroom curricula, school/ classroom environment, community crime prevention, alcohol and drug prevention	School, community

NOTE: The information provided in Table 5-3 is meant to illustrate core features of program elements and focus rather than provide a detailed assessment of all aspects of a program or its demonstrated effects. The table is not intended to be an exhaustive list of all prevention programs.

Targeted Population	Age Range of Children Served	Program Goals
Children exposed to violence or other traumatic events		• To reduce symptoms related to trauma. • To build resilience. • To increase peer and parent support.
Children exposed to violence and their families	3-14	• To treat serious emotional problems such as posttraumatic stress, fear, anxiety, and depression by teaching children and parents new skills to process thoughts and feelings resulting from traumatic events.
Young offenders and their families	11-18	• To decrease risk factors and increase protective factors that directly affect adolescents, with a particular emphasis on familial factors.
Children at risk for substance abuse and behavior problems and their families	6-17	• To improve youth's behavior by improving family interactions that are presumed to be directly related to the child's symptoms, thus reducing risk factors and strengthening protective factors for adolescent drug abuse and other conduct problems.
Children and their families	6-18	• To keep youths with delinquent behavior at home and out of institutions.
Young offenders and their families	12-17	• To alter the youth's ecology in a manner that promotes prosocial conduct while decreasing problem and delinquent behavior.
Infant, early childhood-preschool, late childhood, kindergarten-elementary school, early adolescence, middle school, late adolescence, high school, early adulthood	0-18	• To create a "community prevention board" comprising public officials and community leaders to identify and reduce risk factors while promoting protective factors by selecting and implementing tested interventions throughout the community.

SOURCE: Program information was obtained from Blueprints for Healthy Youth Development at http://www.blueprintsprograms.com/programs and CrimeSolutons.gov at http://www.crimesolutions.gov/ [June 2016].

TABLE 5-4 Summary of Ecological Contexts in which the selected Selective and Indicated Prevention Programs Operate

	INDIVIDUAL	PEERS	FAMILY	SCHOOL	COMMUNITY	HEALTHCARE
PROGRAM						
Coping Power Program (CPP)	●		●	●		
Incredible Years	●		●	●	●	●
Family Check-Up (Formerly Adolescent Transitions)	●		●	●		
Triple P			●	●	●	●
Cognitive Behavioral Intervention for Trauma in Schools	●		●	●		
Trauma Focused Cognitive Behavioral Therapy	●		●			●
Functional Family Therapy	●		●		●	●
Brief Strategic Family Therapy	●		●		●	
Wraparound/Case Management	●		●	●	●	
Multisystemic Therapy	●	●	●	●	●	
Communities that Care	●		●	●	●	

NOTE: The information provided in Table 5-4 is meant to illustrate core features of program elements and focus rather than provide a detailed assessment of all aspects of a program or its demonstrated effects. The table is not intended to be an exhaustive list of all prevention programs.

SOURCE: Program information was obtained from Blueprints for Healthy Youth Development at http://www.blueprintsprograms.com/programs [June 2016] and CrimeSolutons.gov at http://www.crimesolutions.gov/ [June 2016].

Examples of Preventive Intervention to Address
Cyberbullying and Related Behaviors

In a review of interventions to reduce cyberbullying, Mishna and colleagues (2012) found some gains in knowledge about Internet safety, but psychoeducational interventions had little effect on changing risky online behavior. Ryan and Curwen (2013) noted the lack of evidence-based interventions for victims of cyberbullying in their review of evidence regarding the occurrence, impact, and interventions for targets of cyberbullying. Given that cyberbullying takes place online and that the vast majority of youth are online, online resources to prevent or address cyberbullying may have broad reach. At present, online resources exist that were created to address or provide support regarding cyberbullying; one example is the website STOP Cyberbullying.[5] There have also been social marketing campaigns tied to online resources that include resources to counter cyberbulling; one example is the It Gets Better Project.[6] To the committee's knowledge, none of these online programs has undergone empirical evaluation yet.

Across social media sites, there is no consistent information about bullying policies, resources, or tracking of behaviors. Facebook is the most popular social media site and provides a Webpage of bullying resources.[7] Instagram is also popular among teens and provides its own Webpage discussing cyberbullying.[8] Both of these sites provide links where bullying can be reported to site administrators, but there are no published reports of this information or empirical studies evaluating prevalence of what is reported. The committee found no studies of the effectiveness of these sites or of the resources they provide.

In the family context, however, recent correlational studies suggest that spending time together, such as through family meals, may provide an important context for disclosure of being a target of bullying, which in turn buffers some of the subsequent effects of bullying on social-emotional adjustment (Elgar et al., 2014).

Some recent research, predominantly in Europe, has examined the effectiveness of preventive interventions specifically on cyberbullying. These programs are school based and were designed for students between the ages of 13 and 17. Many of these evaluation studies used randomized designs, including studies of Cyber Friendly Schools and the Viennese Social Competence Program. Cyber Friendly Schools is a whole-school, online cyberbullying prevention and intervention program that is based on a

---

[5] See http://www.stopcyberbullying.org [April 2016].
[6] See http://www.itgetsbetter.org/ [April 2016].
[7] See *Put a Stop to Bullying* at https://www.facebook.com/safety/bullying [February 2016].
[8] See *Learn How to Address Abuse* at https://help.instagram.com/527320407282978/ [October 2015].

social–ecological approach and considers the many factors that influence students' vulnerability to cyberbullying at multiple levels (Cross et al., 2015). The Viennese Social Competence Program is a primary preventive program that includes secondary preventive elements to reduce aggressive behavior and bullying and to foster social and intercultural competencies in schools (Gradinger et al., 2015). These programs have been associated with declines, from program pretest to post-test, in both cyberbullying perpetration and being targeted.

The German program Medienhelden ("Media Heroes"), which was originally designed for traditional bullying, has also been used as a cyberbullying intervention. This program is a universal, modularized, and theoretically based preventive intervention for the school context that builds on previous knowledge about potential risk and protective factors such as cognitive and affective empathy. An evaluation of this program showed that while the intervention was associated with reductions in both traditional and cyberbullying perpetration for both short-intervention conditions (mean difference = –0.29, p = .00) and long-intervention conditions (mean difference = –0.32, p = .00), it was not associated with reductions in being targets of either kind of bullying (Chaux et al., 2016).

Other studies used a quasi-experimental design. For example, an evaluation of the NoTrap! Program, which is a school-based intervention, and utilizes a peer-led approach to prevent and combat both traditional bullying and cyberbullying, showed a decrease over time in being targeted for traditional bullying or cyberbullying ($F(1, 457)$ = 5.379, p = .02; $\eta^2 p$ = .012) and in perpetrating bullying ($F(1, 457)$ = 9.807, p =. 002; $\eta^2 p$ = .021) (Palladino et al., 2016). Evaluation of the ConRed Program (Ortega-Ruiz et al., 2012), which is a theory-driven program designed to prevent cyberbullying and improve cyberbullying coping skills, showed that individuals who had been targets of cyberbullying reported decreased incidence of being bullied for both traditional bullying (F = 7.33, p = .008, d = 0.46) and cyberbullying (F = 7.73, p = .03, d = 0.56) (Del Rey et al., 2015). Finally, a study focused on college students used the theory of reasoned action (Ajzen, 1985) in a cyberbullying prevention program involving an educational video. One month follow-up found that the intervention group had increases in cyberbullying knowledge (d = 0.85), as well as decreases in approving attitudes (.24 < ds < .48) toward online behaviors such as unwanted contact, public humiliation, and deception (Doane et al., 2015).

As a whole, this body of research supports a finding that interventions designed to target one type of bullying can have spillover effects on another. This is not surprising, given the overlap between cyberbullying and traditional bullying (Waasdorp and Bradshaw, 2015). A common issue and limitation of this body of work is that all the studies involved self-report by students. Future research opportunities include triangulating this data with reports from parents or teachers. All of the preventive interventions reviewed in this section, despite their focus on cyberbullying, are implemented in the offline world and specifically in schools.

RECOMMENDED COMPONENTS AND CONSIDERATIONS FOR BULLYING PREVENTION

In the committee's broader reflections on the literature about and practice of bullying prevention, a number of core elements or critical features consistently emerged. In this section, we summarize those elements for which there is a converging body of supporting evidence. However, a challenge in this area is the limited documentation on the effectiveness of particular components or programmatic elements. Much of what has been reported about what works in bullying prevention comes from randomized trials of programs and meta-analyses summarizing effective models, with limited post hoc exploration into programmatic elements associated with the greatest effect sizes. Although few studies were appropriately designed to discern particular effective components or elements of an entire model, separate from other elements, the following frameworks and core components are among the most promising within the extant research.

As noted above, there is a growing emphasis on the use of multi-tiered approaches—those which leverage universal, selective, and indicated prevention programs and activities. For example, a tiered approach might include lessons on social-emotional skill development for all students—thus making it a universal program. In fact, research highlights the importance of providing class time to discuss bullying (Olweus, 1993) and the use of lessons to foster skills and competencies, effective communication, and strategies for responding to bullying (Farrington and Ttofi, 2009); such strategies can also have a positive impact on academic and other behavioral outcomes (Durlak et al., 2010). Effective classroom management is also critical, as well-managed classrooms are rated as having a more favorable climate, being safer and more supportive, and having lower rates of bullying compared to less-well-managed classrooms (Koth et al., 2008). At Tier 2, selective interventions may include social skills training for small groups of children at risk for becoming involved in bullying. Finally, an indicated preventive intervention (Tier 3) may include more intensive supports and programs tailored to meet the needs of students identified as a perpetrator or a target of bullying and the needs of their families (Espelage and Swearer, 2008; Ross and Horner, 2009).

Consistent with the social–ecological framework (Espelage et al., 2004), schools should address the social environment and the broader culture and climate of bullying (Bradshaw and Waasdorp, 2009). Research documents the importance of schoolwide prevention efforts that provide positive behavior support, establish a common set of expectations for positive behavior across all school contexts, and involve all school staff in prevention activities (Ross and Horner, 2009). Effective supervision, especially in bullying "hot spots," and clear anti-bullying policies are essential elements of a successful schoolwide prevention effort (Olweus, 1993). The playground appears to be a particularly important context for increasing supervision in order to prevent bullying (Farrington and Ttofi, 2009; Frey et al., 2005). Collecting data on bullying via anonymous student surveys can inform the supervision and intervention process. These data can identify potential areas for intensive training of school staff, which is an essential element of successful bullying prevention efforts (Farrington and Ttofi, 2009). Data are also critical for monitoring progress toward the goal of reducing bullying (Olweus, 1993).

Families also play a critical role in bullying prevention by providing emotional support to promote disclosure of bullying incidents and by fostering coping skills in their children. Parents need training in how to talk with their children about bullying (Johnson et al., 2011), how to communicate their concerns about bullying to the school, and how to get actively involved in school-based bullying prevention efforts (Waasdorp et al., 2011). There also are important bullying prevention activities that can occur at the community level, such as awareness or social marketing campaigns that encourage all youth and adults—including doctors, police officers, and storekeepers—to intervene when they see bullying and to become actively involved in school- and community-based prevention activities (Olweus, 1993).

It is also important to consider how schools can integrate prevention efforts with their other existing programs and supports. Research by Gottfredson and Gottfredson (2001) indicates that, on average, schools are using about 14 different strategies or programs to prevent violence and promote a safe learning environment. This can often be overwhelming for school staff to execute well, thereby leading to poor implementation fidelity. Therefore, schools are encouraged to integrate their prevention efforts so that there is a seamless system of support (Domitrovich et al., 2010), which is coordinated, monitored for high fidelity implementation, and includes all staff across all school contexts. Instead of adopting a different program to combat each new problem that emerges, schools can develop a consistent and long-term prevention plan that addresses multiple student concerns through a set of well-integrated programs and services. Such efforts would address multiple competencies and skills in order to prevent bullying, while helping students cope and respond appropriately when bullying does occur. Programs should include efforts to enhance resilience and positive behaviors and not just focus on reductions in bullying perpetration. The three-tiered public health model provides a framework for connecting bullying prevention with other programs to address bullying within the broader set of behavioral and academic concerns.

Collectively, the extant research suggests that there are a number of universal prevention programs that are effective or potentially promising for reducing bullying and related behavioral and mental health concerns. With regard to selective and indicated prevention programs, the focus of the model tends to be more generally on other behavioral concerns, with relatively few programs at these levels being tested using RCT designs to determine impacts on bullying specifically. Additional research is clearly needed to better understand the impacts of programs across all three tiers, as well as the combined impacts of such programs.

NONRECOMMENDED APPROACHES

There has been an emerging concern that some programs and strategies commonly used with the goal of preventing or stopping bullying may actually increase bullying or cause other harm to youth or the school community. For example, suspension and related exclusionary techniques are often the default response by school staff and administrators in bullying situations; however, these approaches do not appear to be effective and may actually result in increased academic and behavioral problems for youth. Encouraging youth to fight back when bullied is also not a recommended strategy, as it suggests that aggression is an effective means for responding to victimization and may perpetuate the cycle of violence. Furthermore, such an aggressive response may escalate the level of violence and the risk of harm for all parties involved. While there is still much to be learned about effective youth responses to bullying across the different age groups and social–ecological contexts, recommended responses may include deflecting, seeking peer and adult support, and avoidance of situations that may increase the likelihood of exposure to bullying (Waasdorp and Bradshaw, 2011). Yet there are characteristics of some youth that may make some of these responses easier to display than others. For example, youth who have challenges regulating emotions and inhibiting aggressive responses are more likely to use violence when bullied.

Given that bullying is a complex peer behavior, it may seem wise to leverage peers in attempting to intervene in bullying situations. In fact, there is a large and growing literature supporting the potential effectiveness of bystander interventions (Polanin et al., 2012). However, caution should be taken about the types of roles youth play in bullying prevention. Youth- or peer-facilitated programs, such as peer mediation, peer-led conflict resolution, forced apology, and peer mentoring may not be appropriate or effective in bullying prevention.

There are concerns about approaches based on forced apology or the use of peer-mediated conflict resolution within the context of bullying programs, in part because of the face-to-face interactions between the youth who have been perpetrators and those who have been targeted. Such approaches are rarely structured in a way to address peer abuse of power, as it occurs in bullying behavior, as compared to the original focus of such approaches on conflict (Bradshaw, 2013). The systematic review and meta-analysis of school-based anti-bullying programs by Ttofi and Farrington (2011) found that programs that were peer-led often produced null or even iatrogenic effects. Some programs appeared to increase attitudes supportive of bullying, whereas others showed an increase in incidents of targeting rather than a reduction in bullying-related behaviors. There is also a large body of violence- and delinquency-related research (see Dodge et al., 2006, for review) suggesting that grouping youth who bully together may actually reinforce their aggressive behaviors and result in higher rates of bullying. In these situations, a contagion process likely occurs, whereby the youth learn more aggressive and bullying behaviors from each other and are reinforced for their aggressive behavior. Furthermore, conflict resolution approaches, even when facilitated by adults, are not typically recommended in situations of bullying, as they suggest a disagreement between two peers of equal status or power, rather than an instance of peer abuse. These approaches also typically bring targets and youth who bully face to face, which may be especially hurtful for the youth who is bullied. It is important to note, however, that there may be other forms of delinquent and problem behavior, such as property offenses or threats toward staff, which may be more appropriate for these types of conflict resolution approaches. Although additional research is certainly needed to determine the appropriateness of these and other youth-facilitated practices in the context of bullying prevention, it is likely that structured and well-supervised youth leadership activities can have a positive impact on bullying prevention; however, more RCT-designed studies that document outcomes associated with these approaches are needed.

There is also little evidence that one-day awareness raising events or brief assemblies are effective at changing a climate of bullying or producing sustainable effects on bullying behavior (Farrington and Ttofi, 2009). Some of these types of efforts have focused largely on instances of youth suicides, which may have been linked in some way with bullying. Given growing concerns about the potential association between bullying and youth suicide, and more generally issues related to suicidal contagion among adolescents (Duong and Bradshaw, 2015; Romer et al., 2006), practitioners and researchers should be cautious in highlighting such a potential link, as it may result in confusion and misattribution among families as well as in the media. Rather, it is critical to state the epidemiologic evidence that suicide is extremely complex and generally associated more directly with mental health concerns such as anxiety and depression. Bullying could, therefore, serve as a risk factor for youth who are also experiencing mental health concerns (Klomek et al., 2011). This underscores the importance of multicomponent programs that address social, behavioral, and mental health concerns.

AREAS FOR FUTURE RESEARCH RELATED TO BULLYING PREVENTION PROGRAMMING

This final major section of the chapter identifies a number of areas that require additional research and focus in order to advance bullying prevention programming.

Implementation of Bullying Prevention Programming

There is a need for more implementation-focused research aimed at improving the adoption and implementation of evidence-based programs. Numerous studies have documented challenges with implementation fidelity of school-based programs, most of which suggest that the programs themselves are not difficult to implement; rather, constraints such as lack of buy-in, limited time to implement programs, competing priorities, lack of organizational capacity to coordinate the effort, and insufficient administrative support are all factors that may contribute to the relatively slow adoption of school-based programs and that compromise implementation fidelity (Beets et al., 2008; Domitrovich et al., 2008; Vreeman and Carroll, 2007). Commitment not only to the implementation of a model but also to its sustainment and authentic integration with other efforts is needed for any such program to become routinized. For example, teacher attitudes about the potential effectiveness of the program, as well as school-related factors that support successful implementation with fidelity, have been shown to be important predictors of successful implementation of universal character education programs (Beets et al., 2008).

A need also exists for sustained investment in data systems to guide the identification of strengths and gaps in implementation programming, as well as to track progress toward outcomes (Bradshaw, 2013). Adequate time for ongoing quality professional development, coaching supports, and performance feedback are essential features of an implementation support system for achieving high-quality implementation of any evidence-based practice; positive effects cannot otherwise be expected (Domitrovich et al., 2008; Fixsen et al., 2005).

Bullying prevention programming could also benefit from adopting practices and principles from the field of implementation science (Fixsen et al., 2005). It may be that potentially effective programs already exist and that the field just needs to make a more sustained commitment to implementing the existing models with fidelity and testing them with RCT designs to better understand what works for whom, and under what conditions. This may be especially relevant when considering the broader set of youth violence prevention programs, which have rarely been evaluated to determine the impacts of these interventions on bullying specifically. The field of bullying prevention could benefit from the development and implementation of additional innovative and novel approaches that use emerging technologies and strategies. Furthermore, more research is needed to better understand the effective mechanisms of change and strategies to optimize the effect size of prevention programs.

The Role of Peers and Peer-Led Programming

There is no question that peers have a significant influence on youth development (Collins et al., 2000; Dodge et al., 2006) including their involvement in and responses to bullying (Paluck et al., 2016; Salmivalli, 2010). In fact, correlational studies have found that having more friends was associated with increased bullying perpetration but less risk of being bullied (Wang et al., 2009), whereas other studies found that the way in which peers respond to witnessing bullying may help buffer the effects for the targeted youth (Salmivalli et al., 1996). As a result, there is an increasing interest in leveraging these relationships and influences to prevent and intervene in bullying situations (Paluck et al., 2016). However, the empirical findings on the role of peers in bullying prevention have been mixed, with some researchers suggesting the need for more peer-based interventions (Paluck et al., 2016), such as friendship-making components (Leff and Waasdorp, 2013), and others calling for more caution, particularly regarding implementation of selected or indicated interventions (Dodge et al., 2006). Clearly, there is a need to distinguish between the role of peers as bystanders in bullying situations and peers as potential leaders or implementers of intervention programs.

Within group-based interventions, which is often a modality used for selective and some indicated preventive interventions, studies show that there is the potential for deviance training and a shift in attitudes that actually favor aggression and deviant behavior (Dodge et al., 2006). While there are certainly structures and procedures that adult facilitators of such groups can put in place to try to mitigate these potentially iatrogenic effects, caution should be taken when implementing group-based programs for youth who are aggressive, such as those who bully.

One particular area of interest is intervention programs that operate through peer bystander behavior. This is a topic that is gaining attention, both within practice and within the research literature (Cunningham et al., 2011; Polanin et al., 2012; Salmivalli, 2014). A bystander is defined as an onlooker who is present during the bullying event but remains neutral (passive), helping neither the victim nor the bully (Salmivalli, 2010). A meta-analysis by Polanin and colleagues (2012) reviewed 12 school-based bullying prevention approaches that focused on bystanders' behaviors as a component of the intervention. They found that bystander-involved models were generally effective at reducing bullying (overall effect size as measured by Hedge's $g = 0.20$, $p < .001$, 95% CI [0.11, 0.29]). Although overall these programs were successful at increasing bystanders' intervention in bullying situations, Polanin and colleagues (2012) did not find any improvement in bystander empathy for the victims. This is consistent with other recent meta-analyses on a smaller set of studies that included bystander effects (Merrell et al., 2008). Developmentally, Polanin and colleagues (2012) also found that bystander intervention effects were larger for older youth compared to younger children. Specifically, the effects were typically stronger in high schools (ES = 0.43) compared to students in younger grades (ES = 0.14; $p < .05$). Polanin and colleagues (2012) noted that their meta-analysis was limited to a relatively small number of studies, so they called for more research on the effects of peers on bullying, especially regarding the distinction between peers as bystanders and peers as leaders of intervention programming.

There are some potentially promising findings emerging from a few peer-led educational models that have been used successfully to address bullying and cyberbullying in Italy (Menesini et al., 2012). Other youth-led programs have demonstrated some potentially promising effects in the context of bullying, sexual harassment, and dating violence prevention (Connolly et al., 2015). However, a study by Salmivalli (2001) testing a peer-led intervention campaign against school bullying found that it produced mixed effects, with an increase in pro-bullying attitudes among boys. Additional research is clearly needed with larger samples and more RCT designs to determine the extent to which these and the other peer-led models are truly effective and robust against potentially iatrogenic effects. Other potentially promising findings are in the area of gay-straight alliances, which were discussed in Chapter 3 (Poteat et al., 2013, 2015). Such resources appear to be an important buffer for LGB youth and may contribute to a shift in the norms regarding stereotype-driven targeting of LGB youth. There is also growing interest in programming focused on issues related to equity in relation to both sexual and racial minorities (Bulanda et al., 2014; Polanin and Vera, 2013). Similarly, there is increasing interest in the use of restorative practice-based models with the goal of preventing bullying and providing more equitable disciplinary practices in response to other behavioral violations (Bradshaw, 2013). However, much of the work on this topic has been descriptive and conceptual, with few randomized and controlled studies assessing behavioral or bullying-related outcomes for youth. Additional research is needed to leverage findings from the extant research on equity and inclusion for subpopulations (e.g., minorities; youth with disabilities; lesbian, gay, bisexual, and transgender [LGBT] youth) to inform bullying prevention programming.

Role of Educators and School-Based Programming

Given the amount of time youth spend in school and the overall rates of school-based bullying, it is not surprising that teachers and other education support professionals play an important role in bullying prevention (Bradshaw et al., 2013b). Teachers often serve as implementers of programs as well as frontline interveners in bullying situations (Goncy et al., 2014; Holt et al., 2013); however, they vary in their willingness to intervene and in their skills to intervene effectively (Biggs et al., 2008; Bradshaw et al., 2009c; Hektner and Swenson, 2011). In fact, there appears to be a disconnect between students' and educators' perceptions and experiences of bullying behavior. Several studies found that educators underestimated the impact and prevalence of bullying behavior (Bradshaw et al., 2009c), which in turn likely contributes to youth's hesitance to report bullying to adults at school. Furthermore, many adults lacked skills to intervene effectively, and potentially even overestimated their efficacy and ability to detect bullying-related problems. Studies have found that many youth perceived teachers as not effective in preventing or intervening in bullying situations (Berguno et al., 2004; Bradshaw et al., 2009c).

In contrast, teachers' perceived efficacy has been associated with an increased likelihood of intervening in a bullying situation, although this was also affected by perceived threat and the teachers' years of experience (Duong and Bradshaw, 2013), as well as their feelings of connection to the school (Bradshaw et al., 2013b; O'Brennan et al., 2014). There is research to suggest that professional development can have a positive effect on teacher efficacy with respect to increasing teachers' willingness to intervene in bullying incidents (Bell et al., 2010). Nevertheless, it is clear that more work is needed to better understand ways that educators can bridge with students to improve prevention and intervention in bullying situations.

Teachers are not the only adults working in schools or outside of schools who have a role to play in bullying prevention (see Box 5-1). There is emerging research on the important, but often overlooked, group of education support professionals (ESPs), including bus drivers, cafeteria workers, and other paraprofessionals, in bullying prevention (Bradshaw et al., 2013b). The U.S. Department of Education's Office of Safe and Healthy Students provides guidance on how bus drivers can effectively respond to and prevent bullying (U.S. Department of Health and Human Services,

2015). These individuals are rarely provided training in bullying prevention and their school's policies related to bullying. They are seldom engaged in schoolwide bullying prevention efforts, despite witnessing rates of student bullying similar to teachers.

School resource officers (SROs) are also an increasing presence in schools (James and McCallion, 2013), but their engagement in prevention programming is rare. Most SROs are engaged primarily in law enforcement–related activities, such as patrolling school grounds, responding to crime/disorder reports, and investigating leads about crime (Coon and Travis III, 2012; James et al., 2011). The SRO role is traditionally viewed as a triad of law enforcement, teacher, and counselor, so it makes sense that an officer can play a potentially important role on school safety teams and in bullying prevention efforts. However, few studies have examined their role in implementing anti-bullying policies and interventions (James and McCallion, 2013; Robles-Piña and Denham, 2012). The limited research on this topic acknowledges a tension between two different perspectives. The first is that SROs should not be involved in bullying interventions because many acts that individuals report as bullying are not criminal matters (Broll and Huey, 2015; Parr et al., 2012). In contrast, others view the SRO as not just a sworn law enforcement officer but also an important member of the school staff who can and should be trained to engage in teaching- and counselor-related activities (Coon and Travis III, 2012; Robles-Piña and Denham, 2012). Although SROs are often called in when there is a problem, additional research is needed on how best to leverage their expertise and role to promote a positive school climate and prevent bullying.

The Role of Parents

Not surprisingly, parents play an important role in helping youth navigate social challenges and adapting to stress (Collins et al., 2000). There is a large and growing body of research documenting the efficacy and effectiveness of preventive interventions that involve parents, particularly at the selective and indicated levels. However, the vast majority of these programs focus on youth violence prevention, social-emotional development, and academic outcomes, with virtually no RCT-design evaluations of programs that were developed specifically to prevent bullying. Yet, intervention research consistently highlights the importance of parents in shaping positive outcomes for youth. The meta-analysis by Ttofi and Farrington (2009) found that several family factors were important elements of effective bullying prevention programs, including parent training and informing parents about bullying. However, few of the evaluations of universal programs reviewed by the committee collected comprehensive data on the penetration or uptake of those parent-focused elements. For example, sending home

---

BOX 5-1
Who Are the Adult Professionals and Volunteers
Who Work with Children and Adolescents?

There are many different professionals and volunteers who interact on a regular basis with children and youth, ranging from teachers and education support professionals (ESPs), to health care professionals, to youth development and afterschool program staff and volunteers. The role of health care professionals in bullying prevention is discussed below in this section. As mentioned in Chapter 3, teachers are unlikely to intervene if they do not have proper training (Bauman et al., 2008). The U.S. Department of Health and Human Services has developed various Web-based resources, including training presentations and toolkits, to help educators, ESPs, parents, and community members train themselves on bullying prevention practices (U.S. Department of Health and Human Services, 2015).[a] The National Center on Safe Supportive Learning Environments, a Technical Assistance Center under contract to the U.S. Department of Education, has also created bullying prevention training toolkits aimed at educators and school bus drivers.[b]

The U.S. Department of Education provides the *You for Youth* resource through its 21st Century Community Learning Centers. This is an online professional learning community that helps state and local centers connect with each other and share best practices for creating positive experiences for all children. However, these trainings do not directly deal with bullying prevention (U.S. Department of Education, 2015). The National Education Association has developed training materials and other resources for educators as well as a toolkit, *Bully Free: It Starts With Me,* aimed at all ESPs including bus drivers, custodial, food service, and clerical staff, among others.[c] Violence Prevention Works provides a 2-day committee training for the Olweus Bullying Prevention Program conducted by a certified Olweus trainer. These are just a few of the toolkits and training resources available to adult professionals and volunteers who interact with children. However, data are not available on how the toolkits are being implemented at the local level and how many teachers and ESPs are using these resources. It is also unclear whether all of these resources have been evaluated.

About 10.2 million children (18%) participate in an afterschool program. This is an increase of nearly 60 percent—or 4 million additional children—in the past decade (Afterschool Alliance, 2014). The U.S Census Bureau found that, in 2013, 57 percent of children between the ages of 6 and 17 participated in at least one afterschool extracurricular activity (U.S. Census Bureau, 2014). Precise national

---

information to parents and offering workshops is much easier than ensuring parents' engagement, program attendance, and actual use of those materials (Bradshaw et al., 2009b). It is quite possible that parent-focused programming for school-age youth is more efficient and effective at the selective and indicated levels than at the universal level (Arseneault et al., 2010).

estimates for the number of paid staff and volunteers who work with children and youth in the out-of-school time sector are not available but the National Collaboration for Youth, an affinity group of 50 national, nonprofit youth development organizations, notes that their member organizations employ over 100,000 paid staff and engage more than six million volunteers.[d] Member organizations include groups such as Girl Scouts of the USA and Big Brothers Big Sisters.

There are currently nearly one million adult 4-H volunteers.[e] While organizations such as Girl Scouts and 4-H place a significant emphasis on physical and emotional safety in their trainings for volunteers, it is not clear whether evidence-based trainings are used with these volunteers or if resources are limited to toolkits and fact sheets. For example, Girl Scouts of the USA offers the Be a Friend First Program aimed at preventing bullying among girls but it does not currently offer training for adult volunteers on how to intervene or prevent bullying.[f]

As mentioned in Chapter 3, 80 percent of American youth ages 6-17 participate in extracurricular activities, which include sports and clubs (Riese et al., 2015). The Census Bureau reported that, in 2013, about 35 percent of children who participated in at least one afterschool activity participated in sports, around 29 percent participated in clubs, and approximately 29 percent participated in lessons such as music, dance, or language (U.S. Census Bureau, 2014). It is unclear if the adults who run these extracurricular activities receive any formalized training on how to handle bullying situations. More than 3 million youth sports coaches have been certified by the National Alliance for Youth Sports,[g] a nonprofit organization focused on positive instruction of youth sports coaches. The National Standards for Youth Sports, established by this same organization, does not specifically address bullying.

---

[a]For additional information, see http://www.stopbullying.gov [December 2015].

[b]See *Creating a Safe and Respectful Environment on Our Nation's School Busses*. National Center on Safe Supportive Learning Environments. See https://safesupportivelearning.ed.gov/events/conferences-learning-events/creating-safe-and-respectful-environment-our-nations-school-buses [April 2016].

[c]For additional information, see http://www.nea.org/home/neabullyfree.html [June 2016].

[d]For additional information, see http://www.collab4youth.org/Default.aspx [June 2016].

[e]For additional information, see http://www.reeis.usda.gov/reports-and-documents/4-h-reports [June 2016].

[f]For additional information, see http://www.girlscouts.org/en/our-program/ways-to-participate/series/bff.html [June 2016].

[g]For additional information, see http://www.nays.org/about/about-nays/faqs/ [June 2016].

The notion that "violence begets violence" also applies to the need for interventions targeted to individuals who bully and are bullied by others. Espelage and colleagues (2012) examined the relationship between peer victimization and family violence in early adolescence and found that youth who were identified as poly-victims[9] or who reported relational bullying were more likely to also endorse witnessing domestic violence and being physically or sexually abused at home when compared to nonvictimized youth. Similarly, parents also need to be wary of behavior akin to bullying in the home, such as among siblings or cousins (Jones et al., 2013), which speaks to the need for increased parent awareness of the signs and symptoms of bullying and its impact on the youth and family.

Hawley and Williford (2015) specifically called for the active and consistent involvement of parents in anti-bullying interventions, particularly with respect to the prevention of cyberbullying. In a study of late adolescent victims of bullying, Hemphill and colleagues (2014) found that having opportunities for prosocial involvement in the family lessened subsequent involvement in nonviolent antisocial behaviors. Wang and colleagues (2009) also found that parental support may protect adolescents from multiple forms of bullying, including cyberbullying, which makes parental involvement a potentially critical intervention target.

Health Care Professionals and Bullying Prevention and Intervention

Health care clinicians, including mental and behavioral health experts, can be important players in bullying prevention, especially when they can collaborate with teachers and other education professionals. Evidence of the physical, mental, and behavioral health issues of children who bully, are bullied, or observe bullying incidents (Borowsky et al., 2013; Vessey et al., 2013; Wolke and Lereya, 2015) provides child health and mental health clinicians in community and acute care settings with knowledge to engage in bullying prevention interventions.

Child health care providers can address biological and psychological consequences of bullying in many ways (Fekkes, 2006). Although their clinical roles and responsibilities may vary, community- and hospital-based child health care providers have opportunities to identify and support children, family members, and school personnel in need of care or advice. In addition to physicians and nurses, other health care providers, such as psychologists, dentists, social workers, physical therapists, occupational therapists, and speech and language professionals, may encounter children and youth who have been bullied, who bully, or who have been bystanders to bullying incidents.

Bullying raises complex issues for health care providers because of the associations among bullying and many physical, emotional, behavioral, and social issues such as depression, anxiety, suicide, psychosomatic complaints,

---

[9]The term "poly-victim" for individuals who experience multiple types of victimization is discussed in Chapter 4.

substance abuse, school truancy and delinquency (Borowsky et al., 2013; Dale et al., 2014; Gini and Pozzoli, 2009). Clinicians in schools, clinics, primary care practices, schools, and school-based health centers have opportunities to discuss bullying during visits for well-child care, annual school or sports exams, and routine acute care (Magalnick and Mazyck, 2008). Because middle school students experience higher rates of being bullied than students in high school (Robers et al., 2015), encounters with early adolescents might be especially important for prevention and anticipatory guidance. Because of possible long-term effects of bullying (and other early childhood adversity or toxic stresses) (Lereya et al., 2015; Shonkoff et al., 2012), youth in high school might have emotional or mental health issues that relate to previous bullying incidents.

In addition to children and youth who have been bullied, those who bully may have specific health care needs. They might have family situations that are characterized by violence, abuse, neglect, low socioeconomic status, or other stressful issues. Perpetrating bullying might be the manifestation of other underlying issues, such as mental or behavioral health problems, alienation, homelessness, or undetected learning disabilities.

Because some children internalize victimization or emotional difficulties (Adams et al., 2013; Borowsky et al., 2013), the physical or emotional impacts of bullying on children who bully, have been bullied, or have been bystanders to bullying might not be readily apparent to family members, educators, or health care professionals. Therefore, during child health encounters, clinicians might inquire about changes in behavior, appetite, and sleep and about children's attitudes toward school as ways of screening for involvement with bullying.

Given possible somatization of symptoms among children who have been bullied (Gini and Pozzoli, 2009), health care professionals who see children for purported acute care problems that don't show evidence of illness might consider experience of being bullied among many other possible reasons for the symptoms claimed for the visit or for parents' or children's concerns. Children and youth with certain diagnoses and conditions might be at higher risk for being targets of bullying than others. This includes children with chronic illnesses (e.g., diabetes, obesity, or cerebral palsy), autism spectrum disorders, attention deficit disorders, learning disabilities, congenital anomalies, and behavioral or emotional illnesses (Adams et al., 2013; Pittet et al., 2009; Storch et al., 2006; Twyman et al., 2010).

Health care professionals might also consider protective factors for youth involved with bullying and could provide guidance to parents and children regarding the importance of certain supports. For example, parent connectedness and perceived caring by friends and nonparental adults can be protective factors for some children and youth involved with bullying (Borowsky et al., 2013).

Because most bullying occurs at school (Robers et al., 2015), school nurses are often on the frontlines of caring for children and youth involved in bullying. They might be the first health care professional involved with children and youth who have been bullied in school settings, especially some groups of children who are particularly at risk. As noted above, counselors are often called upon to respond to bullying prevention situations, but they rarely use evidence-based bullying-intervention approaches when providing counseling services to youth who bully or who are victims of bullying. Additional research is needed on the selective and indicated mental health interventions referenced above (e.g., CBITS, MST, FFT, Wraparound/Case Management), as they, too, may be effective for youth involved in bullying. Moreover clinicians should inquire about bullying, even when the youth presents with symptoms that seem consistent with other mental health problems, as bullying may be a contributing factor.

Bullying prevention intervention presents inherent challenges to pediatric health care providers. For example, if a health care professional suspects or identifies a child who has been involved with bullying, effective mechanisms for referral and collaboration with education and other professionals are typically lacking. Appropriate counseling or other services may be in short supply in communities, especially in remote rural areas or other underserved areas. Sharing patient or student information across settings presents legal and logistical challenges. Involvement of parents may be difficult. Reporting mechanisms under state and local laws and other policies might not pertain to situations in which a child health professional detects that bullying has occurred. Finally, best practices or procedures for follow-up by health care professionals are lacking from the evidence-based literature.

Other challenges reside in integrating bullying prevention intervention into the daily responsibilities and realities of health care professionals, regardless of setting. Mechanisms to compensate for time spent on screening, referral, counseling, follow-up of bullying incidents among patients and school or community education may lack public or private sources of financing and reimbursement.

Organizations such as the American Academy of Pediatrics and the National Association of School Nurses have issued statements on the bullying prevention role of their respective members (Committee on Injury, Violence, and Poison Prevention, 2009; DeSisto and Smith, 2015). Interdisciplinary collaboration in this area and identification of effective intervention for best child health outcomes need further study.

The Role of Media

As noted in previous sections of this report, the media serves as both a positive and negative influence on youth with respect to bullying behavior.

There are relatively few RCT studies of social norm campaigns focused on bullying awareness and prevention, despite the large body of public health research suggesting such approaches may be effective at shifting norms, attitudes, and behavior (Wakefield et al., 2010). For example, there have been programs that have delivered normative information as a primary tool for changing socially significant behaviors, such as alcohol consumption (Neighbors et al., 2004), tobacco and drug use (Donaldson et al., 1994), and gambling (Larimer and Neighbors, 2003). Additional work is clearly needed to better understand both the risks and the opportunities associated with media-focused campaigns and social norms–based interventions in relation to bullying.

Social Media

Social media offers both intervention challenges and opportunities for cyberbullying. A challenge is that social media provides a platform on which bullying can occur. This may include bullying by private messages sent within a site, by posting public and embarrassing content about a peer, or by creating a "false" profile of the target and posting embarrassing or untruthful content. Because of the multimedia capacity of these sites, embarrassing content may include text, photos, or even video. Social media allows this content to be spread rapidly within a network, as well as shared through others' networks. Even if the original post is removed, content that has been shared may be difficult to locate and remove.

Social media also provides opportunities to prevent and intervene with bullying. Organizations dedicated to intervention for preventing and treating consequences of bullying may use social media to maintain a presence in those electronic communities where bullying is taking place and to use their platforms for positive messages. Social media may be used to promote prevention messages, such as the It Gets Better campaign,[10] although the committee recognizes that this use of social media, as well as many other intervention approaches, needs further evaluation to determine if it helps or harms children involved in bullying. Social media may also provide opportunities for those who have experienced bullying to directly communicate with an organization. While limited studies have evaluated these efforts, the platform of social media provides opportunities to test the effectiveness of these approaches.

---

[10] The It Gets Better Program employs user-generated media to reach LGBT youth and ameliorate depression and suicidal thoughts among these individuals during their adolescent years. See http://www.itgetsbetter.org [April 2016].

SUMMARY

Systematic reviews and meta-analyses over the past decade recommend that the most likely effective bullying prevention programs are whole school, multicomponent programs that combine elements of universal and targeted strategies (Bradshaw, 2015; Rigby and Slee, 2008; Vreeman and Carroll, 2007). Yet, most meta-analyses of bullying programs show mixed effects and small to moderate effect sizes, at best. When the effects are positive, they are more likely to be effects on attitudes, knowledge, and perceptions, rather than effects on bullying behavior such as experience as a perpetrator or target of bullying. If a universal program does include elements intended to reduce related risk factors or enhance protective factors such as social competence, these elements tend to be embedded in the program so that it is not easy to discern which program components produce desired results for bullying-related behavior. The effects of preventive interventions tend to be greatest for the highest-risk youth, even for interventions in early elementary school (Bradshaw et al., 2015; Limbos et al., 2007; Petras et al., 2008).

Few bullying programs include specific intervention components for youth at risk for involvement in bullying or for youth already involved in bullying, whether as perpetrators or targets (or both). Other school-based interventions tend to target behaviors associated with bullying (e.g., aggressive behavior, social skill development) or the mental health problems associated with being buillied (depression, anxiety, academic failure). Few of the selective and indicated preventive interventions for identified perpetrators (aggressive youth) or targets (youth with mental health issues or at risk for suicide) are school-based, so there needs to be stronger connections between schools, families, and community-based treatment programs. Moreover, these programs need to be further evaluated with regard to impacts on bullying behavior, as they were originally developed to address violence and mental health problems. Yet, many of these problems co-occur and have overlapping risk and protective factors, which suggests these other evidence-based selective and indicated violence prevention models may also demonstrate positive effects for youth involved in bullying.

There is still a dearth of intervention research on programs related to cyberbullying and on programs targeted to vulnerable populations such as LGBT youth, youth with chronic health problems, or youth with developmental disabilities such as autism (Minton, 2014). The role of peers in interventions for at-risk students or for those who are perpetrators or targets needs further clarification, whether that is for peers as bystanders or peers as interventionists, or peers as fellow perpetrators, or targets. Despite increasing interest in programs aimed at increasing equity, shifting norms related to stereotypes, or the use of restorative practices, there are few fully developed models that target these issues, and virtually no randomized studies documenting outcomes associated with these approaches. Additional work is needed on these models to determine whether broader dissemination of these approaches is warranted.

Schools may want to consider implementing a multicomponent program that focuses on school climate, positive behavior support, social and emotional learning, or violence prevention more generally, rather than implementing a bullying-specific preventive intervention, as these more inclusive programs may reach a broader set of outcomes for students and the school environment. Tiered preventive interventions appear to be a promising model for schools, but the lack of rigorously tested selective and indicated preventive interventions focused specifically on bullying means that other violence and mental health prevention models should be leveraged and integrated to increase efficiency. Regardless of the model selected, issues related to implementation fidelity, spanning initial buy-in, and adoption through sustainability, need careful consideration and an authentic investment of resources in order to achieve outcomes.

FINDINGS AND CONCLUSIONS

Findings

Finding 5.1: The most likely effective bullying prevention programs are whole school, multicomponent programs that combine elements of universal and targeted strategies.

Finding 5.2: The findings from meta-analyses of bullying prevention programs have been mixed, with the largest effects observed for whole school programs implemented in Europe, as compared to programs tested in the United States. The challenge of designing and delivering effective bullying prevention programs in the United States may be due to the greater social and economic complexities, including greater income disparities and racial/ethnic heterogeneity in the United States, compared with European countries. More research is needed in the United States focusing on developing and testing novel models for bullying prevention programming and the identification of strategies for increasing fidelity of implementation and effect sizes.

Finding 5.3: Research on the role of peers in bullying prevention interventions has been mixed, with some studies suggesting the need for more peer-based interventions, such as friendship-making components, and others calling for more caution because peer-based interventions have produced null or even iatrogenic effects.

Finding 5.4: Few bullying programs include specific intervention components for youth at risk for bullying (e.g., ethnic minorities, sexual minorities, youth with disabilities), or for youth already involved in bullying as perpetrators or targets (or both), and the studies examining impacts of bullying prevention programs for these subpopulations are rare.

Finding 5.5: Few of the selective and indicated preventive interventions for identified perpetrators (aggressive youth) or targets (e.g., bullied youth with mental health issues or at risk for suicide) are school-based, so there needs to be stronger connections among schools, families, and community-based treatment programs.

Finding 5.6: There is a growing interest in research documenting the effectiveness of bullying and youth violence preventive interventions that involve parents, particularly at the selective and indicated levels. However, to date few such family-focused programs have been developed or tested in relation to impacts specifically on bullying.

Finding 5.7: There is emerging international research that suggests a variety of models may be effective at reducing both cyberbullying and traditional bullying.

Conclusions

Conclusion 5.1: The vast majority of research on bullying prevention programming has focused on universal school-based programs; however, the effects of those programs within the United States appear to be relatively modest. Multicomponent schoolwide programs appear to be most effective at reducing bullying and should be the types of programs implemented and disseminated in the United States.

Conclusion 5.2: Most of the school, family, and community-based prevention programs tested using randomized controlled trial designs have focused on youth violence, delinquency, social-emotional development, and academic outcomes, with limited consideration of the impacts on bullying specifically. However, it is likely that these programs also produce effects on bullying, which have largely been unmeasured and therefore data on bullying outcomes should be routinely collected in future research.

Conclusion 5.3: There has been limited research on selective and indicated models for bullying intervention programming, either inside or outside of schools. More attention should be given to these interventions in future bullying research.

Conclusion 5.4: The extant, empirically supported selective and indicated preventive interventions for violence and delinquency should also be leveraged to meet the needs of students involved in bullying, or those experiencing the mental and behavioral health consequences of bullying. These programs should be integrated into a multi-tiered system of supports for students at risk for engaging in or experiencing the consequences of bullying.

Conclusion 5.5: The role of peers in bullying prevention as bystanders and as intervention program leaders needs further clarification and empirical investigation in order to determine the extent to which peer-led programs are effective and robust against potentially iatrogenic effects.

Conclusion 5.6: The role of online resources or social marketing campaigns in bullying prevention or intervention needs further clarification and empirical investigation in order to determine whether these resources and programs are effective.

Conclusion 5.7: Since issues of power and equity are highly relevant to bullying, fully developed prevention models that target these issues as an approach for preventing bullying should be conducted using randomized controlled trial designs.

Conclusion 5.8: Additional research is needed on the effectiveness of programs targeted to vulnerable populations such as lesbian, gay, bisexual, and transgender youth, youth with chronic health problems such as obesity, or those with developmental disabilities (e.g., autism), as well as variation in the effectiveness of universal programs for these subpopulations.

Conclusion 5.9: There is a strong need for additional programming and effectiveness research on interdisciplinary collaboration with health care practitioners, parents, school resource officers, community-based organizations (e.g., scouts, athletics), and industry to address issues related to bullying and cyberbullying.

Conclusion 5.10: Regardless of the prevention program or model selected, issues related to implementation fidelity, spanning initial buy-in and adoption through taking programs to scale and sustainability, need careful consideration and an authentic investment of resources in order to achieve outcomes and sustained implementation.

REFERENCES

Adams, R.E., Fredstrom, B.K., Duncan, A.W., Holleb, L.J., and Bishop, S.L. (2013). Using self- and parent-reports to test the association between peer victimization and internalizing symptoms in verbally fluent adolescents with ASD. *Journal of Autism and Developmental Disorders, 44*(4), 861-872.

Afterschool Alliance. (2014). *America after 3 pm: Afterschool Programs in Demand.* Available: http://www.afterschoolalliance.org/documents/AA3PM-2014/AA3PM_Key_Findings.pdf [December 2015].

Ahtola, A., Haataja, A., Kärnä, A., Poskiparta, E., and Salmivalli, C. (2012). For children only? Effects of the KiVa Anti-Bullying Program on teachers. *Teaching and Teacher Education, 28*(6), 851-859.

Ajzen, I. (1985). From intentions to actions: A theory of planned behavior. In J. Kuh and J. Beckmann (Eds.), *Action Control: From Cognition to Behavior* (pp. 11-39). Berlin: Springer-Verlag.

Aos, S., Lee, S., Drake, E., Pennucci, A., Klima, T., Miller, M., Anderson, L., Mayfield, J., and Burley, M. (2011). *Evidence-based Options to Improve Statewide Outcomes, July 2011 Update* (Pub. No. 04-07-3901). Olympia: Washington State Institute for Public Policy. Available: http://wsipp.wa.gov/pub. asp [December 2015].

Arseneault, L., Bowes, L., and Shakoor, S. (2010). Bullying victimization in youths and mental health problems: "Much ado about nothing"? *Psychological Medicine, 40*(05), 717-729.

Bagley, C., and Pritchard, C. (1998). The reduction of problem behaviours and school exclusion in at-risk youth: An experimental study of school social work with cost-benefit analyses. *Child and Family Social Work, 3*(4), 219-226.

Barnes, T.N., Smith, S.W., and Miller, M.D. (2014). School-based cognitive-behavioral interventions in the treatment of aggression in the United States: A meta-analysis. *Aggression and Violent Behavior, 19*(4), 311-321.

Barrera Jr, M., Biglan, A., Taylor, T.K., Gunn, B.K., Smolkowski, K., Black, C., Ary, D.V., and Fowler, R.C. (2002). Early elementary school intervention to reduce conduct problems: A randomized trial with Hispanic and non-Hispanic children. *Prevention Science, 3*(2), 83-94.

Batsche, G. (2014). Multi-tiered system of supports for inclusive schools. In J. McLeskey, N.L. Waldron, F. Sponder, and B. Algozzine (Eds.) *Handbook of Effective Inclusive Schools: Research and Practice* (pp. 183-196). New York: Routledge.

Baughman-Sladky, M., Hussey, D., Flannery, D., and Jefferis, E. (2015). Adolescent delinquency and violent behavior. In T.P. Gullotta, R.W. Plant, and M.A. Evans (Eds.), *Handbook of Adolescent Behavioral Problems: Evidence-Based Approaches to Prevention and Treatment, Second Edition* (pp. 445-471). New York: Springer Press.

Bauman, S., Rigby, K., and Hoppa, K. (2008). U.S. teachers' and school counsellors' strategies for handling school bullying incidents. *Educational Psychology, 28*(7), 837-856.

Beets, M.W., Flay, B.R., Vuchinich, S., Acock, A.C., Li, K.-K., and Allred, C. (2008). School climate and teachers' beliefs and attitudes associated with implementation of the Positive Action Program: A diffusion of innovations model. *Prevention Science, 9*(4), 264-275.

Bell, C.D., Raczynski, K.A., and Horne, A.M. (2010). Bully Busters Abbreviated: Evaluation of a group-based bully intervention and prevention program. *Group Dynamics: Theory, Research, and Practice, 14*(3), 257-267.

Berguno, G., Leroux, P., McAinsh, K., and Shaikh, S. (2004). Children's experience of loneliness at school and its relation to bullying and the quality of teacher interventions. *The Qualitative Report, 9*(3), 483-499.

Berry, K., and Hunt, C.J. (2009). Evaluation of an intervention program for anxious adolescent boys who are bullied at school. *Journal of Adolescent Health, 45*(4), 376-382.

Biggs, B.K., Vernberg, E.M., Twemlow, S.W., Fonagy, P., and Dill, E.J. (2008). Teacher adherence and its relation to teacher attitudes and student outcomes in an elementary school–based violence prevention program. *School Psychology Review, 37*(4), 533.

Biglan, A., Flay, B.R., and Wagenaar, A.C. (2015). Commentary on the 2015 SPR Standards of Evidence. *Prevention Science, 16*(7), 927-932.

Borowsky, I.W., Taliaferro, L.A., and McMorris, B.J. (2013). Suicidal thinking and behavior among youth involved in verbal and social bullying: Risk and protective factors. *Journal of Adolescent Health, 53*(1), S4-S12.

Botvin, G.J., Griffin, K.W., and Nichols, T.D. (2006). Preventing youth violence and delinquency through a universal school-based prevention approach. *Prevention Science, 7*(4), 403-408.

Bowes, L., Maughan, B., Caspi, A., Moffitt, T., and Arseneault, L. (2010). Families promote emotional and behavioural resilience to bullying: Evidence of an environmental effect. *Child Psychology and Psychiatry, 51*(7), 809-817.

Bradshaw, C.P. (2013). Preventing bullying through Positive Behavioral Interventions and Supports (PBIS): A multitiered approach to prevention and integration. *Theory into Practice, 52*(4), 288-295.

Bradshaw, C.P. (2015). Translating research to practice in bullying prevention. *American Psychologist, 70*(4), 322.

Bradshaw, C.P. (Ed.). (in press). *Handbook of Bullying Prevention: A Life Course Perspective*: Washington, DC: National Association of Social Workers Press.

Bradshaw, C.P., and Waasdorp, T.E. (2009). Measuring and changing a "culture of bullying." *School Psychology Review, 38*(3), 356-361.

Bradshaw, C.P., Koth, C.W., Bevans, K.B., Ialongo, N., and Leaf, P.J. (2008). The impact of school-wide Positive Behavioral Interventions and Supports (PBIS) on the organizational health of elementary schools. *School Psychology Quarterly, 23*(4), 462-473.

Bradshaw, C.P., Sawyer, A.L., and O'Brennan, L.M. (2009a). A social disorganization perspective on bullying-related attitudes and behaviors: The influence of school context. *American Journal of Community Psychology, 43*(3-4), 204-220.

Bradshaw, C.P., Koth, C.W., Thornton, L.A., and Leaf, P.J. (2009b). Altering school climate through school-wide Positive Behavioral Interventions and Supports: Findings from a group-randomized effectiveness trial. *Prevention Science, 10*(2), 100-115.

Bradshaw, C.P., Zmuda, J.H., Kellam, S.G., and Ialongo, N.S. (2009c). Longitudinal impact of two universal preventive interventions in first grade on educational outcomes in high school. *Journal of Educational Psychology, 101*(4), 926-937.

Bradshaw, C.P., Mitchell, M.M., and Leaf, P.J. (2010). Examining the effects of schoolwide Positive Behavioral Interventions and Supports on student outcomes: Results from a randomized controlled effectiveness trial in elementary schools. *Journal of Positive Behavior Interventions, 12*(3), 133-148.

Bradshaw, C.P., Waasdorp, T.E., and Leaf, P.J. (2012). Effects of school-wide Positive Behavioral Interventions and Supports on child behavior problems. *Pediatrics, 130*(5), e1136-e1145.

Bradshaw, C.P., Waasdorp, T.E., Goldweber, A., and Johnson, S.L. (2013a). Bullies, gangs, drugs, and school: Understanding the overlap and the role of ethnicity and urbanicity. *Journal of Youth and Adolescence, 42*(2), 220-234.

Bradshaw, C.P., Waasdorp, T.E., O'Brennan, L.M., and Gulemetova, M. (2013b). Teachers' and education support professionals' perspectives on bullying and prevention: Findings from a National Education Association study. *School Psychology Review, 42*(3), 280-297.

Bradshaw, C.P., Bottiani, J.H., Osher, D., and Sugai, G. (2014a). The integration of positive behavioral interventions and supports and social and emotional learning. In M.D. Weist, N.A. Lever, and J.S. Owens (Eds.), *Handbook of School Mental Health* (pp. 101-118). New York: Springer.

Bradshaw, C.P., Debnam, K., Johnson, S., Pas, E., Hershfeldt, P., Alexander, A., Barrett, S., and Leaf, P. (2014b). Maryland's evolving system of social, emotional, and behavioral interventions in public schools: The Maryland Safe and Supportive Schools project. *Adolescent Psychiatry, 4*(3), 194-206.

Bradshaw, C.P., Waasdorp, T.E., and Leaf, P.J. (2015). Examining variation in the impact of school-wide Positive Behavioral Interventions and Supports: Findings from a randomized controlled effectiveness trial. *Journal of Educational Psychology, 107*(2), 546-557.

Broll, R., and Huey, L. (2015). "Just being mean to somebody isn't a police matter": Police perspectives on policing cyberbullying. *Journal of School Violence, 14*(2), 155-176.

Brown, E.C., Low, S., Smith, B.H., and Haggerty, K.P. (2011). Outcomes from a school-randomized controlled trial of Steps to Respect: A bullying prevention program. *School Psychology Review, 40*(3), 423-443.

Bruns, E.J., Burchard, J.D., and Yoe, J.T. (1995). Evaluating the Vermont system of care: Outcomes associated with community-based Wraparound services. *Journal of Child and Family Studies, 4*(3), 321-339.

Bulanda, J.J., Bruhn, C., Byro-Johnson, T., and Zentmyer, M. (2014). Addressing mental health stigma among young adolescents: Evaluation of a youth-led approach. *Health & Social Work, 39*(2), 73-80.

Carney, M.M., and Buttell, F. (2003). Reducing juvenile recidivism: Evaluating the Wraparound services model. *Research on Social Work Practice, 13*(5), 551-568.

Catalano, R.F., Mazza, J.J., Harachi, T.W., Abbott, R.D., Haggerty, K.P., and Fleming, C.B. (2003). Raising healthy children through enhancing social development in elementary school: Results after 1.5 years. *Journal of School Psychology, 41*(2), 143-164.

Chaux, E., Velasquez, A.M., Schultze-Krumbholz, A., and Scheithauer, H. (2016). Effects of the cyberbullying prevention program Media Heroes (Medienhelden) on traditional bullying. *Aggressive Behavior, 42*(2), 157-165.

Cohen, J.A., Deblinger, E., Mannarino, A.P., and Steer, R.A. (2004). A multisite, randomized controlled trial for children with sexual abuse–related PTSD symptoms. *Journal of the American Academy of Child & Adolescent Psychiatry, 43*(4), 393-402.

Cohen, J.A., Mannarino, A.P., and Knudsen, K. (2005). Treating sexually abused children: 1-year follow-up of a randomized controlled trial. *Child Abuse & Neglect, 29*(2), 135-145.

Cohen, J., Mannarino, A., and Deblinger, E. (2006). *Treating Trauma and Traumatic Grief in Children and Adolescents.* New York: Guilford Press.

Collins, W.A., Maccoby, E.E., Steinberg, L., Hetherington, E.M., and Bornstein, M.H. (2000). Contemporary research on parenting: The case for nature and nurture. *American Psychologist, 55*(2), 218-232.

Committee on Injury, Violence, and Poison Prevention. (2009). Policy statement—Role of the pediatrician in youth violence prevention. *Pediatrics, 124*(1), 393-402.

Conduct Problems Prevention Research Group. (1999). Initial impact of the Fast Track prevention trial for conduct problems: II. Classroom effects. *Journal of Consulting and Clinical Psychology, 67*(5), 648-657.

Conduct Problems Prevention Research Group. (2002). Using the Fast Track randomized prevention trial to test the early-starter model of the development of serious conduct problems. *Development and Psychopathology, 14*(4), 925-943.

Conduct Problems Prevention Research Group. (2010). Fast Track intervention effects on youth arrests and delinquency. *Journal of Experimental Criminology, 6*(2), 131-157.

Conduct Problems Prevention Research Group. (2011). The effects of the Fast Track preventive intervention on the development of conduct disorder across childhood. *Child Development, 82*(1), 331-345.

Connell, A.M., Dishion, T.J., Yasui, M., and Kavanagh, K. (2007). An adaptive approach to family intervention: Linking engagement in family-centered intervention to reductions in adolescent problem behavior. *Journal of Consulting and Clinical Psychology, 75*(4), 568-579.

Connolly, J., Josephson, W., Schnoll, J., Simkins-Strong, E., Pepler, D., MacPherson, A., Weiser, J., Moran, M., and Jiang, D. (2015). Evaluation of a youth-led program for preventing bullying, sexual harassment, and dating aggression in middle schools. *The Journal of Early Adolescence, 35*(3), 403-434.

Coon, J.K., and Travis III, L.F. (2012). The role of police in public schools: A comparison of principal and police reports of activities in schools. *Police Practice and Research, 13*(1), 15-30.

Cross, D., Shaw, T., Hadwen, K., Cardoso, P., Slee, P., Roberts, C., Thomas, L., and Barnes, A. (2015). Longitudinal impact of the Cyber Friendly Schools program on adolescents' cyberbullying behavior. *Aggressive Behavior, 42*(2), 166-180.

Cunningham, C.E., Vaillancourt, T., Cunningham, L.J., Chen, Y., and Ratcliffe, J. (2011). Modeling the bullying prevention program design recommendations of students from grades five to eight: A discrete choice conjoint experiment. *Aggressive Behavior, 37*(6), 521-537.

Dale, J., Russell, R., and Wolke, D. (2014). Intervening in primary care against childhood bullying: An increasingly pressing public health need. *Journal of the Royal Society of Medicine, 107*(6), 219-223.

Deblinger, E., Mannarino, A.P., Cohen, J.A., Runyon, M.K., and Steer, R.A. (2011). Trauma-focused cognitive behavioral therapy for children: Impact of the trauma narrative and treatment length. *Depression and Anxiety, 28*(1), 67-75.

Del Rey, R., Casas, J.A., and Ortega, R. (2015). The impacts of the ConRed program on different cyberbulling roles. *Aggressive Behavior, 42*(2), 123-135.

DeRosier, M.E. (2004). Building relationships and combating bullying: Effectiveness of a school-based social skills group intervention. *Journal of Clinical Child & Adolescent Psychology, 33*(1), 196-201.

DeRosier, M.E., and Marcus, S.R. (2005). Building friendships and combating bullying: Effectiveness of S.S.GRIN at one-year follow-up. *Journal of Clinical Child & Adolescent Psychology, 34*(1), 140-150.

DeSisto, M.C., and Smith, S. (2015). Bullying prevention in schools: Position statement. *National Association of School Nurses, 30*(3), 189-191.

Dishion, T.J., and Kavanagh, K. (2003). *Intervening in Adolescent Problem Behavior: A Family-centered Approach*. New York: Guilford Press.

Dishion, T.J., Brennan, L.M., Shaw, D.S., McEachern, A.D., Wilson, M.N., and Jo, B. (2014). Prevention of problem behavior through annual family check-ups in early childhood: Intervention effects from home to early elementary school. *Journal of Abnormal Child Psychology, 42*(3), 343-354.

Doane, A.N., Kelley, M.L., and Pearson, M.R. (2015). Reducing cyberbullying: A Theory of Reasoned Action-based video prevention program for college students. *Aggressive Behavior, 42*(2), 136-146.

Dodge, K., Bierman, K., Coie, J., Greenberg, M., Lochman, J., McMahon, R., and Pinderhughes, E. (2015). Impact of early intervention on psychopathology, crime, and well-being at age 25. *The American Journal of Psychiatry, 172*(1), 59-70.

Dodge, K.A., Dishion, T.J., and Lansford, J.E. (2006). Deviant peer influences in intervention and public policy for youth. *Society for Research in Child Development, 20*(1) 1-19.

Domitrovich, C.E., Bradshaw, C.P., Poduska, J.M., Hoagwood, K., Buckley, J.A., Olin, S., Romanelli, L.H., Leaf, P.J., Greenberg, M.T., and Ialongo, N.S. (2008). Maximizing the implementation quality of evidence-based preventive interventions in schools: A conceptual framework. *Advances in School Mental Health Promotion, 1*(3), 6-28.

Domitrovich, C.E., Bradshaw, C.P., Greenberg, M.T., Embry, D., Poduska, J.M., and Ialongo, N.S. (2010). Integrated models of school-based prevention: Logic and theory. *Psychology in the Schools, 47*(1), 71-88.

Domitrovich, C.E., Bradshaw, C.P., Berg, J., Pas, E., Becker, K., Musci, R., Embry, D., and Ialongo, N. (2016). How do school-based prevention programs impact teachers? Findings from a randomized trial of an integrated classroom management and social-emotional program. *Prevention Science, 17*, 325-337.

Donaldson, S.I., Graham, J.W., and Hansen, W.B. (1994). Testing the generalizability of intervening mechanism theories: Understanding the effects of adolescent drug use prevention interventions. *Journal of Behavioral Medicine, 17*(2), 195-216.

Duong, J., and Bradshaw, C.P. (2013). Using the extended parallel process model to examine teachers' likelihood of intervening in bullying. *Journal of School Health, 83*(6), 422-429.

Duong, J., and Bradshaw, C.P. (2015). Bullying and suicide prevention: Taking a balanced approach that is scientifically informed. In P. Goldblum, D.L. Espelage, J. Chu, and B. Bongar (Eds.), *Youth Suicide and Bullying: Challenges and Strategies for Prevention and Intervention* (pp. 19-27). New York: Oxford University Press.

Durlak, J., Weissberg, R., Taylor, R., and Dymnicki, A. (2007). *The Effects of School-based Social and Emotional Learning: A Meta-analytic Review.* Unpublished manuscript, Loyola University, Chicago, IL.

Durlak, J.A., Weissberg, R.P., and Pachan, M. (2010). A meta-analysis of after-school programs that seek to promote personal and social skills in children and adolescents. *American Journal of Community Psychology, 45*(3-4), 294-309.

Durlak, J.A., Weissberg, R.P., Dymnicki, A.B., Taylor, R.D., and Schellinger, K.B. (2011). The impact of enhancing students' social and emotional learning: A meta-analysis of school-based universal interventions. *Child Development, 82*(1), 405-432.

Eddy, J.M., Reid, J.B., and Fetrow, R.A. (2000). An elementary school-based prevention program targeting modifiable antecedents of youth delinquency and violence: Linking the Interests of Families and Teachers (LIFT). *Journal of Emotional and Behavioral Disorders, 8*(3), 165-176.

Elgar, F.J., Napoletano, A., Saul, G., Dirks, M.A., Craig, W., Poteat, V.P., Holt, M., and Koenig, B.W. (2014). Cyberbullying victimization and mental health in adolescents and the moderating role of family dinners. *JAMA Pediatrics, 168*(11), 1015-1022.

Embry, D.D., Flannery, D.J., Vazsonyi, A.T., Powell, K.E., and Atha, H. (1996). Peacebuilders: A theoretically driven, school-based model for early violence prevention. *American Journal of Preventive Medicine, 12*(5), 91-100.

Eron, L., Huesmann, R., Spindler, A., Guerra, N., Henry, D., and Tolan, P. (2002). A cognitive-ecological approach to preventing aggression in urban settings: Initial outcomes for high-risk children. *Journal of Consulting and Clinical Psychology, 70*(1), 179-194.

Espelage, D.L., and Swearer, S.M. (2008). Current perspectives on linking school bullying research to effective prevention strategies. In T.W. Miller (Ed.), *School Violence and Primary Prevention* (pp. 335-353). New York: Springer Science + Business Media.

Espelage, D.L., Gutgsell, E.W., and Swearer, S.M. (2004). *Bullying in American Schools: A Social-ecological Perspective on Prevention and Intervention*. Mahwah, NJ: L. Erlbaum Associates.

Espelage, D.L., Low, S., and De La Rue, L. (2012). Relations between peer victimization subtypes, family violence, and psychological outcomes during early adolescence. *Psychology of Violence*, 2(4), 313-324.

Espelage, D.L., Low, S., Polanin, J.R., and Brown, E.C. (2013). The impact of a middle school program to reduce aggression, victimization, and sexual violence. *Journal of Adolescent Health*, 53(2), 180-186.

Evans, C.B., Fraser, M.W., and Cotter, K.L. (2014). The effectiveness of school-based bullying prevention programs: A systematic review. *Aggression and Violent Behavior*, 19(5), 532-544.

Farrington, D.P., and Ttofi, M. (2009). School-based programs to reduce bullying and victimization: A systematic review. *Campbell Systematic Reviews*, 5(6), 1-148.

Farrington, D.P., and Ttofi, M.M. (2011). Bullying as a predictor of offending, violence, and later life outcomes. *Criminal Behaviour and Mental Health*, 21(2), 90-98.

Fast, J., Fanelli, F., and Salen, L. (2003). How becoming mediators affects aggressive students. *Children & Schools*, 25(3), 161-171.

Fekkes, M. (2006). Do bullied children get ill, or do ill children get bullied? A prospective cohort study on the relationship between bullying and health-related symptoms. *Pediatrics*, 117(5), 1568-1574.

Finkelhor, D., Turner, H.A., and Hamby, S. (2012). Let's prevent peer victimization, not just bullying. *Child Abuse & Neglect*, 36(4), 271-274.

Fixsen, D., Naoom, S., Blasé, K., Friedman, R., and Wallace, F. (2005). *Implementation Research: A Synthesis of the Literature* (FMHI Pub. No. 231). Tampa: University of South Florida, Louis de la Parte Florida Mental Health Institute.

Flannery, D.J., Vazsonyi, A.T., Liau, A.K., Guo, S., Powell, K.E., Atha, H., Vesterdal, W., and Embry, D. (2003). Initial behavior outcomes for the Peacebuilders Universal School-Based Violence Prevention Program. *Developmental Psychology*, 39(2), 292-308.

Flannery, D., Hussey, D., and Jefferis, E. (2005). Adolescent delinquency and violent behavior. In T. Gullotta and G.Adams (Eds), *Handbook of Adolescent Behavioral Problems: Evidence-Based Approaches to Prevention and Treatment* (pp. 415-438). New York: Springer.

Frey, K.S., Nolen, S.B., Edstrom, L.V.S., and Hirschstein, M.K. (2005). Effects of a school-based social–emotional competence program: Linking children's goals, attributions, and behavior. *Journal of Applied Developmental Psychology*, 26(2), 171-200.

Frey, K.S., Hirschstein, M.K., Edstrom, L.V., and Snell, J.L. (2009). Observed reductions in school bullying, nonbullying aggression, and destructive bystander behavior: A longitudinal evaluation. *Journal of Educational Psychology*, 101(2), 466-481.

Fung, A.L. (2012). Group treatment of reactive aggressors by social workers in a Hong Kong school setting: A two-year longitudinal study adopting quantitative and qualitative approaches. *British Journal of Social Work*, 42(8), 1533-1555.

Garandeau, C.F., Poskiparta, E., and Salmivalli, C. (2014). Tackling acute cases of school bullying in the KiVa anti-bullying program: A comparison of two approaches. *Journal of Abnormal Child Psychology*, 42(6), 981-991.

Gartlehner, G., Hansen, R.A., Nissman, D., Lohr, K.N., and Carey, T.S. (2006). A simple and valid tool distinguished efficacy from effectiveness studies. *Journal of Clinical Epidemiology*, 59(11), 1125-1126.

Gini, G., and Pozzoli, T. (2009). Association between bullying and psychosomatic problems: A meta-analysis. *Pediatrics*, 123(3), 1059-1065.

Girl Scouts of the USA. (2015). *Volunteer with Girl Scouts Today!* Available: http://www. girlscouts.org/content/gsusa/en/adults/volunteer.html [February 2016].

Goncy, E.A., Sutherland, K.S., Farrell, A.D., Sullivan, T.N., and Doyle, S.T. (2014). Measuring teacher implementation in delivery of a bullying prevention program: The impact of instructional and procedural adherence and competence on student responsiveness. *Prevention Science, 16*(3), 440-450.

Goodman, R. (1997). The Strengths and Difficulties Questionnaire: A research note. *Journal of Child Psychology and Psychiatry, 38*(5), 581-586.

Gottfredson, G.D., and Gottfredson, D.C. (2001). What schools do to prevent problem behavior and promote safe environments. *Journal of Educational and Psychological Consultation, 12*(4), 313-344.

Gradinger, P., Yanagida, T., Strohmeier, D., and Spiel, C. (2015). Prevention of cyberbullying and cyber victimization: Evaluation of the ViSC Social Competence Program. *Journal of School Violence, 14*(1), 87-110.

Greenwood, P.W., and Welsh, B.C. (2012). Promoting evidence-based practice in delinquency prevention at the state level. *Criminology & Public Policy, 11*(3), 493-513.

Grossman, D.C., Neckerman, H.J., Koepsell, T.D., Liu, P.-Y., Asher, K.N., Beland, K., Frey, K., and Rivara, F.P. (1997). Effectiveness of a violence prevention curriculum among children in elementary school: A randomized controlled trial. *Journal of the American Medical Association, 277*(20), 1605-1611.

Hahn, R., Fuqua-Whitley, D., Wethington, H., Lowy, J., Crosby, A., Fullilove, M., Johnson, R., Liberman, A., Moscicki, E., and Price, L. (2007). Effectiveness of universal school-based programs to prevent violent and aggressive behavior: A systematic review. *American Journal of Preventive Medicine, 33*(2), S114-S129.

Hanewinkel, R. (2004). Prevention of bullying in German schools: An evaluation of an anti-bullying approach. In P.K. Smith, D. Pepler, and K. Rigby (Eds.), *Bullying in Schools: How Successful Can Interventions Be?* (pp. 81-97). Cambridge, UK: Cambridge University Press.

Hatzenbuehler, M.L., Schwab-Reese, L., Ranapurwala, S.I., Hertz, M.F., and Ramirez, M.R. (2015). Associations between antibullying policies and bullying in 25 states. *JAMA Pediatrics, 169*(10), e152-e411.

Hawkins, J.D., Catalano, R.F., Kosterman, R., Abbott, R., and Hill, K.G. (1999). Preventing adolescent health-risk behaviors by strengthening protection during childhood. *Archives of Pediatrics and Adolescent Medicine, 153*(3), 226-234.

Hawkins, J.D., Jenson, J.M., Catalano, R., Fraser, M.W., Shapiro, V., Botvin, G.J., Brown, C.H., Beardslee, W., Brent, D., Leslie, L.K., Rotheram-Borus, M.J., Shea, P., Shih, A., Anthony, E., Bender, K., Haggerty, K.P., Gorman-Smith, E., Casey, E., and Stone, S. (2015). *Unleashing the Power of Prevention.* Institute of Medicine discussion paper. Available: https://nam.edu/perspectives-2015-unleashing-the-power-of-prevention/ [August 2016].

Hawkins, J.D., Kosterman, R., Catalano, R.F., Hill, K.G., and Abbott, R.D. (2005). Promoting positive adult functioning through social development intervention in childhood: Long-term effects from the Seattle Social Development Project. *Archives of Pediatrics and Adolescent Medicine, 159*(1), 25-31.

Hawkins, J.D., Oesterle, S., Brown, E.C., Monahan, K.C., Abbott, R.D., Arthur, M.W., and Catalano, R.F. (2011). Sustained decreases in risk exposure and youth problem behaviors after installation of the Communities that Care prevention system in a randomized trial. *Archives of Pediatrics and Adolescent Medicine, 166*(2), 141-148.

Hawley, P.H., and Williford, A. (2015). Articulating the theory of bullying intervention programs: Views from social psychology, social work, and organizational science. *Journal of Applied Developmental Psychology, 37*, 3-15.

Healy, K.L., and Sanders, M.R. (2014). Randomized controlled trial of a family intervention for children bullied by peers. *Behavior Therapy, 45*(6), 760-777.

Hektner, J.M., and Swenson, C.A. (2011). Links from teacher beliefs to peer victimization and bystander intervention: Tests of mediating processes. *Journal of Early Adolescence, 32*(4), 516-536.

Hemphill, S.A., Tollit, M., and Herrenkohl, T.I. (2014). Protective factors against the impact of school bullying perpetration and victimization on young adult externalizing and internalizing problems. *Journal of School Violence, 13*(1), 125-145.

Henggeler, S.W. (2011). Efficacy studies to large-scale transport: The development and validation of multisystemic therapy programs. *Annual Review of Clinical Psychology, 7*, 351-381.

Henggeler, S.W., and Sheidow, A.J. (2012). Empirically supported family-based treatments for conduct disorder and delinquency in adolescents. *Journal of Marital and Family Therapy, 38*(1), 30-58.

Henggeler, S.W., Pickrel, S.G., and Brondino, M.J. (1999). Multisystemic treatment of substance-abusing and -dependent delinquents: Outcomes, treatment fidelity, and transportability. *Mental Health Services Research, 1*(3), 171-184.

Holt, M.K., Raczynski, K., Frey, K.S., Hymel, S., and Limber, S.P. (2013). School and community-based approaches for preventing bullying. *Journal of School Violence, 12*(3), 238-252.

Hong, J.S., and Espelage, D.L. (2012). A review of mixed methods research on bullying and peer victimization in school. *Educational Review, 64*(1), 115-126.

Horner, R.H., Sugai, G., Smolkowski, K., Eber, L., Nakasato, J., Todd, A.W., and Esperanza, J. (2009). A randomized, wait-list controlled effectiveness trial assessing school-wide positive behavior support in elementary schools. *Journal of Positive Behavior Interventions, 11*(3), 133-144.

Hussey, D.L., and Flannery, D.J. (2007). Implementing and evaluating school-based primary prevention programs and the importance of differential effects on outcomes. *Journal of School Violence, 6*(2), 117-134.

Institute of Medicine. (1994). *Reducing Risks for Mental Disorders: Frontiers for Preventive Intervention Research*. Washington, DC: National Academy Press.

James, N., and McCallion, G. (2013). *School Resource Officers: Law Enforcement Officers in Schools*. Washington, DC: Congressional Research Service.

James, R.K., Logan, J., and Davis, S.A. (2011). Including school resource officers in school-based crisis intervention: Strengthening student support. *School Psychology International, 32*(2), 210-224.

Jaycox, L.H., Cohen, J.A., Mannarino, A.P., Walker, D.W., Langley, A.K., Gegenheimer, K.L., Scott, M., and Schonlau, M. (2010). Children's mental health care following Hurricane Katrina: A field trial of trauma-focused psychotherapies. *Journal of Traumatic Stress, 23*(2), 223-231.

Jiménez-Barbero, J.A., Ruiz-Hernández, J.A., Llor-Zaragoza, L., Pérez-García, M., and Llor-Esteban, B. (2016). Effectiveness of anti-bullying school programs: A meta-analysis. *Children and Youth Services Review, 61*, 165-175.

Johnson, S.R.L., Finigan, N.M., Bradshaw, C.P., Haynie, D.L., and Cheng, T.L. (2011). Examining the link between neighborhood context and parental messages to their adolescent children about violence. *Journal of Adolescent Health, 49*(1), 58-63.

Jones, L.M., Mitchell, K.J., and Finkelhor, D. (2013). Online harassment in context: Trends from three Youth Internet Safety Surveys (2000, 2005, 2010). *Psychology of Violence, 3*(1), 53-69.

Kärnä, A., Voeten, M., Little, T.D., Poskiparta, E., Alanen, E., and Salmivalli, C. (2011a). Going to scale: A nonrandomized nationwide trial of the KiVa antibullying program for grades 1–9. *Journal of Consulting and Clinical Psychology, 79*(6), 796-805.

Kärnä, A., Voeten, M., Little, T.D., Poskiparta, E., Kaljonen, A., and Salmivalli, C. (2011b). A large-scale evaluation of the KiVa Antibullying Program: Grades 4–6. *Child Development, 82*(1), 311-330.

Kellam, S.G., Rebok, G.W., Ialongo, N., and Mayer, L.S. (1994). The course and malleability of aggressive behavior from early first grade into middle school: Results of a developmental epidemiologically-based preventive trial. *Journal of Child Psychology and Psychiatry, 35*(2), 259-282.

Klomek, A.B., Kleinman, M., Altschuler, E., Marrocco, F., Amakawa, L., and Gould, M.S. (2011). High school bullying as a risk for later depression and suicidality. *Suicide and Life-Threatening Behavior, 41*(5), 501-516.

Koth, C.W., Bradshaw, C.P., and Leaf, P.J. (2008). A multilevel study of predictors of student perceptions of school climate: The effect of classroom-level factors. *Journal of Educational Psychology, 100*(1), 96-104.

Kraag, G., Zeegers, M.P., Kok, G., Hosman, C., and Abu-Saad, H.H. (2006). School programs targeting stress management in children and adolescents: A meta-analysis. *Journal of School Psychology, 44*(6), 449-472.

Kutash, K., Duchnowski, A.J., and Lynn, N. (2006). *School-based Mental Health: An Empirical Guide for Decision-makers.* Louis de la Parte Florida Mental Health Institute, Department of Child and Family Studies, Research and Training Center for Children's Mental Health. Tampa: University of South Florida,

Lanza, S.T., and Rhoades, B.L. (2013). Latent class analysis: An alternative perspective on subgroup analysis in prevention and treatment. *Prevention Science, 14*(2), 157-168.

Larimer, M.E., and Neighbors, C. (2003). Normative misperception and the impact of descriptive and injunctive norms on college student gambling. *Psychology of Addictive Behaviors, 17*(3), 235-243.

Leff, S.S., and Waasdorp, T.E. (2013). Effect of aggression and bullying on children and adolescents: Implications for prevention and intervention. *Current Psychiatry Reports, 15*(3), 1-10.

Lereya, S.T., Copeland, W.E., Costello, E.J., and Wolke, D. (2015). Adult mental health consequences of peer bullying and maltreatment in childhood: Two cohorts in two countries. *The Lancet Psychiatry, 2*(6), 524-531.

Lewis, T.J., and Sugai, G. (1999). Effective behavior support: A systems approach to proactive schoolwide management. *Focus on Exceptional Children, 31*(6), 1-24.

Limbos, M.A., Chan, L.S., Warf, C., Schneir, A., Iverson, E., Shekelle, P., and Kipke, M.D. (2007). Effectiveness of interventions to prevent youth violence: A systematic review. *American Journal of Preventive Medicine, 33*(1), 65-74.

Lindsley, O.R. (1992). Why aren't effective teaching tools widely adopted? *Journal of Applied Behavior Analysis, 25*(1), 21-26.

Lochman, J.E., Wells, K.C., Qu, L., and Chen, L. (2013). Three-year follow-up of Coping Power intervention effects: Evidence of neighborhood moderation? *Prevention Science, 14*(4), 364-376.

Magalnick, H., and Mazyck, D. (2008). Role of the school nurse in providing school health services. *Pediatrics, 121*(5), 1052-1056.

Matjasko, J.L., Vivolo-Kantor, A.M., Massetti, G.M., Holland, K.M., Holt, M.K., and Cruz, J.D. (2012). A systematic meta-review of evaluations of youth violence prevention programs: Common and divergent findings from 25 years of meta-analyses and systematic reviews. *Aggression and Violent Behavior, 17*(6), 540-552.

McElearney, A., Adamson, G., Shevlin, M., and Bunting, B. (2013). Impact evaluation of a school-based counselling intervention in Northern Ireland: Is it effective for pupils who have been bullied? *Child Care in Practice, 19*(1), 4-22.

Menesini, E., Nocentini, A., and Palladino, B.E. (2012). Empowering students against bullying and cyberbullying: Evaluation of an Italian peer-led model. *International Journal of Conflict and Violence, 6*(2), 313-320.

Merrell, K.W., Gueldner, B.A., Ross, S.W., and Isava, D.M. (2008). How effective are school bullying intervention programs? A meta-analysis of intervention research. *School Psychology Quarterly, 23*(1), 26-42.

Meyer, N., and Lesch, E. (2000). An analysis of the limitations of a behavioural programme for bullying boys from a subeconomic environment. *Southern African Journal of Child and Adolescent Mental Health, 12*(1), 59-69.

Miles, P., Bruns, E., Osher, T., and Walker, J. (2006). *The Wraparound Process User's Guide: A Handbook for Families.* National Wraparound Initiative Advisory Group, Research and Training Center on Family Support and Children's Mental Health. Portland, OR: Portland State University.

Minton, S.J. (2014). Prejudice and effective anti-bullying intervention: Evidence from the bullying of "minorities." *Nordic Psychology, 66*(2), 108-120.

Mishna, F., Khoury-Kassabri, M., Gadalla, T., and Daciuk, J. (2012). Risk factors for involvement in cyber bullying: Victims, bullies and bully–victims. *Children and Youth Services Review, 34*(1), 63-70.

Mytton, J.A., DiGuiseppi, C., Gough, D.A., Taylor, R.S., and Logan, S. (2002). School-based violence prevention programs: Systematic review of secondary prevention trials. *Archives of Pediatrics and Adolescent Medicine, 156*(8), 752-762.

Nansel, T.R., Overpeck, M.D., Haynie, D.L., Ruan, W.J., and Scheidt, P.C. (2003). Relationships between bullying and violence among U.S. youth. *Archives of Pediatrics and Adolescent Medicine, 157*(4), 348-353.

National Center for Health Statistics and National Center for Health Services Research. (2001). *Health, United States.* Public Health Service, Health Resources Administration, National Center for Health Statistics. Washington, DC: U.S. Department of Health, Education, and Welfare.

National Research Council and Institute of Medicine. (2009). *Preventing Mental, Emotional, and Behavioral Disorders Among Young People: Progress and Possibilities.* Committee on the Prevention of Mental Disorders and Substance Abuse Among Children, Youth, and Young Adults: Research Advances and Promising Interventions. M.E. O'Connell, T. Boat, and K.E. Warner, Editors. Board on Children, Youth, and Families, Division of Behavioral and Social Sciences and Education. Washington, DC: The National Academies Press.

Neighbors, C., Larimer, M.E., and Lewis, M.A. (2004). Targeting misperceptions of descriptive drinking norms: Efficacy of a computer-delivered personalized normative feedback intervention. *Journal of Consulting and Clinical Psychology, 72*(3), 434-447.

Nickel, M.K., Muehlbacher, M., Kaplan, P., and Krawczyk, J. (2006). Influence of family therapy on bullying behaviour, cortisol secretion, anger, and quality of life in bullying male adolescents: A randomized, prospective, controlled study. *Canadian Journal of Psychiatry, 51*(6), 355-362.

O'Brennan, L.M., Waasdorp, T.E., and Bradshaw, C.P. (2014). Strengthening bullying prevention through school staff connectedness. *Journal of Educational Psychology, 106*(3), 870-880.

Olweus, D. (1993). *Bullying at School: What We Know and What We Can Do.* Oxford, UK: Blackwell.

Olweus, D. (2005). A useful evaluation design, and effects of the Olweus Bullying Prevention Program. *Psychology, Crime & Law, 11*(4), 389-402.

Olweus, D., Limber, S., and Mihalic, S.F. (1999). *Bullying Prevention Program: Blueprints for Violence Prevention.* Blueprints for Violence Prevention Series, Center for the Study and Prevention of Violence, Institute of Behavioral Science, University of Colorado. Available: https://www.ncjrs.gov/pdffiles1/Digitization/174202NCJRS.pdf [June 2016].

Ortega-Ruiz, R., Del Rey, R., and Casas, J.A. (2012). Knowing, building and living together on Internet and social networks: The ConRed Cyberbullying Prevention Program. *International Journal of Conflict and Violence, 6*(2), 302-312.

Paluck, E.L., Sheperd, H., and Aronow, P.M. (2016). Changing climates of conflict: A social network experiment in 56 schools. *Proceedings of the National Academy of Sciences of the United States of America 113*(3), 566-571.

Palladino, E., Nocentini, A., and Menesini, E. (2016). Evidence-based intervention against bullying and cyberbullying: Evaluation of the NoTrap! Program through two independent trials. *Aggressive Behavior, 42*(2), 194-206.

Parr, M., Dagley, P.J., Pogrund, A., and MacDonell, L. (2012). *Bullying: A Report from the Huntington Beach Human Relations Task Force.* Available: http://www.ci.huntingtonbeach.ca.us/government/boards_commissions/pdf-files/2800-May-2012-Bullying-Report.pdf [Febuary 2016].

Pepler, D.J., Craig, W.M., and O'Connell, P., and Charach, A. (2004). Making a difference in bullying: Evaluation of a systemic school-based program in Canada. In P.K. Smith, D. Pepler and K. Rigby (Eds.), *Bullying in Schools: How Successful Can Interventions Be?* (pp. 125-140). Cambridge, UK: Cambridge University Press.

Petras, H., Kellam, S.G., Brown, C.H., Muthén, B.O., Ialongo, N.S., and Poduska, J.M. (2008). Developmental epidemiological courses leading to antisocial personality disorder and violent and criminal behavior: Effects by young adulthood of a universal preventive intervention in first-and second-grade classrooms. *Drug and Alcohol Dependence, 95,* S45-S59.

Pittet, I., Berchtold, A., Akre, C., Michaud, P.A., and Suris, J.C. (2009). Are adolescents with chronic conditions particularly at risk for bullying? *Archives of Disease in Childhood, 95*(9), 711-716.

Poduska, J.M., Kellam, S.G., Wang, W., Brown, C.H., Ialongo, N.S., and Toyinbo, P. (2008). Impact of the Good Behavior Game, a universal classroom-based behavior intervention, on young adult service use for problems with emotions, behavior, or drugs or alcohol. *Drug and Alcohol Dependence, 95,* S29-S44.

Polanin, J.R., Espelage, D.L., and Pigott, T.D. (2012). A meta-analysis of school-based bullying prevention programs' effects on bystander intervention behavior. *School Psychology Review, 41*(1), 47-65.

Polanin, M., and Vera, E. (2013). Bullying prevention and social justice. *Theory into Practice, 52*(4), 303-310.

Poteat, V.P., Sinclair, K.O., DiGiovanni, C.D., Koenig, B.W., and Russell, S.T. (2013). Gay–straight alliances are associated with student health: A multischool comparison of LGBTQ and heterosexual youth. *Journal of Research on Adolescence, 23*(2), 319-330.

Poteat, V.P., Yoshikawa, H., Calzo, J.P., Gray, M.L., DiGiovanni, C.D., Lipkin, A., Mundy-Shephard, A., Perrotti, J., Scheer, J.R., and Shaw, M.P. (2015). Contextualizing gay–straight alliances: Student, advisor, and structural factors related to positive youth development among members. *Child Development, 86*(1), 176-193.

Richard, J.F., Schneider, B.H., and Mallet, P. (2012). Revisiting the whole-school approach to bullying: Really looking at the whole school. *School Psychology International, 33*(3), 263-284.

Riese, A., Gjelsvik, A., and Ranney, M.L. (2015). Extracurricular activities and bullying perpetration: Results from a nationally representative sample. *Journal of School Health*, 85(8), 544-551.

Rigby, K., and Slee, P. (2008). Interventions to reduce bullying. *International Journal of Adolescent Medicine and Health*, 20(2), 165-183.

Robbins, M., Szapocznik, J., and Pérez, G.A. (2007). Brief Strategic Family Therapy. In N. Kazantzia and L. L'Abate (Eds.), *Handbook of Homework Assignments in Psychotherapy* (pp. 133-149). New York: Springer.

Robbins, M.S., Bachrach, K., and Szapocznik, J. (2002). Bridging the research-practice gap in adolescent substance abuse treatment: The case of Brief Strategic Family Therapy. *Journal of Substance Abuse Treatment*, 23(2), 123-132.

Robers, S., Zhang, A., Morgan, R.E., Musu-Gillette, L. (2015). *Indicators of School Crime and Safety: 2014* (NCES 2015-072/NCJ 248036). National Center for Education Statistics, U.S. Department of Education, and Bureau of Justice Statistics, Office of Justice Programs, U.S. Department of Justice. Washington, D.C: U.S. Government Publishing Office.

Robles-Piña, R.A., and Denham, M.A. (2012). School resource officers for bullying interventions: A mixed-methods analysis. *Journal of School Violence*, 11(1), 38-55.

Romer, D., Jamieson, P.E., and Jamieson, K.H. (2006). Are news reports of suicide contagious? A stringent test in six U.S. cities. *Journal of Communication*, 56(2), 253-270.

Ross, S.W., and Horner, R.H. (2009). Bullying prevention in positive behavior support. *Journal of Applied Behavior Analysis*, 42(4), 747-759.

Ryan, K.N., and Curwen, T. (2013). Cyber-victimized students: Incidence, impact, and intervention. *SAGE Open*, 3(4), 1-7.

Salmivalli, C. (2001). Peer-led intervention campaign against school bullying: Who considered it useful, who benefited? *Educational Research*, 43(3), 263-278.

Salmivalli, C. (2010). Bullying and the peer group: A review. *Aggression and Violent Behavior*, 15(2), 112-120.

Salmivalli, C. (2014). Participant roles in bullying: How can peer bystanders be utilized in interventions? *Theory into Practice*, 53(4), 286-292.

Salmivalli, C., Lagerspetz, K., Björkqvist, K., Österman, K., and Kaukiainen, A. (1996). Bullying as a group process: Participant roles and their relations to social status within the group. *Aggressive Behavior*, 22(1), 1-15.

Sanders, M.R., Markie-Dadds, C., Tully, L.A., and Bor, W. (2000). The Triple P—Positive Parenting Program: A comparison of enhanced, standard, and self-directed behavioral family intervention for parents of children with early onset conduct problems. *Journal of Consulting and Clinical Psychology*, 68(4), 624-640.

Sapouna, M., Wolke, D., Vannini, N., Watson, S., Woods, S., Schneider, W., Enz, S., Hall, L., Paiva, A., and André, E. (2010). Virtual learning intervention to reduce bullying victimization in primary school: A controlled trial. *Journal of Child Psychology and Psychiatry*, 51(1), 104-112.

Sawyer, A.M., Borduin, C.M., and Dopp, A.R. (2015). Long-term effects of prevention and treatment on youth antisocial behavior: A meta-analysis. *Clinical Psychology Review*, 42, 130-144.

Schaeffer, C.M., and Borduin, C.M. (2005). Long-term follow-up to a randomized clinical trial of multisystemic therapy with serious and violent juvenile offenders. *Journal of Consulting and Clinical Psychology*, 73(3), 445-453.

Sexton, T.L., and Alexander, J.F. (2000). Functional family therapy. *Juvenile Justice Bulletin*, December. Available: https://www.ncjrs.gov/pdffiles1/ojjdp/184743.pdf [June 2016].

Shields, A., and Cicchetti, D. (2001). Parental maltreatment and emotion dysregulation as risk factors for bullying and victimization in middle childhood. *Journal of Clinical Child Psychology*, 30(3), 349-363.

Shonkoff, J.P., Garner, A.S., Siegel, B.S., Dobbins, M.I., Earls, M.F., McGuinn, L., Pascoe, J., and Wood, D.L. (2012). The lifelong effects of early childhood adversity and toxic stress. *Pediatrics, 129*(1), e232-e246.

Smith, J.D., Schneider, B.H., Smith, P.K., and Ananiadou, K. (2004). The effectiveness of whole-school antibullying programs: A synthesis of evaluation research. *School Psychology Review, 33*(4), 547-560.

Storch, E.A., Heidgerken, A.D., Geffken, G.R., Lewin, A.B., Ohleyer, V., Freddo, M., and Silverstein, J.H. (2006). Bullying, regimen self-management, and metabolic control in youth with Type I diabetes. *The Journal of Pediatrics, 148*(6), 784-787.

Stuart-Cassel, V., Bell, A., and Springer, J.F. (2011). *Analysis of State Bullying Laws and Policies.* Washington, DC: Office of Planning, Evaluation and Policy Development, U.S. Department of Education.

Sugai, G., and Horner, R.R. (2006). A promising approach for expanding and sustaining school-wide positive behavior support. *School Psychology Review, 35*(2), 245-259.

Sugai, G., Horner, R.H., and Gresham, F.M. (2002). Behaviorally effective school environments. In M.R. Shinn, H.M, Walker, and G. Stoner (Eds.*), Interventions for Academic and Behavior Problems II: Preventive and Remedial Approaches.* Washington, DC: National Association of School Psychologists.

Swearer, S., Espelage, D., Koenig, B., Berry, B., Collins, A., and Lembeck, P. (2012). A social-ecological model of bullying prevention and intervention in early adolescence. In S.R. Jimberson, A.B. Nickerson, M.J. Mayer, and M.J. Furlong (Eds.), *Handbook of School Violence and School Safety: International Research and Practice* (pp. 333-355). New York: Routledge.

Swearer, S.M., Espelage, D.L., Vaillancourt, T., and Hymel, S. (2010). What can be done about school bullying?: Linking research to educational practice. *Educational Researcher, 39*(1), 38-47.

Swearer, S.M., Wang, C., Collins, A., Strawhun, J., and Fluke, S. (2014). Bullying: A school mental health perspective. In M.D. Weist, N.A. Lever, C.P. Bradshaw, and J.S. Owens (Eds.), *Handbook of School Mental Health: Research, Training, Practice and Policy* (pp. 341-354). New York: Springer.

Szapocznik, J., and Williams, R.A. (2000). Brief Strategic Family Therapy: Twenty-five years of interplay among theory, research and practice in adolescent behavior problems and drug abuse. *Clinical Child and Family Psychology Review, 3*(2), 117-134.

Tierney, T., and Dowd, R. (2000). The use of social skills groups to support girls with emotional difficulties in secondary schools. *Support for Learning, 15*(2), 82-85.

Ttofi, M.M., and Farrington, D.P. (2009). What works in preventing bullying: Effective elements of anti-bullying programmes. *Journal of Aggression, Conflict and Peace Research, 1*(1), 13-24.

Ttofi, M.M., and Farrington, D.P. (2011). Effectiveness of school-based programs to reduce bullying: A systematic and meta-analytic review. *Journal of Experimental Criminology, 7*(1), 27-56.

Ttofi, M.M., and Farrington, D.P. (2012). Risk and protective factors, longitudinal research, and bullying prevention. *New Directions for Youth Development, 2012*(133), 85-98.

Ttofi, M.M., Eisner, M., and Bradshaw, C.P. (2014). Bullying prevention: Assessing existing meta-evaluations. In G. Bruinsma and D. Weisburd (Eds.), *Encyclopedia of Criminology and Criminal Justice* (pp. 231-242). New York: Springer.

Twyman, K.A., Saylor, C.F., Saia, D., Macias, M.M., Taylor, L.A., and Spratt, E. (2010). Bullying and ostracism experiences in children with special health care needs. *Journal of Developmental & Behavioral Pediatrics, 31*(1), 1-8.

U.S. Census Bureau. (2014). *Nearly 6 out of 10 Children Participate in Extracurricular Activities, Census Bureau Reports* (U.S. Census Bureau press release). Available: https://www.census.gov/newsroom/press-releases/2014/cb14-224.html [December 2015].

U.S. Department of Education. (2015). *21st Century Community Learning Centers—Resources.* Available: http://www2.ed.gov/programs/21stcclc/resources.html [December 2015].

U.S. Department of Health and Human Services. (2015). *Bullying Prevention Training Center.* Available: http://www.stopbullying.gov/prevention/training-center/ [December 2015].

van der Stouwe, T., Asscher, J.J., Stams, G.J.J., Deković, M., and van der Laan, P.H. (2014). The effectiveness of Multisystemic Therapy (MST): A meta-analysis. *Clinical Psychology Review, 34*(6), 468-481.

Vannini, N., Enz, S., Sapouna, M., Wolke, D., Watson, S., Woods, S., Dautenhahn, K., Hall, L., Paiva, A., and André, E. (2011). "FearNot!": A computer-based anti-bullying-programme designed to foster peer intervention. *European Journal of Psychology of Education, 26*(1), 21-44.

Veenstra, R., Lindenberg, S., Huitsing, G., Sainio, M., and Salmivalli, C. (2014). The role of teachers in bullying: The relation between antibullying attitudes, efficacy, and efforts to reduce bullying. *Journal of Educational Psychology, 106*(4), 1135-1143.

Vessey, J.A., DiFazio, R.L., and Strout, T.D. (2013). Youth bullying: A review of the science and call to action. *Nursing Outlook, 61*(5), 337-345.

Vreeman, R.C., and Carroll, A.E. (2007). A systematic review of school-based interventions to prevent bullying. *Archives of Pediatrics and Adolescent Medicine, 161*(1), 78-88.

Waasdorp, T.E., and Bradshaw, C.P. (2011). Examining student responses to frequent bullying: A latent class approach. *Journal of Educational Psychology, 103*(2), 336-352.

Waasdorp, T.E., and Bradshaw, C.P. (2015). The overlap between cyberbullying and traditional bullying. *Journal of Adolescent Health, 56*(5), 483-488. Available: http://dx.doi.org/10.1016/j.jadohealth.2014.12.002 [November 2015].

Waasdorp, T.E., Bradshaw, C.P., and Duong, J. (2011). The link between parents' perceptions of the school and their responses to school bullying: Variation by child characteristics and the forms of victimization. *Journal of Educational Psychology, 103*(2), 324-335.

Waasdorp, T.E., Bradshaw, C.P., and Leaf, P.J. (2012). The impact of schoolwide positive behavioral interventions and supports on bullying and peer rejection: A randomized controlled effectiveness trial. *Archives of Pediatrics and Adolescent Medicine, 166*(2), 149-156.

Wakefield, M.A., Loken, B., and Hornik, R.C. (2010). Use of mass media campaigns to change health behaviour. *The Lancet, 376*(9748), 1261-1271.

Walker, H.M., Horner, R.H., Sugai, G., Bullis, M., Sprague, J.R., Bricker, D., and Kaufman, M.J. (1996). Integrated approaches to preventing antisocial behavior patterns among school-age children and youth. *Journal of Emotional and Behavioral Disorders, 4*(4), 194-209.

Wang, J., Iannotti, R.J., and Nansel, T.R. (2009). School bullying among adolescents in the United States: Physical, verbal, relational, and cyber. *Journal of Adolescent Health, 45*(4), 368-375.

Webster-Stratton, C. (1999). *How to Promote Children's Social and Emotional Competence.* London: Paul Chapman.

Webster-Stratton, C., Jamila Reid, M., and Stoolmiller, M. (2008). Preventing conduct problems and improving school readiness: Evaluation of the Incredible Years teacher and child training programs in high-risk schools. *Journal of Child Psychology and Psychiatry, 49*(5), 471-488.

Weisz, J.R., Sandler, I.N., Durlak, J.A., and Anton, B.S. (2005). Promoting and protecting youth mental health through evidence-based prevention and treatment. *American Psychologist, 60*(6), 628-648.

Wilcox, H.C., Kellam, S.G., Brown, C.H., Poduska, J.M., Ialongo, N.S., Wang, W., and Anthony, J.C. (2008). The impact of two universal randomized first-and second-grade classroom interventions on young adult suicide ideation and attempts. *Drug and Alcohol Dependence, 95,* S60-S73.

Wilson, S.J., and Lipsey, M.W. (2007). School-based interventions for aggressive and disruptive behavior: Update of a meta-analysis. *American Journal of Preventive Medicine, 33*(2), S130-S143.

Wolke, D., and Lereya, S.T. (2015). Long-term effects of bullying. *Archives of Disease in Childhood, 100*(9), 879-885.

Ybarra, M.L., and Mitchell, K.J. (2004). Online aggressor/targets, aggressors, and targets: A comparison of associated youth characteristics. *Journal of Child Psychology and Psychiatry, 45*(7), 1308-1316.

Yeager, D.S., Fong, C.J., Lee, H.Y., and Espelage, D.L. (2015). Declines in efficacy of anti-bullying programs among older adolescents: Theory and a three-level meta-analysis. *Journal of Applied Developmental Psychology, 37,* 36-51.

6

Law and Policy

Law and policy can be used for a range of functions, including preventing undesirable behaviors and securing desirable ones (Raz, 1979). Both the mandate of a particular law and the presence of the law itself can help shape attitudes and behaviors. Public health has long relied on law and policy as components of a response to threats to human health and safety, from the control of infectious diseases to motor vehicle safety to safer foods and drinking water (Goodman et al., 2006). Law has also been employed to address various forms of violence against children, such as mandatory reporting laws, which were adopted to address child abuse (Institute of Medicine and National Research Council, 2014). For examples of the role of law in addressing public health issues, see Table 6-1.

Bullying implicates a breadth of federal and state laws and policies. In this chapter, the committee provides an overview of relevant laws and policies that relate to bullying at the federal and state level and discusses selected litigation efforts aimed at addressing bullying. The committee also reviews recent research on the impact of state anti-bullying laws and policies on bullying, as well as the implementation of these laws and policies, and discusses existing gaps in this literature that warrant additional research.

Before we begin, the committee provides a brief discussion on the rationale for the inclusion/exclusion criteria for the studies that are reviewed in this chapter. This chapter sets out the federal and state law and policy

TABLE 6-1 Ten Great Public Health Achievements and Selected Supportive Laws and Legal Tools, United States, 1900-1999

Public Health Achievement	Local	State	Federal
Control of Infectious Diseases	Sanitary codes and drinking water standards; quarantine and isolation authority; zoning ordinances and building codes; mosquito- and rodent-control programs; inspection of food establishments	Authority to conduct disease surveillance, require disease reports, and investigate outbreaks; regulation of drinking water, waste disposal, and food supplies; licensure of health professionals	Public Health Service Act of 1944; Safe Drinking Water Act of 1974; National Environmental Protection Act of 1976
Motor Vehicle Safety	Speed limits; limitation on liquor store hours; penalties for serving inebriated bar patrons	Seatbelt, child-safety-seat, and motorcycle-helmet laws; vehicle inspections; drive licensing and graduated driver's license systems; authorization to conduct sobriety checkpoints; zero tolerance for alcohol among drivers under age 21 years; prohibition on alcohol sales to minors; 0.08% blood alcohol content per se laws; speed limits	Performance and crash standards for motor vehicles; standards for road and highway construction; safety-belt use in some commercial vehicles; financial assistance to states to promote and enforce highway safety initiatives; airbag warning labels; creation of state offices of highway safety; federal court ruling upholding motorcycle-helmet use
Fluoridation of Drinking Water	Ordinances authorizing fluoridation; referenda and initiatives authoring fluoridation	Legislation authorizing fluoridation; court ruling upholding fluoridation	Federal court rulings upholding fluoridation of public drinking water supplies; Environmental Protection Agency caps on fluoride levels

TABLE 6-1 Continued

Public Health Achievement	Local	State	Federal
Recognition of Tobacco Use as a Health Hazard	Excise taxes; restrictions on retail sale to minors; clean indoor air laws	Excise taxes; restrictions on retail sale practices; clean indoor air laws; funding for public antismoking education; lawsuits leading to the Master Settlement Agreement of 1998	Excise tax mandated warning labels; prohibition of advertising on radio and television; penalties on states not outlawing sale of tobacco products to persons under 18 years of age; financial assistance to state and local tobacco-control programs; Department of Justice lawsuit to recover health care costs
Vaccination	School board enforcement of school entry vaccination requirements	Court rulings supporting mandatory vaccination; school entry admission laws	Court rulings supporting mandatory vaccination; licensure of vaccines; financial aid to state vaccination programs
Decline in Deaths from Coronary Heart Disease and Stroke	Education and information programs	Tobacco control laws; education and information programs	Food-labeling laws; Department of Transportation funding for bikeways and walking paths; National High Blood Pressure Education Program
Safer and Healthier Foods	Standards for and inspection of retail food establishments	Mandated niacin enrichment of bread and flour; standards for and inspection of foods at the producer level; limits on chemical contamination of crops	Pure Food and Drug Act of 1906 and later enactments to regulate foods and prescription drugs; mandated folic acid fortification of cereal grain products; limits on chemical contamination of crops; food stamps; Women, Infants, and Children Program; school meals

continued

TABLE 6-1 Continued

Public Health Achievement	Local	State	Federal
Healthier Mothers and Babies	Sewage and refuse ordinances; drinking water codes; milk pasteurization	Establishment of maternal and child health clinics; licensure of health-care professionals in obstetrics; mandated milk pasteurization; funding for Medicaid services	Drinking water quality standards; creation of the Children's Bureau (1912) with education and service programs; licensure of sulfa drugs and antibiotics; creation of the Medicaid program; Infant Formula Act of 1980
Family Planning	Funding for family planning clinics	Authorization to provide birth control services; authority to provide prenatal and postnatal care to indigent mothers	Family Planning Services and Population Research Act; Supreme Court rulings on contraceptive use
Safer Workplaces	Authority to inspect for unsafe conditions; building and fire safety codes	Laws to inspect and regulate workplace safety practices, including toxic exposures; criminal penalties for grossly negligent worker injury or death	Minimum safety standards for federal contractors; inspection and regulation of mine safety; mandates on states to adopt minimum workplace safety standards; Occupational Health and Safety Health Act of 1970

SOURCE: Adapted from Centers for Disease Control and Prevention (2006).

framework. Except for one study[1] and a brief committee overview on zero tolerance policies, the committee does not include local and school policy for several reasons. First, few systematic evaluations of local or school-specific policies exist. Second, there is great diversity of practice at the local

---

[1] The one exception was a study that provided evidence for the effectiveness of school district anti-bullying policies that enumerate protected groups. This study was included because it was one of the few studies on this topic that used an objectively coded measure of the anti-bullying policy.

and school level, and local policies and practices are shaped by a breadth of factors, including perceptions, traits unique to a particular school, and others. Third, in many jurisdictions, state law provides the mandate that local entities adopt measures to address bullying in their district or schools. Thus, we view local or school policies largely as measures taken to implement federal or state law and policy.

Additionally, the committee recognizes that various laws use different terms to address bullying. For example, federal law typically refers to "harassment" rather than "bullying." In some instances, the terms have important distinctions; for example, bullying definitions typically include power imbalance as an element, while laws on harassment do not necessarily require a power imbalance (Cornell and Limber, 2015). Yet, as Cornell and Limber explain, "The term *harassment* is often used interchangeably with bullying, [even though] it has an established history in civil rights law and policy that precedes the fledgling laws and developing policies concerning bullying" (Cornell and Limber, 2015, p. 335). The committee's review includes laws and policies that refer to bullying (as defined in Chapter 1) as well as other laws and policies—most notably, federal laws—that are recognized as applying to bullying even though they use other terms such as "harassment" instead of "bullying."

OVERVIEW OF RELEVANT LAW AND POLICY

Federal Law and Policy

There is no specific federal law on bullying. However, federal law and policy provide a framework for many of the responses to bullying. Federal law offers protections and remedies for certain individuals, while federal agency guidelines provide recommendations to states and localities developing and assessing their responses to bullying.

Civil rights and antidiscrimination laws secure rights for protected classes of individuals if they have been subjected to harassment. Relevant federal law—which is overseen and enforced by the U.S. Departments of Justice and Education—prohibits discrimination based on the following traits (U.S. Department of Education Office of Civil Rights, 2010b; U.S. Government Accountability Office, 2012):

race, color, or national origin;[2,3]
sex;[2,3,4]
disability;[5,6,7] and
religion.[2]

Schools can be found in violation of these federal laws and relevant implementing regulations when bullying is based on race, color, national origin, sex, disability, or religion and is "sufficiently serious that it creates a hostile environment and such harassment is encouraged, tolerated, not adequately addressed, or ignored by school employees" (U.S. Department of Education Office of Civil Rights, 2010b, p. 1). In other words, schools have a legal responsibility for maintaining safe environments that enable children and adolescents to pursue the education and other services or opportunities available at that school. Under the same authorities, schools are responsible for addressing harassment that school administrators and teachers are aware of or that they should reasonably have known about. In such cases, schools must take immediate and appropriate action to address the harassment.

In addition to the above, the Individuals with Disabilities Education Act (IDEA) offers further protections for select students.[8] It requires states that receive federal education funding to provide children with disabilities *a free appropriate public education.* That education must be provided in the *least restrictive environment* and in conformity with an *individualized education program.*[9] Therefore, if bullying interferes with a covered child's access to an appropriate public education, a claim can be brought against the school for failing to secure such an environment. Unlike remedies under the civil rights laws cited above, an IDEA claim typically does not lead to compensatory damages. Instead it can result in the school being required to take specific steps to ensure the child has access to an appropriate education. The U.S. Departments of Education and Justice oversee and enforce federal law addressing discrimination and harassment. Individual com-

---

[2] Civil Rights Act of 1964, tit. IV, 42 U.S.C. §§ 2000c to 2000c-9 (2012).

[3] Civil Rights Act of 1964, tit. VI, 42 U.S.C. §§ 2000d to 2000d-4 (2012).

[4] Education Amendments of 1972, tit. IX, 20 U.S.C. §§ 1681-88 (2012). Title IX protects students—including lesbian, gay, bisexual, and transgender (LGBT) students—from sex discrimination but does not expressly prohibit discrimination based on sexual orientation. Title IX has been held in select cases to include protection from harassment for failing to conform to stereotypical norms of masculinity or femininity, but those decisions do not equate to a guarantee of protection for LGBT students.

[5] Section 504 of the Rehabilitation Act of 1973, 29 U.S.C. § 794 (2012).

[6] Title II of the Americans with Disabilities Act of 1990, 42 U.S.C. §§ 12101-12213 (2012).

[7] Title III of the Americans with Disabilities Act of 1990, 42 U.S.C. §§ 12181-12189 (2012).

[8] 20 U.S.C. §§ 1400–1482 (2012).

[9] 20 U.S.C. §§ 1412, 1414 (2012).

plaints can be filed with either Department, depending on the nature of the allegations. Complaints filed with the Department of Education's (DOE's) Office for Civil Rights are typically resolved through agreements entered into with schools to take specific actions to address the harassment, and these actions can be individual or systemic (such as adopting policies and procedures, training staff, or addressing the specific incidents). Complaints filed with the Department of Justice can lead to, among other things, consent decrees and negotiated settlements that require schools to address bullying. In addition, individuals can pursue civil actions, discussed below in the "Litigation" section (U.S. Government Accountability Office, 2012).

As the above discussion of federal law indicates, federal law is limited to recognized protected classes, so if a child is not a member of a protected class and is subjected to bullying, he or she might not have a remedy under federal law. However, state or local remedies might be available; that is, federal law establishes a floor, rather than a ceiling, and individual states, districts, or schools can create anti-bullying laws and policies that include traits not expressly covered by federal law (discussed in the "State and Local Law and Policy" section below).

In addition to offering potential remedies, federal law also enshrines protections of individual rights, which limit the actions schools and other government entities can take. In particular, constitutional protections on speech and privacy, which guard against undue government intrusion on liberty, have implications in the context of bullying. In the landmark case *Tinker v. Des Moines Independent Community School District*, the U.S. Supreme Court stated that students do not "shed their constitutional right to freedom of speech or expression at the schoolhouse gate."[10] Similarly, the Supreme Court has recognized that students are entitled to constitutional protections against unlawful searches and seizures.[11] In both areas, the courts have granted schools latitude, allowing schools to impose some limitations on students' rights in order to preserve a positive educational environment and to ensure student safety. This permits schools to limit speech at schools that is lewd, obscene, hateful, or threatens violence. It also has allowed schools to adopt drug-testing policies for athletes (Hanks, 2015). Balancing schools' authority to police students and students' constitutional rights is an ongoing challenge. As state laws expand schools' authority beyond school grounds, particularly in the context of cyberbullying (see discussion on scope of schools' authority in "State and Local Law and Policy" below), the parameters of schools' authority and students' constitutional rights will be revisited in future cases.

Beyond existing federal statutes, the federal government also has the ca-

---

[10] Tinker v. Des Moines Independent Community School District, 393 U.S. 503, 506 (1969).
[11] New Jersey v. TLO, 469 U.S. 325 (1985).

pacity to proffer policies and more informal guidelines that have significant influence on state and local responses. Two notable initiatives include the Dear Colleague Letter of October 26, 2010, from the DOE Office for Civil Rights (U.S. Department of Education Office of Civil Rights, 2010b), and DOE's suggested list of key components for state and local laws and policies, which was distributed to governors and chief state school officers as part of the Dear Colleague Letter of December 16, 2010. (Dear Colleague Letters are formal memos to relevant state and local officials offering guidance on a particular issue) (U.S. Department of Education Office of Civil Rights, 2010a).

The Dear Colleague Letter of October 26, 2010, provides an overview of relevant federal law and delineates schools' responsibilities to address various forms of bullying (U.S. Department of Education, Office of Civil Rights, 2010b). It also provides examples of school-based bullying and details how a school should address the issue in each case.

Also in 2010, DOE identified 11 recommended components for state and local laws and policies on bullying, including (1) a purpose statement; (2) a statement of scope; (3) specification of the prohibited conduct; (4) enumeration of specific characteristics—actual or perceived—of students who have historically been targets of bullying; (5) development and implementation of local education area policies; (6) essential components of local education area policies; (7) provision for regular review of local policies; (8) a communication plan for notifying students, students' families, and staff of policies related to bullying; (9) training and prevention education; (10) transparency and monitoring; and (11) and a statement that the policy does not preclude those who are bullied from seeking other legal remedies (U.S. Department of Education, Office of Civil Rights, 2010a). DOE developed these criteria to provide states and localities with technical assistance as they consider new or revised legislation or policies to address bullying. Although the committee finds that these recommended components are relevant, it recognizes that there is limited evidence-based research on what components of a state or local law or policy must have, in order to have a positive impact in addressing bullying (see section below, "Impact of Laws and Policies on Bullying").

These two Dear Colleague Letters provide important guidance that can help state and local actors strengthen law and policy and improve responses to bullying in compliance with federal law.

State and Local Law and Policy

State and local law and policy constitute a key component of current responses to bullying. Given the substantial amount of childhood spent at school, the fact that most responses to bullying to date have been school-centered, and that education has historically been the primary responsibility of state and local government, it is important to ensure that appropriate laws and policies are in place to promote and support anti-bullying programs. For the reasons explained in the introduction to this chapter, this section focuses on state law and policy and does not include local or school-based policies. In view of the significant attention given to school-based zero tolerance policies, the committee included Box 6-1, which reviews the research on that strategy for responding to bullying. In addition, the committee cites a number of individual state statutes in this section. These examples are illustrative of the range of existing law and policy responses to bullying and should not be viewed as an endorsement of the effectiveness of particular laws or policies. (See section "Impact of Laws and Policies on Bullying" for a discussion of the effectiveness of anti-bullying policies.)

In the past 15 years, all 50 states and the District of Columbia have adopted or revised laws on bullying (Child Trends, 2015). Forty-nine states and the District of Columbia include electronic forms of bullying (cyberbullying) in their anti-bullying statutes.[12] Many state laws require school districts or schools to implement policies but allow school districts or schools to determine specific policy content (Hinduja and Patchin, 2011). Thus, policies may vary across schools and communities. Most states now also have model bullying policies.[13]

While all 50 states and the District of Columbia have adopted anti-bullying laws, there are significant differences in the content of these laws. To begin, although most states' laws include a definition of bullying, the states do not use a uniform definition to outline the proscribed behaviors. Therefore, an act or series of actions may constitute bullying in certain states but not others. For example, in New Jersey, bullying can be "a single incident or a series of incidents," while in Nebraska, bullying is defined as "any ongoing pattern" of abuse.[14,15] Adding to the differences, select state laws direct the state department of education or similar agency to develop a definition (e.g., Wisconsin) or delegate that decision to local school districts (e.g., Arizona) (Sacco et al., 2012). In addition, state law definitions of bullying do not necessarily conform to bullying definitions used in social science research or in anti-bullying programs.

---

[12] Alaska does not include electronic forms of bullying in its anti-bullying law, but it amended its definition of "the crime of harassment in the second degree" in 2014 to include electronic forms of harassment of an individual under 18 years of age. See Alaska Stat. Ann. § 11.61.120 (West 2015).

[13] For detailed state-by-state information on state laws and model policies, see the Department of Health and Human Services Website for its Stop Bullying initiative, see http://www.StopBullying.gov [August 2015].

[14] N.J. Stat. Ann. § 18A:37-14 (West 2015).

[15] Neb. Rev. Stat. Ann. 79-2,137(2) (West 2015).

BOX 6-1
Zero Tolerance Policies

In some instances, so-called "zero tolerance" policies have been adopted by schools, in which schools use automatic suspensions for certain events within the school, like bullying or fighting (American Psychological Association Zero Tolerance Task Force, 2008; Boccanfuso and Kuhfeld, 2011). The term "zero tolerance" describes a range of policies that impose severe sanctions on students, typically suspension and expulsion for minor offenses in hopes of preventing more serious ones (Borum et al., 2010). Zero tolerance became widely adopted in schools in the early 1990s. Zero tolerance policy is defined as

> a philosophy or policy that mandates the application of predetermined consequences, most often severe and punitive in nature, that are intended to be applied regardless of the gravity of behavior, mitigating circumstances, or situational context.
> (American Psychological Association Zero Tolerance Task Force, 2008, p. 852).

Zero tolerance policies were originally created to provide a uniform punishment for specific behaviors related to drug use and violence (Skiba and Rausch, 2006), but in practice, discipline can be arbitrary and the punishments given out do not always match the offense (Wilson, 2014). While these policies were put in place to protect students and maintain a safe school environment, research has found that zero tolerance policies have not had the intended effect in making schools safer (Evans and Lester, 2012; Pitlick, 2015; Skiba, 2014; Wilson, 2014). As a part of preventive intervention efforts for bullying, many U.S schools have zero tolerance policies for bullying, even though zero tolerance has not been shown to improve school climate or school safety (American Psychological Association Zero Tolerance Task Force, 2008).

Although ensuring the safety of the victim is critical, and the consistent use of discipline is strongly recommended for reducing bullying (Farrington and Ttofi, 2009), zero tolerance policies may also lead to underreporting of bullying incidents because the consequence of suspension is perceived as too harsh or punitive. Furthermore, there is limited evidence that the policies are effective in curbing aggressive or bullying behavior (American Psychological Association Zero Tolerance Task Force, 2008; Boccanfuso and Kuhfeld, 2011), as many youth who bully may also be victims of bullying and may have other behavioral, social, or mental health problems requiring support (O'Brennan et al., 2009; Swearer et al., 2010). Not only are there growing concerns about the limited opportunity for effective intervention and learning associated with suspension but there is also evidence of disproportionate use of these types of disciplinary approaches for students of color (American Psychological Association Zero Tolerance Task Force, 2008; Boccanfuso and Kuhfeld, 2011).

Similarly, as states have moved to address the emerging threat of cyberbullying, definitions of cyberbullying used among the states vary greatly. While some states use the term "cyberbullying," others simply refer to any "electronic" communication. For example, Iowa prohibits any "electronic, written, verbal, or physical act or conduct toward a student" that constitutes bullying (emphasis added). It defines "electronic" as "any communication involving the transmission of information by wire, radio, optical cable, electromagnetic, or other similar means. "Electronic" includes but is not limited to communication via electronic mail, Internet-based communications, pager service, cell phones, and electronic text messaging."[16] The Massachusetts' definition of cyberbullying includes many of the same means, but also explicitly includes the act of assuming someone else's identity online in a way that causes harm to or fear in another student, creates a hostile school environment for another student, infringes on another student's rights, or disrupts the school environment.[17] The Massachusetts' definition of cyberbullying includes

> bullying through the use of technology or any electronic communication, which shall include, but shall not be limited to, any transfer of signs, signals, writing, images, sounds, data or intelligence of any nature transmitted in whole or in part by a wire, radio, electromagnetic, photo electronic or photo optical system, including, but not limited to, electronic mail, internet communications, instant messages or facsimile communications. Cyber-bullying shall also include (i) the creation of a web page or blog in which the creator assumes the identity of another person or (ii) the knowing impersonation of another person as the author of posted content or messages, if the creation or impersonation creates any of the conditions enumerated in clauses (i) to (v), inclusive, of the definition of bullying. Cyber-bullying shall also include the distribution by electronic means of a communication to more than one person or the posting of material on an electronic medium that may be accessed by one or more persons, if the distribution or posting creates any of the conditions enumerated in clauses (i) to (v), inclusive, of the definition of bullying.[18]

The specific mention of electronic forms of bullying, or cyberbullying, in these state laws does not create separate policies for cyberbullying but rather adds cyberbullying as a type of bullying covered by the particular anti-bullying law or policy of that state. These broad definitions of bullying, encompassing both traditional forms and cyberbullying, when combined with the expanded scope of school authority in many states (described

---

[16] Iowa Code § 280.28(2)(b) (2015).
[17] Mass. Gen. Laws Ann. Ch 71, §370(a) (West 2015).
[18] Mass. Gen. Laws Ann. Ch 71, §370(a) (West 2015).

below), allow schools to address bullying in a range of locales—real and virtual.

In addition, while many states provide an enumerated list of protected or vulnerable groups, others do not. Among those states that provide an enumerated list, some are more extensive than others. For example, Massachusetts' law provides that certain students may be more vulnerable based on "actual or perceived differentiating characteristics, including race, color, religion, ancestry, national origin, sex, socioeconomic status, homelessness, academic status, gender identity or expression, physical appearance, pregnant or parenting status, sexual orientation, mental, physical, developmental or sensory disability or by association with a person who has or is perceived to have 1 or more of these characteristics."[19] Vermont's anti-bullying law explicitly recognizes vulnerability based on a "student's or a student's family member's actual or perceived race, creed, color, national origin, marital status, sex, sexual orientation, gender identity, or disability."[20] In contrast, a number of states—for example, Arizona, Ohio, and Texas—do not enumerate protected classes in their anti-bullying laws.[21,22,23,24] There is some debate over whether it is better to enumerate protected classes or to have nonspecific language that does not enumerate specific groups. In general, the enumeration of protected classes in a law can be used in two ways: either to explicitly limit a statute's coverage or to highlight the need to address particular individuals or situations. In the context of bullying, it has been argued that "a more inclusive approach is to enumerate the groups deemed most vulnerable for bullying, but to explicitly recognize in the law that any form of bullying against any student is prohibited" (Cornell and Limber, 2015, p. 340). However, there is a dearth of research on the extent to which enumeration of protected classes is effective in addressing bullying among at-risk youth. For more on the existing evidence of the effectiveness of enumerating protected classes in reducing bullying, see the section on "Impact of Laws and Policies on Bullying" below.

There are also significant differences in the scope of schools' jurisdiction. Some states limit schools' authority to school grounds and other sites or events controlled by schools. For example, North Carolina's anti-bullying law is limited to any act that "takes place on school property, at any school-sponsored function, or on a school bus."[25] Other states have granted authority to schools to address bullying that occurs elsewhere but

---

[19] Mass. Gen. Laws Ch 71, § 37O (d)(3).
[20] Vt. Stat. Ann. tit. 16 § 11(a)(26)(a) (West 2015).
[21] Ariz. Rev. Stat. Ann. § 15-2301 (2015).
[22] Ohio Rev. Code Ann. § 3313.666 (West 2015).
[23] Tex. Educ. § 37.0832 (West 2015).
[24] Arizona classified bullying as hazing.
[25] N.C. Gen. Stat. Ann. § 115C-407.15 (West, 2015).

affects the school environment for the child who is bullied. For example, Maryland's statute covers any act that "[o]ccurs on school property, at a school activity or event, or on a school bus; or . . . [s]ubstantially disrupts the orderly operation of a school."[26] The Maryland law and more than 20 other similar state statutes implicitly grant schools authority over acts that have no nexus with the school (Suski, 2014). This expansive authority is particularly pertinent to cyberbullying because in many cases, electronic forms of bullying occur when students are neither at a school function nor in each other's presence. The broad authority granted to schools raises questions about both students' rights (e.g., speech and privacy) and the potential additional expectations on schools to police student interactions beyond the school campus (see the section "Future Directions" below for discussion of potential implications).

Differences also exist among the states with respect to other key components of anti-bullying laws, ranging from prevention programs, including training of teachers and other key personnel, to reporting procedures and related protections for students who are bullied (Sacco et al., 2012; Stuart-Cassel et al., 2011). In Massachusetts, for example, school districts' plans must include "professional development to build the skills of all staff members, including, but not limited to, educators, administrators, school nurses, cafeteria workers, custodians, bus drivers, athletic coaches, advisors to extracurricular activities and paraprofessionals, to prevent, identify and respond to bullying."[27] Such plans must also include "provisions for informing parents and guardians about the bullying prevention curriculum of the school district." In terms of reporting incidents of bullying, many state laws require school districts to establish reporting procedures—in some cases, making school personnel mandatory reporters—and mandate protections against retaliation for reporting bullying.[28]

Finally, most laws that address bullying establish an unfunded mandate (Sacco et al., 2012). Although providing a safe learning environment can be viewed as part of schools' core responsibilities and thus covered by general education funding, many anti-bullying laws specifically ask school districts and schools to take on additional tasks—such as providing training on bullying for teachers and other school personnel—without allocating additional funds for these tasks. Insufficient funding can impose limitations on implementation and enforcement of these laws. (See "Implementation of Anti-Bullying Laws and Policies" later in this chapter for further discussion of these limitations.)

A small number of studies have assessed the content of state laws, each

---

[26] Md. Code Ann., Educ. § 7-424 (West, 2015).
[27] Mass. Gen. Laws Ch 71, § 37O(d).
[28] See, for example, Ga. Code Ann. § 20-2-751.4(c) (West, 2015).

using its own criteria. As described above, DOE recommends inclusion of 11 components in state and local laws. Employing a public health framework, Srabstein and colleagues (2008) suggested that anti-bullying laws should include (1) a clear definition of bullying, (2) an explicit articulation of prohibition against bullying, (3) funded prevention and treatment programs, and (4) recognition of the association between bullying and public health risks (Kosse, 2005; Srabstein et al., 2008). Kosse (2005) proposed a legal framework that recommends 10 components for state legislatures to require of school districts: (1) a general statement of the policy that a school district values a learning and working environment that is free from any type of violence and harassment, (2) consistent statewide definitions of the types of violence and harassment prohibited, (3) specific reporting procedures, (4) specific investigation procedures, (5) a consistent range of school district actions, (6) a reprisal provision prohibiting retaliation, (7) a statement that the policy does not prohibit other procedures available or required under law, (8) provisions describing how the policy will be disseminated and employees and students trained, (9) penalty provisions for schools that fail to adopt or enforce anti-bullying policies, and (10) a requirement that policies be submitted for review to the state's Department of Education.

Each of these frameworks identifies important components of law- and policy-based responses to bullying. As described later in this chapter, research on the impact of law on the prevalence of bullying is limited. Therefore, while the above frameworks can help guide the development of anti-bullying policies and programs, these frameworks have not been fully evaluated in order to determine which components must be included in an anti-bullying law to ensure a positive impact. As with all new law, there is typically a time lag from adoption to full implementation and subsequent population impact. Given that many of the state laws have been adopted relatively recently, evidence on implementation and impact is still emerging.

Finally, in addition to anti-bullying laws, states' civil rights laws might offer protections for individuals who are not members of groups enumerated under federal law (U.S. Government Accountability Office, 2012). However, no assessment has been conducted of state civil rights laws to identify available protections against bullying and procedures for filing complaints under those state laws (U.S. Government Accountability Office, 2012). Further research is needed to determine the full range of remedies available under state and local law and policies. Finally, see Box 6-1 (above) for an overview of zero tolerance policies, why they were created, and why there are concerns about them.

Litigation

While anti-bullying statutes provide a mandate to create a framework for preventing and responding to bullying, litigation offers another avenue to pursue a remedy for harms suffered as a result of bullying. This section reviews litigation efforts, providing details on the types of claims brought and their success. The committee does not include specific cases and fact patterns, both because litigation is a narrow remedy and because these claims filed in court typically represent the more severe cases of bullying and thus are not representative of the range of cases. The committee did not want to suggest that a particular case or two was paradigmatic of bullying incidences.

Litigation presents an opportunity to secure a remedy in select cases; however, the great majority of instances of bullying do not reach litigation. Any review of case law on bullying therefore captures neither instances that do not result in a legal claim nor those cases that are settled before a judgment is issued. Thus, the case law on bullying represents a small percentage of bullying cases and is not necessarily representative. Given the cost of pursuing litigation, it is likely that the case law reflects more severe cases in which there is better evidence that a school or its employees were aware of the bullying.

There are few empirical studies of bullying-related litigation. Holben and Zirkel (2014) reviewed cases for more than 20 years (1992 to 2011) and found 166 court decisions on bullying claims. The overwhelming majority of cases (89%) were litigated in federal court, as opposed to state court. Plaintiffs were a member of a protected class in 84 percent of the cases, with the most frequent protected traits being gender, disability, perceived sexual orientation, and race/ethnicity. School districts and school employees were named as defendants in the majority of cases, with defendants more likely to be institutions than individuals (Holben and Zirkel, 2014).

Plaintiffs' claims relied most often on the following laws: Title IX of the Civil Rights Act of 1964, Fourteenth Amendment substantive due process, Fourteenth Amendment equal protection, negligence, and state civil rights or equal protection claims. Plaintiffs' greater reliance on federal rather than state law might reflect an effort to avoid state law–based immunities for schools and their employees, which may bar legal claims against schools and their employees. It might also reflect the fact that state law opinions are often unpublished. In only 6 of the 166 cases were the rulings based on anti-bullying laws (Holben and Zirkel, 2014). This limited use of anti-bullying laws reflects in part the constraint that in many states such laws do not create a separate private right of action.

Over this 20-year period, court decisions consistently favored the defendant. Holben and Zirkel (2014) reported that only 2 percent of the

742 claim rulings (many cases involve multiple claims) were conclusively decided for the plaintiff, whereas 65 percent were conclusively for the defendant. Analyzing court decisions, rather than individual claims, revealed a similar, although less pronounced, slant toward defendants: 5 percent of decisions conclusively favored the plaintiffs, while 41 percent conclusively favored the defendants. Of the remaining court decisions, 34 percent were inconclusively for the plaintiffs (e.g., denial of a motion for dismissal), 15 percent were inconclusively for the defendants (e.g., denial of plaintiff's motion for summary judgment), and 5 percent were relatively evenly split between the parties (Holben and Zirkel, 2014). Although plaintiffs' claims brought under Title IX or the IDEA had the best success rates (Holben and Zirkel, 2014), most Title IX and IDEA cases still favored the defendants.

Both the limited number of bullying-related cases and the evidence that results tend to favor defendants indicate that litigation is a limited remedy. Though some individuals have been successful in pursuing remedies through the courts for bullying-related harms, plaintiffs face several challenges in pursuing litigation. They must prove severity of harm and the lack or ineffectiveness of a school's response once the school knew or should have known about the bullying. Qualified immunity—which protects "government officials . . . from liability for civil damages insofar as their conduct does not violate clearly established statutory or constitutional rights of which a reasonable person would have known"[29]—also presents a significant hurdle in many cases.[30] Finally, anecdotal evidence suggests that it is important to educate judges and other professionals in the legal system on the harms inflicted by bullying, as litigation efforts addressing other forms of discrimination have benefited from the incorporation of social science research.[31]

Although landmark cases can spur changes in law and policy, the evidence suggests that only a limited number of children who are bullied will be able to secure a remedy through the courts. These limitations highlight the importance of ensuring that anti-bullying laws and policies produce robust prevention programs.

---

[29] Quoted passage is from the decision in Harlow v. Fitzgerald, 457 U.S. 800, 818 (1982).

[30] From a presentation by Craig Goodmark (Atlanta Legal Aid Society) at a public information-gathering session to the Committee on the Biological and Psychosocial Effects of Peer Victimization: Lessons for Bullying Prevention, National Academy of Sciences, June 24, 2015, Washington, DC.

[31] Brief of social psychologists as Amici Curiae in support of plaintiff-appellants, in NAACP v. Horne (9th Cir. 2013) (No. 13-17247).

Future Directions

As federal antidiscrimination laws continue to evolve, additional research will be needed to assess the extent to which federal law protects all children and adolescents who are vulnerable to bullying. Further research is also needed on state civil rights laws and state antiharassment laws: their coverage, procedures for filing complaints under such laws, and their viability in addressing bullying (U.S. Government Accountability Office, 2012). State anti-bullying laws have emerged quickly and changed considerably in the past 15 years in order to address various forms of bullying, including cyberbullying. The impact of this body of law is inherently limited by the requirement not to violate constitutional rights of individuals. Important questions exist about the balance between schools' authority to address bullying and students' rights to freedom of expression and privacy (Hanks, 2015). Further research is needed in this area to ensure that state and local laws and policies provide schools sufficient authority to prevent and respond to bullying, while also ensuring that schools' actions in particular cases do not violate students' constitutional rights, particularly with respect to school policing of electronic communications that do not occur at any school event. Additional research is also needed to assess the impact of litigation, including the threat of litigation, on schools. Finally, as detailed above, there is considerable variation among state laws in terminology and definitions of bullying that are used. Further research is needed to better understand whether and how these differences affect responses to bullying.

IMPACT OF LAWS AND POLICIES ON BULLYING

Despite the proliferation and ubiquity of anti-bullying legislation, there has been very little empirical examination of the effectiveness of such laws in reducing bullying. Instead, existing research on anti-bullying laws has focused almost exclusively on content analyses of anti-bullying laws, as discussed in the previous section (e.g., Limber and Small, 2003; Srabstein et al., 2008; Stuart-Cassel et al., 2011). In a 2003 review of the literature on anti-bullying laws and policies, Limber and Small noted that "the question of whether state laws can provide a useful vehicle for reducing bullying behavior among children remains unanswered" (p. 448). In a follow-up review paper written over a decade later, Cornell and Limber (2015) similarly stated, "Although the content of state anti-bullying laws has been evaluated and contrasted, remarkably little research has been conducted to study how these laws and policies are implemented and to what effect" (p. 341). While this literature is still in its early stages, there are now a handful of published studies that have examined the effectiveness of anti-bullying policies, which the committee discusses below.

Single-State Evaluations

One approach to examining effectiveness has been to conduct single-state evaluations over time. In this approach, researchers use quasi-experimental data to examine whether rates of bullying victimization within a single state are lower after the implementation of an anti-bullying law, compared to rates before the law was implemented. In an example of this work, Schwab-Reese and colleagues (2016) conducted an evaluation of Iowa's anti-bullying law (Iowa Code 280.28), which was passed in 2005. The law required schools to adopt an anti-bullying policy that defines acts of bullying, to establish a process for reporting incidents, and to describe consequences and actions for bully perpetrators. To evaluate the effectiveness of this law, the researchers used data from sixth, eighth, and eleventh graders from Iowa who completed the Iowa Youth Survey (similar to the Youth Risk Behavior Surveillance System dataset; see Chapter 2) in 2005, 2008, and 2010. The odds of respondents reporting that they were frequently bullied increased in the first year after the law was passed, possibly due to improved reporting. However, odds of reporting being bullied decreased from 2008 to 2010 (though not below pre-law levels) (Schwab-Reese et al., 2016). Similar delayed or gradual effects of laws have been observed in other types of public health law studies (e.g., Wagenaar and Komro, 2013; Webster et al., 2002).

Multistate Evaluations

Research has also examined associations between anti-bullying laws and bullying outcomes in multistate evaluations. In one study, investigators examined how bullying rates were associated with 25 state anti-bullying laws. Specifically, data on reports of being the target of bullying or cyberbullying in the past 12 months came from students in grades 9-12 who were participating in the 2011 Youth Risk Behavior Surveillance System study ($n = 63,635$). These data, which were obtained from DOE, were linked to anti-bullying laws from 25 states. Students living in states with anti-bullying policies that had at least one DOE-recommended legislative component had 24 percent reduced odds of reporting being bullied and 20 percent reduced odds of being a target of cyberbullying, compared to students living in states whose laws had no DOE-recommended legislative components (Hatzenbuehler et al., 2015). These analyses controlled for relevant state-level confounders such as violent crime rates in the state. In addition, three individual components of anti-bullying laws were consistently associated with decreased odds by 20 percent or more for being a target of either bullying or cyberbullying. First, a *statement of scope* was included in the law that describes where the law applies and the circumstances under which the school has the authority to take action (e.g., whether the law applies if students are off-campus but the event is sponsored by the school). Second, the law included a *description of prohibited behaviors* that defined the behaviors that are considered bullying, in some cases differentiating bullying behavior from what may be developmentally appropriate peer interactions and in other cases specifying that the behavior must be repeated to be a bullying behavior. Third, the state law included *requirements for districts to develop and implement local policies*, requirements that dictated the components that must be included in local policies and that may set a timeline in which the local policy must be developed. These three components, noted by Hatzenbuehler and colleagues (2015), offer details and specificity that provide clarity for school administrators and may increase the likelihood that they feel empowered to act.

Countrywide Evaluations

Australia in 2003 became one of the first countries to implement a national policy (the National Safe Schools Framework, NSSF) for the prevention of aggressive behaviors among youth, including bullying. The NSSF specified and discussed six key elements that schools were expected to measure as part of their implementation of the policy: (1) schools' values, ethos, culture, structures, and student welfare; (2) policies, programs, and procedures; (3) education/training for school staff, students, and parents; (4) managing incidents of victimization; (5) providing support for students; and (6) working closely with parents. To evaluate the effectiveness of the NSSF, Cross and colleagues (2011) collected data in 2007 from 7,418 students, ages 9-14, from 106 representative Australian schools and compared that data with similar data collected in 1990. In 1990, 24.9 percent of students, ages 9-14, reported being bullied "at least once a week." In contrast, 16 percent of students ages 9-14 reported being bullied "at least once a week" in 2007. The authors suggested that there was a "downward trend" in reports of being bullied between the two time periods (Cross et al., 2011, p. 5). However, the prevalence of students who reported bullying others was similar between the two time periods.

Effects of Anti-Bullying Laws on At-Risk Populations

As reviewed in Chapter 2, several groups are disproportionately targeted by bullying, including sexual minorities (i.e., lesbian, gay, bisexual, and transgender [LGBT] youth; Berlan et al., 2010), overweight/obese adolescents (Puhl and Latner, 2007), and students with disabilities (Rose et al., 2010). Few studies have examined whether anti-bullying policies are effective in protecting at-risk groups against peer victimization and associated adverse outcomes (Hatzenbuehler and Keyes, 2013). In one study, Hatzenbuehler and Keyes (2013) coded school district Websites and student handbooks across 197 school districts in Oregon to determine whether the districts had any anti-bullying policies (harassment and antidiscrimination policies were not included in this category) and, if so, whether these policies contained sexual orientation as a protected class (referred to in the literature as an "enumerated group"). Thus, these data made it possible to differentiate between three combinations of anti-bullying policies: (1) the absence of anti-bullying policies; (2) the presence of anti-bullying policies that either did not include any enumerated groups or, if groups were enumerated (e.g., gender, race, religion), sexual orientation was not specifically mentioned (referred to below as "restrictive" policies); and (3) anti-bullying policies that were inclusive of sexual orientation (referred to below as "inclusive" policies). These policy data were then linked to 3 years of pooled data from the Oregon Healthy Teens survey, a population-based dataset of eleventh- grade public school students (n = 1,413 lesbian, gay, and bisexual students, or 4.4%). Because information on location of residence for the study participants was only available at the county level, the measures of anti-bullying policies were aggregated from the district to the county level by dividing the number of school districts with anti-bullying policies by the total number of school districts in the county. Variables were then created for the proportion of school districts that had restrictive and inclusive anti-bullying policies within each of 34 Oregon counties (Hatzenbuehler and Keyes, 2013).

This study revealed three noteworthy findings. First, although the study did not assess bullying, it did include one measure of peer harassment/ victimization ("During the last 30 days, have you been harassed at school or on the way to or from school?"). Peer harassment/victimization of all youth (heterosexual and those who were lesbian, gay, or bisexual) was less likely to occur in counties with a greater proportion of school districts with inclusive anti-bullying policies, although the effect was small (harassment/ victimization was 6 percent less likely to occur in countries with inclusive policies).

Second, researchers were also interested in whether anti-bullying policies were effective in reducing the risk of suicide attempts among lesbian and gay youth, given previously reported relationships between bullying and suicide attempts among this population (e.g., Rivers, 2004; Russell et al., 2011). Results indicated that lesbian and gay youths living in counties with the fewest number of school districts with inclusive anti-bullying policies were 2.25 times (OR = 2.25; 95% CI [1.13, 4.49]) more likely to have attempted suicide in the past year compared to those living in counties with the most number of school districts with inclusive policies. Moreover, inclusive anti-bullying policies were significantly associated with a lower risk of suicide attempts among lesbian and gay youths even after controlling for sociodemographic characteristics (sex, race/ethnicity) and exposure to peer harassment/victimization ($OR = 0.18$; 95% CI [0.03-0.92]).

Third, anti-bullying policies that did not include sexual orientation (i.e., "restrictive" policies) were not associated with lower suicide attempts among lesbian and gay youth. These results suggest that policies had to include sexual orientation in the list of protected classes in order to be effective in protecting lesbian and gay youths from attempting suicide. The results also suggest the importance of specifically including sexual orientation in anti-bullying policies that enumerate protected groups, in order to signal supportive and inclusive school environments for lesbian and gay students.

There is considerable debate regarding the enumeration of protected groups in bullying laws, with some researchers arguing that enumeration highlights the importance of administrators protecting youth that are most vulnerable to bullying, and others saying that enumeration protects only a small subset of youth that are targets of bullying (Cornell and Limber, 2015). The Oregon study by Hatzenbuehler and Keyes (2013) did not code the other groups that were protected in the inclusive policies; consequently, it was not possible to test whether enumerated policies were effective in reducing risk of peer harassment/victimization among other at-risk groups (e.g., overweight/obese youth).

Methodological Assessment of Existing Literature

The studies discussed above have provided important initial insights into the efficacy of anti-bullying policies, but the findings should be considered in light of certain methodological limitations. Two of these studies (Hatzenbuehler and Keyes, 2013; Hatzenbuehler et al., 2015) were cross-sectional. Thus, researchers inferred, but could not test, causal relationships between anti-bullying policies and bullying behavior. For instance, although the studies controlled for potential confounders, an unmeasured common factor may be responsible for the observed relationship between anti-bullying laws and bullying outcomes. In the Australian study, researchers compared rates of bullying from two cross-sectional studies before and after the implementation of a national policy aimed at addressing bullying and other aggressive behaviors among youth (Cross et al., 2011). Although this pre-post analysis improves upon single-time-period cross-sectional designs, numerous events occurred during the implementation of the policy that could also affect bullying behaviors (e.g., media coverage, the implementation of whole-school programs that address the same outcomes), introducing a threat to the internal validity of the study (known as a history threat; see Shadish, 2002). Moreover, bullying was merely one of a number of issues that were targeted through this policy in Australia. It is therefore possible that the policy did not adequately address bullying behaviors.

The study by Schwab-Reese and colleagues (2016) improved upon these methodological limitations through the use of a quasi-experimental design, which afforded the opportunity to examine whether bullying was reduced following the implementation of Iowa's anti-bullying policy. However, this study did not have a comparison group—for example, a state that did not currently have an anti-bullying policy—which would have strengthened the study's ability to determine whether it was the policy, rather than some other factor, that was responsible for the observed relationships. Further, the study demonstrated the importance of having data before and after the bullying legislation was passed, given the initial uptick followed by a reduction in bullying at subsequent assessments. However, it is often quite difficult to obtain data before a policy is enacted, particularly given that all states currently have anti-bullying laws. Time-series analyses are therefore likely to be particularly important in future studies exploring the impact of anti-bullying policies. Finally, none of the studies included information on implementation of these laws (see "Implementation of Anti-Bullying Laws and Policies" later in this chapter) to evaluate the prevalence of bullying across different levels of implementation (i.e., examining implementation as a moderator of the law's impact on bullying behavior).

Future Directions

The study of the impact of anti-bullying laws and policies on bullying is in its relative infancy. Therefore, several critical directions for future inquiry remain in order to advance this literature (for a review, see Hatzenbuehler et al., 2014). These directions are explored below.

Research on mediating mechanisms is needed to uncover why anti-bullying laws or policies are effective in reducing bullying. There are multiple ways in which anti-bullying policies could reduce bullying behaviors, ranging from changing social norms in the school to improving opportunities for reporting bullying. It is currently unknown which of these mechanisms is an "active ingredient" in effective anti-bullying policies. Thus, an important direction for future studies is to identify the processes linking anti-bullying policies to reductions in bullying behavior, which will inform the development of more effective anti-bullying policies that can target these specific mechanisms.

Additionally, research into moderating factors can provide critical information on youth for whom anti-bullying policies are most effective and, conversely, youth for whom these policies are less effective. In particular, it is currently largely unknown whether anti-bullying policies are effective in protecting youth known to be at disproportionate risk for bullying victimization (but see Hatzenbuehler and Keyes, 2013). Whether anti-bullying laws—including the enumeration of specific groups—are effective in reducing disparities in bullying victimization is therefore largely unknown. Furthermore, youth with intersectional identities (i.e., with more than one stigmatized characteristic or identity, such as being a black lesbian) could potentially benefit from anti-bullying policies; the conceptual literature on intersectionality (e.g., McCall, 2005) provides a framework for evaluating the impact of anti-bullying policies on adolescents with multiple marginalized statuses.

Existing studies have focused on anti-bullying laws as a primary prevention strategy for preventing bullying behavior. However, it is also plausible that such policies might prevent bullying *perpetration* and other forms of peer aggression and violence (e.g., weapon carrying, physical fights), a topic that deserves attention in future studies. In addition, anti-bullying laws can also be conceptualized as a *secondary* prevention strategy for reducing the adverse sequelae among those who are bullied. For instance, is the relationship between being the target of bullying and adverse health outcomes (e.g., depression, suicide attempts, substance use, retaliatory aggression) attenuated (or even eliminated) among those youth who attend schools with more comprehensive anti-bullying policies? Addressing these and other questions will help inform the potential reach of anti-bullying policies.

As discussed above, there are several frameworks for understanding and evaluating anti-bullying policies. Currently, only the DOE framework has been evaluated. Given that existing frameworks highlight different foci, results from the DOE framework may not be generalizable to other anti-bullying law frameworks, such as the public health framework mentioned above (Srabstein et al., 2008). Future studies need to compare these frameworks and identify best practices.

Finally, as previously mentioned, the first anti-bullying law was implemented more than 15 years ago, and this was followed by a fairly rapid policy response in other states. These laws have largely been reactive to particular events, such as the Columbine High School shootings in 1999 and suicides among youth who were reportedly bullied. (See Chapter 4 for more detail on school shootings.) There is substantial heterogeneity across states in terms of what is included in anti-bullying laws. Little is known, however, about how emerging evidence, sustained advocacy, and political opportunity converged to create this proliferation of laws to address the issue of bullying across the nation, despite the fact that the field of public health policy research has made clear that the range of possible policy solutions is shaped by the ways in which problems emerge and are framed (e.g., see Table 6-1). A social history of the emergence of bullying as a focus of public policy concern is therefore needed, as understanding the circumstances under which any issue gains traction and draws attention as needing remediation is critical in crafting effective policy responses (e.g., Lerner, 2011).

In order for many of these questions to be addressed in future research; it will be necessary for new data structures to be created, as well as for modifications to be made to existing data structures. In particular, one of the methodological challenges confronting researchers is that many population-based studies that include bullying outcomes do not provide information at geographic units of analysis (e.g., state, school district, or school levels) that would enable researchers to evaluate the implementation and impact of anti-bullying policies. Collaborations between researchers and the federal agencies that create these datasets are therefore needed to address these barriers in order to further facilitate research on this topic.

IMPLEMENTATION OF ANTI-BULLYING LAWS AND POLICIES

If there is a dearth of research on the effectiveness of anti-bullying laws and policies, there is even less empirical research on the implementation of these policies. This is due, in part, to the relatively recent focus on law and policy specifically within the context of bullying, as well as to the lack of attention more generally to the factors that determine how social policies are implemented (Burris et al., 2010). In this section, the committee provides a review of the existing evidence on the implementation of anti-bullying policies. We first discuss the methods that have been used, then review and evaluate the literature, and finally consider important directions for future inquiry.

Several methods have been used to evaluate the implementation of anti-bullying policies, including: (1) content reviews of school and district policies to determine compliance with anti-bullying laws (e.g., Temkin et al., 2014), (2) quantitative surveys of teachers and administrators to identify perceived barriers to implementation (e.g., Cross et al., 2011), and (3) in-depth qualitative interviews that seek to understand institutional forces that hinder or support policy implementation (e.g., EMT Associates Inc., 2013). These implementation studies span different geographic scales, ranging from single cities (e.g., Washington, DC, in Temkin et al., 2014) to single states (e.g., Iowa in Ramirez et al., 2014) to multiple states (e.g., EMT Associates Inc., 2013) and, in one study, a countrywide evaluation in Australia (Cross et al., 2011). Impact evaluations of the implementation of anti-bullying policies have thus far largely been conducted either by task forces appointed by members of the executive and legislative branches (e.g., the New Jersey Anti-Bullying Task Force) or by independent contractors who were hired by agencies (e.g., DC Office of Human Rights; Temkin et al., 2014). In one instance, the U.S. Government Accountability Office (GAO) initiated a performance audit at the request of Congress (U.S. Government Accountability Office, 2012). Although not designed as an implementation study per se, the GAO audit did include several interviews with school administrators and parents in an attempt to ascertain challenges that hindered anti-bullying efforts, including difficulties in the implementation of anti-bullying policies.

Research Approaches

Similar to the previous section on the effectiveness of anti-bullying policies, the review in this section of the existing research evidence on implementation is organized by geographic scope of the study, starting with a single state, moving to multistate assessments, and finally to a countrywide implementation analysis.

A mixed-methods study in Iowa examined how schools in that state implemented its anti-bullying law (Ramirez et al., 2014). Researchers conducted quantitative surveys of (n = 145) and qualitative interviews with (n = 27) middle school administrators. Although administrators in general reported being successful in developing an anti-bullying policy for their school as mandated by state law, the implementation of the policy presented certain challenges. Specifically, in qualitative interviews, administrators reported difficulties in interpreting the legal definitions of bullying, which created challenges both in confirming bullying cases as well as in disciplining bullying behaviors (Ramirez et al., 2014). Further, administrators reported challenges in obtaining the financial resources that were necessary to support the successful implementation of certain components of the anti-bullying policies (e.g., teacher training).

Two multistate studies have examined the implementation of anti-bullying policies, and both reported findings similar to those obtained in the single-state analysis in Iowa. In the first study, researchers who were contracted by DOE conducted site visits in 11 school districts and 22 middle schools (diverse with respect to ethnicity, urbanicity, and socioeconomic status) in four states selected from different regions in the United States (the states are not named in the report). The study's stated goals were to "describe how schools were implementing components of their states [sic] bullying laws, to determine how differences in state legislation influenced school responses to bullying on school campuses, and to identify challenges and school supports associated with the implementation process" (EMT Associates Inc., 2013, p. iii). At the site visits, 281 semistructured qualitative interviews were conducted with numerous constituencies such as state education agency representatives, school and district personnel, school principals, school counselors, teachers, and bus drivers.

Results from these interviews revealed some positive aspects related to anti-bullying law and policy. For instance, many respondents reported that their ability to identify and effectively respond to bullying incidents was strengthened by the policies' requirements that schools develop procedures for handling bullying. Moreover, nearly all respondents supported the policies' emphasis on raising expectations that schools were responsible for preventing and addressing bullying (EMT Associates Inc., 2013). At the same time, a number of barriers to implementation were observed. Although teachers and other school staff were typically aware of the existence of anti-bullying policies, many were not familiar with the particular details of the policies, which in turn hindered implementation. Additional impediments to the effective implementation of anti-bullying policies included (1) teachers' confusion over whether certain behaviors constituted bullying (versus other forms of peer aggression) and therefore whether these behaviors warranted reporting and any disciplinary responses, as required by the state legislation; (2) district administrators' stated difficulties over how to investigate and resolve incidents of cyberbullying and other forms of bullying that occurred off campus (i.e., understanding the scope of anti-bullying policies); and (3) perceived pressures of time and cost in responding to new mandates resulting from anti-bullying policies, such as completing reporting requirements and formal complaint procedures (EMT Associates Inc., 2013).

In addition to documenting particular challenges to implementation, the report revealed several institutional factors, identified by school staff, that supported the implementation of anti-bullying policies, including: "strong school leadership, effective communication, a sense of collaboration among school and district staff, and school structures that helped cultivate relationships among faculty and students and that encouraged information-sharing and problem-solving to achieve resolution of incidents" (EMT Associates Inc., 2013, p. v).

In the second multistate study, the GAO sampled six school districts across eight states (Arkansas, California, Illinois, Iowa, Massachusetts, New Mexico, Virginia, and Vermont) that varied with respect to several dimensions, including geography, student enrollment, and the state's anti-bullying policies (e.g., how bullying was defined in the policy, which protected classes of students were enumerated in the policy). The audit conducted interviews with central administrators, principals, school staff, and parents (the number of interviews that were conducted is not provided in the report). The results from these interviews revealed three areas of concern—each of which is covered in anti-bullying law and/or policy—among state and local officials: (1) challenges in determining appropriate responses for out-of-school incidents, including cyberbullying; (2) difficulties in helping parents and youths distinguish between bullying versus other forms of peer aggression and conflict; and (3) obstacles presented by lack of funding available for training teachers and staff in bullying prevention, identification, and response (U.S. Government Accountability Office, 2012).

Only one study has evaluated the implementation of anti-bullying policies at the country level (this study evaluated a broader school safety framework in Australia known as the National Safe Schools Framework, or NSSF, of which bullying prevention was only one component). In this study, Cross and colleagues (2011) collected data from 106 schools that were surveyed as part of the Australian Covert Bullying Prevalence Study. In each school, four teachers who taught grades 4 through 9 and two senior staff (typically the principal and deputy principal) completed quantitative surveys, in which they rated both their school's implementation of the 23 whole-school policy and practice strategies as part of the NSSF and their school staff's expertise in addressing bullying. A quarter of the teachers were unsure about the contents of the school's policy, rendering implementation of the policy recommendations and practices difficult. Furthermore, fewer than half of the schools reported using more than half of the strategies in the NSSF policy, indicating the implementation rates were low (Cross et al., 2011).

Methodological Assessment of Existing Studies

Research on the implementation of anti-bullying policies, while sparse, has begun to provide some valuable initial insights regarding challenges to the implementation of these policies, such as lack of awareness of the specific components of the policies among school administrators and teachers, as well as confusion over the scope of the policies and the specific behaviors that meet the definition of bullying (Ramirez et al., 2014; U.S. Government Accountability Office, 2012). On the other hand, this research has noted some positive aspects of the policies, including focusing greater attention on bullying within schools. In addition, certain supports were identified that have facilitated the successful implementation of these policies, including strong leadership and effective communication (EMT Associates Inc., 2013).

At the same time, there are important limitations to this research. Only one of these studies used a probability design (Cross et al., 2011); the others relied on purposive sampling to obtain states, and school districts within states, that varied on dimensions hypothesized to affect implementation (e.g., rurality, socioeconomic characteristics). Consequently, results from the majority of evaluation studies are not generalizable to the population of school-based youths. In addition, the implementation studies vary widely in terms of their purpose: some were not designed specifically to address implementation of anti-bullying policies (e.g., Cross et al., 2011; U.S. Government Accountability Office, 2012), whereas others (e.g., Temkin et al.,

2014) evaluated some components of implementation—compliance with establishing a policy—but not others (e.g., fidelity of the implementation). In short, very few studies have been designed with the stated purpose of comprehensively examining the implementation of anti-bullying policies.

The methods employed have also varied substantially across studies, and in some instances it is unclear what methods were used. For instance, the GAO (2012) report stated, "We analyzed narrative responses thematically" (p. 33) but did not provide specific details about whether statistical programs for qualitative data were used (e.g., NVivo) or what particular approaches guided the data analysis (e.g., grounded theory and open and axial coding strategies; Strauss and Corbin, 1990). In the absence of such information, it is difficult to evaluate the validity of the study's results. Furthermore, most of these studies lacked an explicit theoretical framework that would help guide the data collection, methodologies, research questions, and interpretation of study findings. Though many social science theories and approaches could be appropriate for implementation studies of anti-bullying policies, the theories and methods of implementation science (Lobb and Colditz, 2013) offer one widely used paradigm that may be fruitfully applied to the context of anti-bullying policies. In addition, research on evidence-based public health policies (e.g., Brownson et al., 2009) provides several theoretical frameworks for evaluation, such as the RE-AIM policies (Glasgow et al., 1999), that could be adapted to understand the variability in the specific case of implementing anti-bullying policies.

Future Directions

The circumstances that shape both institutional commitment to the implementation of anti-bullying policies and the characteristics of that implementation require future research. Specifically, practitioners, school administrators, and other stakeholders would benefit from an understanding of the process of anti-bullying policy implementation and the complex social processes involved in the transformation of institutional climate that occurs as a result of anti-bullying policies. For instance, little is currently known about how the school's institutional climate around bullying changes during the implementation of these policies (e.g., how school norms around bullying are altered). A better understanding is needed of the institutional and cultural barriers that prevent the uptake and/or maintenance of anti-bullying policies in situations in which the school climate related to bullying does not change following adoption of a new policy. Indeed, there is often a general resistance to policy implementation, (e.g., Brownson et al., 2009) and neither the sources of resistance related to anti-bullying policies nor how such resistance may be overcome is well understood (Hatzenbuehler et al., 2014). Finally, political factors may often determine the development of anti-bullying laws (e.g., which enumerated groups are included) as well as their passage and implementation; however, these political factors are not well understood and deserve more attention in future research. Mixed-methods studies that combine quantitative and qualitative designs are uniquely suited to address these questions but are thus far largely missing from the literature (see Schwab-Reese et al., 2014 for a notable exception).

SUMMARY

In the past 15 years, all 50 states and the District of Columbia have adopted anti-bullying laws. The majority of states have supplemented that law with additional policies. Together with existing federal civil rights and anti-discrimination law and state civil rights laws, this wave of state anti-bullying legislation provides a mandate to address bullying and its harmful consequences. Despite the substantial legislative and policy action on bullying, the variations in law and policy across jurisdictions, as well as the early stage of implementation and evaluation of anti-bullying laws, indicate that considerable work remains to identify the most effective law and policy frameworks for addressing bullying.

Public health policy frameworks (e.g., Srabstein et al., 2008) posit that anti-bullying laws can exert a salubrious influence on youth by preventing bullying behaviors before they occur (thereby serving as a primary prevention strategy), and by reducing the adverse sequelae—such as depression, anxiety, suicidality, and social isolation—among those who are already bullied (thereby serving as a tertiary prevention strategy). While this framework is theoretically sound, research has only recently begun to evaluate whether anti-bullying laws and policies are, in fact, effective in preventing bullying. Two studies have shown positive benefits of the laws in reducing bullying and related constructs (Hatzenbuehler and Keyes, 2013; Hatzenbuehler et al., 2015), whereas two other studies have found more mixed results (Cross et al., 2011; Schwab-Reese et al., 2016). Furthermore, a handful of studies have highlighted both barriers to implementation of anti-bullying policies as well as supports that have facilitated their implementation (EMT Associates Inc., 2013; Ramirez et al., 2014; U.S. Government Accountability Office, 2012); however, variation in the type and quality of methods used in these studies limits the inferences that can be drawn. Little is known about the potential adverse consequences of anti-bullying laws on children and adolescents. For instance, many states' laws significantly expand school surveillance authority, potentially raising privacy and free speech concerns (Suski, 2014). These and other unintended consequences merit further attention.

At the same time, legal content analyses of anti-bullying policies (e.g., Cornell and Limber, 2015; Limber and Small, 2003), and of state civil rights laws (e.g., U.S. Government Accountability Office, 2012), indicate that there is substantial heterogeneity across states regarding the content of anti-bullying policies and the legal protections conferred to students (e.g., the domain of protected classes). As one report concluded, the nature and extent of protections available to students who are bullied "depend on the laws and policies of where they live or go to school" (U.S. Government Accountability Office, 2012, p. 26). Consequently, the full impact of anti-bullying (and related) laws is currently muted—because some state anti-bullying laws and policies appear to be less effective than others in reducing bullying and its adverse consequences (e.g., Hatzenbuehler et al., 2015), because some institutional and social factors prevent these laws and policies from being fully implemented (e.g., EMT Associates Inc., 2013; Ramirez et al., 2014), and because some state civil rights laws offer incomplete protections to certain categories of youths (U.S. Government Accountability Office, 2012).

Much remains to be learned about the effectiveness of anti-bullying laws and policies and about the factors that contribute to their successful implementation. To be maximally effective, the study of anti-bullying laws and policies requires an interdisciplinary, team-based response, drawing on and integrating theories and methods from such diverse fields as law, public policy, psychology, anthropology, sociology, and history (Hatzenbuehler et al., 2014). There are several potential benefits of an interdisciplinary approach to the study of anti-bullying laws and policies, including the triangulation of multiple sources of data to strengthen causal inferences and the ability to address certain issues related to this topic that are not possible with other disciplinary approaches. For instance, whereas quantitative analyses can provide information on the prevalence and correlates of different features of the implementation process (e.g., type and quality of teacher training that is mandated by the policy, political and social characteristics of school districts that fail to implement the policy), detailed, theory-driven ethnographic research in schools can uncover more covert barriers and facilitators of policy implementation so that effective dissemination of policies across diverse social contexts becomes possible. Although the importance of team-based approaches in science is increasingly recognized (National Research Council, 2015), very little work to date—with rare exceptions (e.g., Hatzenbuehler et al., 2015; Ramirez et al., 2014)—incorporates this sort of interdisciplinary, multimethod approach to address the broad questions of how, to what extent, and under what circumstances anti-bullying laws and policies can effectively reduce the prevalence of bullying and its adverse health, academic, and social consequences.

FINDINGS AND CONCLUSIONS

Findings

Finding 6.1: Federal civil rights and anti-discrimination laws offer important protections against bullying, but may be limited in addressing bullying of individuals who are not a member of an enumerated protected class.

Finding 6.2: States and localities have been exploring law and policy solutions to bullying. There is substantial heterogeneity across states, with state laws differing on a number of critical issues, including how bullying is defined and the scope of schools' authority to respond to bullying. In addition, these legal definitions sometimes differ from definitions used in research and in anti-bullying programs.

Finding 6.3: There is limited evidence on the consequences (either positive and/or unintended) of expanding schools' authority to address bullying that occurs off-campus. Such consequences include the impact on students' privacy and speech rights, schools' potential liability and their capacity to address off-campus bullying, and the prevalence of bullying.

Finding 6.4: Litigation offers a potential remedy for victims of bullying. Although some claimants have been successful in pursuing a remedy through the courts, significant challenges exist in pursuing litigation, and most cases litigated to date have favored defendants (most commonly, schools).

Finding 6.5: There are limited evaluations of the effectiveness of bullying laws in preventing bullying behaviors and in reducing the deleterious consequences of bullying among those who are targets of bullying.

Finding 6.6: Emerging evidence exists to suggest that anti-bullying laws and policies can have a positive impact on reducing bullying and on protecting groups that are disproportionately vulnerable to bullying, such as gay and lesbian youth.

Finding 6.7: As with research on effectiveness, there is limited investigation of the implementation of anti-bullying laws and policies. The few studies that do exist suggest general support for anti-bullying policies by district and school personnel, as well as some factors that facilitate implementation of these policies. But there are several barriers to successful implementation of anti-bullying laws and policies, including lack of awareness of the specific components of the laws and policies among school administrators and teachers, confusion over the scope of the laws and policies and the bullying behaviors they cover, and the ability of local jurisdictions to fulfill mandates required by law (e.g., teacher training) without additional resources.

Finding 6.8: There is limited investigation of potential adverse consequences of anti-bullying laws, including their potential impact on students' privacy and free speech rights.

Finding 6.9: There is a lack of analysis of bullying issues and prevention efforts in the context of nonschool settings including, but not limited to, juvenile justice facilities and residential treatment facilities.

Finding 6.10: Zero tolerance policies have not had an impact in keeping schools safer and could have adverse consequences.

Conclusions

Conclusion 6.1: Law and policy have the potential to strengthen state and local efforts to prevent, identify, and respond to bullying.

Conclusion 6.2: The development of model anti-bullying laws or policies should be evidence-based. Additional research is needed to determine the specific components of an anti-bullying law that are most effective in reducing bullying, in order to guide legislators who may amend existing laws or create new ones.

Conclusion 6.3: Further research is needed to assess the implications for both students and schools of expanding schools' authority to address bullying beyond the school campus and school functions.

Conclusion 6.4: Additional research is needed to further evaluate the effectiveness of anti-bullying laws and policies, including determining (1) whether anti-bullying laws and policies are effective in reducing bullying perpetration; (2) the mechanisms through which anti-bullying laws and policies reduce bullying (e.g., change in perceptions of school safety or norms around bullying); (3) whether anti-bullying laws and policies impact all forms of bullying (e.g., relational, physical, reputational, and cyberbullying) or merely a subset; (4) whether the beneficial consequences of these laws and policies also extend to other forms of youth violence (e.g., weapons carrying, fighting) and risky behaviors (e.g., drug/alcohol use); (5) whether, among those who are bullied, anti-bullying laws and policies are effective in reducing the adverse sequelae associated with exposure to bullying (e.g., poor academic achievement, depression, suicidal ideation); and (6) subgroups for whom anti-bullying laws and policies are most, and least, effective—and in particular, whether these laws and policies are effective in reducing disparities in bullying.

Conclusion 6.5: Future studies are needed to more fully elucidate the institutional, contextual, and social factors that impede, or facilitate, the implementation of anti-bullying laws and policies. Such studies should be grounded in social science theory and conducted with larger and more representative samples, and with state-of-the-science methods.

Conclusion 6.6: Evidence-based research on the consequences of bullying can help inform litigation efforts at several stages, including case discovery and planning, pleadings, and trial.

Conclusion 6.7: There is emerging research that some widely used approaches such as zero tolerance policies are not effective at reducing bullying and thus should be discontinued, with the resources redirected to evidence-based policies and programs.

REFERENCES

American Psychological Association Zero Tolerance Task Force. (2008). Are zero tolerance policies effective in the schools?: An evidentiary review and recommendations. *American Psychologist, 63*(9) 852-862.

Berlan, E.D., Corliss, H.L., Field, A.E., Goodman, E., and Austin, S.B. (2010). Sexual orientation and bullying among adolescents in the Growing up Today study. *Journal of Adolescent Health, 46*(4), 366-371.

Boccanfuso, C., and Kuhfeld, M. (2011, March). *Multiple Responses, Promising Results: Evidence-Based Nonpunitive Alternatives to Zero Tolerance.* Research to Results Brief, Child Trends Publication No. 2011-09. Available: http://www.childtrends.org/wp-content/uploads/2011/03/Child_Trends-2011_03_01_RB_AltToZeroTolerance.pdf [August 2016].

Borum, R., Cornell, D.G., Modzeleski, W., and Jimerson, S.R. (2010). What can be done about school shootings? A review of the evidence. *Educational Researcher, 39*(1), 27-37.

Brownson, R.C., Chriqui, J.F., and Stamatakis, K.A. (2009). Understanding evidence-based public health policy. *American Journal of Public Health, 99*(9), 1576-1583.

Burris, S., Wagenaar, A.C., Swanson, J., Ibrahim, J.K., Wood, J., and Mello, M.M. (2010). Making the case for laws that improve health: A framework for public health law research. *Milbank Quarterly, 88*(2), 169-210.

Centers for Disease Control and Prevention. (2006). 60 years of public health science at CDC. *Morbidity and Mortality Weekly Report* (55), 1-38.

Child Trends. (2015). *All 50 States Now Have A Bullying Law. Now What?* Available: http://www.childtrends.org/all-50-states-now-have-a-bullying-law-now-what/ [May 2015].

Cornell, D., and Limber, S.P. (2015). Law and policy on the concept of bullying at school. *American Psychologist, 70*(4), 333-343.

Cross, D., Epstein, M., Hearn, L., Slee, P., Shaw, T., and Monks, H. (2011). National Safe Schools Framework: Policy and practice to reduce bullying in Australian schools. *International Journal of Behavioral Development*, 1-7. doi: 10.1177/0165025411407456.

EMT Associates, Inc. (2013). *Middle School Implementation of State Bullying Legislation and District Policies* Washington, DC: U.S. Department of Education.

Evans, K.R., and Lester, J.N. (2012). Zero tolerance: Moving the conversation forward. *Intervention in School and Clinic*, 48(2), 98-114.

Gartlehner, G., Hansen, R.A., Nissman, D., Lohr, K., and Carey, T.S. (2006). Criteria for distinguishing effectiveness from efficacy trials in systematic reviews. *Technical Review 12*. Rockville, MD: Agency for Healthcare.

Glasgow, R.E., Vogt, T.M., and Boles, S.M. (1999). Evaluating the public health impact of health promotion interventions: The RE-AIM Framework. *American Journal of Public Health*, 89(9), 1322-1327.

Goodman, R.A., Moulton, A., Matthews, G., Shaw, F., Kocher, P., Mensah, G., Zaza, S., and Besser, R. (2006). Law and public health at CDC. *Morbidity and Mortality Weekly Report*, 55, 29-33.

Hanks, J.C. (2015). *Schooly Bullying: How Long Is the Arm of the Law?* (Second Ed.). Chicago: American Bar Association, Section of State and Local Government Law.

Hatzenbuehler, M.L., and Keyes, K.M. (2013). Inclusive anti-bullying policies and reduced risk of suicide attempts in lesbian and gay youth. *Journal of Adolescent Health*, 53(1), S21-S26.

Hatzenbuehler, M., Hirsch, J., Parker, R., Nathanson, C., Fairchild, A., Goldblum, P., Espelage, D., Chu, J., and Bongar, B. (2014). The mental health consequences of antibullying policies. In P. Goldblum, D.L. Espelage, J. Chu, and B. Bongar (Eds.), *Youth Suicide and Bullying: Challenges and Strategies for Prevention and Intervention* (pp. 288-303). Oxford: Oxford University Press.

Hatzenbuehler, M.L., Schwab-Reese, L., Ranapurwala, S.I., Hertz, M.F., and Ramirez, M.R. (2015). Associations between antibullying policies and bullying in 25 states. *JAMA Pediatrics*, 169(10), 1-8.

Hinduja, S., and Patchin, J.W. (2011). Cyberbullying: A review of the legal issues facing educators. *Preventing School Failure: Alternative Education for Children and Youth*, 55(2), 71-78.

Holben, D.M., and Zirkel, P.A. (2014). School bullying litigation: An empirical analysis of the case law. *Akron Law Review*, 47(299), 299-328.

Institute of Medicine and National Research Council. (2014). *New Directions in Child Abuse and Neglect Research*. Washington, DC: The National Academies Press.

Klomek, A.B., Kleinman, M., Altschuler, E., Marrocco, F., Amakawa, L., and Gould, M.S. (2011). High school bullying as a risk for later depression and suicidality. *Suicide and Life-Threatening Behavior*, 41(5), 501-516.

Kosse, S.H. (2005). How best to confront the bully: Should Title IX or antibullying statutes be the answer. *Duke Journal of Gender Law & Policy*, 12, 53-80.

Lerner, B.H. (2011). *One for the Road: Drunk Driving since 1900*. Baltimore: Johns Hopkins University Press.

Limber, S.P., and Small, M.A. (2003). State laws and policies to address bullying in schools. *School Psychology Review*, 32(3), 445-455.

Lobb, R., and Colditz, G.A. (2013). Implementation science and its application to population health. *Annual Review of Public Health*, 34, 235-251.

McCall, L. (2005). The complexity of intersectionality. *Journal of Women in Culture and Society*, 30(3), 1771-1800.

National Research Council. (2015). *Enhancing the Effectiveness of Team Science*. Washington, DC: The National Academies Press.

O'Brennan, L.M., Bradshaw, C.P., and Sawyer, A.L. (2009). Examining developmental differences in the social-emotional problems among frequent bullies, victims, and bully/victims. *Psychology in the Schools, 46*(2), 100-115.

Pitlick, N.E. (2015). *Alternatives to Zero Tolerance Policies Affecting Students of Color: A Systematic Review.* Master of Social Work Clinical Research Papers, #502, St. Catherine University. Available: http://sophia.stkate.edu/msw_papers/502 [August 2016].

Puhl, R.M., and Latner, J.D. (2007). Stigma, obesity, and the health of the nation's children. *Psychological Bulletin, 133*(4), 557-580.

Ramirez, M., Schwab-Reese, L., Spies, E.L., Peek-Asa, C., and Onwuachi-Willig, A. (2014). *Evaluation of the Implementation of Anti-Bullying Legislation in Schools.* Paper presented at the 142nd APHA Annual Meeting and Exposition, November 18, New Orleans, LA. Available: https://apha.confex.com/apha/142am/webprogram/Paper307377.html [February 2016].

Raz, J. (1979). *The Authority of Law: Essays on Laws and Morality.* Oxford, UK: Clarendon Press.

Rivers, I. (2004). Recollections of bullying at school and their long-term implications for lesbians, gay men, and bisexuals. *Crisis, 25*(4), 169-175.

Rose, C.A., Monda-Amaya, L.E., and Espelage, D.L. (2010). Bullying perpetration and victimization in special education: A review of the literature. *Remedial and Special Education,* 1-17. doi: 10.1177/0741932510361247.

Russell, S.T., Ryan, C., Toomey, R.B., Diaz, R.M., and Sanchez, J. (2011). Lesbian, gay, bisexual, and transgender adolescent school victimization: Implications for young adult health and adjustment. *Journal of School Health, 81*(5), 223-230.

Sacco, D., Baird Silbaugh, K., Corredor, F., Casey, J., and Doherty, D. (2012). *An Overview of State Anti-Bullying Legislation and Other Related Laws.* Cambridge, MA: Berkman Center Research.

Schwab-Reese, L., Ramirez, M., Peek-Asa, C., and Onwuachi-Willig, A. (2016). Evaluation of Iowa's Anti-Bullying Law. Submitted to *Injury Epidemiology.*

Shadish, W.R. (2002). Revisiting field experimentation: Field notes for the future. *Psychological Methods, 7*(1), 3-18.

Skiba, R.J. (2014). The failure of zero tolerance. *Reclaiming Children and Youth, 22*(4), 27-33.

Srabstein, J.C., Berkman, B.E., and Pyntikova, E. (2008). Antibullying legislation: A public health perspective. *Journal of Adolescent Health, 42*(1), 11-20.

Strauss, A.L., and Corbin, J.M. (1990). *Basics of Qualitative Research* (vol. 15). Newbury Park, CA: Sage.

Stuart-Cassel, V., Bell, A., and Springer, J.F. (2011). *Analysis of State Bullying Laws and Policies.* Washington, DC: Office of Planning, Evaluation and Policy Development, U.S. Department of Education.

Suski, E. (2014). Beyond the schoolhouse gates: The unprecedented expansion of school surveillance authority under cyberbullying laws. *Case Western Reserve Law Review, 65*(1). Available: http://scholarlycommons.law.case.edu/caselrev/vol65/iss1/9/ [August 2016].

Swearer, S.M., Espelage, D.L., Vaillancourt, T., and Hymel, S. (2010). What can be done about school bullying? Linking research to educational practice. *Educational Researcher, 39*(1), 38-47.

Temkin, D., Horton, S., and Kim, A. (2014). *Bullying Prevention in District of Columbia Educational Institutions: School Year 2013-14 Compliance Report.* Washington, DC: Child Trends.

U.S. Department of Education, Office of Civil Rights. (2010a). *Dear Colleague Letter, December 16, 2010.* Available: http://www2.ed.gov/about/offices/list/ocr/letters/colleague-201010.html [October 2015].

U.S. Department of Education, Office of Civil Rights. (2010b). *Dear Colleague Letter, October 26, 2010.* Available: http://www2.ed.gov/about/offices/list/ocr/letters/colleague-201010. html [October 2015].

U.S. Government Accountability Office. (2012). *School Bullying—Extent of Legal Protections for Vulnerable Groups Needs to Be More Fully Assessed.* Washington, DC: U.S. Government Printing Office.

Wagenaar, A.C., and Komro, K.A. (2013). *Natural Experiments: Research Design Elements for Optimal Causal Inference without Randomization.* Public Health Law Research: Theory and Methods Monograph Series. Washington DC: Robert Wood Johnson Foundation.

Webster, D.W., Vernick, J.S., and Hepburn, L.M. (2002). Effects of Maryland's law banning "Saturday night special" handguns on homicides. *American Journal of Epidemiology, 155*(5), 406-412.

Wilson, H. (2014). Turning off the school-to-prison pipeline. *Reclaiming Children and Youth, 23*(1), 49.

7

Future Directions for Research, Policy, and Practice

The committee was charged with critically examining the state of the science on the biological and psychosocial consequences of bullying and on the risk factors and protective factors that, respectively, increase or decrease bullying behavior and its consequences. The previous chapters in this report have addressed these two primary tasks. Despite the challenges, as detailed in Chapter 2, in deriving consistent prevalence rates for bullying across major national-level surveys, bullying and cyberbullying in the United States is common and warrants commensurate attention at the federal, state, and local levels. Chapter 3 focused on the social contexts that can either attenuate or exacerbate (i.e., moderate) the effect of individual characteristics on bullying behavior. In addition, as described in Chapter 3, bullying does not just affect the children and youth who are most directly involved in the bullying dynamic. Bullying is a group phenomenon in which peers play a number of different complex roles. As discussed explicitly in Chapter 4 and reflected throughout this report, bullying behavior is a serious public health issue with significant negative consequences, in both the short and long term, for the children who are bullied, the children who perpetrate bullying behavior, and children who are both perpetrators and targets of bullying.

As stated in Chapter 5, the committee finds that universal prevention programs do exist that either have demonstrated effectiveness or hold promise for reducing bullying and related behavioral and mental health problems, although the effectiveness of current programs is relatively modest. Multicomponent schoolwide programs appear to be most effective at reducing bullying. Moreover, the committee finds that while federal civil rights and antidiscrimination laws can offer some protections against bullying, these laws have important limitations. State anti-bullying laws differ substantially with regard to how bullying is defined and the scope of schools' authority to respond to bullying, as noted in Chapter 6.

In this chapter, the committee presents its overall conclusions and recommendations as they relate to the study's statement of task. In addition, the committee provides recommendations for addressing the research needed to improve policy and practice that address bullying behavior. Finally, the committee summarizes a proposed research agenda, in which gaps in the current evidence base are noted.

OVERALL CONCLUSIONS CONCERNING SCIENCE, POLICY, AND PRACTICE

Although the committee identified specific conclusions in each chapter, below are the major overall conclusions for the report.

Definitional and measurement inconsistencies in national datasets lead to a variation in estimates of the prevalence of youth being bullied; considerably less is known about the number of perpetrators, and even less is known about the number of bystanders. The prevalence of bullying at school ranges from 17.9 percent to 30.9 percent of youth, whereas the prevalence of cyber victimization ranges from 6.9 percent to 14.8 percent of youth. However, the prevalence of bullying among some groups of youth (e.g., youth who are lesbian, gay, bisexual, or transgender [LGBT], youth with disabilities) appears to be even higher. (Chapter 2)

Youth are embedded in multiple contexts, ranging from peer and family to school and community. Each of these contexts can affect individual characteristics of youth (e.g., race/ethnicity, sexual orientation) in ways that either exacerbate or attenuate the association between these individual characteristics and being the perpetrator or target of bullying, or both. (Chapter 3)

Bullying behavior has significant negative consequences on physical, mental, and behavioral health and on academic performance. Bullying behavior leads to biological changes, although more research is needed to fully understand how changes in the brain associated with bullying lead to increased risk for mental and physical health problems. (Chapter 4)

Multicomponent schoolwide programs appear to be the most effective approach for reducing bullying and should be implemented along with rigorous evaluations of their effects when applied to large populations of youth. Some widely used approaches such as zero tolerance policies and school assemblies are not effective at reducing bullying and may even be harmful; they should be discontinued with resources redirected to evidence-based programs. (Chapter 5)

Law and policy can play a significant role in strengthening state and local efforts to prevent, identify, and respond to bullying. However, data on how these laws and policies affect the prevalence of bullying and its consequences are extremely limited. (Chapter 6)

RECOMMENDATIONS FOR MOVING FORWARD

The committee has developed seven recommendations to make progress in monitoring, preventing, and intervening in bullying. These recommendations are organized around the following four categories: Surveillance and Monitoring, State and Local Policies, Preventive Intervention Programming, and the Social Media Industry. The committee's recommendations are described in more detail below, and the chapter-specific conclusions that support these recommendations are identified.

Surveillance and Monitoring

The first two recommendations are concerned with addressing the challenges in reliably and ethically measuring the incidence of bullying and surveilling its prevalence.

Recommendation 7.1: The U.S Departments of Agriculture, Defense, Education, Health and Human Services, and Justice, and the Federal Trade Commission, which are engaged in the Federal Partners in Bullying Prevention interagency group, should foster use of a consistent definition of bullying. These agencies should

- Promote wide adoption and use of this definition by all federal surveillance efforts on bullying prevalence, by investigators studying bullying, and by schools and other organizations.
- Encourage research that compares different methods and operational definitions of bullying to determine the impact of different definitions on prevalence and incidence rates, change over time, or effects of interventions on outcome behaviors.
- Mandate that prevalence of bullying behaviors be included with other outcome measures in any evaluations of youth violence prevention programs, in order to also determine their effects on bullying.

There are many violence prevention programs that have been implemented to reduce youth interpersonal violence. While these programs may very well have an effect on bullying behavior, few of these programs explicitly measure bullying behavior as an outcome. As described earlier in this report (Chapter 1), bullying behavior is characterized by an imbalance of power, an intention to harm, and repeated perpetration.

Supporting Evidence for the Recommendation:

> **Conclusion 2.3:** Cyberbullying should be considered within the context of bullying rather than as a separate entity. The Centers for Disease Control and Prevention definition should be evaluated for its application to cyberbullying. Although cyberbullying may already be included, it is not perceived that way by the public or by the youth population.

> **Conclusion 2.4:** Different types of bullying behaviors—physical, relational, cyber—may emerge or be more salient at different stages of the developmental life course.

> **Recommendation 7.2: The U.S. Departments of Education, Health and Human Services, and Justice, and other agencies engaged in the Federal Partners in Bullying Prevention interagency group should gather longitudinal surveillance data on the prevalence of all forms of bullying, including physical, verbal, relational, property, cyber, and bias-based bullying, and the prevalence of individuals involved in bullying, including perpetrators, targets, and bystanders, in order to have more uniform and accurate prevalence estimates.**

- This should include at a minimum all school-age children (ages 5-18) who might be involved in or affected by bullying behavior.
- This should include nationally representative data on groups that are identified in this report as being at increased risk for bullying behavior (for example, but not limited to, LGBT students, students with disabilities, and youth living in poverty).
- These agencies should develop mechanisms for sharing bullying data at geographic units of analysis other than the national level (e.g., state and school district level) that will allow communities, organizations, and researchers to evaluate the implementation and impact of policies and programs.

The committee has stated in Chapter 6 that there is much to be learned about the effectiveness of anti-bullying policies and about the factors that can contribute to their successful implementation. The committee also articulated the methodological challenges involved in conducting research on the implementation of anti-bullying policies, including the creation of data structures that permit the evaluation of anti-bullying policies. Sharing data at geographic units of analysis that align with policies and programs (e.g., state, school district, school) will provide important uniform and economical information that can be used to evaluate the impact of programs and policies, guide investigators and policy makers to high prevalence areas in need of intervention, serve to improve the methodological rigor of the studies, and promote further research in this area.

Supporting Evidence for the Recommendation:

Conclusion 2.1: Definitional and measurement inconsistencies lead to a variation in estimates of bullying prevalence, especially across disparate samples of youth. Although there is a variation in numbers, the national surveys show bullying behavior is a real problem that affects a large number of youth.

Conclusion 2.2: The national datasets on the prevalence of bullying focus predominantly on the children who are bullied. Considerably less is known about perpetrators, and nothing is known about bystanders in that national data.

Conclusion 3.1: Youth are embedded in multiple contexts, ranging from peer and family to school, community, and macrosystem. Each of these contexts can affect individual characteristics of youth (e.g., race/ethnicity, sexual orientation) in ways that either exacerbate or attenuate the association between these individual characteristics and perpetrating and/or being the target of bullying behavior.

Conclusion 3.2: Contextual factors operate differently across groups of youth, and therefore contexts that protect some youth against the negative effects of bullying are not generalizable to all youth. Consequently, research is needed to identify contextual factors that are protective for specific subgroups of youth that are most at risk of perpetrating or being targeted by bullying behavior.

State and Local Policies

The following recommendation addresses state and local policies.

Recommendation 7.3: The U.S. Department of Education's Office of Civil Rights, the state attorneys general, and local education agencies together should (1) partner with researchers to collect data on an ongoing basis on the efficacy and implementation of anti-bullying laws and policies; (2) convene an annual meeting in which collaborations between social scientists, legislative members, and practitioners

responsible for creating, implementing, enforcing, and evaluating anti-bullying laws and policies can be more effectively facilitated and in which research on anti-bullying laws and policies can be reviewed; and (3) report research findings on an annual basis to both Congress and the state legislatures so that anti-bullying laws and policies can be strengthened and informed by evidence-based research.

The committee believes that state-level laws and policies aimed at reducing bullying should be evidence-based. Establishing best practices for this legislation will involve an iterative process of conducting additional research on and evaluation of anti-bullying laws outlined in this report, followed by fine-tuning of the laws, followed by more research and evaluation. Such an endeavor will also involve more interdisciplinary and cross-sectoral collaborations between social scientists, practitioners, and legislative members than currently exist.

These researchers should come from varied disciplines including public health, justice, law, behavioral health, implementation science, and economics. These public-private collaborations should also focus on the dissemination and sharing of what is learned through their data collection efforts.

Supporting Evidence for the Recommendation:

Conclusion 6.1: Law and policy can play a significant role in strengthening state and local efforts to prevent, identify, and respond to bullying.

Conclusion 6.2: The development of model anti-bullying laws or policies should be evidence-based. Additional research is needed to determine the specific components of an anti-bullying law that are most effective in reducing bullying, in order to guide legislators who may amend existing laws or create new ones.

Conclusion 6.4: Additional research is needed to further evaluate the effectiveness of anti-bullying laws and policies, including determining: (1) whether anti-bullying laws and policies are effective in reducing bullying perpetration; (2) the mechanisms through which anti-bullying laws and policies reduce bullying (e.g., change in perceptions of school safety or norms around bullying); (3) whether anti-bullying laws and policies impact all forms of bullying (e.g., relational, physical, reputational, and cyberbullying) or merely a subset; (4) whether the beneficial consequences of these laws and policies also extend to other forms of youth violence (e.g., weapons carrying, fighting) and risky behaviors (e.g., drug/alcohol use); (5) whether, among those who are bullied, anti-bullying laws and policies are effective in reducing the adverse sequelae associated with exposure to bullying (e.g., poor academic achievement, depression, suicidal ideation); and (6) subgroups for whom anti-bullying laws and policies are most, and least, effective—and in particular, whether these laws and policies are effective in reducing disparities in bullying.

Conclusion 6.5: Future studies are needed to more fully elucidate the institutional, contextual, and social factors that impede, or facilitate, the implementation of anti-bullying laws and policies. Such studies should be grounded in social science theory and conducted with larger and more representative samples, and with state-of-the-science methods.

Conclusion 6.6: Evidence-based research on the consequences of bullying can help inform litigation efforts at several stages, including case discovery and planning, pleadings, and trial.

Preventive Intervention Programming

The following three recommendations address preventive intervention programming.

Recommendation 7.4: The U.S. Departments of Education, Health and Human Services, and Justice, working with other relevant stakeholders, should sponsor the development, implementation, and evaluation of evidence-based programs to address bullying behavior. These programs should

- Include the needs of students already involved in bullying, either as individuals who bully, who are targets of bullying, or who are bystanders.
- Be specifically evaluated to determine their impact on vulnerable populations, including but not limited to children living in poverty and children with disabilities.
- Include parents, other adult caregivers, and families.
- Test and incorporate the use of emerging and innovative technologies to reach youth.

Ineffective or harmful programs and practices such as zero tolerance should be immediately discontinued.

These should include programs consistent with a public health approach to bullying, which includes universal, targeted, and indicated prevention programming. It is also important to address the need for more intensive interventions and mental health services for youth already involved in bullying and experiencing behavioral and mental health consequences.

There should be a particular emphasis on research that identifies effective programs for youth who appear to be at elevated risk for involvement in bullying (e.g., youth with disabilities, LGBT youth, and culturally diverse youth). There is also a need for studies that can enhance understanding of the extent to which extant, empirically supported selective and indicated preventive interventions for violence, aggression, and delinquency could be leveraged to meet the needs of students involved in bullying behavior or experiencing the mental and behavioral health consequences of bullying.

Research should also assess the impact of preventive interventions and how these impacts interplay with the factors known to influence bullying behavior (e.g., age, gender, school climate, peers). In addition, it should assess the extent to which novel technologies (e.g., social media), innovative approaches, and youth voice could be leveraged to improve the impact of prevention programs.

Supporting Evidence for the Recommendation:

Conclusion 5.1: The vast majority of research on bullying prevention programing has focused on universal school-based programs; however, the effects of those programs within the United States appear to be relatively modest. Multicomponent schoolwide programs appear to be most effective at reducing bullying and should be the types of programs implemented and disseminated in the United States.

Conclusion 5.5: The role of peers in bullying prevention as bystanders and as intervention program leaders needs further clarification and empirical investigation in order to determine the extent to which peer-led programs are effective and robust against potentially iatrogenic effects.

Conclusion 5.7: Since issues of power and equity are highly relevant to bullying, fully developed prevention models that target these issues as an approach for preventing bullying should be conducted using randomized controlled trial designs.

Conclusion 5.8: Additional research is needed on the effectiveness of programs targeted to vulnerable populations such as lesbian, gay, bisexual, and transgende youth, youth with chronic health problems such as obesity, or those with developmental disabilities (e.g., autism), as well as variation in the effectiveness of universal programs for these subpopulations.

Conclusion 5.9: There is a strong need for additional programming and effectiveness research on interdisciplinary collaboration with health care practitioners, parents, school resource officers, community-based organizations (e.g., scouts, athletics), and industry to address issues related to bullying and cyberbullying.

Conclusion 5.10: Regardless of the prevention program or model selected, issues related to implementation fidelity, spanning initial buy-in and adoption through taking programs to scale and sustainability, need careful consideration and an authentic investment of resources in order to achieve outcomes and sustained implementation.

Conclusion 6.7: There is emerging research that some widely used approaches such as zero tolerance policies are not effective at reducing bullying and thus should be discontinued, with the resources redirected to evidence-based policies and programs.

Recommendation 7.5: The U.S. Departments of Education, Health and Human Services, and Justice, working with other relevant stakeholders, should promote the evaluation of the role of stigma and bias in bullying behavior and sponsor the development, implementation, and evaluation of evidence-based programs to address stigma- and bias-based bullying behavior, including the stereotypes and prejudice that may underlie such behavior.

As noted in Chapter 3 of this report, bias-based bullying due to one or more stigmatized social identities (e.g., race/ethnicity, LGBT, weight, disability status) is understudied in the bullying literature, and the committee believes that greater cross-fertilization between the stigma and bullying literatures is needed to advance the effectiveness of anti-bullying efforts.

Supporting Evidence for the Recommendation:

Conclusion 3.1: Youth are embedded in multiple contexts, ranging from peer and family to school, community, and macrosystem. Each of these contexts can affect individual characteristics of youth (e.g., race/ethnicity, sexual orientation) in ways that either exacerbate or attenuate the association between these individual characteristics and perpetrating and/or being the target of bullying behavior.

Conclusion 3.2: Contextual factors operate differently across groups of youth, and therefore contexts that protect some youth against the negative effects of bullying are not generalizable to all youth. Consequently, research is needed to identify contextual factors that are protective for specific subgroups of youth that are most at risk of perpetrating or being targeted by bullying behavior.

Conclusion 3.4: Other conceptual models—particularly stigma—have been under-utilized in the bullying literature and yet hold promise (1) for understanding the causes of disproportionate rates of bullying among certain groups of youth, (2) for identifying motivations for some types of bullying (i.e., bias-based bullying), and (3) for providing additional targets for preventive interventions.

Conclusion 3.5: Studying experiences of being bullied in particular vulnerable subgroups (e.g., those based on race/ethnicity or sexual orientation) cannot be completely disentangled from the study of discrimination or of unfair treatment based on a stigmatized identity. These are separate empirical literatures (school-based discrimination versus school-based bullying) although often they are studying the same phenomenon. There should be much more cross-fertilization between the empirical literatures on school bullying and discrimination due to social stigma.

Recommendation 7.6: The U.S. Departments of Education and Health and Human Services, working with other partners, should support the development, implementation, and evaluation of evidence-informed bullying prevention training for individuals, both professionals and volunteers, who work directly with children and adolescents on a regular basis.

Training should occur on an ongoing basis (1) to ensure retention of information and to sustain competence, (2) to account for turnover of personnel in these positions, and (3) to promote high quality implementation of evidence-informed bullying prevention practices. The competence of these individuals to address bullying behavior appropriately should be periodically monitored.

These individuals can include educators; education support professionals such as school bus drivers, school resource officers, and others who interact on a regular basis with children and youth; health care professionals, including pediatricians, school nurses, and counselors; and other adults such as youth development staff at after-school programs, sports coaches, religious staff, Scout leaders, camp counselors, and the like. As described in earlier chapters, especially Chapter 5, these paid and unpaid professionals are often at the "front lines" and may witness bullying or want to intervene but feel poorly equipped to do so. In some cases, their interventions may actually be harmful to both the child who is bullied and the child who perpetrates the bullying behavior. A more consistent, intentional, and evidence-based system of training is needed to support these professionals.

Supporting Evidence for the Recommendation:

    Conclusion 5.9: There is a strong need for additional programming and effectiveness research on interdisciplinary collaboration with health care practitioners, parents, school resource officers, community-based organizations (e.g., scouts, athletics), and industry to address issues related to bullying and cyberbullying.

    Conclusion 5.10: Regardless of the prevention program or model selected, issues related to implementation fidelity, spanning initial buy-in and adoption through taking programs to scale and sustainability, need careful consideration and an authentic investment of resources in order to achieve outcomes and sustained implementation.

    Conclusion 6.7: There is emerging research that some widely used approaches such as zero tolerance policies are not effective at reducing bullying and thus should be discontinued, with the resources redirected to evidence-based policies and programs.

Social Media Industry

The following recommendation addresses the social media industry.

    Recommendation 7.7: Social media companies, in partnership with the Federal Partners for Bullying Prevention Steering Committee, should adopt, implement, and evaluate on an ongoing basis policies and programs for preventing, identifying, and responding to bullying on their platforms and should publish their anti-bullying policies on their Websites.

This report has illustrated that the majority of U.S. adolescents are online and most use social media sites. Social media sites such as Facebook provide a venue in which adolescents communicate with others, observe peers, build an online identity, and may be exposed to cyberbullying. Some of these social media sites provide bullying reporting options and resources, but little is known regarding how that information is used by the sites and whether their resources are effective. Previous research work confirms that the prevalence of cyberbullying is high, particularly among adolescents, and that being online more is associated with a higher risk of exposure to cyberbullying. Therefore, the online context now appears to be the second most common venue where bullying takes place. Evidence suggests that traditional adult role models such as teachers may not be effective in supporting youth in the online context. Thus, it is important that social media companies, whose platforms provide a venue for bullying, become proactively involved in this issue and provide transparency in their efforts.

Supporting Evidence for the Recommendation

Conclusion 2.4: Different types of bullying behaviors—physical, relational, cyber—may emerge or be more salient at different stages of the developmental life course.

Conclusion 2.5: The online context where cyberbullying takes place is nearly universally accessed by adolescents. Social media sites are used by the majority of teens and are an influential and immersive medium in which cyberbullying occurs.

Conclusion 3.1: Youth are embedded in multiple contexts, ranging from peer and family to school, community, and macrosystem. Each of these contexts can affect individual characteristics of youth (e.g., race/ethnicity, sexual orientation) in ways that either exacerbate or attenuate the association between these individual characteristics and perpetrating and/or being the target of bullying behavior.

Conclusion 5.6: The role of online resources or social marketing campaigns in bullying prevention or intervention needs further clarification and empirical investigation in order to determine whether these resources and programs are effective.

Conclusion 5.9: There is a strong need for additional programming and effectiveness research on interdisciplinary collaboration with health care practitioners, parents, school resource officers, community-based organizations (e.g., scouts, athletics), and industry to address issues related to bullying and cyberbullying.

RESEARCH NEEDS

Throughout the report, the committee has identified specific research gaps and future needs that will lead to a more comprehensive understanding of the consequences of bullying for the children and youth who are engaged in the bullying dynamic; more fully elucidate the dynamic between the bullying perpetrator and target; and more systematically examine factors that contribute to resilient outcomes of children and youth involved in bullying, whether as the child who bullies, the child who is bullied, or a bystander. Table 7-1 summarizes the research needs identified by the committee.

TABLE 7-1 Research Needs to Inform Policies and Programs to Improve Bullying Outcomes

General Category	Specific Research Needs
Behavioral Health Consequences of Bullying	Conduct longitudinal research to track children through adulthood in order to more fully understand links among being bullied, substance abuse, and other behaviors including violence and aggression.
Consequences of Bullying on Brain Function	Probe how and why bullying alters brain functioning.
Digital Devices and Cyberbullying	Better understand usage of digital devices among younger children and how these devices are used in cyberbullying.
Educators and Education Support Professionals	Better understand the roles of educators, education support professionals (e.g., cafeteria workers, school bus drivers), and school resource officers in preventing and intervening in bullying.
Epigenetic Consequences of Bullying	Investigate epigenetic changes, such as in DNA methylation and bullying.
Genetic Predisposition to Mental Health Outcomes and Bullying	Understand the role of genetic influences on both bullying and victimization; for example, studies that examine bullying perpetration in relation to serotonin transporter polymorphisms.
Health Care Professionals	Investigate evidence-based practices for integrating content on bullying preventive interventions into curricula for health care professionals.
Law and Policy	• Conduct systematic evaluation of local policies to: (1) understand which components of anti-bullying policies must be included in an anti-bullying law to ensure a positive impact; (2) determine the full range of remedies available under state and local laws and policies; and (3) assess the capacity of federal antidiscrimination laws to address various forms of bullying. • Investigate state civil rights laws, the balance between schools' authority and students' rights to freedom of expression and privacy, and moderating factors to more fully understand for whom anti-bullying policies are most and least effective, including whether they are effective in reducing disparities in bullying. • Investigate anti-bullying policy implementation.

continued

TABLE 7-1 Continued

General Category	Specific Research Needs
Media	• Understand the risks and opportunities associated with media-focused campaigns and social-norms-based interventions in relation to bullying. • Conduct research on cyberbullying prevention programs. • Track bullying incidents and conduct research on the effectiveness of media companies' policies in addressing cyberbullying.
Neuroendocrinology of Stress	• Examine the relation between bullying, sleep, learning/memory, and cortisol dysregulation. • Explore how testosterone and cortisol interact together in relation to being a target or perpetrator of bullying, or both.
Parents	• Explore the role parents play in helping youth navigate social challenges and adapting to stress. • Support additional research and evaluation of programs developed specifically to prevent bullying.
Peers as a Context	Explore the effects of peers on bullying, especially peers as bystanders and as leaders of anti-bullying programming.
Physical Health Consequences of Bullying	Examine the physical health consequences for children and youth who bully and for those who both bully and are bullied, including how outcomes vary over time for different groups of youth, why individuals with the same bullying and victim experiences may have different physical health outcomes, and how physical and emotional health outcomes intersect over time.
Prevalence of Bullying	Study the disparities in prevalence between different groups (e.g., LGBT youth, overweight/obese youth, youth with specific developmental disabilities, socioeconomic status, immigration status, minority religious status, youth with intersectional identities, urbanicity).

TABLE 7-1 Continued

General Category	Specific Research Needs
Preventive Interventions	• Understand the role of social-cognitive and emotion regulation processes as targets for preventive interventions. • Conduct more large-scale, rigorous studies on the combined effects on bullying of multi-tiered programs. • Develop systematic studies to assess the impacts of selective and indicated programs on bullying. • Investigate evidence-based interventions that are targeted toward youth from vulnerable populations (e.g., LGBT youth, youth with chronic health problems, and youth with developmental disabilities) to reduce bullying-related disparities. • Study how to improve the adoption and implementation of evidence-based programs, including testing models to better understand what works for whom and under what conditions.
Protective Factors and Contexts	• Identify contexts that are uniquely protective for subgroups of youth, particularly those who are vulnerable to bullying. • Explore more fully the ways in which school ethnic diversity can be a protective factor, the contextual factors that make teachers more or less likely to intervene; and the role(s) of school diversity clubs, extracurricular programs, acculturation, virtual and media contexts, and the policy context.

CONCLUSION

While the study of bullying behavior is a relatively recent field, much has been learned over the past few decades that has significantly improved evidence-based knowledge of what bullying behavior is, how it can be measured, and the contexts that can ameliorate or potentiate the association between individual characteristics and being a bully, a target of bullying, or a bystander to the behavior. This research has established that bullying negatively impacts the child who is bullied, the child who is the bully, the child who is both a bully and a victim, and the bystanders. Finally, the research is beginning to show ways in which law and policy can play an important role in strengthening state and local efforts to prevent, identify, and respond to bullying. This is a pivotal time for bullying prevention, and there is not a quick fix or one-size-fits-all solution. Nevertheless, science and policy have provided, and will continue to improve, tools needed to tackle this complex and serious public health problem.

Reducing the presence and impact of bullying in the lives of youth will involve multifaceted efforts at the level of federal and state governments and agencies, communities, schools and families, health care, media and social media. The committee believes the recommendations laid out in this report are an important roadmap for achieving this goal.

Appendix A

Public Session Agendas

April 7, 2015
Open Session Sponsor Briefing

National Academy of Sciences
Keck Room 206
500 Fifth Street, NW
Washington, DC

1:00 PM   Welcome
*Frederick Rivara, Committee Chair, Seattle Children's
Guild Endowed Chair in Pediatrics and Professor of
Pediatrics, University of Washington School of Medicine*

1:05 PM   **Remarks on Study Statement of Task from Sponsors**
(5 minutes for each organization/agency)
- *Yvonne Cook, President, Highmark Foundation*
- *Ingrid Donato, Chief, Mental Health Promotion
  Branch, Division of Prevention, Traumatic Stress, and
  Special Programs, Substance Abuse and Mental Health
  Services Administration, U.S. Department of Health
  and Human Services*
- *Elizabeth Edgerton, Director, Division of Child,
  Adolescent, and Family Health, Maternal and Child
  Health Bureau, Health Resources and Services
  Administration, U.S. Department of Health and Human
  Services*
- *Jennifer Ng'andu, Program Officer, Robert Wood
  Johnson Foundation (via phone)*
- *Alana Vivolo-Kantor, Health Scientist, National
  Center for Injury Prevention and Control, Centers for
  Disease Control and Prevention, U.S. Department of
  Health and Human Services*

- *Phelan Wyrick, Division Director, Crime and Crime Prevention Research Division, National Institute of Justice, U.S. Department of Justice*

1:35 PM   Committee Discussion with Sponsors

2:40 PM   Public Comment and Questions from Audience

3:10 PM   Concluding Remarks
Frederick Rivara

3:15 PM   Adjourn Open Session

PUBLIC INFORMATION-GATHERING SESSION
June 24, 2015

National Academy of Sciences
Keck Room 101
500 Fifth Street, NW
Washington, DC

Purpose of this session: This meeting is part of an Institute of Medicine/National Research Council project. The project's statement of task and committee roster have been provided with the meeting materials. Throughout this session, the committee will gather information to help conduct its study. This session is not designed to be a comprehensive information-gathering effort; it is one among many means for the committee to assemble relevant resources, materials, and input to examine and discuss in the course of its deliberations. At this time, the committee has made no conclusions or recommendations. Comments and questions should not be interpreted as positions of the individual committee members, the committee as a whole, nor the Institute of Medicine and National Research Council.

9:00 AM   Welcome and Introductory Remarks
Frederick Rivara, Committee Chair, Seattle Children's Guild Endowed Chair in Pediatrics and Professor of Pediatrics, University of Washington School of Medicine

9:15 AM   The Neurobiology of Bullying
                Frederick Rivara, Moderator
                • *Daniel Pine, Chief, Section on Development and
                  Affective Neuroscience, National Institute of Mental
                  Health*

9:45 AM   • *Wendy Craig, Interim Head of Department of
                  Psychology, Professor, Queen's University, Kingston,
                  Ontario, Canada*

10:30 AM   BREAK

10:45 AM   Bullying as a Group Phenomenon and the Role of
                Bystanders
                Sandra Graham, Moderator
                • *Christina Salmivalli Professor of Psychology,
                  University of Turku, Finland (via WebEx)*
                • *Karin Frey Research Associate Professor, Educational
                  Psychology, University of Washington*
                • *Wendy Craig,Interim Head of Department of
                  Psychology, Professor, Queen's University, Kingston,
                  Ontario, Canada*

12:00 PM   LUNCH [3rd Floor Atrium Cafeteria-Lunch on Your
                Own]

1:00 PM   The Role of Media in Bullying Prevention [Web-Ex
                panel]
                *Megan Moreno, Associate Professor, Seattle Children's
                Hospital, Session Moderator*
                • *Kaveri Subrahmanyam, Professor, California State
                  University*
                • *Larry Magid, CEO, ConnectSafely.org and Founder,
                  SafeKids.com, and On-Air Technology Analyst, CBS
                  News*
                • *Rosemarie Truglio, Senior Vice President of
                  Curriculum and Content, Sesame Workshop*

2:30 PM   BREAK

2:45 PM   The Intersection of Social Science, the Law, and Bullying and Peer Victimization (Web-Ex panel)
Jonathan Todres, Moderator
- *Sarah Sisaye, Management and Program Analyst, Office of Safe and Healthy Students, U.S. Department of Education*
- *Sarah Burns, Professor of Clinical Law, Faculty Director, Carr Center for Reproductive Justice, New York University School of Law*
- *Craig Goodmark, Consultant, Atlanta Legal Aid Society*

4:00 PM   Perspectives from Stakeholders

                     Format: Stakeholders will have 3-5 minutes to provide comments

4:30 PM   **Closing Remarks and Adjourn**

Appendix B

Information-Gathering from the Field

SITE VISIT OVERVIEW

As part of the study charge, the committee conducted a site visit to a northeastern city.[1] The location enabled the study staff to draw participants from a wide and diverse variety of school districts, community-based organizations, and philanthropies. The site visit included a series of four group interviews with the following types of individuals: (1) school personnel; (2) representatives from community-based organizations; (3) representatives from the philanthropic community; and (4) young adults between the ages of 18-26 who may have experienced examples of bullying in their schools, communities, or on-line when they were younger. Individuals were recruited through purposeful sampling.

The purpose of the site visit was to provide the committee with an opportunity for place-based learning about bullying prevention programs and best practices with a goal of identifying characteristics of promising initiatives, strategies, and opportunities for feasible change, as well as understanding ongoing challenges. Questions related to participants' experiences with bullying and peer victimization were asked to help committee members and staff better identify characteristics of promising initiatives, strategies, and opportunities for prevention, as well as to understand ongoing challenges. The focus group interviews were not intended to be a

---

[1] The name of the city is not identified to protect the confidentiality of the focus group participants.

comprehensive research effort but served as an important complement to the committee's other information-gathering activities and approaches.

Participating Groups

Below is a listing of the relevant characteristics of the individuals who participated in the four focus groups/interviews:

School Personnel
* Guidance counselor of a local middle school
* Principal of a local high school
* Bullying prevention consultant
* Manager of a school-based research institute

Community-Based Service Providers
* Program manager of a local community-based organization
* Program coordinator of a local community-based organization
* Youth mentor of a local community-based organization
* Senior supervisor of a community-based organization

Philanthropic Organizations
* Senior program officer of a local foundation
* Program officer of a local foundation
* Senior program officer of a local foundation
* President of a local foundation

Young Adults
* Recent high school graduate
* Recent college graduate

Key Themes from the Site Visit

Overall Key Messages[2]

* Bullying is a public health issue.
* The definition of bullying is still a struggle. Bullying is not well defined.
* Although much has been done on bullying prevention, much work needs to be done.

---

[2] These overall messages represent themes that emerged across all the groups in the focus groups.

- It is important to educate parents on bullying and encourage them to take action.
- It is important to include parents in bullying prevention programs.
- There is no specific program for the child who bullies.
- Bullying doesn't just happen in schools; it happens in school yards, playgrounds, at home—everywhere.

Key Messages from School Personnel[3]

- Evidence-based practices are not always best practices. Evidence-based practices cannot always be applied in a real world. There is a disconnect between the practice of interventions and the skills needed to implement them.
- Every adult in the school is responsible for bullying prevention.
- The real motivation for bullying prevention is to ensure a high level of learning for any student. Any student who comes to school should have a good environment to learn. A student who comes to school worrying about bullying is not in a position to learn and does not feel safe.
- There is no program or intervention for the child who bullies (perpetrator). The resources for children who bully are lacking. Discipline actions are mostly used.
- Disciplinary measures that are punitive in nature are not very effective.
- Any student has the potential to be a perpetrator of antisocial behavior.
- It is important to train adults to intervene appropriately, address the specific behavior, and then follow up with the student who has been bullied.
- There are still some antiquated resources that schools hold on to in bullying prevention.
- The goal of bullying prevention programs are to: (1) stop the behavior as it is occurring, and (2) prevent future incidents of the same behavior.
- Bullying is human behavior.
- Funding for bullying prevention programs is moving more toward evidence-based programming.
- The community-based programs are not always synced with the evidence-based programs going on in the schools. There is a need to bring school-based programs to community-based organizations that provide services in schools.

---

[3] These key messages represent themes that emerged from the School Personnel focus group.

- A lot of students do not get health services that they need because their parents do not work and they do not have health insurance.
- Program evaluation is important because it enables educators to strengthen the quality of existing programs.
- Bullying prevention successes include (1) breaking the stigma around bullying and other antisocial behaviors and increasing the level of education and awareness among children; (2) shifting the norm and creating common expectations with teachers, students, parents, and community members; (3) creating greater parental awareness about bullying behavior; and (4) using data to drive decisions.
- Bullying prevention challenges include (1) lack of time and human resources in the day for pro-social activities; (2) the use of antiquated resources, such as victim blaming and peer mediation, that are being used in schools; (3) lack of culturally responsive leadership in schools; and (4) confusion about cyberbullying and what occurs at home on social media and how that affects the school environment.

Key Messages from the Community-Based Service Providers[4]

- The consequences of bullying on the child who is bullied include isolation, lack of self-esteem, feelings of not being accepted, anger, being withdrawn, truancy, and poor eating habits.
- Bullying is brought up about 80 percent of the time as one of the main reasons for children not wanting to attend school, dropping out of school, or transferring to a charter school. Children who bully others have issues of anxiety, lack self-confidence, and are looking for ways to be loved.
- The child who bullies needs attention just as much as the child who is bullied.
- Some children who are bullied end up bullying other children as their way of expressing anger.
- It is important for researchers to pay attention to practice-based evidence and not just evidence-based practice.
- It is important for parents to model appropriate behaviors and believe in treating others with respect.
- It is challenging to know the effective ways of dealing with the child who bullies.

---

[4]These key messages represent themes that emerged from the Community-based Service Providers focus group.

- There is no clear path for fostering partnerships between community service providers and school districts.
- There is not enough capacity to handle the issue of cyberbullying since most of the time, service providers do not even know what is going on in the virtual world.
- Bullying prevention programs are not evenly distributed. There are disparities in accessing available programs.
- In bullying prevention, it is important to think about culture and socioeconomic backgrounds and not just race.
- Bullying prevention successes include both the creation of awareness of the issue as well as increased tolerance of differences among children and youth.
- Bullying prevention challenges include (1) a lack of access to treatment services; (2) poor coordination of care and services; (3) promoting information sharing and awareness about the issue of bullying; (4) lack of a good resource pool or resource list where children who bully and children who are bullied could be referred to for help; and (5) lack of relationships and partnerships with other stakeholders.

Key Messages from the Philanthropic Organizations[5]

- Bullying is certainly a problem in schools and it is a concern of the philanthropic community.
- School programs have to be evidence-based before they can be funded.
- It is often hard to assess the impact of bullying prevention interventions.
- Bullying prevention is complex and requires a larger strategy from different disciplines and stakeholders to address the issue at different levels.
- There is a disconnect in terms of messaging and resources at the school level between the superintendent, the school board, and then the actual teachers. The quality of school leadership matters in whether bullying prevention works.
- It is a challenge to bring all the stakeholders in bullying prevention together.
- It is important for the community to understand the real impacts and implications of bullying.

---

[5] These key messages represent themes that emerged from the Philanthropic Organizations focus group.

- Philanthropic organizations invest in bullying prevention programs because of the following:
  - o Children have a right to be safe and comfortable as much as adults do. It is the responsibility of adults to keep children safe and healthy.
  - o It is a requirement of a civil society.
  - o Bullying can turn into a lifetime of behavioral and health issues.
  - o Bullying can present a higher cost to society in the long run if not prevented early.
- The challenges faced in funding bullying prevention programs include
  - o A lot of adults in the school system that are involved with children and bullying prevention think that some amount of bullying is normal. Schools have to realize that there is an issue and own up to it.
  - o Lack of commitment from schools and teachers implementing bullying prevention programs.
  - o There are so many programs out there that are evidence-based, but it is a challenge to know which ones are effective.

Key Messages from the Young Adults[6]

- Bullying someone emotionally and mentally puts them down.
- Bullying is an awkward subject to talk about but everyone has experienced or witnessed bullying before.
- Some adults see bullying as normal.
- Children pride themselves on how they are presented in social media. Social media can have both negative and positive impacts and it depends on the age range and who you are following or talking to. Videos and fights online could be very disturbing.
- Different forms of bullying are experienced throughout life, and people bully because they want to get a social reward or they want to retaliate.
- A lot of children who witness bullying do not like the bullying, and they may not know what to do to stop it.
- When bullying happens, the bystanders feel helpless, get the feeling that bullying is a way of life, and are scared that it could happen to them tomorrow.
- Bullying programs work if they are culturally receptive, the leaders of the program are committed, and they involve positive reinforcement from peers.

---

[6] These key messages represent themes that emerged from the Young Adults focus group.

- Bullying can be prevented by encouraging bystanders to stand up against the child who bullies, educating parents and children on the consequences of bullying, educating children on how to deal with bullying, and having more children as role models to talk about their experiences.
- Young adults can help children who are targets of bullying by rallying around them, by identifying and understanding what makes them easy targets, and by being a friend to them.
- Young adults can help children who bully by asking them what is going on in their lives and understanding what they are going through.

GROUP INTERVIEW AGENDA

June 12, 2015

9:00 AM   **Group Interview 1:** Educational systems' response to committee members
Facilitator: committee member

10:30 AM   **BREAK**

10:45 AM   **Group Interview 2:** Service providers' response to committee members
Facilitator: committee member

12:15 PM   **LUNCH**

1:30 PM   **Group Interview 3:** Philanthropies' response to committee members
Facilitator: committee member

3:00 PM   **BREAK**

3:15 PM   **Group Interview 4:** Young adults' response to committee members
Facilitator: committee member

4:45 PM   **CONCLUDE DAY—DEBRIEF**

Appendix C

Bullying Prevalence Data from National Surveys

TABLE C-1 School Crime Supplement to the National Crime Victimization Survey: Students Who Reported Being Bullied at School during School Year 2012-2013

Student Characteristic	Students Bullied	Students Not Bullied	Student Was Injured[b]	Adult Was Notified
Total	21.5	78.5	05.8	38.9
Sex				
Male	19.5	80.6	07.8	38.5
Female	23.7	76.3	04.1	39.3
Race/Ethnicity[c]				
White, not Hispanic or Latino	23.7	76.3	05.8	40.5
Black, not Hispanic or Latino	20.3	79.7	04.6 !	40.0
Hispanic or Latino	19.2	80.8	06.0	37.5
Asian, not Hispanic or Latino	09.2	90.8	17.6 !	¥
All other races, not Hispanic or Latino	25.2	74.8	¥	36.8
School Level[d]				
Primary	27.6	72.4	10.5	51.8
Middle	25.0	75.0	09.1	51.2
High	19.2	80.8	02.8 !	29.7
Other	22.4	77.6	09.2	37.9
Grade[d]				
6	27.8	72.2	10.6	58.3
7	26.4	73.6	10.5	52.3
8	21.7	78.3	06.2 !	38.1
9	23.0	77.0	03.9 !	35.2
10	19.5	80.5	04.0 !	34.6
11	20.0	80.0	¥	25.8
12	14.1	85.9	¥	22.4

Key to Symbols
! Interpret data with caution. The standard error for this estimate is 30 to 50 percent of the estimate's value
¥ Reporting standards not met. The standard error for this estimate is equal to 50 percent or more of the estimate's value

NOTE: "Bullied" includes students being made fun of, called names, or insulted; being the subject of rumors; being threatened with harm; being pushed, shoved, tripped, or spit on; being pressured into doing things they did not want to do; being excluded from activities on purpose; and having property destroyed on purpose. "At school" includes the school building, school property, school bus, or going to and from school. Missing data are not shown for household income.

[a]Students who responded "don't know" when asked about the frequency of bullying are treated as missing in calculating frequencies.

[b]Injury includes bruises or swelling; cuts, scratches, or scrapes; black eye or bloody nose;

Percentage Distribution of the Frequency of Bullying among Bullied Students[a]

Once or Twice in the School Year	Once or Twice a Month	Once or Twice a Week	Almost Every Day
67.3	19.4	07.6	05.7
68.0	19.2	07.4	05.5
66.6	19.6	07.8	06.0
64.6	20.6	09.1	05.7
70.2	18.0	05.6 !	06.2 !
73.8	17.9	04.4	04.0 !
57.3	18.3 !	¥	¥
66.9	15.2 !	¥	12.8 !
68.0	14.5	12.6	04.9 !
62.7	20.8	07.8	08.7
70.4	19.7	06.2	03.7
67.3	17.3	07.8 !	07.5 !
62.4	22.7	06.5 !	08.4 !
63.8	17.3	11.4	07.5
64.0	19.1	07.9	09.1
67.4	24.7	03.7 !	04.2 !
65.6	21.5	07.8	05.0 !
75.8	12.9	08.2	03.2 !
75.2	17.4	06.1 !	¥

teeth chipped or knocked out; broken bones or internal injuries; knocked unconscious; or other injuries. Only students who reported they were pushed, shoved, tripped, or spit on were asked if they suffered injuries as a result of the incident.

[c]Respondents who were reported as being of Hispanic or Latino origin were classified as "Hispanic or Latino" regardless of their race. "Black, not Hispanic or Latino" includes African Americans. "All other races, not Hispanic or Latino" includes Native Hawaiians or Other Pacific Islanders, American Indians or Alaska Natives, and respondents of two or more races (4% of all respondents).

[d]The School Crime Supplement sample includes students ages 12–18 and, therefore, might not be representative of students in sixth grade. Comparisons between students in sixth grade and those in other grades should be made with caution.

SOURCE: Data from National Center for Education Statistics. (2015). *Student Reports of Bullying and Cyber-Bullying: Results from the 2013 School Crime Supplement to the National Crime Victimization Survey* (NCES 2015-056).Washington, DC: U.S. Department of Education. Available: http://nces.ed.gov/pubs2015/2015056.pdf [May 2016].

TABLE C-2 School Crime Supplement to the National Crime Victimization Survey: Students Who Reported Being Bullied at School during School Year 2012-2013

Student Characteristic	Among Bullied Students: Location of Bullying						
	In a Classroom	In a Hallway or Stairwell	In a Bathroom/ Locker Room	Cafeteria at School	Outside on School Grounds	School Bus	Somewhere Else at School
Total	33.6	45.6	09.1	18.9	22.9	7.8	0.8
Sex							
Male	31.1	45.8	11.6	17.9	22.3	08.9	¥
Female	35.8	45.3	07.0	19.7	23.4	06.9	1.2
Race/ Ethnicity[a]							
White, not Hispanic or Latino	33.9	46.9	11.0	19.8	22.9	09.6	0.8
Black, not Hispanic or Latino	28.7	39.5	05.1 !	19.2	18.7	06.4 !	¥
Hispanic or Latino	35.6	44.8	07.1	15.5	26.4	02.3 !	¥
Asian, not Hispanic or Latino	41.9	53.4	16.7 !	32.4 !	¥	¥	#
All other races	31.9	48.3	¥	14.3 !	25.1	17.0 !	#
School Level[b]							
Primary	40.1	22.9	07.4 !	09.7 !	46.6	08.7 !	¥
Middle	34.4	45.0	10.0	20.0	24.6	12.7	¥
High	31.6	49.2	08.6	19.2	17.5	04.4	1.0 !
Other	33.2	39.6	07.1 !	16.7	32.0	11.3	¥
Grade[b]							
6	34.9	40.9	07.3 !	11.6	36.4	17.1	#
7	32.4	43.6	12.9	20.8	26.8	10.2	¥
8	38.0	41.2	07.7	18.0	26.1	08.7	¥
9	29.9	42.0	09.5	23.9	19.0	05.7 !	¥
10	40.1	52.6	09.0	19.2	20.0	07.9	¥
11	29.5	52.2	08.2	18.8	16.6	¥	¥
12	30.1	47.4	06.2 !	14.9	14.1	¥	¥

Type of Bullying						
Made Fun of, Called Names, or Insulted	Spread Rumors	Threatened with Harm	Pushed, Shoved, Tripped, or Spit on	Tried to Make Do Things They Didn't Want to Do	Exclude from Activities on Purpose	Property Destroyed on Purpose
13.6	13.2	3.9	6.0	2.2	4.5	1.6
12.6	09.6	4.1	07.4	2.4	3.5	1.8
14.7	17.0	3.7	04.6	1.9	5.5	1.3
15.6	14.6	4.4	06.1	2.0	5.4	1.5
10.5	12.7	3.2	06.0	2.7	2.7	2.0
12.1	11.5	4.0	06.3	1.6	3.5	1.4
7.5	3.7	¥	02.0 !	3.8 !	2.2 !	1.6 !
16.5	17.3	4.3 !	08.5	4.0 !	6.5	2.1 !
19.1	14.5	4.7	08.9	1.6 !	7.0	1.7 !
17.4	14.6	6.0	09.8	3.1	5.7	2.4
11.3	12.0	2.6	04.0	1.8	3.3	1.1
12.5	16.0	6.0	04.5	2.3	6.8	1.0 !
21.3	16.1	5.9	11.0	3.4	6.5	3.1
17.9	15.5	6.1	11.6	3.0	6.3	2.2
14.5	12.7	3.9	6.5	2.3	5.2	1.5 !
13.7	13.8	3.6	04.9	2.6	4.3	1.2 !
12.9	12.9	4.3	03.7	1.7	4.6	1.3
11.2	12.5	3.0	03.4	1.5	2.4	1.6 !
6.4	9.7	1.0 !	03.0	1.3 !	2.6	0.7 !

TABLE C-2 Continued

Key to Symbols

\# Rounds to zero

! Interpret data with caution. The standard error for this estimate is 30 to 50 percent of the estimate's value

¥ Reporting standards not met. The standard error for this estimate is equal to 50 percent or more of the estimate's value

NOTE: "Bullied" includes students being made fun of, called names, or insulted; being the subject of rumors; being threatened with harm; being pushed, shoved, tripped, or spit on; being pressured into doing things they did not want to do; being excluded from activities on purpose; and having property destroyed on purpose. "At school" includes the school building, school property, school bus, or going to and from school. Missing data are not shown for household income.

[a]Respondents who were reported as being of Hispanic or Latino origin were classified as "Hispanic or Latino" regardless of their race. "Black, not Hispanic or Latino" includes African Americans. "All other races, not Hispanic or Latino" includes Native Hawaiians or Other Pacific Islanders, American Indians or Alaska Natives, and respondents of two or more races (4 percent of all respondents).

[b]The School Crime Supplement sample includes students ages 12-18 and, therefore, might not be representative of students in sixth grade. Comparisons between students in sixth grade and those in other grades should be made with caution.

SOURCE: Data from National Center for Education Statistics. (2015). *Student Reports of Bullying and Cyber-Bullying: Results from the 2013 School Crime Supplement to the National Crime Victimization Survey* (NCES 2015-056).Washington, DC: U.S. Department of Education. Available: http://nces.ed.gov/pubs2015/2015056.pdf [May 2016].

TABLE C-3 School Crime Supplement to the National Crime Victimization Survey: Students Who Reported Being Cyberbullied Anywhere, School Year 2012-2013

Student Characteristic	Students Cyber-bullied	Students not Cyber-bullied	Adult Was Notified	Frequency of Cyberbullying among Cyberbullied Students (%)			
				Once or Twice in the School Year	Once or Twice a Month	Once or Twice a Week	Almost Every Day
Total	06.9	93.1	23.3	73.2	15.0	07.9	3.8
Sex							
Male	05.2	94.8	10.5	75.2	09.3	08.1	7.4 !
Female	08.6	91.4	31.6	71.9	18.8	07.9	¥
Race/Ethnicity[a]							
White	07.6	92.4	24.4	76.9	15.2	04.6 !	3.3 !
Black	04.5	95.5	24.5 !	68.2	18.9 !	¥	#
Hispanic or Latino	05.8	94.2	23.7	73.5	08.9 !	12.5 !	¥
Asian,	05.8	94.2	¥	42.9 !	32.6 !	24.5 !	#
All other races, not Hispanic or Latino	13.4	86.6	21.0	65.2	¥	¥	¥
School Level[b]							
Primary	04.6	95.4	54.2	79.1	¥	¥	¥
Middle	06.6	93.4	23.7	68.3	20.4	6.4	4.9 !
High	07.2	92.8	20.3	73.9	15.3	7.3	3.6
Other	07.3	92.7	19.7	84.1	¥	¥	¥
Grade[b]							
6	05.9	94.1	17.5	82.3	¥	¥	¥
7	07.0	93.0	28.0	65.5	24.9	¥	¥
8	06.4	93.6	30.4	70.5	17.2 !	08.6 !	¥
9	06.7	93.3	12.4	79.6	07.7 !	09.2 !	¥
10	08.6	91.4	23.9	73.8	16.7 !	06.7 !	¥
11	06.8	93.2	26.7	71.4	14.2!	12.3 !	¥
12	05.9	94.1	21.0	74.6	13.3 !	¥	¥

Key to Symbols
Rounds to zero
! Interpret data with caution. The standard error for this estimate is 30 to 50 percent of the estimate's value
¥ Reporting standards not met. The standard error for this estimate is equal to 50 percent or more of the estimate's value

NOTE: "Bullied" includes students being made fun of, called names, or insulted; being the subject of rumors; being threatened with harm; being pushed, shoved, tripped, or spit on; being pressured into doing things they did not want to do; being excluded from activities on purpose; and having property destroyed on purpose. "At school" includes the school building, school property, school bus, or going to and from school. Missing data are not shown for household income.

Type of Cyberbullying (%)

Hurtful Information on Internet	Purposely Shared Private Information	Unwanted Contact via E-mail	Unwanted Contact via Instant Message	Unwanted Contact via Text Message	Unwanted Contact via Online Gaming	Purposeful Exclusion from an Online Community
2.8	0.9	0.9	2.1	3.2	1.5	0.9
1.2	0.4	0.2 !	1.0	1.6	2.5	0.9
4.5	1.5	1.7	3.4	4.9	0.4	0.9
2.9	1.0	0.8	2.2	3.8	1.8	1.0
2.2	¥	0.8 !	1.8 !	1.9	¥	¥
2.6	1.0 !	0.8 !	1.9	2.6	0.9 !	1.0
1.8 !	#	¥	¥	¥	3.1 !	¥
6.9	1.9	4.7 !	4.9 !	6.2	3.2 !	¥
¥	¥	1.4 !	¥	2.7	¥	¥
2.4	0.8	0.9	2.6	3.2	2.0	1.0
3.2	0.9	0.8	2.1	3.2	1.3	0.9
¥	¥	1.6 !	¥	3.7	¥	¥
1.4 !	¥	¥	1.2 !	2.3 !	1.5 !	¥
2.1	1.1 !	1.0 !	2.3	3.8	1.8	0.8 !
3.1	0.9 !	1.5 !	2.3	3.2	1.7	1.5 !
2.0	¥	¥	2.9	2.8	1.6	1.4
4.1	1.2 !	1.4	2.8	4.5	1.0 !	1.0 !
3.9	1.3 !	¥	1.1 !	2.7	1.3	¥
2.6	¥	1.1 !	1.9	2.3	1.4 !	¥

[a]Respondents who were reported as being of Hispanic or Latino origin were classified as "Hispanic or Latino" regardless of their race. "Black, not Hispanic or Latino" includes African Americans. "All other races, not Hispanic or Latino" includes Native Hawaiians or Other Pacific Islanders, American Indians or Alaska Natives, and respondents of two or more races (4% of all respondents).

[b]The School Crime Supplement sample includes students ages 12–18 and, therefore, might not be representative of students in sixth grade. Comparisons between students in sixth grade and those in other grades should be made with caution.

SOURCE: Data from National Center for Education Statistics. (2015). *Student Reports of Bullying and Cyber-Bullying: Results from the 2013 School Crime Supplement to the National Crime Victimization Survey* (NCES 2015-056).Washington, DC: U.S. Department of Education. Available: http://nces.ed.gov/pubs2015/2015056.pdf [May 2016].

TABLE C-4 Youth Risk Behavior Surveillance Data: 2012-2013 School Year

	Bullied on School Property[a] (%)			Electronically Bullied[a b] (%)		
	Female	Male	Total	Female	Male	Total
Race / Ethnicity						
White[c]	27.3	16.2	21.8	25.2	08.7	16.9
Black[c]	15.1	10.2	12.7	10.5	06.9	08.7
Hispanic	20.7	14.8	17.8	17.1	08.3	12.8
Grade						
9	29.2	20.8	25.0	22.8	09.4	16.1
10	28.8	15.8	22.2	21.9	07.2	14.5
11	20.3	13.1	16.8	20.6	08.9	14.9
12	15.5	11.2	13.3	18.3	08.6	13.5
Total	23.7	15.6	19.6	21.0	08.5	14.8

[a]During the 12 months before the survey.
[b]Including being bullied through e-mail, chat rooms, instant messaging, Websites, or texting.
[c]Non-Hispanic.
SOURCE: Data from Centers for Disease Control and Prevention. (2014). Youth Risk Behavior Surveillance—United States. *Morbidity and Mortality Weekly Report, 64*(4).

TABLE C-5 National Survey of Children's Exposure to Violence II: Bullying and Cyberbullying Prevalence Rates 2012, Data from 2011

| Victimization Type | All Victims (%) | | Victim Gender (%) | | | | Victim Age (%) | | | | |
| | | | Male | | Female | | | | | | |
	Last Year	Lifetime	Last Year	Lifetime	Last Year	Lifetime	0-1 Last Year	2-5 Last Year	6-9 Last Year	10-13 Last Year	14-17 Last Year
Assault by peer, nonsibling	17.9	27.8	**22.8**	**34.1**	12.8	21.3	3.7	16.4	20.6	23.5	18.4
Assault by gang or group[a]	01.7	3.60	2.50	05.2	00.9	02.0	+	00.1	01.2	02.5	02.9
Bias attack[a]	01.8	02.8	2.20	03.6	01.4	02.0	+	00.8	01.9	02.6	01.9
Threatened assault[a]	08.8	17.8	9.10	**19.5**	08.4	16.1	+	03.9	05.7	13.1	12.4
Internet/cell phone harassment[b]	06.0	08.5	3.80	05.8	08.3	11.3	+	00.0[c]	00.5	04.4	13.9

Key to Symbols
+ Not available

NOTE: Values in boldface are significantly different at $p < .05$ by Pearson χ^2 test.

[a]Among those 2 years or older.
[b]Among those 5 years or older.
[c]Includes 5-year-olds only.

SOURCE: Data from Finkelhor, D., Turner, H.A., Shattuck, A., and Hamby, S.L. (2015). *Violence, Crime, and Abuse Exposure in a National Sample of Children and Youth: An Update.* Washington, DC: U.S. Department of Justice, Office of Justice Programs, Office of Juvenile Justice and Delinquency Prevention. Available: http://www.ojjdp.gov/pubs/248547.pdf [June 2016].

TABLE C-6 Health Behavior in School-Age Children: Bullying and Cyberbullying Frequency for Children Who Are Bullied, 2009-2010 School Year

	Frequency (%)[a]					
Question Asked	Zero Times	Once or Twice	2 or 3 Times per Month	Once a Week	Several Times a Week
Bullied at school	69.1	16.0	4.1	2.6	4.0
Called names/teased	64.4	16.9	3.3	3.2	5.5
Left out of things	69.8	13.3	3.1	2.9	3.7
Hit/kicked/pushed	79.1	07.3	2.0	1.8	2.2
Others lied about me	65.4	15.8	4.4	2.7	4.6
Bullied for race/color	80.4	05.9	1.8	1.6	2.7
Bullied for religion	83.5	04.3	1.4	1.0	1.9
Made sexual jokes to me	72.4	10.2	3.2	2.7	4.0
Bullied using a computer/e-mail	85.2	03.5	1.5	0.9	1.2
Bullied using a computer/e-mail, outside of school	85.2	03.7	1.4	0.8	1.4
Bullied using a cell phone	85.2	03.4	1.2	0.9	1.2
Bullied using a cell phone, outside of school	85.5	03.2	1.3	0.9	1.3

NOTE: Being bullied is defined as when another student, or a group of students, say or do nasty or unpleasant things to him or her. It is also bullying when a student is teased repeatedly in a way he or she does not like or when they are deliberately left out of things. But it is NOT BULLYING when two students of about the same strength or power argue or fight. It is also not bullying when a student is teased in a friendly and playful way.

[a]During the 12 months before the survey.

SOURCE: Data from Iannotti, R.J. (2010). *Health Behavior in School-Aged Children (HBSC), 2009-2010* (ICPSR 34791). U.S. Department of Health and Human Services, National Institutes of Health, Eunice Kennedy Shriver National Institute of Child Health and Human Development. Available: http://www.icpsr.umich.edu/icpsrweb/NAHDAP/studies/34792 [May 2016].

TABLE C-7 Health Behavior in School-Age Children: Bullying and Cyberbullying Frequency for Children Who Bully, 2009-2010 School Year

Question Asked	Frequency (%)				
	Zero Times	Once or Twice	2 or 3 Times/Month	Once a Week	Several Times a Week
Bullied another student	68.2	19.1	3.6	1.7	1.9
Called another student names/teased	70.0	15.7	2.4	1.6	2.3
Left another student out of things	76.5	10.3	1.9	1.2	1.7
Hit/kicked/pushed another student	80.7	06.3	1.5	1.3	1.6
Others lied about another student	82.8	05.2	1.3	1.0	1.2
Bullied another student for race/color	84.4	03.8	1.2	0.8	1.3
Bullied another student for religion	85.8	02.8	1.0	0.8	1.2
Made sexual jokes to another student	82.3	05.0	1.5	1.1	1.5
Bullied another student using a computer/e-mail	86.3	02.4	0.8	0.7	1.2
Bullied another student using a computer/e-mail, outside of school	86.0	02.7	0.9	0.7	1.1
Bullied another student using a cell phone	85.9	02.8	0.9	0.8	1.0
Bullied another student using a cell phone, outside of school	86.0	02.7	0.9	0.5	1.2

NOTE: Being bullied is defined as when another student, or a group of students, say or do nasty or unpleasant things to him or her. It is also bullying when a student is teased repeatedly in a way he or she does not like or when they are deliberately left out of things. But it is NOT BULLYING when two students of about the same strength or power argue or fight. It is also not bullying when a student is teased in a friendly and playful way. SOURCE: Data from Iannotti, R.J. (2010). *Health Behavior in School-Aged Children (HBSC), 2009-2010* (ICPSR 34791). U.S. Department of Health and Human Services, National Institutes of Health, Eunice Kennedy Shriver National Institute of Child Health and Human Development. Available: http://www.icpsr.umich.edu/icpsrweb/NAHDAP/studies/34792 [May 2016]

Appendix D

Selected Federal Resources
for Parents and Teachers

Below is a list of selected federally funded and free resources on bullying prevention for parents and teachers:

General Resources
- Centers for Disease Control and Prevention
  - Prevent Bullying
    http://www.cdc.gov/features/prevent-bullying/

- Eunice Kennedy Shriver National Institute of Child Health and Human Development
  - Bullying: Overview
    https://www.nichd.nih.gov/health/topics/bullying/Pages/default.aspx

- Health Resources and Services Administration
  - Bullying Prevention
    http://mchb.hrsa.gov/programs/bullying/
  - Children Safety Network; Bullying Prevention
    http://www.childrenssafetynetwork.org/injury-topics/bullying-prevention
  - Bullying Prevention: 2015 Resource Guide
    http://www.childrenssafetynetwork.org/sites/childrenssafetynetwork.org/files/Bullying%20Prevention.pdf
  - Bullying Prevention Training
    http://www.stopbullying.gov/training

- Substance Abuse and Mental Health Services Administration (SAMHSA)
  - o Bullying Prevention
    http://www.samhsa.gov/tribal-ttac/resources/bullying-prevention
  - o KnowBullying mobile app
    http://store.samhsa.gov/apps/knowbullying/index.html

- The Ad Council
  - o "Be More Than A Bystander"
    http://www.adcouncil.org/Our-Campaigns/Safety/Bullying-Prevention

- PACER.org
  - o PACER's National Bullying Prevention Center
    http://www.pacer.org/bullying/

- United States Department of Education
  - o Creating a Safe and Respectful Environment on Our Nation's School Buses
    https://safesupportivelearning.ed.gov/creating-safe-and-respectful-environment-our-nations-school-buses-training-toolkit
  - o Creating a Safe and Respectful Environment in Our Nation's Classrooms
    https://safesupportivelearning.ed.gov/creating-safe-and-respectful-environment-our-nations-classrooms-training-toolkit

- United States Department of Health and Human Services
  - o Stopbullying.gov

- United States Department of Justice Office of Justice Programs Office of Juvenile Justice and Delinquency Prevention
  - o Bullying in Schools: An Overview
    http://www.ojjdp.gov/pubs/234205.pdf

Resources Targeted to Parents
- Centers for Disease Control and Prevention
  - o Bullying Prevention for Parents: Podcast
    http://www2c.cdc.gov/podcasts/player.asp?f=8622473

- U.S. Department of Education
  - o What You Can Do: Parents
    http://www.stopbullying.gov/what-you-can-do/parents/
  - o Understanding the Roles of Parents and Caregivers in
    Community-Wide Bullying Prevention Efforts
    http://www.stopbullying.gov/prevention/training-center/hrsa_
    guide_parents-and-caregivers_508v2.pdf
  - o Prevent Bullying: Engage Parents and Youth
    http://www.stopbullying.gov/prevention/at-school/
    engage-parents/
  - o Bullying at Camp–What Parents Should Know!
    http://www.stopbullying.gov/blog/2013/07/30/
    bullying-camp-what-parents-should-know
  - o Take Action Today: How Families and Students Can Take the
    Lead in Creating Safer School Environments
    http://www.stopbullying.gov/blog/2014/09/16/take-action-
    today-how-families-and-students-can-take-lead-creating-safer-
    school

Resources Targeted to Teachers

- Centers for Disease Control and Prevention
  - o School Violence: Prevention Tools and Resources
    http://www.cdc.gov/violenceprevention/youthviolence/
    schoolviolence/tools.html
  - o Electronic Media and Youth Violence: A CDC Issue Brief for
    Educators and Caregivers
    http://www.cdc.gov/violenceprevention/pdf/ea-brief-a.pdf
  - o School Connectedness: Strategies for Increasing Protective
    Factors Among Youth
    http://www.cdc.gov/healthyyouth/protective/pdf/
    connectedness.pdf
  - o Measuring Bullying Victimization, Perpetration, and Bystander
    Experiences: A Compendium of Assessment Tools
    http://www.cdc.gov/violenceprevention/pdf/
    bullycompendium-a.pdf
  - o Bullying Surveillance Among Youths: Uniform Definitions for
    Public Health and Recommended Data Elements
    http://www.cdc.gov/violenceprevention/pdf/bullying-
    definitions-final-a.pdf

- U.S. Department of Education (stopbullying.gov)
  - What You Can Do: Educators
    http://www.stopbullying.gov/what-you-can-do/educators/index.html
  - Understanding the Roles of School Administrators in Community-Wide Bullying Prevention Efforts
    http://www.stopbullying.gov/prevention/training-center/hrsa_guide_school-administrators_508.pdf
  - Creating a Safe and Respectful Environment in Our Nation's Classrooms: Training Toolkit
    https://safesupportivelearning.ed.gov/creating-safe-and-respectful-environment-our-nations-classrooms-training-toolkit

Appendix E

Biosketches of Committee Members and Project Staff

COMMITTEE MEMBERS

Frederick P. Rivara (*Chair*) holds the Seattle Children's Hospital Guild Endowed Chair in pediatrics and is a professor of pediatrics and adjunct professor of epidemiology at the University of Washington. While continuing his work as clinician, teacher, investigator, and advocate at the University of Washington and Seattle Children's Hospital, he is also vice chair of the Department of Pediatrics in the School of Medicine and editor-in-chief of *JAMA Pediatrics*. His research interests, spanning 30 years, include the efficacy and promotion of bicycle helmets, prevention of pedestrian injuries, youth violence, the epidemiology and prevention of firearm injuries, intimate partner violence, traumatic brain injury including sports concussion, interventions for alcohol abuse in trauma patients, and effectiveness of trauma systems in caring for pediatric and adult trauma patients. He was founding director of the Harborview Injury and Research Center, Seattle, founding president of the International Society for Child and Adolescent Injury Prevention, and a founding board member of the Washington State Academy of Science. His honors include the Charles C. Shepard Science Award (Centers for Disease Control and Prevention), Distinguished Career Award (American Public Health Association, Injury Control and Emergency Health Services Section), Physician Achievement Award (American Academy of Pediatrics, Injury and Poison Prevention Section), Distinguished Alumni Award (University of Washington School of Public Health), and election to the Institute of Medicine in 2005.

Angela Amar is associate professor and assistant dean for BSN education in the Nell Hodgson Woodruff School of Nursing, Emory University. Her research, focused on African American women, includes dating violence and sexual assault, mental health responses to trauma, and strategies to increase help-seeking behavior. She is active in university service related to violence and diversity. She received her B.S.N. and M.S.N. from Louisiana State University Medical Center and her Ph.D. from the University of Pennsylvania. At the University of Pennsylvania, she was a Fontaine Fellow and a Pre-Doctoral Fellow in the International Center for Research on Women, Children, and Families. She is a fellow of the American Academy of Nursing, member of its Expert Panel on Psychiatric and Substance Abuse Care, and cochair of its Expert Panel on Violence. She is board-certified as an Advanced Forensic Nurse, a Distinguished Fellow with the International Association of Forensic Nurses, and certified as a Clinical Nurse Specialist in Advanced Practice Adult Psychiatric and Mental Health. She is on the National Advisory Committee for the Robert Wood Johnson Future of Nursing Scholars program, a Public Voices Fellow with the Op-Ed project, and an associate editor for *Journal of Forensic Nursing.*

Catherine Bradshaw is a professor and associate dean for research and faculty development at the Curry School of Education, University of Virginia. She is also deputy director of the Center for the Prevention of Youth Violence and codirector of the Center for Prevention and Early Intervention, both at The Johns Hopkins University. Prior positions include associate professor and associate chair, Department of Mental Health of The Johns Hopkins Bloomberg School of Public Health. Her research, focused on the development of aggressive behavior and school-based prevention, includes bullying and school climate; development of aggressive and problem behaviors; effects on children of exposure to violence, peer victimization, and environmental stress; and design, evaluation, and implementation of evidence-based prevention programs in schools. She collaborates on randomized trials of school-based prevention programs, including Positive Behavioral Interventions and Supports and social-emotional learning curricula. Her expertise includes implementation science, coaching models, and cultural proficiency. She works with the state of Maryland and several school districts on development and implementation of programs and policies to prevent bullying and school violence while fostering safe and supportive learning environments. She is an associate editor for the *Journal of Research on Adolescence,* editor of *Prevention Science,* and a co-editor of *Handbook of School Mental Health.* She holds a Ph.D. in developmental psychology from Cornell University and a M.Ed. in counseling and guidance from the University of Georgia.

Daniel Flannery is director of the Begun Center for Violence Prevention Research and Education at Case Western Reserve University's (CWRU's) Mandel School of Applied Social Sciences. He is the Dr. Semi J. and Ruth W. Begun Professor at CWRU's Jack, Joseph and Morton Mandel School of Applied Social Sciences; adjunct associate professor in the Department of Pediatrics, Rainbow Babies and Children's Hospital, and in psychiatry at CWRU; and adjunct professor, University of Notre Dame Masters in Education Program. He was founding director of the Institute for the Study and Prevention of Violence at Kent State University, where he also was a professor in both the Department of Justice Studies and the College of Public Health. His published work covers areas such as school violence, violence and mental health, and violent behavior and aggression. His most recent book chronicles his work in the U.S. Marshal Services' Fugitive Safe Surrender Program. He is a member of the Research and Training Committee, Mandel School of Applied Social Sciences; a permanent review board member for the U.S. Department of Education, Institute for Education Science, Social and Behavior Sciences; and a past member and chair of the Board of Directors for the Sisters of Charity Foundation and the Saint Ann Foundation of Cleveland. He holds a Ph.D. in clinical-child psychology from The Ohio State University.

Sandra Graham is a professor in the Human Development and Psychology Division, Department of Education, at the University of California, Los Angeles (UCLA) and holds the University of California Presidential Chair in Education and Diversity. Her research includes the study of academic motivation and social development in children of color, particularly experiences of peer victimization in school contexts that vary in racial/ethnic diversity. She has published in developmental, social, and educational psychology journals and has received many awards, including in 2011 the Distinguished Scientific Contributions to Child Development Award from the Society for Research on Child Development and the 2014 E. L. Thorndike Career Award for Distinguished Contributions to Educational Psychology, Division 15, of the American Psychological Association. She received her M.A. in history from Columbia University and her Ph.D. in education from UCLA.

Mark L. Hatzenbuehler is associate professor of sociomedical sciences and codirector of the Center for the Study of Social Inequalities and Health at Columbia University's Mailman School of Public Health. He holds a Ph.D. in clinical psychology from Yale University and was a postdoctoral fellow at Columbia University, where he was a Robert Wood Johnson Foundation Health & Society Scholar. His research includes the social determinants of sexual orientation health disparities; the health consequences of structural forms of stigma, including social policies; and the identification of biopsy-chosocial mechanisms linking stigma to adverse health outcomes among members of socially disadvantaged groups. He has published 86 peer-reviewed articles and book chapters. He received the 2015 Louise Kidder Early Career Award from the Society for the Psychological Study of Social Issues and the 2016 Early Career Award for Distinguished Contributions to Psychology in the Public Interest from the American Psychological Association. His work has been cited in several amicus curiae briefs for court cases on status-based discrimination, and he served on an expert panel on bullying at the Centers for Disease Control and Prevention. He is currently funded by the National Institute on Drug Abuse to study social determinants of substance use and other health outcomes among sexual minority youth.

Matthew Masiello has led or collaborated on clinical and public health teams in the support, development, and implementation of evidence-based, clinical/health promotion initiatives, including school-based bullying prevention initiatives, in the United States and internationally. He has taught courses for physician's assistants on the public health role and graduate courses on delivering heath care using a systems approach. His team of public health and educational professionals at the Center for Health Promotion and Disease Prevention, Windber, PA, where he is director, is completing a 6-year initiative in implementing, monitoring, and evaluating U.S. evidence-based bullying prevention. He is co-editor of *The Public Health Approach to Bullying Prevention*. In 2012 he received the Pennsylvania Public Health Association Keystone Award for Distinguished Service in Public Health. He consults to to school systems, colleges, universities, health systems, and clinical sites on developing undergraduate public health curriculum, becoming a health-promoting hospital, and developing medical home activities within pediatric practices. He was recently appointed Chief Medical Officer at the Children's Institute of Pittsburgh. He has served as a U.S. Network Coordinator and Governance Board member for the International Health Promoting Hospital Network. He holds a M.D. from the University of Guadalajara and a M.P.H. from George Washington University.

Megan A. Moreno is a member of the Division of Adolescent Medicine at Seattle Children's Hospital and an associate professor of pediatrics and adjunct associate professor of health services at the University of Washington. Her research, which focuses on the intersection of adolescent health and technology use, is housed at the Center for Child Health Behavior and Development, where she is principal investigator of the Social Media and Adolescent Health Research Team. With her team, she conducts research on educating adolescents and families toward safe Internet use and on developing tools to assess Internet use, to define problematic Internet use, and to both create and interpret messages within social media that promote healthy behaviors. She received her M.D. degree from George Washington University School of Medicine and completed a residency in pediatrics and a M.Ed. in education at the University of Wisconsin-Madison. She was a fellow in adolescent medicine at the University of Washington, where she also completed a M.P.H.

Regina Sullivan is a professor of child and adolescent psychiatry at the New York University School of Medicine and a developmental behavioral neurobiologist in the Emotional Brain Institute at the Nathan Kline Institute for Psychiatric Research. Her research interests include the neurobiology of infant attachment to the caregiver and the developmental neurobiology of fear, including how the young brain processes trauma and fear differently than the adult brain and how the caregiver's presence and behavior can alter this unique infant neural processing of trauma. She has served on numerous National Institutes of Health working groups and has organized specialized meetings on select developmental issues. She also serves as scientific advisor to the Child Mind Foundation and holds editorial and advisory positions for *Frontiers in Behavioral Neuroscience, Developmental Cognitive Neuroscience* and *Developmental Psychobiology*. She received her Ph.D. in biopsychology from City University of New York. She completed post-doctoral training at Duke University and the University of California-Irvine.

Jonathan Todres is professor of law at Georgia State University College of Law. His research focuses on children's rights and child well-being, with a particular emphasis on vulnerable populations. His primary research areas include trafficking and related forms of child exploitation, domestic implementation of children's rights law, economic and social rights issues, and legal and cultural constructs of childhood. He has authored numerous publications on a range of children's rights issues and serves as a regular advisor to nongovernmental organizations working to address violence against children, including serving as child rights advisor to End Child Prostitution and Trafficking–USA. He serves on the board of the Georgia Asylum and Immigration Network and is a Fellow of the American Bar Foundation. He received a B.A. in international development from Clark University and a J.D. from Columbia Law School.

Tracy Vaillancourt is Canada Research Chair in Children's Mental Health and Violence Prevention at the University of Ottawa, where she is also a full professor in the Faculty of Education (counseling program) and in the School of Psychology, Faculty of Social Sciences. Her research examines the links between aggression and children's mental health functioning, with particular focus on the neurobiology of peer victimization. She is currently funded by the Canadian Institutes for Health Research. She is a Fellow of the College of the Royal Society of Canada and a core member of the Offord Centre for Child Studies at McMaster University. She received her B.A., M.A., and Ph.D. in human development from the University of British Columbia, her postdoctoral diploma from the University of Montreal and Laval University in developmental psychology, and postdoctoral respecialization in applied child psychology (clinical) from McGill University.

PROJECT STAFF

Suzanne Le Menestrel (*Study Director*) is a senior program officer in the Board on Children, Youth, and Families at the National Academies of Sciences, Engineering, and Medicine. Previously she was National Program Leader for Youth Development Research at 4-H National Headquarters, National Institute of Food and Agriculture, U.S. Department of Agriculture (USDA), where she provided national leadership for youth development research programs, with an emphasis on building capacity for research and evaluation and bridging research and evaluation with program development and implementation. She represented USDA on the Federal Partners in Bullying Prevention Interagency Group and was involved in both the research and youth engagement working groups. Before that, she served as the research director in the Academy for Educational Development's Center for Youth Development and Policy Research and was a research associate at Child Trends, a nonprofit research organization. She was a founder of the *Journal of Youth Development: Bridging Research and Practice* and chaired its Publications Committee for 8 years. She is on the editorial board of *Applied Developmental Science*. She received the 2012 Outstanding Leadership and Service to the Extension Evaluation Profession award from the American Evaluation Association's Extension Education Evaluation Topical Interest Group. She has an M.S. and Ph.D. in human development and family studies from Pennsylvania State University.

Francis K. Amankwah is a research associate in the Board on Global Health, at the National Academies of Sciences, Engineering, and Medicine. Previously, he worked in the Board on Children, Youth, and Families. His research interests include population health management and international development. He has an M.P.H. and Graduate Certificate of Global Planning and International Development from Virginia Polytechnic Institute and State University. Mr. Amankwah was raised in Ghana and earned his B.S. in agricultural science from Kwame Nkrumah University of Science and Technology.

Kelsey Geiser is a research assistant with the National Academies of Sciences, Engineering, and Medicine's Board on Children, Youth, and Families. She has a B.A. and M.A. in history from Stanford University, where she gained extensive research and writing experience on the historical treatment of women's and family health issues, for which she received a grant to conduct original research in the Italian National Archives in Rome and Florence. She also wrote for the Stanford News Service and worked in the Palo Alto district office of Congresswoman Anna Eshoo.

Annalee Gonzales is a senior program assistant with the National Academies of Sciences, Engineering, and Medicine's Board on Children, Youth, and Families. Previously, she was an administrative/editorial coordinator for the National Association for Bilingual Education where she assisted in planning the yearly conference and editing the bimonthly magazine and journal for the organization. She also worked at Lauinger Library at Georgetown University. She has a B.A. in communication arts from Trinity University.